ZooA -

Defining Americans

Defining Americans

The Presidency and National Identity

Mary E. Stuckey

UNIVERSITY PRESS OF KANSAS

Published by the University Press of Kansas (Lawrence, Kansas 66049),
which was organized by the Kansas Board of Regents and is operated and
funded by Emporia State University, Fort Hays State University, Kansas
State University, Pittsburg State University, the University of Kansas, and
Wichita State University

Library of Congress Cataloging-in-Publication Data

Stuckey, Mary E.
Defining Americans : the presidency and national identity /
Mary E. Stuckey
p. cm.
Includes bibliographical references and index.
ISBN 0-7006-1349-8 (cloth : alk. paper)
1. Group identity—United States—History.   2. Political culture—United
States—History.   3. National characteristics, American.   4. Presidents—
United States—History.   I. Title.
E169.1.S934 2004
973—dc22
2004013592

British Library Cataloguing-in-Publication Data is available.

Printed in the United States of America

10 9 8 7 6 5 4 3 2 1

The paper used in this publication meets the minimum requirements of
the American National Standard for Permanence of Paper for Printed
Library Materials Z39.48-1984.

Where the mind is without fear and the head is held high;
Where knowledge is free;
Where the world has not been broken up into fragments by narrow
domestic walls;
Where words come out from the depths of truth;
Where tireless striving stretches its arms towards perfection;
Where the clear stream of reason has not lost its way into the
dreary desert sand of dead habit;
Where the mind is led forward by thee into ever-widening thought
and action—
Into that heaven of freedom, my Father, let my country awake.
—Rabindranath Tagore, *Gitanjali*

Contents

ACKNOWLEDGMENTS / ix

Introduction: Presidential Rhetoric and National Identity / 1

Chapter 1. Land, Citizenship, and National Identity in Jackson's America / 21

Chapter 2. Temperance, Character, and Race in the Antebellum United States / 61

Chapter 3. The Business of Government during the Democratic Interregnum of Grover Cleveland, 1885–1889 / 106

Chapter 4. Establishing a Transcendent International Order under Woodrow Wilson, 1913–1921 / 151

Chapter 5. Balancing the Nation: Brokering FDR's Economic Union, 1932–1940 / 198

Chapter 6: Citizenship Contained: Domesticating God, Family, and Country during the Eisenhower Years / 243

Chapter 7: Managing Diversity in a Fragmented Polity: The Post–Cold War World of George H. W. Bush / 288

Conclusion: Choosing Our National Identity / 335

NOTES / 359

INDEX / 405

Acknowledgments

This book took forever to write, and there are a good many people to thank. As always, I need first to thank my family: my mother, brother, sister-in-law, and sister. There are also many special children in my life, and much of what I write is influenced by what I hope they will be learning and by the world in which I hope they will be living. They don't know it, but I am indebted to all of them: Amanda, Robert, Phillip, Dakota, Brave Heart, Anthony, Daniel, Nolan, Art, Natasha, Alexandra, Eric, and those whom I see less often, but whose faces grace my refrigerator and whose presence enriches my life. My friends Scott Altus, Jeannie Barbour, Jennifer and Jim Beese, Tom Carroll and Sarina Russoto, Michael Ferry, Ellen Gardiner, Gary Grigsby, Raba Gunasekera, Beth Gylys, Rachel Howse, Alice Lambert, Chuck and Linda McCarty, Gary Miller, Indrajit Obeyesekera, Victoria and John Sanchez, Greg Shelnut, Ira Strauber, Melanie and Joel Trexler, Niromi Wijewantha, and Anil Weerakoon know, I hope, what they mean to me and how grateful I am to them.

At the University of Mississippi, Robert C. Khayat, Bill Staton and Carolyn Ellis Staton, Gloria Kellum, Billy Barrios, and Glenn Hopkins provided support and encouragement when I needed it most. At Georgia State University I have been blessed with not only one, but two terrific chairs: Mary Ann Romski and Carol Winkler. Our associate chair, Carolyn Codamo and the staff in the Department of Communication make my day-to-day life much easier, and I appreciate their patience with me. I am especially grateful to my colleagues in rhetoric: Michael Bruner, David Cheshire, and James Darsey. A departmental summer research grant was instrumental to the completion of the manuscript.

The first writing for the book came as a lecture for the Mississippi Humanities Council. I thank them, and the University of Mississippi for giving me the opportunity to participate in it. Part of this book was presented at Vanderbilt University as part of the Communication Studies Speaker Series. Special thanks to Chuck Morris for inviting me to Vanderbilt, and especially for his questions about the political consequences of varying degrees of visibility. Thanks to both Chuck and Anne Demo for their hospitality. Part of chapter 4 appeared in *Rhetoric and Public Affairs;* my thanks to the reviewers for their help in improving that work and to Martin J. Medhurst for permission to include it here. An early version of part of chapter 7 is included in *In the Public Domain: Presidents and the Challenges of Public Leadership,* edited by Lori Cox Han and Diane J. Heith. My thanks to them and to State University of New York Press.

Fred Woodward is everything an editor ought to be and more. I am fortunate to have had the opportunity to work with him and the rest of the staff at the University Press of Kansas. Among her other talents, Susan Schott was a loyal partisan in the Great Bobblehead War. Larisa Martin handled the details of production with aplomb. David Henry, Karen Hoffman, Chuck Morris, and John Murphy all read drafts of chapters; I am grateful to them. David Zarefsky did his best to improve this work through a number of helpful readings. The anonymous reviewers were patient and helpful. Their contributions vastly improved the book, and any remaining faults are mine alone.

My final thanks are for Greg Smith, who sees beauty in unexpected places and who taught me to love the shade.

Introduction:
Presidential Rhetoric and
National Identity

> With the exception of ancient Israel, no people
> have argued more than Americans about the
> terms of their own existence. No other people
> at all have made the argument a major reason
> for their being. The quarrel begins with the
> contradiction between what Jefferson wrote and
> the continuing realities of American life.
> —Edward Countryman, *Americans: A Collision
> of Histories*

DURING the summer of 1999, while I was beginning to think about
the complexities of national identity, cultural interactions, what
"diversity" means, and this book, I attended a Fourth of July fireworks celebration in Athens, Georgia. The festivities included fireworks synchronized with patriotic music. I was a Mississippi resident at the time, and it surprised me that the ubiquitous "Dixie"
was not included in the selections. I was equally surprised that the
themes from *Indiana Jones* and *Star Wars* were included, as I had not
known that John Williams had become a "patriotic composer." But
both these facts are, in their own curious way, relevant to our national self-identity. I was most moved that, amid songs like "You're a
Grand Old Flag" and "America the Beautiful," event organizers had
included an excerpt from Martin Luther King, Jr.'s "I Have a Dream"
speech, and did so in a way that accentuated how King's vision
remained more dream than reality. To hear King included as a voice
of patriotism was important, especially given the Southern setting

and the criticism conveyed by his words. That such inclusion aroused so little comment was still more important. Martin Luther King, Jr., and Luke Skywalker, equally American and equally heroic, were being valorized in the hometown of the author of the Confederate Constitution. The creators of that evening had offered a vision of the American empire truly worthy of celebration.

Presidents, no less than the architects of fireworks displays, articulate national identity and, to be successful, must do so in ways that will be accepted as obvious, even inevitable.[1] Like choreographers of Fourth of July celebrations, presidents must unite contemporaneous occasions with appropriate traditions and innovations so that enough of us will continue to see ourselves—and sometimes maybe even our better selves—reflected in the national mirror of public discourse. Not all of us, mind you, but enough of us must recognize ourselves in presidential formulations of national identity to legitimate and sustain the projects of national leadership. Although always diverse and always multicultural,[2] the colonies and the nation that sprang from them have also always been exclusionary.[3] Not everyone has been invited to the national party; just enough of us to keep the party going, to sustain the fragile consensus allowing us to function more or less collectively most of the time.

This collectivity has often been premised on the deliberate and sustained exclusion of specific groups: American Indians, African Americans, propertyless white males, immigrants, women, gays, and lesbians to name just a few. The nation has always seen itself, and its presidents have incessantly talked about it, in more inclusive terms than it has enacted. In so doing, the nation has given itself a standard of judgment it has been unable to meet. By celebrating itself beyond its deserts, the United States has caused enormous pain and anger among those whose lives were damaged by the seeming invisibility of their exclusion.[4] It has also, however, enabled the topoi of successful resistance within the broad structures of national governance. Thus, pain and anger are as much a part of our national identity as are the celebrations of the freedom and ideals that mark our national history. King's pain is as much a part of us as is his dream. They are not so much opposite sides of the same coin as they are equal components of the amalgam melded together to create the coin.

This book is an analysis of the metallurgy of our national coin, an exploration of how the differing elements of discourse and constitutive claims come together to forge our national identities.[5] I use the plural here for a variety of reasons. First, American self-identity is different now than it was even forty years ago, when public adulation of King on the Fourth of July would have been unthinkable in most of the nation's white communities, let alone Southern ones. Second, Americans at any given time have different sets of identities, which, taken together in their contradictory complexity, are variously composed of their experiences of national and international history, race(s), class, gender, region, sexuality, and life history. Presidents reduce these complex identities to a unidimensional point and then assign this overarching identity to individuals based primarily on demography—whether sexuality, gender, race, region, or religion. Historically, we have found enough overlap among these identities to make this idealized reduction the basis for collective action. However, as difference becomes increasingly salient in the national conversation, perhaps the central question of presidential leadership is whether any universal vision of the national character can create a collective culture without necessarily enacting the vilest forms of exclusion and scapegoating. I think that it can. By analyzing instances of failure to live up to our national promise, this book points to at least one way that we can avoid continued failures without sacrificing our joint identity.

Our national history offers plentiful examples of both inclusion and exclusion, often justified in exactly the same terms. Because the overwhelming majority of our national narratives stress the inclusive aspects of our shared history, this analysis seeks to complicate (rather than to contradict) those narratives. I therefore focus on the tensions and limits of inclusion and on outright, overt exclusion. I do not believe that the presidents included here—or indeed any of the others—are malicious men, seeking to exclude others from "their" polity and intent on reifying and maintaining existing structures of power and hierarchy. I do believe that often, by rhetorically instantiating and relying on the prevalent ideologies of their times, these presidents did in fact naturalize and propagate many exclusions. I also believe that they laid the groundwork for later inclusions, often through the same rhetoric that justified contemporaneous exclusions. This book provides documentation for both these beliefs. It concludes with some ideas about how we can preserve national unity even given generalized tolerance for national diversity, largely through the cultivation of a less centralized understanding of cultural respect.

Specifically, I demonstrate three things. First, I show that the dual processes of inclusion and exclusion are enacted through presidential rhetoric; that these processes are enabled through the institution's definitional power. Second, I show how presidents enact these processes through specific rhetorical and political choices. Finally, I provide evidence that these processes occur and have occurred throughout our history through specific attention to individual cases. These individual cases are not entirely discrete and isolated instances of presidential speech, for of course presidents draw on one another as well as on the same sets of traditions and values. Although the structure of the book centers on the presentation of specific moments in the development of American national identity, it also shows considerable, albeit uneven, linear progression as well.

Clear themes run throughout presidential address on issues of diversity. I have chosen to focus on three of those themes that connect and bind the cases I examine. The first is balance. Presidents, as has long been noted, are charged with the difficult task of balancing competing interests and claims in their efforts to imagine and articulate the basis for a shared and stable polity. They are both implicitly and explicitly concerned with this balancing act, sometimes in surprising ways. Generally, although balance is always a concern for American presidents, it is the earlier presidents—those in office before the twentieth century—who were most concerned with balance, as they were charged with maintaining a balance between stability and change in a rapidly growing territory. The bursts of inclusion that accompanied that growth had to be accommodated and disciplined, and balance became a key theme for these presidents. The accommodations and accompanying discipline tended to be overt and explicit; when presidents relied on balance, the inclusion of some groups and the exclusion of others tended to be equally overt and explicit.

The second theme has to do with our generally accepted cultural prescriptions about what constitutes citizenship, the idea that belonging in the United States is often less about birthright and more about capacity, and the tensions that are played out between these two ways of understanding membership in the polity. To be considered a "good" citizen in this democracy, for instance, one must demonstrate self-discipline, independence, productivity, and temperance. Since these attributes are often rhetorically associated with membership in certain groups, they naturalize and sustain many of the created hierarchies among citizens. In general, it is the presidents who served in the twentieth century who were most concerned with the parameters of citizenship. As Rogers M. Smith notes, questions of citizenship have been crucial to our national development since the nation's inception.[6] As the country moved from overt means of exclusion in the twentieth century to a more inclusive self-understanding, distinctions among citizens and the political hierarchies that rested on those distinctions became more difficult to justify. As exclusions became more readily contested and therefore subtler, citizenship became a key theme for presidential discussions of national identity and diversity.

Woven throughout these two centuries and their concern for balance and citizenship are questions of visibility. The third theme thus involves interesting tensions between what is rendered visible—and is also often valorized—and what is made invisible, left unmentioned, and is thus marginalized or erased altogether. Politicians, after all, debate only contingent issues. Presidents both determine and reflect what (and who) is visible as well as what (and who) remains outside their national vision. A good bit of the analysis that follows centers on these determinations and reflections.

For most groups, the process of becoming visible and the process of becoming citizens overlap. That is, many immigrant groups, women, the poor, and others were politically invisible at the time of the founding. Their exclusion was considered natural if not inevitable, and no serious political debates included them. For members of these groups, the struggle toward citizenship was a gradual process of, first, becoming politically visible. Then they were differentiated into "good" and "bad" members of their groups. The "good" members were declared acceptable candidates for limited inclusion and were deemed acceptable citizens, at which point they often vanished as politically meaningful groups—the Irish, the Italians, and other groups, for example.[7]

Each stage in this process is accompanied by specific presidential rhetoric, which remains consistent (at least in its broad outlines) across time. Excluded groups are first ignored by presidents—

politically invisible, they are utterly absent from presidential speech. As groups become politically visible, they are labeled as political problems and are subject to several possible sorts of presidential rhetoric. At the outset, they are frequently asked to be patient, as their inclusion is deferred. Presidents offer them some rhetorical legitimacy as a group but delay policy initiatives (ranging from the granting of citizenship to the franchise or other sorts of legal protections). Once their political presence has been legitimated, groups become open to rhetorical differentiation by the president, who divides group members into "good" and "bad" members. This differentiation lays out the terms for eventual inclusion in the polity and also delineates the nature of citizenship for that president. Finally, once groups have attained both political visibility and at least some measure of political legitimacy, as their members become absorbed into the larger polity, they are also included as "Americans" in presidential rhetoric, often retaining their ethnic or racial identities but on terms that stress their belonging to the polity rather than their exclusion from it.

Historically, not all groups followed this path at the same rate. It is an upward progression, to be sure, but one that was followed in anything but straightforward ways. Nor was full inclusion open equally to all groups. The United States was and remains a hierarchical polity, and these hierarchies are both reflected in and reinforced by presidential speech on national identity, in both the past and present.

In the contemporary era, when overt exclusion is itself politically problematic, presidents often rely on rhetoric that ostensibly includes everyone while still maintaining hierarchies of belonging among citizens. I call this rhetoric "celebratory othering," for it appears inclusive, even laudatory, but does so on terms that maintain existing stratifications and exclusions. It differs from real inclusion in its stress on inclusion not as accepting difference, but on disciplining it into the terms preferred by the dominant culture.

In other words, Smith is right in asserting that there have always been forms of second-class citizenship in the United States, that it has often been premised on ascriptive hierarchies of race and gender, and that the processes of inclusion have operated along with the processes of exclusion. What Gary Gerstle has called the nation's traditions of civic nationalism are interwoven in complicated ways with its more racialized nationalism.[8] These interwoven processes were interacting long before the inception of what Gerstle calls the "Rooseveltian nation," and the disciplinary project of citizenship can be seen as it operated for several groups across time.

This book offers a detailed analysis of how the processes observed by Smith and Gerstle are reflected in and reinforced by the rhetoric of our chief executives. There is a tension between locating a group of "us" and the inclusive ideals that "we" can be presumed to share. What Smith sees as fluctuations in the dominance of liberal, republican, and ascriptive elements of national identity can be clearly observed during the key moments that are the basis for this study. That presidents have such a prominent role in determining the parameters of citizenship through their attempts to balance competing claims using—and sometimes stretching—broadly accepted notions of who ought to be included and under what terms once again demonstrates the constitutive capacities and conservative tendencies of this important institution.

The President Speaks

More than for any other participant in the national conversation, the task of articulating the collective culture, like the responsibility for managing the collective action, belongs to the president.[9] As the only elected politician answerable to all Americans, the president is in a unique position both in terms of policy and in the more ceremonial and symbolic aspects of the office. At least that is how we portray the office to our students.[10] But we also modify that portrayal, even for those same students, because although the president does speak for all of us, he doesn't actually represent the entire polity. He (and the pronoun is revealing) represents those interests large enough, organized enough, resource-rich enough, to merit his attention. He represents the coalition that elected him, and the one that will allow him to govern.[11]

All presidents face tensions between preservation and progress. All presidents face questions of who and what to include—and exclude—as they seek to craft a coalition capable of sustaining both instrumental and constitutive goals. And all presidents may rightly celebrate the expanding inclusion of new groups, a celebration that is bittersweet because of the recognition that we have failed to live up to the promise of our national ideals. Most of all, however, all presidents are inherently conservative in their political as well as their rhetorical choices.[12] This conservatism is a natural product of the presidency as an institution.[13] Its electoral, structural, and political incentives all tend toward the creation and maintenance of broadly based national constituencies, comprising large diverse majorities. The presidency is the repository of a certain amount of cultural consensus. Presidents do not often venture into the truly controversial but instead exercise considerable caution. Before they lead, they want reassurance that their constituents will follow—and this is not a new phenomenon, driven by polls and mass media.[14] Presidents have never been in the vanguard of social or political change. By the time they enunciate a set of beliefs, values, or policies that they claim as "national," those beliefs, values, and polices are in fact widely supported—at least among members of their coalitions.

This is not to deny that presidents take risks; clearly, they do. But they are carefully calculated risks. It is also not to deny that presidents can be forward-thinking and moved by an impulse for justice; obviously they can be. But their calls for justice are calibrated within a context promising some political reward. It certainly doesn't mean that presidents are never controversial; of course they are. But in the normal course of their public pronouncements, the broadly accepted values of their day are the driving impetus of their rhetoric because presidents, for the most part, seek broad agreement and not national polarization.

When presidents speak, they speak to both immediate, policy-oriented goals and to longer-term, constitutive ends. Often this means presidents rely on epideictic oratory, which sometimes takes ceremonial form.[15] By grounding public speech in their own characters, presidents inhabit a larger representative role and reshape the office to their own personalities. Rather than merely speaking to the people, they claim to become something of a surrogate of "the people," simultaneously enacting and enunciating our national values and national identity.[16] There is, consequently, an emphasis throughout this book on these occasions. Although I examined all the rhetoric of the presidents included here, there is a good bit of emphasis on presidential addresses that deal with the rhetoric of nation building, such as inaugurals and annual messages. In addition, much of the material included here can be described as formulaic. Presidents, like other speakers, often rely on platitudes. Rather than dismiss this speech as "merely" platitudinous, I treat it seriously. Much of what is important in a culture is that which is so taken for granted as to be platitudinous, to be "mere rhetoric." It is precisely the taken-for-granted that I want to examine, for community depends on such shared assumptions.

Nations, as Ernest Gellner notes, are not inevitable. There are a variety of ways for humans to organize themselves and their lives, and doing so around the idea of nationality is but one such way, reflecting one set of historical, political, and economic circumstances.[17] The idea of a nation embodying a people is, as many have argued, a fiction brought about by a specific sort of historical necessity and specific kinds of rhetorical action.[18] Once invented, however, nations require certain elements for their sustenance and growth, and a certain sort of language with which to maintain and perpetuate themselves.

A people's identity, much like that of their nation, is largely imagined, based less on historical or geographical inevitability and more on the power of rhetoric to form and focus allegiances.[19] But often, if not inevitably, the invention of an "us" requires the creation of a "them," a fact that has led leaders to define another group or set of groups as outside the nation, incapable of incorporation into it.[20]

Nation building thus inevitably requires reduction. It therefore also implies inclusion and exclusion. That is, in telling us what sorts of policies we ought to espouse or what sorts of values we hold dear, presidents are also telling us who we are, what kinds of people we have been, and how we will proceed into the future. They are telling us who "we" are—and, by implication, who is not one of "us." And they also render judgments: who has "kept faith" with the past, who represents the promise of the future, and who represents a betrayal of that past or a threat to that future.[21]

The same people are not always included or excluded for the same reasons. To be sure, members of some groups, most notably

African Americans, women, Jews, gays, and lesbians, have generally been marginalized, when not excluded or demonized, and members of other groups, most notably white male Protestant property owners, have always been included, if not welcomed and valorized. But the terms by which this process has occurred have not remained constant. There has not been one set of stable, key values evenly applied to all comers over time.[22]

These varying applications are deployed across the rhetorical spectrum: in public and in private; by men and by women; against, for, and within minority communities; in newspapers and other media; in political speech however broadly defined. By the time these applications filter up to the presidency, they have been distilled to their most generic and ambiguous form, allowing the president to claim a national constituency for the ideals and practices he enunciates. The presidency is thus a single site where articulations of national identity consistently appear backed by sufficient social and political power to render those articulations as matters of custom and law. A central purpose of this project is to explore how presidential pronouncements center on questions of inclusion and exclusion. Through them, often implicitly, the nation's collective identity is articulated.

This work then, is a rhetorical history of sorts, attentive to both "the ways in which rhetorical processes have constructed social reality at particular times and in particular contexts and . . . the nature of the study of history as an essentially rhetorical process."[23] By examining presidential rhetoric, it is possible to examine American history from the top down—but with an understanding that it is also history "from the bottom up."[24] The advantage of doing a top-down history with something of a bottom-up perspective is that the data themselves reveal the contours of these tensions among groups as they are managed and orchestrated by the president. As David Carroll Cochran says, "If we are to come to grips with the profoundly complex phenomenon of race in American life, then it is vitally important not only that we think about race, but also that we think about how we think about it—that is, that we examine the normative understandings we draw upon when doing so."[25] What is true for race is also true for other elements of our national diversity, and presidential rhetoric provides an important and comprehensive perspective on those normative understandings.

The Plural Histories of Our Singular National Identity

American national history is conventionally taught, unsurprisingly, as majority history.[26] This approach has, of course, slowly been changing over the last forty years or so, to the chagrin of those who worry that as a consequence, we are losing our ability to function as a single collectivity, that "our" culture is debased, and that national disintegration is the inevitable result.[27] There is even concern that the accomplishments of the United States and indeed of all of Western civilization are being denigrated, and at great cost.[28]

My position is two-fold. First, I do not see evidence of a loss of respect for the ideals and values represented by the United States. In the current adulation for the "greatest generation," evident in the celebratory nature of television programs like *JAG* and *The West Wing*, there is a certain wistfulness and desire to believe in "America." If anything, the nostalgia in such shows reveals the hold of the dominant culture on our national psyche.[29]

Furthermore, multicultural perspectives, the voices of minorities and "others," have been added to the existing narrative.[30] They have not replaced that narrative, nor have they modified it except through such marginal tinkering as is possible by the addition of scattered alternative voices. "American history" remains very much majority history. The narratives of our textbooks remain very supportive of the processes and policy outcomes of the U.S. government. The dominant culture and its accompanying structures of power are in no immediate danger. That culture and those structures are, however, under some pressure from below, and there are certain constraints on them that differ from those of the past.

Because presidents speak for a democratic nation, there is, especially in more modern contexts, little overt exclusion of domestic "savages," or "barbarians," or other unspeakable hordes. Such overt demonization has been relegated primarily to the foreign policy realm.[31] There is, however, quite a bit of exclusion of internal groups based on some ascribed trait that members of excluded groups are supposed to possess.[32] Women, for instance, were often excluded, not precisely as women, but as members of a caste considered incapable of reasoning.[33] This phenomenon makes the task of arguing against exclusionary policies all the more difficult because it requires first that deeply embedded assumptions be made explicit. But to do so makes the excluded vulnerable to charges of paranoia or stridency, which forces them to somehow prove their worthiness. We did not, for instance, hear the argument that women were indeed incapable of rationality but nonetheless deserved full inclusion in the American polity. Instead, women were forced to prove their rationality, a task made more difficult by the fact that those bent on excluding women controlled the collective sense of what is (and what is not) rational.

Thus, the terms that governed the exclusion of women changed over time, as women went from being politically invisible to politically problematic and back to invisible, emerging again as politically problematic and finally becoming voting citizens. Women as politically relevant beings emerged along a pathway that ascends unevenly from invisible to differentiated to (limited) inclusion. In this outline of the case of women, we can see the broad outline of the arguments of this book. As the case of women also illustrates, the experiences of each group—and of each member in each group—must be dealt with individually. This book can only hope to do that with the broadest of strokes.

It is also important to note that even once a minority has "proven" its worthiness, there has been no immediate move to then assume that other excluded groups are therefore equally capable of citizenship. The battle for inclusion is not fully won even then. Change is slow, incremental, uneven, and often incomplete. To use a well-known example, black males were granted the franchise long before women. But the inclusion of one group never meant the automatic inclusion of others; resistance to such inclusion may even be strengthened. It is not all that useful, in this sense, to talk about inclusion in general terms. It makes more sense to place these discussions precisely within political, social, and economic contexts, to observe the interplay between demands for or even hope of inclusion with the exigencies of a given situation, whether defined materially or in a more ideological sense.

Interpreting America

American intellectuals are fond of asserting that we are the only modern nation founded on an idea.[34] But as the epigraph to this chapter implies, it is more accurate to say that we may be the only modern nation founded on an argument. The idea of equality has been contentious throughout our national history and has provided both the means of excluding members of groups and the basis for the inclusion of groups. The argument that stems from our national devotion to equality can be easily summarized as a debate on the question of "If America is an idea, who gets to interpret its meaning?" Historically, there have been many answers to this question and a variety of arguments that stemmed from it.[35]

Considerable recent scholarship addresses this dynamic of nation building through inclusion, appropriation, and exclusion in the context of the United States. Kenneth L. Karst, for example, has analyzed the historical ambivalence with which Americans have always regarded our commitment to the ideal of equality.[36] For Karst, "equality" and "belonging" are indissolubly linked, so to admit universal equality is to erase the boundaries that define that national community.[37] If all men, are truly created equal, according to this understanding, then they are all also created at least potentially American, an interpretation that then renders the concept "American" ambiguous if not meaningless. Thus, there has always been a philosophical tension that has played out historically between the proponents of the retention of certain stabilizing hierarchies of citizenship and belonging and the advocates of a more generalized claim to inclusion based on fundamental and universal principles.

For Rogers M. Smith, that tension is best understood as a dialectic between an inclusive liberalism and a more cautious republicanism, both of which are influenced and complicated by political demands. These demands, the product of the need to hold political constituencies together through policy incentives and commitments, mean that there is no "pure" liberal and inclusive nationalism politically at odds with a "pure" republicanism, but that these generalized ideologies have engaged one another in particular times and contexts such that it makes little sense to write a singular narrative of the United States that claims a singular set of national ideals and that the forces of progress have been consistently working to foster those ideals ever since the founding. That narrative, ubiquitous as it is in contemporary presidential rhetoric, is not descriptive of national history.[38]

Rather, inclusion and exclusion are mixed—for Smith, progress in applying universal principles to one group or in one arena may well be related to, if not premised on, the exclusion of another arena or group.[39] This is not necessarily the product of ill will or of a perverse desire for domination. It is the result of the need to create a national identity that has discernible limits, because without those limits, it is difficult to create and maintain political identities and obligations and thus political allegiances, either to nations in general or to political parties and coalitions.[40]

Smith thus advocates what he terms a "multiple traditions" approach to analyzing American history, in which that history is best understood as comprising, at any given time, liberal, privatized, rights-based ideals alongside communitarian and republican principles, both of which are complicated by the presence of ascriptive and exclusionary hierarchies of race, gender, class, and ethnicity.[41] Leaders will, at any given moment and in varying ways, call on these various traditions to craft the coalitions that make their leadership possible.[42] Thus, rather than a straight line of ever-increasing inclusion and acceptance of diversity, our national history is better graphed as a series of fluctuations as groups are included and excluded, and as the justifications for these varying boundaries alter depending on the exigencies of the historical moment.

Smith's formulation complicates the idea that our national history can best be understood as a conflict between a rights-based liberalism that individuates issues of inclusion and exclusion, and the more republicanist need to conceive of some sort of community in order to function collectively. Those who see history in such stark terms tend to view inclusive rhetoric as hypocritical cant.[43] Worse, others see exclusion as so deeply embedded in even the most hopeful of our shared ideals as to compromise those ideals beyond repair.[44] For these authors, exclusion is understood as inextricably part of the liberal democratic republicanism of the United States, because the suppression of diversity was—and often still is—perceived as the only way to sustain political community. As Desmond King would have it, "A political system that celebrates, both rhetorically and institutionally, individualism and plurality of group identity and allegiance has historically subscribed to a unifying conception of Americanization: this is the only politically plausible means of overcoming a diversity that, left without such a unifying, ideological support, might become politically destructive."[45] According to authors such as King, we have celebrated our diversity even as we have striven to contain it. Indeed, it often appears that we celebrate diversity largely because we *can* contain it.[46]

This seeming contradiction is possible because the processes of exclusion are masked by our celebratory rhetoric and by real acts of political inclusion.[47] Put in its strongest and most negative formulation, as David Carroll Cochran does, "the uniform rights, difference-neutral procedures, and public-private dichotomy instituted by liberalism all obscure and thereby contribute to deeply-rooted social policies and cultural meanings that oppress certain groups based on differences like race, gender, ethnicity, sexual preference, age, or disability."[48] According to this argument, such masking is essential if we are to retain our national belief in the purity of our intentions, goals, and actions. The masking obscures the differences between power and privilege, and allows individuals who lack institutional power to ignore the degree to which they possess a significant degree of privilege.[49] According to this line of argument, privilege allows us to demand that others need only to behave "normally" to be fully included. Exclusion is not the fault of the privileged, but of the excluded. They have choices. Assimilation is simply the only "reasonable" one to make. Other choices lead to other consequences— exclusion is thus framed as the product of individual choice and not as a result of institutional structures and informal practices.

Authors such as Rogers Smith, Gary Gerstle, and Matthew Frye Jacobsen offer a way out of understanding our history as either one of Panglossian progress or a more negative view of our national history as one of continued compromise or corruption of our foundational principles. They also allow us to understand how idealized conceptions of national identity can coexist, however uneasily, with the most perniciously exclusive interpretations of the American mission. They both offer and facilitate a more nuanced view of U.S. history. American citizenship, our national identity, has always been contested terrain. But it hasn't always been contested on the same terrain. It has always been influenced and complicated by the tensions caused by conflicting notions of hierarchy and freedom.

For Gary Gerstle, that tension, which he understands as existing between a philosophical conception of the United States as grounded in adherence to a set of agreed-upon principles (citizenship determined by belief, or civic nationalism) and a sense of nationality grounded in ascribed notions of race, class, ethnicity, and gender (or racial nationalism), is integral to the development of the American polity, especially in the twentieth century.[50] For Gerstle, these two conceptions of citizenship exist side by side and reinforce one another as often as they conflict. The disciplinary project of enforcing assimilation and therefore national unity is, for example, grounded in notions of racial nationalism but also helps to stabilize the otherwise potentially inchoate nation.

Although Gerstle does not argue this explicitly, the task of engaging in this "disciplinary project," or at least the task of using it for nation building, belongs to the president. It is the president's job to exploit some of the differences, heal some of the fractures, and elide the existence of still other oppositions to craft a workable logic of nationality that will cement enough allegiances to ensure the maintenance of both his particular administration and the nation as a whole. This task is profoundly rhetorical and rests on his ability to create a univocal understanding of a broadly shared cultural history and sense of national mission. As noted earlier, that understanding tends to be built on a foundation of support for the status quo rather than risk-taking ventures into new territories of inclusion. Even in their most progressive moments, presidential articulations of national identity are deeply conservative.

It is easy to cite, as nearly all presidents do, the existence of a certain amount of cultural consensus when only one segment of the population controls all the public discourse.[51] The president as a repository of cultural power has enormous influence over the polity's most important conversations on national identity. His (and again I use the pronoun advisedly) real power lies in his ability to make certain practices seem both natural and inevitable.

Those claims to consensus, based on a model of Americanization and assimilation, have required a seamless, linear, univocal articulation of "America" and its history, one that tends to suppress alternative voices and restrict political options. This is not to argue that all voices should receive equal weight or that all political options are equally viable. But plainly, a focus on a white, Anglo-Saxon conception of the American culture has been and remains consequential. Not the least of those consequences is a cultural myopia, where the rich variety of American subnational life is reflected, ignored, forgotten, or trivialized.

The alternative to a monolithic and oppressive dominant culture is not necessarily separatist or even sectarian, despite the plethora of arguments to that effect.[52] It is possible to celebrate a plurality of identities, to rejoice in common ground while still cherishing difference. It is possible to make a distinction between a dominant culture that proposes to share that which it is most proud of and one that imposes its entirety on all comers; this is the difference between respect and disrespect.[53] A more respectful politics is possible, but only if a working political coalition demands it through policy preferences advocated and enacted by leaders.

Thus, this book is grounded in a profound belief in the ideals and accomplishments of Western civilization and the United States. It is not, however, therefore bound to neglect their limitations, faults, or failures. It is written in the hope of opening up more spaces for the celebration of difference on common ground and is dedicated with immense gratitude to all those people in my life whose generous, gracious, and eloquent responses to their often painful experiences of difference have informed the work that follows.

Plan of the Book

This book is neither a seamless nor a comprehensive account of all American history as articulated in the speeches of all its presidents. Instead, I offer a series of snapshots, moments in time that reveal the complexities, movement, continuity, and changes in our national self-understanding as interpreted though presidential rhetoric. It is an episodic rhetorical history of American national identity as seen through the words of some of its presidents. All presidents draw on the same set of national ideals, values, and events; they all call on them in similar situations and for similar purposes.[54] But not all presidents use identical ideas in precisely the same ways, and their individual choices are revealing—both of the presidents and of the people they were elected to lead.

The specific presidents who figure in this study were chosen less for any inherent characteristics and more because of the circumstances of their governance. Presidents who served during the nation's first century were preoccupied with questions of balance and were blunt in their limits on inclusion. Andrew Jackson, for example, whose rhetoric is far too often ignored, decisively shaped the sense of national identity from the period of founding into the next fifty years. His presidency thus allows both a forward and a backward view of American national identity and persistent issues of inclusion and exclusion. Similarly, the period immediately before the Civil War obviously provoked heated debate concerning national identity: the three presidents of the 1850s are taken together to place the contours of that debate in a new light. As the nation moved out of that war and toward a new understanding of itself, Grover Cleveland offered a particularly useful way to understand those changes. He represents a transitional moment between preoccupations with balance and a primary concern with the contours of citizenship. That concern is clear in the public discourse of Woodrow Wilson, who helped us understand the international implications of a new transcendent international order. Franklin Roosevelt helped us come to terms with the economic devastation that accompanied that order. Dwight Eisenhower was in office as the international context was refined into a cold war between two great powers, and the elder George Bush managed the transition into a single superpower.

All these moments were fraught with consequences for how we understand ourselves. They signal choices about who we are and how we should function in the world. They also have enduring implications both for the nation and for the rhetorical and political choices that their successors faced. They are thus worthy of close examination.

Most of these presidents happen to be Democrats. Interestingly, we seem to elect Democrats during periods of particular kinds of internal crises. It is also interesting that Republicans have dominated the institution since the 1940s, mainly because of the external threats that lent themselves to conservatism. The partisanship of the various presidents matters, but presidents, even more than other political actors, act as presidents more than they act as partisans. Moreover, to the extent that they do act as partisans, finding exclusionary implications in the rhetoric of Democrats is, with the exception of the antebellum period, making the harder case. Republicans are traditionally more suspect on issues of national identity, and the ways in which that has come about and continues to operate are already well known.[55] The book begins with Democrats and ends with Republicans, a circumstance driven both by the historical longevity of the Democratic party and by the new political dominance of the Republicans.[56]

Andrew Jackson is the starting point for two reasons. He presided over the first great explosion of inclusion in American politics, the first great expansion of the national franchise.[57] And, to accomplish that expansion, he had to justify it philosophically. Given his times, this meant that he had to explain change in terms essentially consistent with the founders' rhetorical canon. Thus, in analyzing Jackson, I also attend to earlier presidents, specifically Washington and Jefferson.

With the exception of Eisenhower, the cold war presidents, who presided over the most rapid and inclusive social change in American history, are not included here. Partly, this is because the cold war presidents have been and are being extensively studied.[58] Despite this attention, I demonstrate that Eisenhower's rhetorical and political standards most definitely characterized the times, and after including him, the rhetoric of his successors amounts to little more than variations on a theme.[59]

Some groups also get little attention. American Hispanics and Latinos/Latinas, for instance, remain still all but invisible in presidential rhetoric, as are gays, lesbians, the disabled, and members of many other groups. This invisibility is interesting, and merits discussion, but discussing absence poses a tremendous series of problems.[60] Women also receive only sporadic attention, in this book as in presidential speech. American Indians on the other hand, represent an important—and too often neglected—set of anomalies. They are the only group to reverse the historical trend of moving from invisibility through differentiation to limited inclusion. American Indians were anything but politically powerless or politically invisible at the time of the founding. Enormous amounts of presidential attention and rhetoric were focused on American Indians. That attention and rhetoric has been steadily waning since, although American Indians have been consistently viewed as prime targets for disciplinary projects designed to create specific kinds of citizens. Early presidents had to balance the nation's hunger for new territory with the political and military threats and opportunities offered by different groups of American Indians. Because of the perspective offered by presidential rhetoric on American Indians, they get a good bit of analytic attention here.

In treating these groups in various ways throughout this book, my focus is less on how specific groups are treated throughout history, and more on the parameters that presidents articulate as the boundaries for inclusion. Groups vary in their liminality and in the ideological justifications for their exclusion. So some groups are more useful as examples of some periods than others. The focus on members of one group or another is a product of the data, not of a decision made according to an abstract rule prior to—or during—the analysis.

The first part of the book is dominated by the trope of balance. The first chapter is a discussion of land, citizenship, and democracy in the 1830s, with reflections on how Andrew Jackson amended the framer's understandings of these issues, and a discussion of the consequences of those changes. Chapter 2 explores the rhetoric of the three single-term presidents of the 1850s—Millard Fillmore, Franklin Pierce, and James Buchanan—and how their shared conception of citizenship and inclusion gradually shrank the polity as the nation stumbled into war. The third chapter focuses on how the model of business came to be applied to the government during Grover Cleveland's first term and how that trope helped him to manage both concerns of balance and emerging issues involving the nature of citizenship and its boundaries.

The second section of the book is dominated by concern over patrolling the parameters of citizenship and increasingly subtle forms of inclusion and exclusion. Cleveland is followed by an exegesis of the transcendent world order envisioned by Woodrow Wilson, which is in turn followed by an analysis of FDR's rhetoric during the 1930s, and how he defined and articulated the American dream during a time of national depression. The next snapshot is of Dwight Eisenhower and his articulation of cold war policy through its governing metaphor, containment. The final picture is of George H. W. Bush, who struggled to give meaning to America in its new position as the sole remaining superpower. His presidency has set the uncertain stage for those who have followed and reveals the schisms that now dominate our discussions of democracy, diversity, inclusion, and national identity, issues that are discussed in terms of Bill Clinton and George W. Bush in the conclusion.

1 / *Land, Citizenship, and National Identity in Jackson's America*

It is interesting to note that not until political democracy was achieved in America—the creation of a mass electorate, the rise of the common man, the respect for the popular will, the notion that political leaders must serve as representatives of the people, and the rest—not until then did the country decide to get rid of its Indians. And it fell to Andrew Jackson, the symbol of the great democracy, to run the Indians off their ancestral lands and dump them unceremoniously in remote and desolate corners of the United States where they barely survived.
—Robert V. Remini, *The Revolutionary Age of Andrew Jackson*

BY SPEAKING in universals as a way of building political coalitions that answer contemporary political exigencies, presidents manage the nation's citizenry and thus both include and exclude members of specific groups. Andrew Jackson, for instance, relied on his interpretation of Jefferson's legacy and crafted a nation that managed an explosion of white male citizenry. In so doing, he relied on a specific and limited view of national history that marginalized some groups—especially those who did not own property—and forcibly excluded others, such as American Indians. Jackson achieved balance among some interests that he deemed important to his coalition—white male farmers, slave owners, those favoring the expansion of commercial growth and immigration policies that increased white, Western European movement to the nation and thence to the frontier—at the expense of those who did not contribute to that coalition—women, slaves, American Indians, those whose livelihoods depended on a localized or subsistence economy. Citizenship was placed at the service of national balance, and some groups were made politically visible and valorized while others were marginalized or rendered politically invisible.

For Jackson, the key to citizenship was not character, as it had been understood by members of the founding generation, but land. Ownership of land taught one how to be a good citizen in a democracy. Specifically, in Jackson's union, Jefferson's peaceful yeoman farmer—a product of the early need for stability—became an adventurous pioneer, opening up the nation and increasing its territory. Jackson's model of citizenship made the union more dynamic, and its emphasis on land helped render that dynamism politically stable. The nation expanded both geographically and politically, and cast the founders' hierarchies into contention.

According to Rogers M. Smith, these "pervasive hierarchies" were a legacy from the Old World, but remained an important constituent part of the politics of the New.[1] In fact, the founders could propose such sweepingly inclusive politics because of the invisibility of groups that they had no intention of including. Thus, the myths of the American founding, according to Smith, did some important political work in that they legitimated certain sorts of political arrangements, binding together key constituencies on which the survival of the early colonies and the nation that sprang from them depended. This political work included justifying the occupation of contested land, legitimating chattel slavery, and rendering women politically invisible.[2] Some sorts of diversity were allowed and even encouraged. Other sorts were suppressed or ignored.[3] The advocacy of some sorts of national diversity and the suppression of other sorts—the rhetorical creation of a specific kind of citizen—was and is primarily the task of the president.

Gary Gerstle identifies this process most clearly with a twentieth century "Rooseveltian nation," which included also a strong sense of civic nationalism, a stress on political and social equality that existed along with racial hierarchy, and a regulated economy.[4]

But one of the most important aspects of Gerstle's work, his notion of a disciplinary project by which people were rendered citizens through assimilation and adoption of a civic nationalist creed, had its roots much earlier than the twentieth century. Theodore Roosevelt rested his idea of nationhood on the frontier myth. Gerstle does not explicitly recognize that this myth originated in the presidencies of Jefferson and Jackson, in their rhetorical treatments of farmers, pioneers, and American Indians. The processes set forth by Smith and Gerstle have never been more clear than in the case of Jacksonian America, which saw the explosion of democracy in the Age of the Common Man, as well as one of the earliest instances of ethnic cleansing, in the removal of some seventy thousand American Indians from what is now the southeastern United States.[5] These events had their roots in the ideologies and politics of the early republic, when national identity was first being crafted.

Balance and Citizenship in the Early Republic

There were two dominant strains of thought among the founders.[6] The first, which became widely identified with the Federalists and most closely associated with Washington, Hamilton, and Adams, eventually contrasted sharply with the views espoused by Madison and Jefferson, which became associated with the Democratic Republicans. Although the history of the early republic was in many ways a history of the accords, strains, tensions, compromises, and victories of these groups, for my purposes here it is sufficient to restrict the analysis to the founders' views of "the people."

One of the most important elements of these views was the political context in which they were embedded. Despite the rhetoric of equality and universalism that characterized much of the Revolutionary era, the political culture of the founders was an exclusionary one, based largely on the deference of the majority of white males toward an educated elite and the general acquiescence of everyone else. That elite could afford to assume that they knew and understood "the people," and could speak for them because they also assumed that they shared a common culture. Yet this assumption was not always borne out.

There were, in fact, two interwoven notions of national identity,

notions that would become increasingly delineated but that at the time coexisted and mutually reinforced one another. The first, stronger claim was that Americans were essentially an Anglo-Saxon people, chosen by the Protestant God to carry forth His work on earth. At the same time, America was considered something of an "asylum nation," a home for the dispossessed.[7] Even in this more "cosmopolitan" version of national identity, it is important to note that these "dispossessed" were European. Even in its most inclusive version, American national identity was still exclusive.

Indeed, consistent rhetorical insistence on homogeneity masked a great deal of social tension in the founding era, tension that was driven as much by gender, social class, and economic circumstance as by what the framers would have understood as culture. This masking resulted from the founders' understanding of citizenship. Democratic citizenship, in the founders' eyes, was not an easy matter. At a minimum, it required two things: an appropriate character and experience with democracy and its demands. Both of these depended on and were derived from a shared, Anglo-Saxon cultural heritage. "Foreigners" were acceptable, even welcome, so long as they did not act "foreign."[8]

Thus, one could be excluded from the polity because one lacked the experience of democracy (someone of, say, Eastern European descent), the strength of character for a democratic citizen (women, for instance, or African Americans), or the cultural referents required for participation in democratic institutions ("uneducated" American Indians, or "foreigners"). In time, of course, provided one had the potential character (was a willing American Indian, or most preferably, a white male), the culture and experience could presumably be gained, at least after an appropriate period was spent in apprenticeship. The Constitution, for instance, made clear distinctions between "the people," "free inhabitants," and "free citizens," with separate rights, duties, and responsibilities attached to each. Even those who appeared to have appropriate qualifications could still become more of a liability to the polity than an asset and could be encouraged to endanger liberty and the republic. The burgeoning nation was not so easily balanced, as the Whiskey Rebellion made clear.[9]

So important was the rebellion that it prompted a mention from President Washington in his Third Annual Address, where he tried to minimize the significance of the events in Pennsylvania, saying that

the impressions with which this law has [*sic*] been received by the community have been upon the whole such as were to be expected among enlightened and well-disposed citizens from the propriety and necessity of the measure. The novelty, however, of the tax in a considerable part of the United States and a misconception of some of its provisions have given occasion in particular places to some degree of discontent; but it is satisfactory to know that this disposition yields to proper explanations and more just apprehensions of the nature of the law, and I entertain full confidence that it will in all give way to motives which arise out of a just sense of duty and a virtuous regard to the public welfare.[10]

Washington's optimism was not well founded. Within the year, he was compelled to issue a proclamation concerning "proceedings [that] are subversive of good order, contrary to the duty that every citizen owes to his country and to the laws, and of a nature dangerous to the very being of a government."[11] In this proclamation, he expressed the need to "most earnestly admonish and exhort all persons whom it may concern to refrain and desist from all unlawful combinations and proceedings whatsoever."[12] This personal plea for a return to good order had little noticeable effect.

Plagued also with Indian hostilities and the viciousness of whites on the frontier,[13] Washington began his Fourth Annual Address with "some abatement of . . . satisfaction."[14] Between his inability to control either the American Indians or whites and the insurrection in Pennsylvania, Washington and his government seemed to have only the most tenuous control over the nation. As would be the case in later domestic upheavals, the Whiskey Rebellion was so significant because it illustrated to the founders exactly how ready the people could be to alter or abolish their new government. But in the history of the colonies and the new republic, mob violence and insurrection were hardly unique. Not only were violence against American Indians and international war endemic, but mob action, riots, and other forms of antigovernment violence were common.[15] This violence was not new, but the threat that it posed to the new government was real.[16] Stability was essential to prosperity. Measures designed to promote and protect stability were thus imperative.

The national history of violence and mob action provided ample justification for the powerful fear of public opinion and public action that had long prevailed among the founders. The philosophical necessity of basing a government on the consent of the people and the practical necessity of then creating structures designed to insulate that government from the passions of those people was most clearly expressed in *Federalist No. 10*, devoted to the need to "break and control the violence of faction."[17]

> Complaints are everywhere heard from our most considerate and virtuous citizens, equally the friends of public and private faith, and of public and personal liberty, that our governments are too unstable, that the public good is disregarded in the conflicts of rival parties, and that the measures are too often decided, not according to the rules of justice and the rights of the minor party, but by the superior force of an interested and overbearing majority. However anxiously we may wish that these complaints held no foundation, the evidence of known facts will not permit us to deny that they are in some degree true.[18]

Stability depended on the creation of a workable political coalition that would balance the dominant interests—which were understood in exclusively economic terms—and ensure that any instability would be caused by minorities, who could be controlled and contained, not by majorities, whose dissatisfaction could threaten the system. The founders, of course, considered faction the price of freedom and thought that it arose more perniciously and most often from the "unequal distribution of property," which they deemed the inevitable consequence of liberty.[19] Public opinion was dangerous because individuals could learn to see themselves as the majority, and as a majority could endanger liberty. Thus, while the founders in general and the authors of the *Federalist* in particular clearly understood the evocative power of "the people," however constituted, they also clearly understood that this power could be evoked against the government as easily as in its support. In *Federalist No. 51*, therefore, Madison declared that "you must first enable the government to control the governed," an aspect of democracy he considered no less important than the requirement that "in the next place oblige it to control itself."[20] Stability and order were necessary and preceded the defense of individual liberty. Such stability required a government ultimately answerable to, but safely removed from, the people.

It also required a limitation on the number and kind of people deemed fit for citizenship, and the cultivation of a certain kind of citizenship. Stability (balance) required the creation of a governable citizenry—the American penchant for mob violence made this all the more imperative. As antebellum presidents would eventually insist, balance was best understood as the maintenance of public order, and a temperate citizenry was crucial to that project. Those who disrupted the public order disrupted the balance and threatened the nation. They should therefore be excluded from it. Balance required overt exclusion.

Not only were the mass of people removed from the day-to-day workings of their government, but even their representatives were shielded in every way from the will and passions of the mass public. None of the important powers of the Constitution are exercised without very large majorities, and none of them allow for the unfettered expression of the people's will. If a temperate citizenry could not be guaranteed, then government must be temperate for the citizens.

Although the prevailing understanding of democracy seemed to limit it to small republics, for Publius, the most efficacious way of preventing the threat that a majority faction posed was territorial expansion. As *Federalist No. 51* put it, "Different interests necessarily exist in difference classes of citizens. If a majority be united by a common interest, the rights of the minority will be insecure. There are but two methods of providing against this evil: the one by creating a will in the community independent of the majority—that is, of the society itself; the other, by comprehending in the society so many separate descriptions of citizens as will render an unjust combination of a majority of the whole very improbable, if not impracticable."[21] It is important to underline the fact that by "separate descriptions of citizens," Madison was referring to *economic* differences, not to cultural or ethnic ones. He was assuming a homogenous *cultural* community, in which different classes would have different interests, not envisioning a multicultural but peaceful polity. Certain kinds of diversity—mainly economic—were to be actively encouraged. Other kinds of diversity—racial, ethnic, cultural—were erased. Those who did not fit into the culturally homogeneous understanding of the nation were to be actively excluded from it.

The terms by which these politically invisible inhabitants could be made visible and eventually included in the nation were already being set. "Good" citizens were white, Protestant, Anglo-Saxon males who shared specific cultural values and a specific understanding of nationhood that was simultaneously inclusive and exclusive. Exclusion could be based on ascriptive traits such as race or gender, class, or ideological terms, if one were insufficiently committed to the nation or its view of things. Some of the invisible—women and African Americans especially—had at this time no real chance of citizenship, even if envisioned in some distant future time. Others, especially the male immigrant poor, could hope to attain inclusion if they worked hard and came to believe in the right ideals—and assumed the correct ideological trappings of citizenship. Until then, their exclusion was overt and mandatory, for they were considered dangerous to liberty.

For Madison, and later for Jefferson as well, the surest route to the prevention of a majority faction injurious to liberty was the geographical expansion of the polity. Expansion would provide an outlet for the dangerous members of the polity and could thus help promote balance and stability. In *Federalist No.10*, Madison argued that the solution to the danger of majority faction was expansion: "Extend the sphere, and you take in a greater variety of parties and interests; you make it less probable that a majority of the whole will have a common motive to invade the rights of other citizens."[22] And, in defending the Louisiana Purchase during his presidency, Jefferson asserted, "the larger our association the less it will be shaken by local passions."[23] Both of these formulations depended on a notion of balance that meant spreading out discontent and localizing loyalty to the new regime. In both cases, they were, of course, defending specific policy choices by whatever means were at hand. But in both cases, the principle articulated through those choices would later be used by Andrew Jackson to defend greater territorial expansion than either Madison or Jefferson could possibly have foreseen.

Even in their own time, however, there was a tension between maintaining order through expansion and the dilution of discontent and the need to offer a recognizable national identity over a large territory. Ideologically, this tension was resolved by emphasizing both inclusion—who was an "American" regardless of how far from the capital they might reside—and exclusion—who could never be really "American" no matter how central their location. By rendering citizenship in terms of ideology as well as ascriptive characteristics, the founders argued for a cohesive national identity that encompassed a large and varied territory as well as diffusing potential causes for conflict. The power of this solution to the problem of national identity in a diverse republic was amply displayed in the effectiveness with which the nation was managed until the pressures of slavery would push it to the breaking point and the antebellum presidents would have to find other ways of reinforcing a fractured national identity.

As they talked about enlarging the nation, neither Madison nor Jefferson argued that expansion would dilute or even alter the common culture on which the health of the nation depended. Jefferson's defense of the Louisiana Purchase concluded with the question, "and in any view, is it not better that the opposite bank of the Mississippi should be settled by our own brethren and children than by strangers of another family?"[24] Americans were all part of a single family, culture, and political ideology. Anyone falling outside this definition was simply and invisibly, if not necessarily intentionally, excluded. "Our brethren" were ideologically members of one family, on the one hand, and members of a shared and exclusive cultural family on the other. Those who were politically visible could claim one or the other birthright; others were simply erased.

This conception of national identity had at least two important consequences. First, it revealed the extent to which the United States polity has depended on balancing competing interests since its inception. To grow, but to keep the culture and ideology that these presidents understood as characterizing the nation and defining its success, required a careful modulation of competing, if not contradictory, claims. Growth required laborers, both slave and free, for instance. It necessitated the acquisition of territory, which meant the incorporation of others into the nation. This meant in turn that it required a disciplinary project, a way to either exclude those foreign others or to render them less foreign.[25] So the second consequence was the fact of erasure. By simply assuming a homogeneous polity, and by enacting—or refusing to enact—specific legislation that supported—or refused to support—that homogeneity, the disciplinary project would be carried out, but largely invisibly. By promoting certain kinds of diversity, other kinds would be ignored or suppressed. The national balance would be maintained by enforcing the borders of citizenship on both ascriptive and idcological levels. The presidential rhetoric of the era reveals how the nation's traditions of civic and racial nationalism were united and reinforcing.

Both Madison and Jefferson retained a belief in the importance of "democratic character" and common culture as the basis for representative government. Both men also believed strongly that liberty was the prime political value. As Anthony F. C. Wallace notes in the case of Jefferson, a commitment to liberty, however passionate, does not also imply a commitment to equality.[26] In fact, the liberty so vaunted by Jeffersonians allowed them to revel in their citizenship while denying it to others. Indeed, "the presence in the nation's political culture of well-established arguments for the divine mission of the American people, the superiority of Anglo-Saxon civilization, patriarchal rule in the family and polity, and white racial supremacy all not only permitted white American Christian men of the Jeffersonian age to be proud, rather than apologetic, about their exclusive possession of full citizenship."[27] The exclusionary nature of the polity was celebrated, not deplored, and this celebration became intertwined with the myths of that age that undergird the national identity that stemmed from those myths.

This point is particularly important, because some of the founders included yet another protection from the people, first with the Naturalization Act of 1790, and most definitively and dangerously with the Alien and Sedition Acts of 1798, which were passed, ironically enough, soon after the Bill of Rights was ratified. This legislation was clearly designed to protect the government by limiting those who had access to it, for the founders feared the influence of foreign ideas that would be inevitable if immigration were totally unrestricted.

The comparatively benign Naturalization Act addressed the need all nations have to determine citizenship. Essentially, the act delineated three requirements for citizenship: a two-year residence in the United States, proof of good character, and an ethnicity understood at the time as "white." None of these elements received any significant debate or even consideration, as this formulation of widely accepted ascriptive hierarchies seemed too natural for comment. Those hierarchies were instantiated with the force of positive law even while disappearing from public debate.

The Alien and Sedition Acts were another matter altogether. Indeed, they caused a constitutional crisis and were instrumental in John Adams's defeat at the hands of Jefferson in the election of 1800. The Jeffersonians, it should be noted, objected more on the grounds of the implications for federal and state relations than on the grounds that they were exclusionary or restrained the people's right to free speech. Although these acts affected the rights and actions of members of the polity rather than of those denied such membership, they were both more visible and more likely to cause controversy.[28]

Urging their repeal in his first annual message, Jefferson said, "I can not omit recommending a revisal of the laws on the subject of naturalization . . . the Constitution indeed has wisely provided that for certain offices of important trust a residence shall be required sufficient to develop character and design. But might not the general character and capabilities of a citizen be safely communicated to everyone manifesting a bona fide purpose of embarking his life and fortunes permanently with us?"[29] Jefferson argued that the "American" culture was transmittable, that given willingness, time, and education, many of those not born to an appropriately democratic character had the potential to acquire it. Notice, however, that only some immigrants were thought likely to be able to acquire appropriately democratic traits and that those immigrants were, first and foremost, willing to subject themselves to the disciplinary project of assimilation by the act of "embarking his life and fortunes permanently with us." The willingness to assimilate was as important as having the capacity to do so, and even while reinforcing some aspects of racial nationalism by limiting those able to be naturalized, this rhetoric did not preclude the power of civic nationalism. The terms by which the politically invisible could eventually find some measure of inclusion and acceptance were clear. Also clear were the topoi through which they could make their arguments for inclusion. The disciplinary project of citizenship that Gerstle sees as defining, in important ways, twentieth-century America, had it roots in the ideological origins of the nation and in the public speech of its presidents.

Those ideological origins can be traced to a mythic understanding of the nation, an understanding that began as the nation itself began. In Jefferson's America, an idealized corps of yeoman farmers—not those who participated in the Whiskey Rebellion, but sober, hardworking, independent and deferential small landholders—would gradually spread across the continent, bringing democratic mores and institutions with them. In Jefferson's rhetoric lie the seeds of American Indian Removal and Manifest Destiny. In Jefferson's rhetoric also lie the moral justifications for both. It is no surprise then, that Andrew Jackson was an ardent Jeffersonian. Nor is it surprising that it was to Thomas Jefferson that Jackson looked for inspiration and justification.

Jackson and the Republican Tradition: "Justice and Fear"

Like many people of his generation, Jackson revered the founders, considering those of the Revolutionary era to be the models for appropriate action and belief. Yet, also like many of his generation, Jackson's reverence for the founding presidents was enacted through his understanding of his own time, not through an effort to bring their times current. Thus, rather than trying to decide what they would have done in his position, or trying to render them politically contemporary, as Fillmore, Pierce, and Buchanan would later do, Jackson's interpretations of the founding tended to assume that the framers would approve of his actions. As imbued in the "true" republican tradition as he was, he considered his voice the contemporary expression of theirs.

Jackson was greatly influenced by Jefferson.[30] Two main themes in Jefferson's thought—the idealization of the yeomanry and an interpretation of national history that depended heavily on the inevitable, but tragic passing of indigenous peoples—were especially important to Jackson.[31] Balance and stability were to be managed by Andrew Jackson as expansion, but as an ideological expansion of Jefferson's idealized white, yeoman, farming republic, not as the unfettered inclusion of new territory and new peoples. Indeed, racial superiority and entitlement were crucial elements in Jackson's understanding of the expanding republic.[32] Expansion was the national destiny, and natural forces would provide the necessary leaven to maintain the national balance.

Jefferson believed that Americans were essentially homogeneous and were adherents of a particular culture. Using his first inaugural to rhetorically unite a nation bitterly divided by the partisan rivalry of the election, Jefferson asked for national reconciliation and declared that "we are all Republicans, we are all Federalists."[33] More than that, however, the citizens of the United States were not only ideologically connected, but also joined by fate, history, and Divine Providence. Jefferson is worth quoting at length:

> Kindly separated by nature and a wide ocean from the exterminating havoc of one quarter of the globe; too high-minded to endure the degradations of the others; possessing a chosen country, with room enough for our descendants to the thousandth and thousandth generation; entertaining a due sense of our equal right to the use of our own faculties, to the acquisitions of our own industry, to honor and confidence from our fellow citizens, resulting not from birth, but from our actions and their sense of them; enlightened by a benign religion, professed indeed, and practiced in various forms, yet all of them increasing honesty, truth, temperance, gratitude, and the love of man; acknowledging and adoring an overruling Providence, which by all its dispensations proves that it delights in the happiness of man here and in his greater happiness hereafter—with all of these blessings, what more is necessary to make us a happy and a prosperous people?[34]

Jefferson here created a specific sort of citizen, a creation that has never lost its hold on the American imagination. According to this formulation, Americans were heirs to a political tradition that, despite its roots in Europe, owed nothing to contemporaneous Europe. Americans were chosen by a (Protestant) God; they inhabited an (empty) continent; and they were a righteous and Christian people, who were thankful for God's bounty and deserving of it. This language was clearly, for its time, inclusive. All inhabitants of the nation were, at least potentially, equally able to share in this vision. But this language also excluded even as it included. There were those in the United States, not all of them slaves, but including all slaves, who did not trace their ancestry to Europe. There were those in the United States who were not Protestant, those who were not Christian. Not only were they excluded, but the differences that directly led to their exclusion were themselves erased. Those who did not fit Jefferson's mold were not only excluded, but also rendered invisible. This formulation was all the more important because Jefferson combined a clear definition of a good citizen with the past and future of the nation. Good citizens not only accepted this rather narrow view of the nation's history, but promulgated it into the nation's future. Those whom Jefferson excluded were likely to remain invisible for the foreseeable future.

There were two elements in this rhetorical construction of nation and citizen: the yeomanry and the "vanishing Indian." In defining these two groups and the relationship between them, Jefferson also defined those who were to be central to the American polity and national self-understanding and those who were to have no place in either. This ideological creation of a specific kind of citizen was represented not as an actual construction, a political fiction, but as the result of historical inevitability. The nation's balance would be maintained not by the actions of the nation's elites, nor by the political choices of the mass of citizens, but by an implacable fate.

JEFFERSON'S RED BRETHREN AND WHITE YEOMEN

There were two obvious changes in Jefferson's rhetoric regarding American Indians from that of previous presidents. First, where Washington and Adams generally referred to American Indians in the context of war or treaties, by Jefferson's time the United States' military position had been sufficiently consolidated to allow him to see American Indians as clearly subordinate trading partners. Rather than referring to American Indians as "brothers," as George Washington had, Jefferson and his successors (until Woodrow Wilson) preferred to address them as their "red children,"[35] a locution that clearly denoted the change in power relations between the U.S. government and the various indigenous nations with which it dealt. By Jefferson's time, American Indians may have posed occasional minor threats, but not with the sense of military and national peril that characterized the earlier relationship—or that would characterize the nation's later relationships with certain indigenous nations.[36]

Although still factors in the presidential calculus, American Indians were becoming less politically visible. As white men were becoming more of a presence on the frontier, and more of a presence in presidential rhetoric, they were doing so at the expense of American Indians, who would have less political and rhetorical prominence as whites took more of their land.

Discussing American Indians in a letter to Benjamin Hawkins, Jefferson said, "The attention which you pay to their rights also does you great honor, as the want of that is a principal source of dishonor to the American character, the two principles on which our conduct toward the Indians should be founded are justice and fear. After the injuries we have done them they cannot love us, which leaves us no alternative but that of fear to keep them from attacking us, but justice is what we should never lose sight of & in time it may recover their esteem."[37] This was the analysis of one who had little cause to think of American Indian attacks as much more than an inconvenience. It was also the analysis of one who did not envision a nation in which American Indians were likely to play a significant role.

Rather than seeing in American Indians a danger to the union, Jefferson saw in them only land—the source of the nation's future. By his fourth annual message, in fact, Jefferson was recommending that Congress should put its resources into trade with American Indians rather than in war against them. He sought to maintain national stability through expansion, and expansion required land. He therefore sought to co-opt American Indians rather than make direct war upon them:

> By pursuing a uniform course of justice toward them, by aiding them in all the improvements which may better their condition, and especially by establishing a commerce on terms which shall be advantageous to them and only not losing to us, and so regulated as that no incendiaries of our own or any other nation may be permitted to disturb the natural effects of our just and friendly offices, we may render ourselves so necessary to their comfort and prosperity that the protection of our citizens from their disorderly members will become their interest and voluntary care. Instead therefore, of an augmentation of military force proportioned to our extension of frontier, I propose a moderate enlargement of

the capital employed in that commerce as a more effectual, economical, and humane instrument for preserving peace and good neighborhood with them.[38]

Jefferson thus sought to create a particular kind of citizen on the frontiers of the expanding nation. His ideal citizens would treat with the American Indians but would also dominate them. They would take American Indians into their paternal care and would help to tame them, calm their disorderliness, and make them effectual partners in national expansion. American Indians as members of distinct nations with distinct traditions and relationships with the U.S. government were being undifferentiated, subsumed into a mass that could then be rendered impotent and invisible.

American Indians were no longer threats; they had become a potential national resource. If they could be persuaded to develop these trade relationships, either because of debt or through choice, the vast tracts of land still controlled by American Indian nations would end up in the hands of the American government.[39] In addition, the American Indians themselves would be brought into market relationships with the United States. The ideal relationship between those who were included in the nation and those who were not was established. Those relationships were to be literally profitable—based on trade, and on terms that favored the expanding nation. Through such relationships, potential citizens could be trained in the practice of citizenship, their merit periodically evaluated. In the case of American Indians, their inclusion would depend on their ability to evaporate into the nation's population. Inclusion for them meant invisibility.

Prefiguring future American presidential rhetorical and political choices, Jefferson here relied on trade relations to foster more pacific political relations, erasing the cultural antecedents of strained relations and attempting to view all relationships through the lens of economics, arguing that cultural change would accompany economic advantage and rational self-interest. He, like many of his successors, tried to balance competing interests through a selective interpretation of the nature of those interests. All differences could be interpreted as a lack of "development." Through development, then, all (politically important) differences could be made to disappear. This conception of citizenship did the political work of helping to balance the young nation and promote its stability on terms that favored existing elites. Jefferson thus provided an important model for future presidents.[40]

By understanding cultural differences in terms of economics, Jefferson minimized the importance of culture. All cultures, in this (widely shared) understanding were on the same trajectory; they all started as "primitive" and slowly advanced. American Indians were not understood to be on a culturally contingent path, but as further behind white Europeans and Americans on a universal path. Cultural distinctiveness was erased, and the obvious, the humane option was for Americans to help American Indians to achieve an "American" level of development. Conquest was understood as a humanitarian mission. This constituted an important part of the ideological justification for westward expansion and the establishment of an "American empire." In presidential terms, it began with Jefferson.

The second and related obvious change in Jefferson's rhetoric from that of past presidents was the emphasis he placed on the importance of "civilizing" the American Indians, whom he paternalistically "regarded with the commiseration their history inspires."[41] Consistently with the analysis in the preceding paragraph, Jefferson understood American Indians as having two choices: they could adopt the culture of the encroaching whites or they could perish. If they did not develop, according to the model articulated by Jefferson, they would inevitably die. American Indians could either become invisible by disappearing into the American body politic, or they could become invisible by literally disappearing. In either case, they were understood as doomed, not by the political choices of Americans, but by the processes of a neutral nature.

It is well known and well understood how the narrative of the "vanishing Indian" served American expansionist goals.[42] But embedded in the description of American Indians that represented a key part of that narrative was a definition of American citizenship, an ideological argument that underpinned the disciplinary project of citizenship as early as Jefferson's day. By using American Indians as a negative example whose "faults" would inevitably lead to their demise, Jefferson also instructed non–American Indians in the behavior that would lead to their prosperity. Jefferson said, "But the endeavors to enlighten them on the fate which awaits their present course of life, to induce them to exercise their reason, follow its dictates, and change their pursuits with the change of circumstances have powerful obstacles to encounter; they are combated by the habits of their bodies, prejudices of their minds, ignorance, pride, and the influence of interested and crafty individuals among them who feel themselves something in the general order of things and fear to become nothing in any other."[43] American Indians ignored his enlightened instruction, they refused to follow his guidance and their reason, and they continued in their traditional ways, oblivious to their changed circumstances. This was a choice. It was not that they were unable to reason, but they chose and continued to choose the life of bodily satisfaction, either because they preferred pleasure to reason or because they were manipulated by "interested and crafty individuals." American Indians were condemned not by the actions of the American government or its citizens, but by their own stubborn disregard of the laws of nature and natural progress. According to this argument, history, nature, and their inexorable laws doomed the American Indians, not governmental policies. The national balance was the product of a wise God who interceded through natural forces to ensure the future of His chosen nation. Exclusion—forcible or otherwise, was necessary to the nation's development. American Indians were understood as hapless victims of an implacable fate.

That this analysis was demonstrably specious is well documented.[44] There is abundant evidence that amid the complexities inherent in the experiences of various indigenous nations and their reactions to Europeans, many American Indians well understood the Americans' expansionist goals and how those goals would affect their lives.[45] There is abundant evidence that in response to American incursions, many American Indians used artful combinations of resistance, accommodation, avoidance, and confrontation.[46] There is no evidence that Jefferson's analysis was accurate.

But its inaccuracy is also completely beside the point. Jefferson's description of American Indian predilections and behavior, which he undoubtedly offered in perfectly good faith, served at least two important functions. First, it placed the fate of American Indians in American Indian hands. Since it was their choice to refuse "civilization," their inevitable destruction could not be blamed on Americans or on the American government. In this formulation, neither Americans nor their government could be fairly accused of pursuing intentional strategies of physical or cultural genocide. They simply followed the inescapable dictates of history. American Indians had the ability to understand and obey these dictates as well. If they chose to forgo that opportunity or disobey those dictates, history would settle with them in its own way. The Americans were the neutral instruments of an ultimately disinterested fate.[47]

But they must be prepared and suited to serve as that instrument, which was the second function of Jefferson's description. As Smith's analysis would lead us to expect, the parameters of citizenship were related to the political work of nation building. In using the example of the misguided and doomed American Indians to describe those who would be crushed by the advancing American frontier, Jefferson also constructed their opposite—the white American yeoman farmer. Through contradefinition, Jefferson made it clear that good citizens would be attentive to "endeavors to enlighten them," would "exercise their reason," and "change their pursuits as their circumstances change." They would not give in to the "habits of their bodies" nor to the "prejudices of their minds," and they would remain resolute in the face of attempted manipulation by those who desired personal power over the public good. Thus, those citizens who wished to be included in the nation had a standard of belief, a standard of behavior, and an ascriptive standard to meet. Failure in any one realm was justification for exclusion, for the nation's balance depended on the maintenance of the borders of citizenship.

That this was a spectacularly poor description of those who settled the frontier would have interested Jefferson not at all. But that Andrew Jackson saw himself in this description would have powerful consequences for the nation and its definition of its citizens, for this is the beginning of the "frontier myth" that so many later presidents depended on in articulating the national identity. This myth helped to set the standard for citizenship and excluded many who aspired to it, for the language associated with maintaining the national balance is overtly exclusionary.

Jacksonian Democracy: Land, Democracy, and Citizenship

Jacksonian America is one of the most studied eras in our nation's history. It was a time when the issues of nationhood and political process, fought over in the Revolution and quarreled about since, were largely resolved; when the issues of inclusion that were to erupt into the Civil War were first becoming increasingly divisive and dangerous; and when the West was "opened," and the frontier was a place of settlement, war, and possibility. So significant was this age in our national development and so dominant was its leader that Andrew Jackson remains the only figure in American political history to give his name to an entire era. Jackson's presidency also provides valuable insight into the rhetorical processes of nation building and citizenship. It is a locus of ideological enactment of balance, invisibility, and citizenship.

And yet perhaps nothing better illustrates the complexities of American national identity and the president's role in defining it than Andrew Jackson. A hero to some, vilified by others, Jackson's example represents, if nothing else, the dangers of assuming too much about a singular and unified America, or a singular and unified American national identity. Jackson represents American military prowess. He represents the open-ended and democratic possibilities of a country where even the self-made—where especially the self-made—can attain and wield power. He represents the possibilities for the corruption and rapaciousness of that power. He represents the triumph of the "common man" as well as the fall of Man as deference was lost and the muddied masses literally occupied the White House. And, he represents an important moment in the creation and valorization of the American frontier as the key to American national identity, and an important mechanism through which we can begin to understand how the frontiersman became such an ideologically important figure in the creation of what Gerstle has dubbed the "Rooseveltian nation."

Amid all the meanings attributed to Jackson, he is probably best known for three things: his stress on states' rights, illustrated in the Nullification crisis, the expansion of democracy during his presidency, often exemplified by his "war" on the Bank of the United States, and American Indian Removal. These are often considered in isolation from one another, or removal is ignored altogether.[48] Schlesinger's Pulitzer Prize–winning biography of Jackson, for instance, contains not one mention of American Indian Removal, or even of American Indians.[49] Some want to praise Jackson for spearheading the first great movement toward true inclusiveness, for truly including the "common man" in important political debates.[50] Others want to condemn him for the genocidal policies he pursued toward the continent's first inhabitants.[51] And many try to rescue him from the charges of racism on the grounds that his personal feelings toward individual American Indians were neutral or even benign.[52]

Given this complexity, it is important to understand the context as well as the content of his administration. The crucial fact of his presidency was that the expansion of democracy to include nearly all white men, the explosion of participation in civic life that Tocqueville so brilliantly detailed,[53] was not inconsistent with the intentional genocide of American Indians. That explosion of participation was *premised* on American Indian Removal and American Indian genocide.[54] Andrew Jackson rested his stewardship of the nation on its unimpeded expansion. His political coalition depended on the inclusion of nearly all Christian white men. He couched his policies regarding expansion and inclusion in ideological terms that proffered balance as the natural product of natural forces. He considered expansion and (limited) inclusion to be foreordained, and good republican citizens were those who understood their duty and followed it. In Jackson, the exclusionary nature of purportedly inclusive rhetoric and policy was clear.

It was clear both practically and rhetorically. Practically, the increases in democracy were premised on the increase in the numbers of those who could be presumed to have the character and virtue necessary for democratic citizenship. The single best indicator of such character was land.[55] Land ownership provided for a certain standard of living, it allowed freedom from the imprecations of the wealthy, and, most important, it meant that one had a stake in the system and a commitment to its protection and preservation. Land, in other words, served as an educating force. It trained people, not in the rarified pursuits of scholars like Jefferson, Adams, and Madison, but in the business of citizenship in what was still a predominantly rural and largely unschooled nation. But for land to be useful as an educating force, it had to be worked, not left as wilderness. It had to be taken from American Indians and developed by whites. Stability was vital. But during times of great national expansion such stability was difficult to maintain. For Jackson, as for Jefferson before him and the antebellum presidents who followed him, this stability was best achieved through the creation of a certain sort of citizen. For Jackson, the frontiersman exemplified that citizen. Those who did not live up to the idealized model citizen were to be overtly, explicitly, and intentionally excluded from the nation.

Rhetorically, however, these exclusions could not be announced as integral to the national character, inconsistent as they were with the inclusive national principles. Most presumed incapacities remained invisible; widely agreed upon, perhaps, but nonetheless unmentioned for various reasons. The exclusion of women, for instance, was not a contingent issue. It was too natural to merit discussion.[56] The exclusion of slaves could not be considered a contingent issue—to put slavery into question threatened the national consensus. Slaveholders retained a powerful grip on national institutions, and abolitionists were not yet a force in national politics. Slavery remained largely off the national agenda.[57]

The dispossession of American Indians, however, was an ideal issue for political debate. American Indians were "other," a savage opposite of "us," and could serve as an appropriate vehicle for the construction of an American identity.[58] Members of very different nations, with different cultures, practices, and relationships with one another and with the federal government became increasingly subsumed into the undifferentiated label *Indian*, which served as a metonym, reducing difference, and allowing for singular—usually negative—definitions of them. This reduction was an important marker on their road from politically visible "problems" to invisibility.

As American Indians were becoming more invisible however, they became a powerful educating force for those who aspired to inclusion. On the one hand, there was the idealized frontiersman, a model citizen. On the other was the doomed American Indian. American Indians, by example, could do much of the ideological work of nation building. And they were well situated at this historical moment to provide such an example. American Indian dispossession presented no threat to national unity. At the same time, the undemocratic (if not antidemocratic) actions needed to be both explained and sustained in the language of democracy if they were to have legitimacy in the eyes of the nation and the world.[59] It is not surprising, then, that Andrew Jackson devoted considerable attention to this subject. In an age when presidents spoke in public infrequently, rarely did Jackson speak without alluding to American Indians. American Indians were mentioned in his first inaugural, in all of his annual messages, in many of his other prominent speeches, and in his farewell address. American Indians and policies concerning them became an important locus for the articulation of national identity.[60]

As they lost individual and tribal (national) identities, American Indians were, paradoxically, among the most visible of American inhabitants. But they were visible in increasingly powerless roles. They featured less as the "merciless savages" of the Declaration and more as the vanishing examples of peoples who failed to make appropriate use of this magnificent continent and were thus doomed to be exiled from its bounty. They provided ideologically important examples of negative citizenship, warnings of where the United States would end if it failed in its mission.

Throughout Jackson's public speech were three main connections between American Indians, democracy, land, and citizenship: a specific narrative of national history, a specific definition of "citizen," and the combination of these two elements into the third, Jackson's specific projection of the national mission, the responsibilities of and entitlements due those included as citizens. In this, Jackson proposed a specific understanding of American national identity, one based on the dominance of Christian white males, participation in a market economy, and the protection of certain ascriptive hierarchies, especially racially based power structures.

In all cases, the result was the same: an articulation of the beliefs that the end of "the Indian" was both inevitable and fast approaching; that the best hope of preserving American Indians from extinction lay in their removal, which made that policy therefore humanitarian; and that democracy would be best served by the replacement of American Indians with whites who would develop the land and make it productive, extending the promise of democratic participation to some while institutionalizing the criteria through which others would be excluded. These institutional structures, in turn, helped to render that exclusion "natural" and thus affected the ways in which the nation understood itself. In Jackson's rhetoric, the political work of creating a civic ideology that would foster a sense of national cohesion depended on both the inclusion of some and the exclusion of others. For that ideology to be widely shared, it had to be grounded in the preexisting understanding of national history and national destiny.

JACKSON'S HISTORICAL JUSTIFICATION

Jackson's rhetoric offered a coherent view of world and national history and of the individual's role in both. His national balance depended on an ideological articulation of the American frontier and the individual's place within it. He picked up the themes of national development from Jefferson and extended them. Jefferson understood continental history as really beginning with European colonization, and he understood historical forces as operating through Americans. Jefferson provided balance between contending interests through reliance on Providence and the explication of natural forces operating through the American yeoman farmer. For Jackson, whose political coalition depended on expanding the Jeffersonian republic, balance was equally a matter of Providence and the American frontier. For him, continental history began before the arrival of Europeans, and the historical forces that would make Americans their instrument predated their appearance. He presented this view of American history in his second annual message, saying, "In the monuments and fortresses of an unknown people, spread over the extensive regions of the West, we behold the memorials of a once powerful race, which was exterminated or has disappeared to make room for the existing savage tribes. Nor is there anything in this which, upon a comprehensive view of the general interests of mankind, is to be regretted. Philanthropy could not wish to see this continent restored to the condition in which it was found by our forefathers."[61] It was quite beyond Jackson, as it was beyond nearly all his contemporaries, to consider the idea that those "monuments and fortresses" were not contrived by an "unknown people" but were constructed by the "savage tribes" whose capabilities were so often misunderstood and denigrated, and who were widely considered incapable of "civilization."[62] Once Europeans came to claim the continent, however, it would not matter what degree of civilization predated their arrival. The continent was theirs by right and the will of Divine Providence. Jackson balanced the pressures for both stability and expansion by justifying expansion in terms of American stability—the nation's destiny was predicated on its growth.

Jackson, like other presidents before him, argued that there were only three choices open to American Indians. They could die or be killed off in the name of progress; they could cease being American Indian and become "civilized," give up all tribal identity, and join white civil society; or they could continue their "savage ways," outside and beyond the domain of the United States. Implicitly, these choices faced all the nation's inhabitants. American Indians became the metonym for the nation's groups—they could all vanish, become assimilated, or live as exiles—until history caught up with them. The example of American Indians thus did more than justify continental conquest. Symbolically American Indians also did much of the political work of nation building for Jacksonians.

In all probability Jackson considered the first option not only the most likely but also the most desirable, as he believed that all attempts to civilize them had failed and that attempts to "save" them were equally doomed. In his first annual message, for instance, in December 1829, he said:

> Our conduct toward these people is deeply interesting to our national character. Their present condition, compared to what they once were, makes a powerful appeal to our sympathies. Our ancestors found them the uncontrolled possessors of these vast regions. By persuasion and force they have been made to retire from river to river and from mountain to mountain, until some tribes have become extinct, and others have left but remnants to preserve for awhile their once terrible names. Surrounded by the whites with their arts of civilization, which by destroying the resources of the savage doom him to weakness and decay, the fate of the Mohegan, the Narragansett and the Deleware is fast overtaking the Choctaw, the Cherokee, and the Creek. That this fate surely awaits them if they remain within the limits of the States does not admit of a doubt. Humanity and national honor demand that every effort should be made to avert so great a calamity.[63]

Several important things are revealed by this quotation. First, note that the parameters of ideal citizenship were made clear here. Indeed, the first line of the quotation reveals that Jackson saw in the national treatment of American Indians a metonym for the nation and its minorities. Good citizens were controlled; the American Indians were not; they did not discipline themselves nor did they discipline their use of the continent. In this lack of achievement their fate was foreordained. Their names, "once terrible," were reduced—both in number and in the fear that they generated. But the warning was clear, despite the reminiscent tone. If Americans chose badly, if they failed in their commitment to the frontier ideology he was outlining, they too would fall victim to history, and their names would be equally lost.

Thus, Jackson clearly validated the historical narrative found in Jefferson's rhetoric. For Jackson as for Jefferson, the need to balance American stability with expansion led inexorably to the forced exclusion of American Indians. The continent was inevitably becoming dominated by whites, whose actions, however unintentionally, doomed the American Indians. American Indian Removal was inevitable, not the product of deliberate choice. Agency was displaced from American political leaders onto "history," and Jackson appeared as a friend of the American Indians rather than as their enemy. That the tribes he named here as already extinct not only continued to exist in his day, but also in ours, undermined only the accuracy, not the persuasive or ideological power, of this narrative. The political work here is clear: Jackson extended and articulated Jefferson's rhetorical construction of American political identity as he extended and articulated Jefferson's physical expansion of the nation.

In becoming the interpreter of history, Jackson also assumed a position as voice of the people. As agency was removed from American political leaders, this move also absolved the American people who sanctioned the actions of those leaders. As the frontiersman in the White House, Jackson stood symbolically for all settlers.[64] He became both symbol of and spokesman for "the people." The president thus assumed the role as spokesman for the historical forces governing the fate of the nation even as he assumed control of the administrative apparatus of that nation. National balance could be achieved by extending the nation and dissipating conflict through extended territorial reach.

The presidents of the founding generation spoke for "the people" as elite interpreters of a shared culture. Their rhetorical authority derived from their ability to instruct and guide the people such that they could fulfill their role in the designs of Providence and history. Andrew Jackson spoke for "the people" as one of them. His rhetorical authority stemmed from his ability to articulate a view of history in which they could see themselves. The nation existed for them and for those like them. This ideologically driven sense of "peoplehood" was profoundly satisfying to those Jackson most needed to satisfy, facilitating the political work of nation building. The processes observed by Smith and Gerstle were instantiated through presidential rhetoric.

In addition, this narrative, like Jefferson's, placed events outside the American government's control. In advocating removal, Jackson believed that he was advocating the only policy option that would not lead to the destruction of the American Indians. Jackson thus positioned himself as the guardian and protector of American Indian peoples.[65] This position had two important qualifications, however. First, as Michael Paul Rogin notes, Jackson claimed the power to protect American Indians once they were removed, and to punish them if they refused to go, but not to protect them if they chose to stay.[66] This claim concerning his limited yet expansive power functioned to absolve him of responsibility for the consequences of American Indian Removal. This tactic will later surface with other presidents as well, as it reveals both an implicit understanding of the nature of the office and the political work with which the office is charged as conservator of the nation and its values.

The second qualification was articulated by Jackson in his first inaugural, during which he said, "It will be my sincere and constant desire to observe toward the American Indian tribes within our limits a just and liberal policy and to give that humane and considerate attention to their rights and their wants which is consistent with the habits of our Government and the feelings of our citizens."[67] Jackson could not have been clearer about the limits he set on American Indian rights. Such as they were, they would be protected only to the point that they did not interfere with the national government, or exceed the past practices of that government or the sentiments of "the people." Jackson's rhetoric thus served to create the very kind of citizens needed to foster a national balance of interests. Citizens were those who were politically visible, even valorized, as the common people. Those who more precisely echoed the refined culture and mores of the founders were no longer emblematic of those founders. Instead, the "common man" replaced a culture of deference with one of (limited) defiance. These people were needed both for Jackson's immediate political purposes and for the longer-term project of opening the frontier and expanding the nation. Those who were unsuitable for urban life found an outlet on the less ordered frontier. Their sentiments, not the sentiments of the effete Eastern bankers, determined the nation's will.

Consistent with his ideological understanding, and because his concern was with creating a certain kind of citizen most acceptable to his governing coalition, Jackson did not consider the fact that the government in question had generally been at war with various American Indian nations who thus had cause to doubt the beneficence of its actions. Jackson's reliance on "the feelings of the people" as a guide for action was also ideologically congruent with his understanding of American national government. Although compatible with his assumption of authority as representative of the people's will, this claim also directly contravened the founders' insistence on reason above passion. Furthermore, it made it very clear that as far as Jackson was concerned, whether they consented to removal or remained within the territory of the United States, American Indians were not part of "the people," and their feelings deserved and would receive absolutely no consideration when compared to the feelings of those who were included in the polity. American Indians were politically visible as outsiders, as useful examples of the fate that awaited Americans who did not accept the nation's purpose. As members of the polity, they were invisible, erased.

Finally, this view of history cast doubt on Jefferson's understanding of American Indian potential and illustrated the tension between understanding American Indians "lack" of civilization as culturally driven and thus amenable to change through assimilation and education, or racially driven, and thus inherent and unchangeable, between civic nationalism and racial nationalism. Both understandings coexisted, often uneasily, throughout the period. American Indians were a crucial locus for tensions between civic and racial nationalism. In the efforts of the government and private organizations to "civilize" them, American Indians also became something of a set of pilot projects for the nation's disciplinary project of citizenship. Jefferson, for instance, argued that if they so chose, American Indians had the capacity to be "civilized." In encouraging trade relations, he also implied that one element of the civilizing process would be routine, if not constant, economic association with whites. Through such associations, American Indians would learn the habits and mores of democracy and would thus eventually be able to participate in republican institutions. Jeffersonian attitudes about the American Indians' capacity to become "civilized" conflicted sharply with Jacksonian ideas about their inherent unsuitability for citizenship. Over the course of national history, government policy alternated between these two poles. In this, American Indians became an important barometer of the nation's willingness to incorporate difference or to force assimilation.

In Jackson's time, while the missionary impulse was still quite strong, there was an increasing sense that exposure to whites was deleterious to American Indians and that the civilizing process would have better success if American Indians were first removed from the pernicious influence of white society, if they were rendered physically as well as politically invisible. As Jackson said in his fifth annual message,

> That those tribes cannot exist surrounded by our settlements and in continued contact with our citizens is certain. They have neither the intelligence, the industry, the moral habits nor the desire of improvement which are essential to any favorable change in their condition. Established in the midst of another and powerful race, and without appreciating the causes of their inferiority or seeking to control them, they must necessarily yield to the force of circumstances and ere long disappear. Such has been their fate heretofore, and if it is to be averted—and it is—it can only be done by a general removal beyond our boundaries and by the reorganization of their political system upon principles adapted to the new relations in which they will be placed.[68]

To be "saved," American Indians had to be rendered invisible. In time, they could return to a less problematic visibility, and once they assumed sufficient levels of civilization, they could even potentially return to the polity. More likely, they would simply die. Unsuitable as they were for the project of nation building, they could not hope to survive the rigors of frontier life. Jackson could thus argue that he was not advocating the physical and cultural genocide of American Indian peoples; he was in fact seeking its opposite, their preservation. Historians such as Francis Paul Prucha and more recently Robert V. Remini have, in fact, argued eloquently in Jackson's defense on this issue, claiming that he did, in fact, act out of humanitarian impulses and that these nations are with us today because of such action.[69]

Jackson summarized the history of American policy toward the American Indians in his first annual message:

> It has long been the policy of Government to introduce among them the arts of civilization in the hope of gradually redeeming them from the wandering life. This policy has, however, been coupled with another wholly incompatible with its success. Professing a desire to civilize and settle them, we have at the same time lost no opportunity to purchase their lands and thrust them farther into the wilderness. By this means not only have they been kept in a wandering state, but have been led to look upon us as unjust and indifferent to their fate. Thus, though lavish in their expenditures upon the subject, Government has constantly defeated its own policy, and the Indians in general, receding farther and farther to the west, have retained their savage habits.[70]

Since the process of making American Indians into "citizens" spelled out in the first part of the quotation did not work, as they were never "redeemed from the wandering life," other measures were clearly called for, measures more consistent with the rigors of nation building, measures that called for their overt, explicit, and determined exclusion. "Savagery" and "a wandering state" were thus explicitly connected to one another. Because American Indians, when they had land, failed to make of that land an educating force, they did not learn the lessons of citizenship so vital to the United States. Furthermore, now that American Indians lacked land on which to settle, Jackson argued, they could not acquire the capacity to learn the lessons of citizenship from the land and therefore had to be literally as well as figuratively removed from the borders of the polity where they had been residing. This was not an act of cruelty, as his critics would have it, but one he understood as being motivated by generosity and compassion. The point of Jackson's actions was not to harm the American Indians; prominent though they were, American Indians were not the focus of his policy. Instead, his attention was on how to balance and stabilize a rapidly expanding nation through specific definitions of citizenship. For Jackson, the best way to make citizens was through land, appropriately owned, worked, and developed.

Given his belief that continued exposure to whites could only cause "weakness and decay" among the American Indians,[71] Jackson could feel secure in the disinterested kindness of his "hope, therefore, that all good citizens, and none more zealously than those who think the Indians oppressed by subjection to the laws of the States, will unite in attempting to open the eyes of those children of the forest to their true condition, and by a speedy removal to relieve them from all the evils, real or imaginary, present or prospective, with which they may be supposed to be threatened."[72] Jackson knew the "true condition" of the American Indians; he understood their historical trajectory, for it had been outlined by Jefferson. He saw in his own time the furtherance of history as predicted by Jefferson and others. It was imperative that the American Indians themselves come to understand this truth, for only if they did could they act to prevent their otherwise inevitable demise.

Having thus first provided for the safety and security of those most helpless denizens of the United States, Jackson could then further his efforts to educate and "civilize" them. Once they were rendered physically as well as politically invisible, they could be remade as citizens, and they could one day hope to return to the polity as visible members of it. As he said in his third annual message,

> But the removal of the Indians beyond the limits and jurisdiction of the States does not place them beyond the reach of philanthropic and Christian instruction. On the contrary, those whom philanthropy or religion may induce to live among them in their new abode will be more free in the exercise of their benevolent functions than if they remained within the limits of the States, embarrassed by their internal regulations. Now subject to no control but the supervising agency of the Central Government, exercised with the sole

view of preserving peace, they may proceed unmolested in the interesting experiment of gradually advancing a community of American Indians from barbarism to the habits and enjoyments of a civilized life.[73]

Thus, like children, American Indians would be sheltered from the dangers inherent in Anglo-American culture until they developed far enough, and became mature and wise enough, to cope adequately with its more negative and destructive qualities. Like children, they were to remain politically invisible until maturity and material conditions rendered them suitable candidates for citizenship.

Certainly, it was possible to read this argument as self-serving, if not hypocritical. But one does not need to demean Jackson's rhetoric to see how it is designed to accomplish instrumental policy goals. Only by taking that rhetoric seriously, however, can its constitutive implications be revealed. For in defending his actions through these particular language choices, Jackson was not merely engaging in an exercise of hypocrisy. He was also defining his ideal of citizenship.

JACKSON'S DEFINITION OF CITIZENSHIP

Primarily, of course, Jackson agreed with Jefferson that ideal democratic citizens were those who exercised their faculties without regard to outside manipulations. For both presidents, "good" citizens contributed to stability in a growing republic by exercising judgment and strength of mind and character. This understanding would also guide the antebellum presidents as they sought to maintain order over an increasingly fractious polity. But where Jefferson understood stability to depend on the use of dispassionate reason, and for Fillmore, Pierce, and Buchanan it would mean a temperate citizenry, for Jackson it meant making independent choices. Thus, rather than the criteria of character and education so central to the founders' conception of republican citizenship, Jackson implicitly relied on land as the surrogate for independence. Jackson governed an expanding nation; it had to be allowed to grow, but growth potentially destabilized the founders' order. Jackson interpreted that order in ways that were consistent with his needs, and Jefferson's yeoman farmer became Jackson's independent frontiersman.

Not only did Jackson refer to "agriculture [as] the first and most important occupation of man"[74] in his seventh annual message, he first congratulated the nation on an increase in land sales, and then on the consequent ability of the populace to resist the forces of tyranny implicit in centralization in general and personified by the Bank of the United States in particular.[75] For Jackson, land equaled independence. It was the independence offered by land ownership that imbued citizens with what Jackson considered a truly democratic character. In this, he consistently distinguished landowners and farmers from the dependent and more easily manipulated people such as women, nonwhites, and the laboring classes.

Land fueled democracy. Land freed servants from the strictures of masters. Land freed sons from their dependence on fathers. Land freed the poor from domination by the rich, and the enterprising from the demands of civilization. Land freed everyone, in fact, except the slaves, who were required to work it; women, who were needed to tend it; those too poor to afford it or too nonwhite to be entitled to it; and American Indians, who were forced to cede it. That land came from the American Indians in ever-increasing amounts, at an ever-increasing pace.[76] By 1850, land sales comprised 80 percent of the revenues in the federal budget.[77] The primary source of new wealth between 1820 and 1860 was land speculation.[78]

Because land was the surrogate for freedom of choice, therefore, it was important if not imperative for the American Indians to *choose* to leave their land in order for removal to be seen as legitimate.[79] It was equally important for their own development that American Indians willingly accept their own invisibility, their own exclusion. As we will see with other groups in other contexts, the acceptance of their (temporary) exclusion becomes a frequently used barometer of the capacity for (eventual) citizenship. Later presidents will call for patience or will defer the demands of groups seeking inclusion; for this time, the harsher choice of accepting removal was the only path toward eventual reincorporation. Citizenship and exclusion were conceived of in terms that Jackson understood as contributing to the national balance.

As Jackson himself said in his first annual message, "This emigration should be voluntary, for it would be as cruel as unjust to compel the Aborigines to abandon the graves of their fathers and seek a home in a distant land. But they should be distinctly informed that if they remain within the limits of the States they must be subject to their laws. . . . Submitting to the laws of the States and receiving, like other citizens, protection in their person and their property, they will ere long become merged with the mass of our population."[80] Note that the best American Indians could ever hope for was some level of invisibility—they would either be forcibly excluded from the polity, or rendered non–American Indian as they are "merged" once again into it.

Removal in Jackson's view was the natural culmination of history, not a choice forced by some people upon other people. It was instead a product of the relentless march of historical inevitability which facilitated national balance and thus, the nation's future. According to this language, it was not political exigency, not the need to build and protect an electoral and governing coalition that motivated governmental policies such as removal, but history. Jackson's political coalition only benefited from these policies because they were on the right side of history. Because American Indians made choices that put them in the way of history's inexorable march, they would lose their land, the marker of independent choice, and thus would be crushed by historical forces. They had proven themselves unworthy of the land and of citizenship, and had to be removed from the one and excluded from the other.

In his second annual message Jackson said, "Rightly considered, the policy of the General Government toward the red man is not only liberal, but generous. He is unwilling to submit to the laws of the States and mingle with the general population. To save him from this alternative, or perhaps utter annihilation, the General Government kindly offers him a new home and proposes to pay the whole expense of his removal and settlement."[81] According to this understanding, now that the American Indians were considered as a single amorphous entity and were relatively powerless vis-à-vis the general government, that government could have chosen harsher methods of exclusion, and the American Indians, as resistant to previous attempts to help them as they had been, would have had no just cause for complaint. Instead, as the mythologized story of the frontier would have it, the government chose to act in ways that would protect both the American Indians and the new, growing nation. It would remove those in need of sanctuary, reeducate them, and allow the progress of the nation to continue without them. The political work of defining the nation and disciplining its citizens was accomplished rhetorically by the president.

Note that American Indians, even in their removal, served as examples of citizenship in a frontier nation. The things the American Indians ought to desire and that the government would provide were a new home and the expenses of settlement. These were precisely those things that American settlers were themselves desiring: the wherewithal to move West and the land to build on once they were there. The hardships experienced by the American Indians during removal were no greater than those whites expected to endure: "Doubtless it will be painful to leave the graves of their fathers; but what do they more than our ancestors did or our children are now doing? ... And is it supposed that the wandering savage has a stronger attachment to his home than the settled, civilized Christian?"[82] American Indians were thus like American citizens in some ways—in what they wanted and in how their suffering could be measured—but unlike those citizens in their capacity to enjoy and understand the benefits of "civilized" society, an incapacity that made removal necessary. Thus, a hierarchy of citizenship was established. American Indians had not yet been taught to want those things that settlers already desired. Rhetorically, they were demarcated as inferior.

The need for balance fed the need for land. Still advocating American Indian Removal as passionately in his second term as he had in his first, Jackson's sixth annual message argued for the necessity of removal, saying, "The experience of every year adds to the conviction that emigration, and that alone, can preserve from destruction the remnant of the tribes yet living amongst us. The facility with which the necessaries of life are procured and the treaty stipulations providing aid for the emigrant Indians in the agricultural pursuits and the important concern of education, and their Removal from those causes that have heretofore depressed all and destroyed many of the tribes, can not fail to stimulate their exertions and reward their industry."[83] Thus, removal would accomplish what decades of policy had not: in rendering them invisible, it would also help American Indians become productive citizens. And for Jackson, the equation of productivity and citizenship would have been very nearly tautological. For Jackson, the ideal citizen was not the idealized farmer of Jefferson's imagining. The ideal citizen was the feeling and passionate settler who would brave all for the opportunity to develop land and be integrated into the market economy.[84] This passion would, by the time of the antebellum presidents, be seen as potentially destructive of the nation, but for now, the ideal citizen was not the effete, citified denizen of the Eastern United States, but the adventurous and passionate hero of the frontier. The ideal freehold was not a family farm geared toward individual subsistence, but an entrepreneurial enterprise dedicated to improving personal and thus national prosperity.

This version of citizenship, history, and the American mission had its origins in Jefferson's day, and its legitimation as a national goal in Jackson's. As Smith's analysis would lead us to expect, the ideology of the frontier was a powerful force in fostering a sense of nationality over a vast territorial expanse. As Jackson himself said in his second annual message, "What good man would prefer a country covered with forests and ranged by a few thousand savages to our extensive Republic, studded with cities, towns, and prosperous farms, embellished with all the improvements which art can devise or industry execute, occupied by more than 12,000,000 happy people, and filled with all the blessings of liberty, civilization, and religion?"[85] Jacksonian democracy hinged on this definition of a "good man." It was these "good men" who were the beneficiaries of historical progress, for they were the ones chosen by God, who providentially was clearing the continent for them. All that was required for these "good men" was to recognize and act upon their chosen status and play their role in the national mission.

This mission and this future were defined in contrast to what the American Indians could expect. The nation, too, had a choice. It could live, like the American Indians, on the fringes of greatness, impoverished, and excluded, never really fit to join the future offered to civilized nations, and thus pass slowly, inexorably into history. Or Americans could choose Jackson's idealized future, one of hope, possibility, and expansion. Only those with the proper ideological commitment, race, gender, or access to and control over land were fit for that future. And so the American frontier myth, purportedly inclusive, contained certain specific exclusions. For Jackson, national destiny rested on these exclusions.

JACKSON'S VISION OF NATIONAL DESTINY

As scholars too numerous to note have indicated, the United States has long considered itself to have unique access to freedom and a unique responsibility to share their experiences and ideals with the rest of the world. By the Jacksonian era, that mission had become inextricably intertwined with an imperative toward national territorial expansion.[86] For Jackson, that mission was symbolized by the frontiersmen, the "adventurous and hardy population of the West,"[87] whose lives served as a synecdoche for the life of the nation. It was this service that made Jackson's rage against what he understood as "artificial distinctions"[88] so complete. These distinctions and the divisions that they caused not only undermined national equality, but interfered with the progress of the national mission.

Jackson's political coalition demanded certain sorts of political actions—many of which have been spelled out here. For Jackson, maintaining the national balance meant expanding the nation's boundaries. It also meant obeying the imperatives of Providence and nature. Failure to understand the inexorable force of history would lead Americans along the doomed path so darkly illustrated by American Indians. This reliance on an inevitable destiny justified political action in the present. It removed agency from the American government and put the onus of genocide on history and Providence while ideologically reinforcing the effects of such policies. All these processes became subsumed into an idealized notion of the American mission.

That mission, as Jackson and his contemporaries understood it, was not to absorb the influences of the many cultures and peoples of the Americas and its immigrants and to create a multicultural polity based on the forbearance and respect that equality demands. His view of the American mission involved an obligation to resist the contagion of "foreign" ideas and to spread the dominant understanding of citizenship through an ever-expanding nation. This ideological dissemination would not occur by educating and including suitable others, as in Jefferson's model, but in relocating or destroying those others and by populating the land thus left "vacant" and by rendering that land productive.

In his fourth annual message Jackson explained this view of

national destiny: "It cannot be doubted that the speedy settlement of these lands constitutes the true interest of the Republic. The wealth and strength of a country are its population, and the best part of that population are the cultivators of the soil. Independent farmers are everywhere the basis of society and the true friends of liberty."[89] For Jackson, the national balance required expansion to promote stability. It was through productivity of the land that the American mission would be fulfilled, and in the virtue of its citizens, "the bone and sinew of the country,"[90] that freedom would be protected. In his farewell address, he said, "It is to yourselves that you must look for safety and the means of guarding and perpetuating your free institutions."[91] The continent had to be settled by the same people who already occupied the United States, and the existing ascriptive hierarchies, accompanied by legitimating democratic ideals, would spread westward. Jackson's America would be secured. Balance, for Jackson, meant an expanded territory, and through the land thus acquired, a specifically educated citizenry. What appeared to be inclusive language—and what was, in fact, inclusive, for the rise in the number of those newly considered politically visible and viable citizens should not be overlooked—was also premised on certain important, if implicit exclusions.

With this, the founders' system of a stable government based on the limited inclusion of a particular class and the deference of the citizenry toward persons of character comprising the ruling elite was gone. In its place was a polity where the important political distinctions were distinctions of race and property. But as the nation expanded, taking ideas of a racialized nation with it, so did its understanding of civic nationalism. The creed that justified some exclusions was also wielded as a powerful tool by those hoping to embrace a more inclusive polity. These tensions would influence politics into the next century and beyond.

Conclusion

For the moment, however, a racialized and class-based understanding of the American citizen and the American mission led to particular consequences. Most fundamentally, of course, this rhetoric had consequences for American Indians. Their descent into invisibility offered a lesson in citizenship to other Americans and a warning about where history might lead a nation inattentive to those lessons. In constructing policies and an ideology that justified those policies, Jackson created an enduring political coalition as well as an enduring definition of American national identity. Invisibility brought with it different lessons from those that Jackson claimed, for both the nation and for those it excluded. It created citizens who believed in specific and select versions of the American frontier and the cultures that thrived on it, versions of citizenship that would begin to prove politically problematic in just a few decades.

This rhetoric also functioned to tie citizenship to land, which was also implicitly predicated on the dispossession of others. It also unintentionally reinforced racialized understandings of nationalism, while doing little to strengthen more civic versions. Thus, to be a citizen meant to formalize the fundamental distinction between "American Indian" and "white." Race became a marker of more than difference between "slave" and "free"; it constituted a specific relationship to land, and through land to political, social, and economic power. "American Indian" came to mean savagery, wildness, freedom, and independence. "White," on the other hand, came to mean entitlement—to "civilization" and land, and to the right to define the terms under which they could both be contained, controlled, and maintained.

For most of those who gained some access to political and cultural power during the Age of Jackson, then, this sense of entitlement was new. They came to understand it as valuable and to cling to it with fervor. This sense of entitlement helped to fuel that other great controversy of Jackson's presidency, his war on the National Bank and the moneyed, privileged interests Jackson felt it represented. That sense of entitlement fueled the focus on "the will of the people," which remains the hallmark of our system and which was, among other things, behind the argument for Nullification. That sense of entitlement fueled among many whites the fear of immigrants, free blacks, and others that would frame politics into the second half of the nineteenth century.

Jackson had to balance the needs and interests of agrarian settlers, the forces of a burgeoning market economy, and the moneyed as well as the laboring classes to provide for the nation's stability. He responded to those pressures by both centralizing power and decentralizing it; by containing the polity and by expanding it; by controlling the energies of the citizenry and by unleashing them. Some citizens were valorized and others rendered invisible as part of the disciplinary project that made expansion possible without sacrificing a sense of encompassing national character and identity. In this process, citizenship, race, and entitlement became inextricably linked, and the linkage was legitimated in presidential speech. Thus, the maintenance of these artificial but politically meaningful categories became important to those who would be included, and the battles over maintaining, modifying, or eliminating those categories as a basis for exclusion became battles over nationally acceptable definitions of citizenship and humanity.

2 / Temperance, Character, and Race in the Antebellum United States

Extremes beget extremes.
—Franklin Pierce, "Fourth Annual Message"

ONE OF THE KEY political questions of the 1850s concerned who would be considered members of the polity and who would continue to be excluded from it. The price of exclusion and the pain of invisibility were laid most obviously on African Americans, both slave and free. Other groups were also actively excluded—for instance, certain immigrants (the Irish, Asians), and members of certain religions (Jews, Catholics, Muslims, Mormons). During these years, few people—none of them in the political mainstream—spoke publicly in favor of the immediate extension of full political or economic rights to members of these groups.[1] Their exclusion remained invisible, generally unmentioned and uncontested. Citizenship remained not a birthright of "all men" (much less all women), but a privilege reserved for those who could demonstrate their democratic character and capacity. Equally important, those new to such privilege were also aware of its tenuous nature and jealously guarded their prerogatives. As regional tensions enveloped the nation, the political balance established by Jefferson and Jackson became ever more precarious. The need to maintain that balance and preserve the power of the governing coalition became more intense and more difficult to accomplish.

Jefferson and Jackson had managed political coalitions that depended on expansion—of the nation, the land available to that nation, and the economy that underpinned both. Inclusion in a burgeoning market economy was the pivotal need for the Jacksonian frontier. By the 1850s, however, that market economy was reasonably well established, and its continued growth depended on the continued supply of labor. And the nature of that labor became *the* issue of the 1850s, as the Jacksonian coalition of slaveholders and free white men, united in their desire for land, began to divide over their interests in the economy.

The political problem of the decade before the Civil War, then, became the problem of reconciling all the differing claims to entitlement and doing so in ways that would not unravel the fragile fabric of the national union. Whereas Jefferson and Jackson had articulated a specific, ideological definition of union to sustain their political coalition and legitimate their policy choices, Presidents Fillmore, Pierce, and Buchanan had to rely on that still powerful ideology while subtly shifting its meaning so that the coalition to which they owed their position and political allegiance could be preserved amid changed circumstances.

The inherent difficulties of this problem were in part why there were three presidents in the single decade of the 1850s.[2] All three of these presidents sought to solve the problem in similar ways, defending the preexisting national balance by defining citizenship in terms of the character, race, and attitudes that would, in their view, hold the union together; rhetoric that resulted in the maintenance of hierarchies among residents, citizens, and inhabitants. They sought to limit the expansionist promise of Jefferson and Jackson, for preservation lay now in contracting, not in expanding, the nation. The challenge was, in this period as so often in our history, to preserve the stability of the past in institutions and terms of the past—terms and institutions that no longer facilitated the compromises necessary for continued stability. If the theme of balance can be seen in the tension between expansion and stability, for these presidents, expansion, which they generally favored, was a more problematic solution to resolving national issues than it had been for Jefferson and Jackson, and the need for stability became paramount. Given this need, the issue thus became an effort to forestall time itself. They argued for a continuance of the union as it had always been. Any attempt to move away from the past was seen as a betrayal of the founders and a descent into chaos. National history, for these presidents, was also national destiny.

For these presidents the union dated not from the Declaration of Independence, as abolitionists and Abraham Lincoln would later have it. Nor did it date from the ratification of the Constitution, as most defenders of slavery argued. Rather, these presidents implicitly dated the defining act of union to the Articles of Confederation, when the states surrendered a modicum of sovereignty to the central government in national matters but retained state sovereignty in "local" or "domestic" areas. These presidents did not reify the Articles of Confederation, but took from those Articles (and the long history that predated them) a reverence for the rights of the states rather than a focused commitment to the rights of individuals as protected by the power of the federal government. That is to say, of the plethora of governmental theories swirling about the nation during this period, these presidents sided not with a relatively powerful federal government, as Jackson had, nor with a strong sense of national identity and cohesion as Lincoln and (much later) Wilson and FDR would. Instead, these presidents understood the presidential task as the preservation of the Constitution as it had often been interpreted by the Supreme Court—to protect states from the federal government and "local arrangements" from national interference.

Sharing this understanding of union and its preservation, as well as the same political imperatives of protecting the political coalition that had brought them to power, Fillmore, Pierce, and Buchanan all relied on similar rhetorical tactics in their efforts to save the union. These tactics, by preserving the nation's existing balance of political and economic interests, also demanded a specific articulation of citizenship that resulted in the maintenance of existing hierarchies. These presidents all encouraged the reification of a specific, ideologically grounded interpretation of the founders and the Constitution, which they hoped would in turn lead to increased respect for the federal structure of the union, allowing for both nationalistic sentiments and local control over institutions such as slavery. This particular definition of the founders and the founding was the rhetorical fulcrum on which the union balanced, the one key value around which these presidents could, in a limited fashion, preserve their political coalition and the union.

These presidents also argued that only certain kinds of citizens could understand and adhere to this complex notion of patriotism. Like Jefferson and Jackson before them, they tried to create these citizens, rhetorically defining them as those who, first, derived from "common stock" and shared a common language, heritage, and sense of honor and obligation. They also offered a more behavioral definition of citizenship, and in this they differed in important ways from Jefferson and Jackson. For these presidents, correct behavior was important—in matters of religion, politics, and economics, "good citizens" differed from others in being Protestant, refusing to agitate (especially on the issue of abolition), and adhering to a primarily agricultural means of subsistence. There was room in their union only for good citizens thus constituted. Those members of previously excluded groups, especially new immigrants, were thus given some evidence as to what sorts of discipline, to borrow Gary Gerstle's phrase, would be required of them as they moved from invisibility to differentiated definitions of their group and then into limited inclusion.[3]

Finally, these presidents defined good citizens through discourse that castigated their opposites. "Others" were less likely to be of Scots-English ancestry, less likely to be Protestant, and consequently more likely to disrupt the fragile peace through vicious acts of marauding malevolence (American Indians), "frenzied fanaticism" (Mormons and abolitionists), or "foreign influence" (immigrants). Those who did not meet the standards for citizenship were exiled, silenced, erased. Groups that were becoming politically visible—and politically problematic—such as free blacks, women, and some immigrants, had to be marginalized and disciplined if both the national balance of interests and the union itself were to be maintained.

These "others" had to be contained and controlled, whatever the price, because for these presidents, the very future of the union depended on such containment and control.[4] Managing the political issues of the decade and protecting the existence of the federal union depended on right action by those who adopted a policy of temperance, and on the exclusion of those who, out of character, race, or choice, refused the temperate path and led the nation toward dissolution and war.[5] Once again, the need to maintain balance required rhetoric that meant the overt inclusion of certain groups—including some of those previously denied entry into the polity—and the overt exclusion of others.

The Genealogy of Union

Given the fractious nature of American politics during the 1850s, the search for stability is easy to understand. The presidency, like the federal government in general, is conservative. Because of the increasingly entrenched and increasingly opposed interests fighting for their preferred national policies, the union appeared more and more fragile. As the political actors most responsible for the continuation of the polity and embedded in a political environment in which all concerned were conscious of the precarious hold of union, these particular presidents were preoccupied with conservation, which they understood as political stasis. Most important, this meant respecting the union as a compact of states with one another, not of individuals with the central government, an understanding of government that depended on the enshrinement of the founders as the architects of that compact.

Just as Jackson had looked back to Jefferson to legitimate his policy preferences, these presidents also looked back to the founding generation to legitimate political action in their day. Their understanding of the nation's founding was ideologically different from Jefferson's or Jackson's however, for their political problems were different. Rather than relying on the founders as exemplars of a frontier morality, for these presidents, the founders were, above all, prudent crafters of a particular sort of political union, one that rested not on individual rights, but on the rights of states.

A COMPACT OF STATES

Arguments over the relative importance of the founding documents were rarely explicit. They took the form of either implicit assumptions contained within arguments or of direct assault on the Constitution as a pact with the devil. Fillmore, Pierce, and Buchanan revered the Constitution with its careful structures of federalism, above the Declaration of Independence with its promise of individual rights, exalting the fact of union above the promise of equality, a position that, intentionally or not, put them on the same side of many policy debates with defenders of slavery. In Pierce's words, "With the Union, my best and dearest hopes are entwined. Without it what are we, individually or collectively?"[6] For these presidents, respecting the union meant respecting the federal structures it embodied, which meant respecting the rights of the states, especially the right of the Southern states to their "peculiar institution." So strongly did these presidents feel about the need to defend this institution that Franklin Pierce included a specific policy-based defense of slavery in his inaugural and tied the defense of slavery directly to the stability of the federal union.[7] That defense was all the more striking because both political parties had insisted on the finality of the Compromise of 1850 during the campaign. That is, there was widespread national agreement at the elite level that the question of slavery in the territories was settled. Nonetheless, Pierce said,

> I believe that involuntary servitude, as it exists in the different States of this Confederacy, is recognized by the Constitution. I believe that it stands like any other admitted right, and that the states where it exists are entitled to efficient remedies to enforce the constitutional provisions. I hold that the laws of 1850, commonly called the "compromise measures," are strictly constitutional and to be unhesitatingly carried into effect. . . . I fervently hope that the question is at rest, and that no sectional or ambitious or fanatical excitement may again threaten the durability of our institutions or obscure the light of our prosperity.[8]

It is especially important to note that Pierce here referred to the union as a confederacy, which placed the states equally at the center, not the national government.[9] As Buchanan had it, "After all, we must mainly rely upon the patriotism and wisdom of the States for the prevention and redress of evil."[10] This represented a specific understanding of the rights and privileges of the states vis-à-vis one another and the central government, one that protected the right of each state to regulate its "domestic" concerns regardless of the wishes of those in other states. The tremendous growth in national territory during this decade was, in fact, premised on the belief in strong, loosely connected state governments.[11] Unusual for presidents, who often tie personal power to federal power (as we will clearly see with Wilson and Roosevelt), these presidents were more concerned with balance as state maintenance rather than with balance as state building. Their political coalitions granted them federal position on the

condition that they not use federal power. States were to be protected from the federal government, not individuals from the power of
the state, whether local or federal.

"Good" citizens in terms of this political arrangement were
those who maintained a passion only for the union and who thus
defended the rights of the several states. In his first annual message,
for example, Pierce said, "The controversies which have agitated the
country heretofore are passing away with the causes that produced
them and the passions which they had awakened; or, if any trace of
them remains, it may be reasonably hoped that it will only be perceived in the zealous rivalry of all good citizens to testify their
respect for the rights of the States, their devotion to the Union, and
their common determination that each one of the States, its institutions, its welfare, and its domestic peace, shall be held alike secure
under the sacred aegis of the Constitution."[12] Note the hierarchy
here: respect for the rights of the states was primary, the union, secondary. States were again included as tertiary, via the Constitution.

For these presidents, respect for the states was reasonable and
appropriate, for not only was the union a "highly decentralized confederation of states"[13] in fact, but also because in their view, the
states and not the people were the constituent parts of the union. In
Pierce's words, "the substantive power, the popular force, and the
large capacities for social and material development exist in the
respective States, which, all being of themselves well-constituted
republics, as they preceded so they alone are capable of maintaining
and perpetuating the American Union."[14] This was clearly an argument for state sovereignty and an implicit claim that ultimate sovereignty resided in the states. "Good" citizens of the national government would thus also be limited citizens, as good national government was understood to be limited government. Good citizens
would defend the power of the states and would do nothing to weak-
en that power. Given the prevailing arguments at the federal level
over whether the national or the state governments were to be dominant, this position had particular resonance.

This position, however, rested on several important, but tenuous
assumptions. The most significant of these assumptions was that all
differences among the states, and all institutions that resulted from
these differences, were both morally neutral and politically equal.
Given this interpretation, one state's unicameral legislature, say,

became undifferentiated in principle from another state's system of chattel slavery. To argue that slavery was morally different from other sorts of domestic institutions was to threaten the very basis of the union. Pierce, for example, said in his first annual message, "It is evident that a confederation so vast and so varied, both in numbers and in territorial extent, in habits and in interests, could only be kept in national cohesion by the strictest fidelity to the principles of the Constitution as understood by those who have adhered to the most restricted construction of the powers granted by the people and the States."[15] Note the importance given to a "most restricted construction" of the federal government's power. National cohesion depended on turning a blind eye to the moral implications of state policies. As he went on to say, "Mutual forbearance, respect, and non-interference in our personal action as citizens . . . are the means to perpetuate that confidence and fraternity the decay of which a mere political Union, on so vast a scale, could not survive."[16] A balanced union, not to mention the survival of his political coalition, depended on a specific imbalance, one that favored the states over the federal government. This imbalance had to be protected by the concerted action of individual citizens. The lack of such forbearance would mean the end of the union itself. Respect for the union of states was the only way to preserve the union.

Another assumption was that the states and not the general government shared responsibility for the common welfare. In vetoing a measure designed to provide public lands for the benefit of the indigent insane, Pierce said,

> I readily and, I trust, feelingly acknowledge the duty incumbent on us all as men and citizens, and as among the highest and holiest of our duties, to provide for those who, in the mysterious order of Providence, are subject to want and disease of body or mind; but I cannot find any authority in the Constitution for making the Federal Government the great almoner of public charity throughout the United States. To do so would, in my judgment, be contrary to the letter and spirit of the Constitution and subversive of the whole theory upon which the Union of these States is formed.[17]

What was true in one policy arena needed to be applied equally in other areas of policy. It was the duty of every citizen to be charitable toward others but not to expect the general government to assist in that effort. That was the responsibility and the prerogative of the several states. In this way, the president could hope to diffuse the effects of difference. If policy was enacted at the national level, it had national consequences. If issues could be kept off the national agenda, on the other hand, these consequences could be averted or localized. This effort contributed to the invisibility of certain groups, especially those advocating change. Citizenship and participation in the national debates of the day were at the service of maintaining national balance—and the political coalition that had brought these presidents to power.

This demand for deference to the states clearly did some important political work. Philosophically, it followed from a theory of union that dated from the Articles of Confederation. Speaking about the American Revolution in his third annual message, Pierce said, "The object of the war was to disenthrall the united colonies from foreign rule, which had proved to be oppressive, and to separate them permanently from the mother country. The political result was the foundation of a Federal Republic of the free white men of the colonies, constituted, as they were, in distinct and reciprocally independent State governments."[18] Note that the republic was presumed to be the province of "free white men." The exclusion of other groups was understood as natural, if not inevitable.

This meant that the potentially inclusive rhetoric of the Declaration, the rhetoric that was increasingly being used as a major topoi for the defense of the liberty of slaves and the rights of unincorporated groups, was explicitly delegitimized by these presidents as topoi worth consideration, for they did not reflect the "true" meaning of the national union. The ideological and political work of rendering certain groups problematic so that they could also be rendered politically invisible was clear.

Dating the union back to the Articles of Confederation was, for Pierce, appropriate because he saw the cession of power from the states to the general government as the defining moment of union. The Constitution was the operative document. The Articles were the relevant philosophical touchstone.[19] Pierce continued his discussion of national history as follows: "Our cooperative action rests in the conditions of permanent confederation prescribed by the Con-

stitution. Our balance of power is in the separate reserved rights of
the States and their equal representation in the Senate. That independent sovereignty in every one of the States, with its reserved
rights of local self-government, assured to each by their co-equal
power in the Senate, was the fundamental condition of the Constitution. Without it the Union would never have existed."[20] Thus, without the states, there was no union, which was understood as written
in the Constitution—thus protecting slavery. The main obligation of
the union therefore, was to defend the Constitution, and thus the
sovereignty of the states, and therefore slavery. Paradoxically, only
the power of the federal government was sufficient to enforce the
power of the states, and so while insisting on the latter, they also had
to lay claim to the former.

The political structures of the time both facilitated and were
reinforced by the prevailing strength of the various political coalitions. Ideological justifications for those structures helped do the
political work of regime maintenance by providing generally acceptable and accepted ways of encouraging a sense of collective identity
that would transcend disagreements on specific issues and provide a
definition of national identity that a majority of citizens could
accept. Others could be safely and, with the help of these justifications, invisibly excluded.

Protecting the federal structure also meant reserving to the
national government its separate sphere of influence and power,
which in turn meant cultivating a national, rather than a regional or
state-based identity. As Fillmore said in his first annual message, "In
fulfilling our Constitutional duties, fellow-citizens, on this subject,
as in carrying into effect all other powers conferred by the Constitution, we should consider ourselves as deliberating and acting for one
and the same country, and bear constantly in mind that our regard
and our duty are due not to a particular part only, but to the
whole."[21] The emphasis on national feeling ran throughout these
presidencies, as the presidents of the 1850s argued in favor of "national" sentiment, but not in favor of the "federal" government. Balancing the political cohesion of their national constituency meant rein-
ing in the power of the national government while encouraging, as
Rogers M. Smith would lead us to expect, a nationalized sense of collective identity.[22] In a veto message addressing precisely this issue,
Pierce put it this way: "All the pursuits of industry, everything

which promotes the material or intellectual well-being of the race, every ear of corn or boll of cotton which grows, is national in the same sense, for each one of these things goes to swell the aggregate of national prosperity and happiness of the United States; but it confounds all meaning of language to say that these things are 'national,' as equivalent to 'Federal,' so as to come within any of the classes of appropriation for which Congress is authorized by the Constitution to legislate."[23]

By making the distinction between "national" and "federal," these presidents encouraged the perpetuation of the union on terms that were consistent with their theory of government. Given their understanding of what they could—and could not—do under the Constitution, they had little room to maneuver even had they wished to do so. This meant that Southerners would have it both ways—slavery as a domestic institution was protected by the federal government and the federal Constitution, and national feeling would continue to cement the union. All would remain unchanged and secure—if the citizenry would but remain stable and temperate, as they would do if they followed the example of the venerated founders. For them, the only way to maintain their increasingly fractured political coalition and thus their interpretation of the national balance was through offering a vision of national identity that was also a version of political stasis.

VENERATING THE FOUNDING

These presidents had to maintain the existing national balance among competing interests, for that balance protected the interests of their political coalition, begun under Jefferson, expanded by Jackson, and increasingly endangered by the changes fomented by national territorial, political, and economic expansion. The presidents of the 1850s sought to maintain a sense of stability in the present through a focus on a revolutionary past. Reverence for the national past and especially for the founding generation was never higher than during the decades before the Civil War. The ceremonial rhetoric of Daniel Webster, that most famous of orators, is full of such references, which are also found in Abraham Lincoln's public speech, most clearly in the Lyceum Address.[24] This focus on the past served to unite the nation in the present by reminding citizens of shared traditions and shared struggles, and through this device these presidents sought to freeze national history, to prevent the effects of changes forced by the march of time. In his first annual message Millard Fillmore put it this way: "I cannot doubt that the American people, bound together by kindred blood and common traditions, still cherish a paramount regard for the Union of their fathers, and that they are ready to rebuke any attempt to violate its integrity, to disturb the compromises on which it is based, or to resist the laws which have been enacted under its authority."[25] It was not merely the contemporaneous union that was so highly regarded, but "the Union of their fathers," the union of the past, before all the changes that were threatening to divide the nation. And what's more, there was no distinction here between past and present.

It is clear who was implicitly included—and who was excluded—as a result of this formulation of national identity. The polity was connected not only by common traditions (civic nationalism) but also by common blood (racial nationalism). Its members were, quite specifically, members also of the same race, of one family. Like all families, they may have had their disagreements, but the ties binding them—primarily ties of blood and only secondarily of belief—were stronger than the forces vying to separate them. Those who were not of that single blood were politically invisible and were invisibly excluded. Had they been politically visible, their interests would have merited some degree of national attention and the fragile balance of the union would have been proportionately imperiled. Balance again became a justification for exclusion.

Unlike Jackson, who relied on the founders (especially Jefferson) to advocate changes in the national order as he built a political coalition, these presidents, charged with protecting that coalition in a changed political context, used reverence for the past to preserve the fragile political unity of the present. As James Buchanan said in his inaugural, "In entering upon this great office, I must humbly invoke the God of our fathers for wisdom and firmness to execute its high and responsible duties in such a manner as to restore harmony and ancient friendship among the people of the several States and to preserve our free institutions throughout many generations."[26] In invoking the founders and the founders' God, Buchanan was invoking the highest authority possible. The founders were the fathers of the political family, which was blessed by their (Protestant) God.

While arguing for union, these presidents based that union on the terms most readily available to them at the time, terms that contained implicit and invisible exclusions such as, in this example, non-Protestants. Despite this invocation, and despite its reinforcement through this disciplinary project, harmony and friendship were not so easily restored.

Even slavery could be defended because it had been explicitly endorsed by the founders. In Pierce's first annual message, for instance, he said,

> The wisdom of men who knew what independence cost, who had put all at stake upon the issue of the Revolutionary struggle, disposed of the subject to which I refer in the only way consistent with the Union of these States and with the march of power and prosperity which has made us what we are. It is a significant fact that from the adoption of the Constitution until the officers and soldiers of the Revolution had passed to their graves, or, through the infirmities of age and wounds, had ceased to participate actively in public affairs, there was not merely a quiet acquiescence in, but a prompt vindication of, the constitutional rights of the States. The reserved powers were scrupulously defended.[27]

This quotation clearly revealed a notion of balance as preservation of the past; preservation of the dominant political coalition and its structures and arrangements, which Pierce legitimated by tying them directly to the founding. In this reading of history, although those of the revolutionary generation were no longer able to protect their legacy, they had understood that legacy as being centered on the protection of state sovereignty. And, just as important, they promptly vindicated that sovereignty. Succeeding generations were bound to protect that legacy now that the founders were no longer able to do so themselves. Only in this way could the balance of interests required for the preservation of the union be maintained. Pierce thus tied defense of states' rights (slavery) to the "revolutionary struggle" (the fight for freedom). The former was not only consistent with, but tantamount to, the latter.

This dependence on the past had both rational and emotional components. Rationally, preserving the union made for greater peace and more prosperity than were otherwise possible. As Pierce put it in his third annual message,

> With freedom and concert of action it [the union] has enabled us to contend successfully on the battlefield against foreign foes, has elevated the feeble colonies into powerful States, and has raised our industrial productions and our commerce which transports them to the level of the richest and greatest nations of Europe. And the admirable adaptation of our political institutions to their objects, combining local self-government with aggregate strength, has established the practicality of a government like ours to cover a continent with confederated states.[28]

Note that at one time, expansion served the national interest—the growing nation was able to preserve itself because of its size and to become great through expansion. But that growth was predicated upon a particular set of political arrangements—political arrangements that brought Pierce's coalition into power and that he therefore needed to preserve. This quotation thus revealed several important things: the importance of confederation, the understanding of balance as a necessary mediating force between stability and change, and the ways in which that worked to render the dynamic union of Jackson and Jefferson static.

But it would be a mistake to base one's loyalty to the union on merely rational or pragmatic grounds, and the tendency to do so was, to Buchanan, "an evil omen of the times."[29] Emotionally, the union was a matter of sacred trust. As Pierce argued in his third annual message: "Our forefathers of the thirteen united colonies, in acquiring their independence and in founding this Republic of the United States of America, have devolved upon us, their descendants, the greatest and most noble trust ever committed to the hands of man, imposing upon all, and especially such as the public may have invested for the time being with political functions, to the most sacred obligations."[30] Balance meant not only preserving his coalition but the nation as well. The ideology thus fostered created both a powerful legitimating force for those with power, and also a particular sense of national identity, a definition that was to be held as sacred as were the obligations "devolved upon us" by the founders.

So sacred were those obligations, and the national identity here associated with them, that Pierce vetoed a reparations bill because to authorize such payments would be tantamount to concluding that Jefferson, Madison, and Monroe had all erred in denying such reparations during their administrations, and this he would not do.[31] His sense of national identity was identical and identified with that of the founders; it had to be held sacred and inviolate. Dynamic union thus became static.

Any problems that the nation was experiencing were thus not treated as inherent to the system nor as cause for reforming that system. To do either of these would be to admit error in the founding, the fulcrum on which the union was balanced. Such error would create an imbalance that would in turn endanger the present union. The presidents of the 1850s had two responses to these problems: one involved action, the other silence. First, they blamed problems on exaggeration, overzealousness, or willful malevolence of an isolated faction. As Franklin Pierce put it, "Whatever of discontent or public dissatisfaction exists is attributable to the imperfections of human nature or is incident to all governments, however perfect, which human wisdom can devise. Such subjects of political agitation as occupy the public mind consist, to a great extent of exaggeration of inevitable evils, or overzeal in social improvement, or mere imagination of grievance, having but remote connection with any of the constitutional functions or duties of a Federal Government."[32] Balance depended not on passion, as Jackson understood it, but on temperance, the avoidance of "overzeal," and a commitment to a limited notion of government inherited from the founders' age.

This fear of uncurbed and unrestrained passion applied to the protests against slavery, and especially to protests against the Fugitive Slave Law. After a mob in Boston forcibly freed a slave being held for return to the South, Fillmore said:

> Whereas information has been received that surely lawless persons, principally persons of color, combined and confederated together for purposes of opposing by force the execution of the laws of the United States, did, at Boston, in Massachusetts, on the fifteenth of the month, make a violent assault on the marshal or deputy marshals of the United States for the district of Massachusetts, in the court-house,

and did overcome said officers, and did by force rescue from their custody a person arrested as a fugitive slave, and then and there a prisoner lawfully holden by the said marshal or deputy marshals of the United States, and other scandalous outrages did commit in violation of the law.[33]

Such people were to be overtly excluded from the polity—not only were they lawless, but they were lawless "persons of color," inclined to "combine and confederate together," and thus offered powerful evidence for what would happen nationally if the abolitionists were to have their way and the existing order disturbed. It would not be replaced with a new order, as a far more extreme revolution had been portrayed by Thomas Paine a generation earlier. The dynamic order established by the Revolution was understood as stable by these presidents, as we have seen, because it respected certain established hierarchies. Jackson tinkered with those hierarchies by including previously disenfranchised white Protestant males. But these white Protestant males had been educated for proper citizenship through the vehicle of land ownership. Now, the hierarchies themselves were being challenged, and in favor of those who had no such education. Thus, unlike the initial or even the Jacksonian revolutions, which altered some few political structures while leaving social structures largely intact, the result of this one would be chaos, slave revolts, mob rule, and an end to all order.

This intemperate behavior was all the more distressing to these presidents because in their view Americans were naturally a temperate, dispassionate, reasonable and reasoning, and thus well-behaved people, who believed in the laws and who would uphold those laws if given the chance (people that Pierce characterized as "otherwise patriotic and law-abiding" now inflicted with "misdirected zeal").[34] Evidence of such temperance was found (for Fillmore) in the election of Pierce, and (for Pierce) in the election of Buchanan.[35] Of his own election, Buchanan said, "The voice of the majority speaking in the manner prescribed by the Constitution, was heard, and instant submission followed. Our own country alone could have exhibited so grand and striking a spectacle of the capacity of man for self-government."[36] That capacity was illustrated in the people's submission to reason, exemplified by law and the Constitution. As Fillmore put it in his first annual message, "without law there can be no practical liberty . . . when law is trampled underfoot tyranny rules; whether it appears in the form of a military despotism or of popular violence. The law is the only sure protection of the weak and the only efficient restraint upon the strong."[37] Self-government depended on such enlightened submission and was endangered by its opposite, self-righteous indulgence in passions. This enlightened submission was a direct result of fidelity to the founders. Any internal problems and tensions were thus not the result of honest, law-abiding people with honest reasons for disagreeing about issues of morality, the law, and their relationship to one another, but were instead the product of the abuse of liberty by those who cared nothing for the law or the stability and security it provides.

Abolitionists (called by Pierce "visionary sophists and interested agitators")[38] fell under this heading, as did those who were tempted to add territory to the United States through any means—the unauthorized invasions of Cuba, Nicaragua, and Mexico were all roundly criticized by these presidents.[39] There was a right way to expand and a wrong way. These presidents supported expansion but not some of the methods private citizens adopted to forward it. "It is beyond question," Buchanan asserted in an 1858 message to the Senate, that "the destiny of our race is to spread themselves over the continent of North America, and this at no distant day should events be permitted to take their natural course. The tide of emigrants will flow to the South, and nothing can arrest its progress. If permitted to go there peacefully, Central America will soon contain an American population which will confer blessings and benefits as well upon the natives as their respective Governments. Liberty under the restraint of law will preserve domestic peace, whilst the different transit routes across the Isthmus, in which we are so deeply interested, will have assured protection."[40] Like Jefferson's question as to whether Americans would prefer to see western lands settled by strangers or by "our brethren," this quotation similarly called upon the same tradition of entitlement and destiny through which Americans would spread over the hemisphere rather than just the continent. That process, Buchanan went on to note, had been "retarded" by "unlawful expeditions."[41] Emigration was the right way to expand the nation. Invasion without government sanction was the wrong way.

Such unauthorized activity delayed the progress of the nation and postponed its destiny. Thus even in the fulfillment of national destiny, temperance was called for or the national balance of interests could be disrupted.

The danger was less that the naturally stable and temperate citizenry would suddenly forsake that moderation and give in to foolish passions, but that the compounding nature of a series of intemperate actions would finally drive moderate citizens to extremes.[42] The national balance required a certain sort of citizen. Citizenship served national interests, which were identical to the interests of the governing coalition. As Buchanan put it, "Those who announce abstract doctrines subversive of the Constitution and the Union must not be surprised should their heated partisans advance one step further and attempt by violence to carry these doctrines into practical effect."[43] "Heated partisans" were easily led into error. Only the sober reflection of the president could systematically reveal such error and put the nation on the right path—the founders' path—to our national destiny. Identity and destiny were thus parts of one ideological whole. To advocate any change in the existing balance was to potentially foment violent action. There was no foreseeing the end to the disastrous consequences of one intemperate action.

If excluding those responsible did not solve the national problems, the second response was to ignore the problems altogether, to rely on silence as the partner of invisibility. Not only did all three presidents continually hope that the nation's political difficulties would soon be over, but they all acted as if they were indeed over.[44] Pierce, for instance, insisted on sending his third annual message to a Congress that was so crippled by dissension that it could not receive it. In that message, despite the fact that Kansas was already erupting into violence, he nonetheless congratulated the nation on its peace and prosperity.[45] By rendering the issues being contested in Kansas invisible, Pierce could hope to render them politically ineffectual as well.

In relying on a specific definition of the founders' union, these presidents hoped to preserve the fractured political coalition they had inherited from Jefferson and Jackson. By rendering a dynamic union into a static polity, they hoped to preserve the union. By identifying their vision of national identity as the definitive vision, the founders' vision, they facilitated the political work of regime maintenance. But the stakes of victory in the political battles that divided the nation also increased. These presidents thus sought to discourage political contention through the creation of a specific sort of citizen—a temperate citizen who would acquiesce to previous political arrangements and hierarchies.

A Stable Citizenry

Neither their interpretation of national union nor their reliance on the founding was sufficient to stave off the momentum of time, however. Immigrants kept coming; the nation kept growing; tensions among the sections were continually exacerbated by both the actions and inactions of the government. The nation, in short, was changing. In response to those changes, these presidents tried to maintain political stasis first by rhetorically creating a stable citizenry and, second, by defining that stable citizenry through the counterexamples of those who threatened unity through intemperance and who consequently had to be excluded if the union was to survive. Taking the dynamic union of Jackson and making it static was critical to the preservation of the balance of interests that Jackson's political coalition depended on. But for it to do the requisite political work, a new way of defining stability had to be devised.

THE OLD MODEL OF STABILITY

In keeping with their political vision of political stasis, these presidents tried to maintain the old Jeffersonian model as articulated by Jackson, the model of creating and maintaining stability through land. In their different ways, Jefferson and Jackson considered land an educative force, a way of training citizens in the lessons of democracy. Allowing the market economy to flourish was a mechanism of political equality for those who would own, work, and render the land profitable. For Jefferson, as for the presidents of the 1850s, the agricultural life fostered temperance, patience, and the attributes of good, stable citizenship. For Jackson, the frontier life provided the hardihood necessary for participation in democracy. Instability

derived from the urban areas, and a wise government policy therefore favored the former. In his second annual message, for example,
Fillmore said,

> Agriculture may justly be regarded as the great interest of our
> people. . . . Justice and sound policy, therefore, alike require
> that the Government should use all the means authorized by
> the Constitution to promote the interests and welfare of our
> citizens. And yet it is a singular fact that while the manu-
> facturing and commercial interests have engaged the Con-
> gress during a large portion of every session and our statutes
> abound in provisions for their protection and encourage-
> ment, little has yet been done directly for the advancement
> of agriculture.[46]

In relying on the frontier myth propagated by Jefferson and Jackson, Pierce put that myth to different ideological ends. He continued
to valorize the farmer, but the frontier was no longer an unmitigat-
ed benefit to the nation and the question of whether new territories
should be slave or free was among the most contentious issues of the
day. So Pierce valorized the farmer but not the frontiersman—rather
than the expansionist vision of Jackson, he harkened back to the
more staid yeoman farmer of Jefferson.

Consistent with Jackson's rhetoric, however, manufacturing and
commercial concerns, not being central to the national interest,
were considered a threat to the peace and stability of the nation by
asking for—and receiving—more than their due from the national
government. Unrest and instability naturally followed. Agriculture—
in the sense of the settled farmer, not the adventurous pioneer—
remained the nation's mainstay and the source of its strength. As
Buchanan put it in his first annual message, "Whilst the public lands,
as a source of revenue, are of great importance, their importance is
far greater as furnishing homes for a hardy and independent race of
honest and industrious citizens who desire to subdue and cultivate
the soil."[47] The lessons so essential to a democratic citizenry that
Jackson saw as inherent in the ownership of land were still vital to
the preservation of the nation two decades later. Even as late as
Buchanan's day, presidents had not entirely given up on the vision of
creating good citizenship through land ownership.

The settled cultivation of the land promoted stability; urban life and commercial occupations were unsettling and destabilizing. Abolitionists hailed from the commercial and urban Northeast; in the South agriculture continued to reign, and thus Southerners were, for these presidents, normally the most forbearing of citizens. The fears of these presidents grew, however. They argued that Southerners' patience was wearing thin by the mid-1850s, as they were pushed to the brink of tolerance by the activities of abolitionists and Republicans, and it became clear that Southern unionism was "a perishable commodity."[48] Their solution was the same as that of Jefferson and Jackson before them: expansion. Balance could thus be maintained, and the existing sets of political arrangements preserved, not by maintaining the size of the union but by carefully extending it while also protecting its political structures. Government-controlled expansion served the national balance. Impetuous actions of private citizens, endorsed by Jackson as contributing to balance, were now understood as potentially undermining that balance.

Some expansion seemed politically and practically possible, however, for both sides shared some common ground: they agreed on the virtues of white male labor and sought to protect its privileges. Both sides thus implicitly denigrated the contributions of African Americans, both slave and free, of many immigrants, and of all women. Without the capacity for eventual citizenship, members of these groups occupied the lowest levels of the developing hierarchies. They remained politically invisible, as neither side wished to risk their political privileges by mobilizing them as potential allies and supporters. And class became identified with race, gender, religion, and country of origin. Through this identification, class became politically invisible and ostensibly irrelevant. As the national identity became overtly racialized, class distinctions became less important to identity as a citizen than racial distinctions. All these distinctions reflected the positions of these groups in the processes of becoming politically visible, then problematic and differentiated, and finally included.

It was the presidents' task to balance these competing claims and do so without incurring public debate on the subject. In so doing they also maintained the national hierarchies. These issues were so fraught, so divisive, the previous attempts at conciliation so fragile that even continued discussion could wreak havoc on the national union. Silence, like stasis, was required, at least until passions had cooled enough for careful deliberation.

The exclusion of certain persons, like the silencing of certain issues, had to be accomplished tacitly, naturally, invisibly, or the ruptures that they threatened would occur. These presidents thus implicitly endorsed and naturalized hierarchies that they took for granted. Farmers were valorized; those held up in opposition to them were not. Many American Indians, for instance, were characterized as "wild and intractable" and were contrasted with the "hardy and independent race of honest and industrious citizens who desire to subdue and cultivate the soil."[49] Although this language reflected the ideology common at the time and was thus in that sense unremarkable, it also reflected the naturalized hierarchies and led to the silencing of certain voices.

Invisibility does its political work best when it can be understood as natural or inevitable. When both the members of the governing coalition and the members of groups who wish to challenge that group for dominance agree on the necessity of excluding others as dangerous to both, then invisibility can be instantiated without protest or comment. Such silencing was possible in this case because both Northerners and Southerners were seeking the same thing: the nationalization of their regional cultures, the national acceptance of the restrictions on citizenship they preferred. Through restricting the available land, Northerners especially hoped to develop the entire polity in their own image. Northern expansionists hoped with equal fervor that by expanding the land base and restricting its ownership to white male laborers, they could extend both the nation and their dominance over it. Southerners, on the other hand, contended that slavery reduced class conflict by promoting equality among white men and urged the adoption of this vision for the nation as a whole and its validation in the West.

Thus, all sides in the emerging conflict believed that they were enacting the "best" and "most equal" version of the founders' vision and that their sense of entitlement was both philosophical, as heirs to the framers, and material, as heirs to the continent. The presidents of the period had to balance these claims without allowing significant change in the original constitutional design. Buchanan, for instance, promised a "strict construction" of the Constitution,[50] and Fillmore asserted that "the Government of the United States is a limited Government."[51] In part, of course, these presidents were expressing the same treatment of government that many presidents do on such occasions. But they were also expressing a deeply felt theory of governmental power that was widely accepted at the time. That theory of government also supported a specific set of institutional arrangements and ideologies that in turn supported a specific political coalition. The theory of government, social ideology, and institutions all combined to render some inclusions inevitable and natural while doing the same for specific exclusions. By limiting government, these presidents could also limit those who had access to it.

Thus, the acceptance of limited government had clear practical consequences. Speaking about the continuing problems in Kansas in his second annual message, for instance, Buchanan blamed the participants' willful disregard of the Constitution, saying, "The past unfortunate experience of Kansas has enforced the lesson, so often already taught, that resistance to the lawful authority under our form of government can not fail in the end to prove disastrous to its authors. Had the people of the Territory yielded obedience to the laws enacted by their legislature, it would at the present moment have contained a large population of industrious and enterprising citizens, who have been deterred from entering its borders by the existence of civil strife and organized rebellion."[52] Prosperity derived from obedience to current laws, from respect for existing hierarchies and structures of power. Failure in these philosophical realms led also to failure in the material realm. Just as Jackson used American Indians and what he considered their philosophical failures to highlight the consequences of faulty citizenship, Buchanan here used Kansas in the same way.

Now of course this quotation was in reference to a particular political problem, and of course it was a justification for Buchanan's position regarding that problem. But as a philosophy of government, it potentially appealed to both sides of the debate: nearly everyone was for law and order under the founders' Constitution. The presidential problem lay in interpreting that ideal in ways that would lead to continued union under circumstances that did not allow for compromise. The problem posed by the necessity of balancing these conflicting interests led to support for the status quo as the only available option. Stability and stasis became one and the same.

Yet the dynamic union also could serve stability. The political problems caused by the addition of new territory and the question of how to distribute it were postponed through the expedient of adding still more territory, "empty" territory, there for the taking and morally, at least, already part of the United States. Politicians such as Henry Clay, more cautious than many Democrats, advocated controlled expansion as the best means of maintaining and extending the national balance.[53] The key here, obviously, was "controlled expansion"—the benefits of land ownership were to be given only to those deemed worthy and under conditions that served the interests of the governing coalition. They could not afford to allow disruptive forces to settle within the boundaries of the union. Good settlers included only those with an intention to cultivate the soil; policies that encouraged speculation and other uses of the land were frowned upon. Jefferson's yeoman farmer was a better citizen during such fragile times than was Jackson's adventurous frontiersman. Yet the addition of still more territory—and the question of who would control it—exacerbated the tensions that expansion was intended to resolve.[54] The addition of land was both potentially stabilizing and destabilizing.

Where once the acquisition of land served as a way to provide stability and a stable citizenry for the polity, it now served to exacerbate the tensions periodically convulsing that polity. Land could not be used to forestall time or the changes it brought. The presidents of the 1850s had to look for other ways to preserve and protect their vision of the national heritage. They thus sought to create rhetorically the sorts of citizens they deemed necessary for the perpetuation of the founders' union.

A STABLE CITIZENRY

The characteristics required to produce a stable and temperate citizenry were, to these presidents, obvious, and were best understood in terms of whom they were not. In his third annual message, for instance, Fillmore explained why the annexation of Cuba was not in the national interest: "Were this island comparatively destitute of inhabitants or occupied by a kindred race, I should regard it, if voluntarily ceded by Spain, as a most desirable acquisition. But under existing circumstances, I should look upon its incorporation into our Union as a very hazardous measure."[55] Specifically, the inhabitants of Cuba were "a population of a different national stock . . . speaking a different language . . . and not likely to harmonize with other members" of the union. Furthermore, the addition of Cuba would have negative economic consequences for the South and would revive sectional tensions.[56] "Acceptable" citizens thus were those who shared the "national stock," who were of a "kindred race" to those who wielded power, and who were likely to share their cultural assumptions and political preferences. They spoke English, would contribute to the national economy without endangering any particular section, and would contribute to national unity, not sectional division. If not already culturally identical to "Americans" thus monolithically understood, they would willingly assimilate and subsume themselves into the whole.

Notice here how racial nationalism and civic nationalism reinforced one another. Those most able to absorb the national ideology and adapt themselves to the requirements of democratic citizenship were also those who came from Western European racial stock. Ideological capacity, race, and national identity were so closely interwoven as to be virtually indistinguishable. Other sorts of beliefs, other interpretations of the national creed, other races were simply excluded or erased. Politically, they had no meaning. They were invisible.

"Good" citizens were also defined by Pierce in his peroration on the founding as creating a "Federal Republic of the free white men of the colonies,"[57] which led in turn to a very specific of idea of who was American and who therefore was not: "As for the subject races, whether American Indian or African, the wise and brave statesmen of that day, being engaged in no extravagant scheme of social change, left them as they were, and thus preserved themselves and their posterity from the anarchy and the ever-recurring civil wars which have prevailed in other revolutionized European colonies of America."[58] He reified the past through a specific and exclusionary interpretation. The founders favored "no extravagant schemes of social change," and their hierarchies should be his hierarchies. Those hierarchies were the mechanism through which the framers preserved the nation; they should also serve as the mechanism through which contemporaneous Americans preserved their inheritance, the nation of the founders.

Those who were "other" were "foreigners," advocates of "foreign rule," anyone who fell outside the category "free white men," any member of "subject races," and those who ascribed to any "extravagant scheme of social change." The "good" citizenry was composed of white male property owners over the age of twenty-one, who possessed the correct democratic character, were loyal to the general government, interested in defending states' rights, and temperate in all passions save dedication to the union. They were, in fact, sober members of the governing coalition, whose preservation was synonymous with the preservation of the nation.

Good citizens were also law abiding. Willful disregard for law and order led Buchanan to reject the Topeka Constitution, considering its supporters "in a state of rebellion against the government under which they live."[59] Ostensibly, he had no intention of rewarding such poor citizenship and thus promoted the Lecompton Constitution, not because of its inherent advantages, but because it was passed in conformity to the law, and process trumped content. The facts of Buchanan's pro-Southern tendencies, his agreement with the content of the latter document and personal involvement in fomenting the disruption that led to its passage, doubtless made his decision easier. He could have the outcome he preferred while upholding the sort of honest, temperate citizenship his politics required.

The problem with this definition of stable and thus good citizens was that as the decade progressed, it applied to fewer and fewer people. As the violence in Kansas persisted in illustrating, fewer citizens were exercising democratic forbearance. The pool of those whose exclusion was required kept growing, making the definitions and philosophies of these presidents increasingly problematic politically.

THREATS TO STABILITY: DEFINING OTHERS

The stable and temperate members of society, its "good citizens," had to expend considerable energy to combat the negative influences of those who, through the unwonted expression of various passions, threatened the polity. All those defined as "other" by these presidents shared this single characteristic: they were, in one way or another, intemperate. Temperance became connected to the frontier themes as articulated by Jefferson and Jackson and, for these presidents, became the single characteristic that linked the union of the founders with the contemporaneous union. It was the cornerstone of their understanding of national identity and thus the dividing line between those who were included and those who were excluded. Balanced on the fulcrum of the founders, the union could only survive if the citizenry imitated the behavior and deportment of the founders.

The most threatening of these others remained American Indians. They were also among the most difficult to deal with, for they held out the promise of potential civilization while remaining maddeningly outside "civilized" parameters. In part, this was a vocabulary problem: non–American Indians insisted on ignoring the enormous diversity among indigenous nations and subsumed them all under the single category, "Indian." This created several layers of analytic and linguistic confusion[60] and served to complicate national policy on the "Indian problem." Thus it was possible for a president to declare in a single speech, as Fillmore did in his second annual message, that "we are at peace with all of them," meaning the American Indians in the Northwest Territory and those west of the Mississippi River, and that these American Indians were "gradually advancing in civilization and the pursuits of the social life," while at the same time deploring those "other" American Indians of the California, Oregon, and Mexican frontiers, where, "there have been occasional manifestations of unfriendly feeling, and some depredations committed."[61] Linguistic confusion underpinned and reinforced political confusion. This understanding of American Indians provided a dual unifying function. American Indians were at once subdued by the nation, thus validating its manifest destiny, and also opposed the nation, thus unifying it against the threat that they posed. In neither case, however, were American Indians considered *of* the nation. They were politically visible, but apart from the nation, a matter of foreign policy, not domestic concerns over citizenship.

For these presidents, American Indians would always represent a threat to the nation, endangering the peace, if not the security, of the United States. This was certainly the lesson that Fillmore offered in his third annual message: "Experience has shown, however, that whenever the two races are brought into contact, collisions will inevitably occur."[62] These "collisions" were not the result of venal behavior on the part of settlers, nor were they the product of government policies aimed at destroying American Indian nations and acquiring their lands. They were not even the result of misunderstandings between two equal peoples. These collisions were the "inevitable" product of racial mixing and as such were indications that all such mixing, not just that with American Indians, must be avoided. National identity was premised on racialized ideas of nationalism, and thus the hierarchies of race had to be preserved.

Previous policies always constrain later policy options. For these presidents, as for Jefferson and Jackson before them, the prevention of racial mixing was best accomplished through American Indian Removal or extermination. By 1854, Franklin Pierce argued for the increase of military forces employed against indigenous nations, thus marking a clear turn in presidential rhetoric away from commemorating the "noble savage" and toward vilifying the "vicious savage." This definitional shift was an important marker in terms of American Indian political visibility, for it signaled that American Indians were now clearly outsiders in the American nation. The Indian Wars that were to be so important a part of Theodore Roosevelt's understanding of American national identity were premised, in large part, on this understanding of American Indians as savage opponents of the nation, whose mettle would be tested and refined in battles with them. American Indians were to become increasingly invisible as potential citizens and more visible as foils to the nation after the Civil War, a move that was prefigured here.

In his second annual message, for instance, Pierce said, "The experience of the last year furnishes additional reasons, I regret to say, of a painful character, for the recommendation heretofore made to provide for increasing the military force employed in the Territory inhabited by the Indians. The settlers of the frontier have suffered much from the incursions of predatory bands and large parties of emigrants to our Pacific possessions have been massacred with impunity. The recurrence of such scenes can only be prevented by teaching these wild tribes the power and their responsibility to the United States."[63] Note here that the adventurous pioneer of Andrew Jackson, the hardy frontiersman who earned his manhood in contests with American Indians was displaced by Jefferson's meeker, yeoman farmer, who was in need of government aid to assist him against the unwarranted assaults of the American Indians. Note also that the American Indians themselves were no longer capable of assimilation; that possibility had disappeared. For the time being, the force of the federal government would be used to instruct the "wild tribes" the cost of inconveniencing "civilized" nations rather than in attempts to assimilate them.

Like American Indians, who skirted the boundary between internal and external threats to the United States, enslaved African Americans posed a threat of their own. First, African Americans were threatening in their own right and had to be excluded, for they were seen as unable to reason. Northerners and Southerners alike widely considered them to be children.[64] As George Fitzhugh wrote in 1854, the Negro "is but a grown-up child, and must be governed as a child, not as a lunatic or a criminal."[65] Note that the choices were not between the self-governance of the adult citizen and the paternalism of the master, but between different degrees of incarceration—as a lunatic, criminal, or slave. Blacks were politically visible and politically problematic. They were not, however, perceived as having political agency. They were always understood as being acted upon, never acting. Lacking agency, they were clearly not candidates for political inclusion. And indeed, no mainstream political actors were calling for their political inclusion. They remained on the margins of visibility.

One implication of this metaphor, although clearly not one intended by its author, was that children eventually grow up. With proper tutelage, then, slaves arguably possessed the capacity to become citizens. Unlike felons or the mad, if slaves were children, then they could be educated out of their racial "faults." Thus, even if only in the most charitable interpretation, the promise of eventual abolition was held out, if only to be endlessly delayed. For the parent decides what rights and responsibilities to bestow upon the maturing children, and others would decide when the slaves were ready for emancipation. They remained politically excluded, but in their burgeoning visibility lay the hope of eventual, if limited, inclusion.

For this reason, orators like Frederick Douglass were particularly disconcerting, for the mastery of language is, above all, a sign of adulthood and civilization, and the public display of eloquence was also a public reproach to paternalism.[66] Orators such as the Grimke sisters offered similar reproaches to those who would exclude women,[67] and Sojourner Truth thus created dissonance on two fronts.[68] That these people used the founders and the principles espoused by the founders in the service of a civic nationalism that required, among other things, abolition, tended to increase rather than diminish them as a threat to the prevailing racialized and balanced order.[69] Lacking agency, those who acted on their behalf threatened the interests represented in the governing coalition, and thus any signs of agency, as markers of capacity for citizenship, were doubly threatening. They challenged both the ideological basis of citizenship and the actual structures of power based on that ideological understanding.

Thus, African Americans and their advocates were threatening because, if freed, they would be responsible for the dissolution of social order. But they also posed a more complicated threat, because of the activities of abolitionists (joined in the mid-1850s by Republicans) on their behalf. In his third annual message, Pierce characterized the abolitionists as follows:

> If the passionate rage of fanaticism and partisan spirit did not force the fact upon our attention, it would be difficult to believe that any significant portion of the people of this enlightened country could have so surrendered themselves to a fanatical devotion to the supposed interests of the relatively few Africans in the United States as totally to abandon and disregard the interests of 25,000,000 Americans; to trample underfoot the injunctions of moral and constitutional obligation, and to engage in plans of vindictive hostility against those who are associated with them in the enjoyment of the common heritage of our national institutions.[70]

The government existed to further the interests of the majority. That this majority also represented the interests of the governing coalition was clear. It was also clear that the members of that coalition were identified with model citizenry. They were temperate, not fanatical, they respected the laws that protected them, and they wanted to protect "our common heritage," the union and the social arrangements of the founders. The terms of the national balance Pierce sought were also clear: Africans on the one side of the equation, and all other Americans, American traditions, and obligations on the other side. For Pierce, passionate rage, fanaticism, and partisan spirit were responsible for causing otherwise responsible citizens to forget where their interests lay and to side with slaves against their own countrymen.

It is notable that some fifty years after the official end of the slave trade, and thus some fifty years after all slaves could be presumed to be "Americans," slaves ("Africans") existed on one side of this rhetorical divide and "Americans" were on the other. Slaves were not just denied citizenship and personhood; they were also denied nationality. They were rendered invisible as Americans and remained only as slaves. They had to be kept as distant as possible. As it had been in the revered past, so must it always be. The changes in the experiences of slaves could not be allowed to matter or to be recognized without threatening the past and thus the present. The national balance depended on the overt exclusion of slaves. Only through their exclusion could the inclusion of others be protected through the preservation of the union. Good citizens recognized this imperative and thus excluded both slaves and their allies—those who were included but who were betraying the union of the founders in favor of a new and dangerous ideological definition of union.

Northerners and Southerners alike resented the antislavery movement because it threatened the tacit and increasingly fragile consensus by forcing both sides to make their unstated principles explicit and to justify those principles and beliefs in terms of the national ideology and founding documents. Even those who advocated union could endanger it, for the impending conflict centered on how that union was to be understood and interpreted. Threatening the prevailing ideological underpinnings of national identity was synonymous with threatening the union itself.

Abolitionists exacerbated these tensions by loudly, publicly, and repeatedly demanding that citizens must choose between civic and racial interpretations of nationalism and union, that attempts to reconcile these interpretations were not only futile but also corrupting to the individual soul and the collective republic. Authors of these attempts even consciously sought to use intemperance as a weapon in their rhetorical arsenal against slavery and the Constitution that allowed it, thus giving ammunition to those who argued that intemperance could lead to the dissolution of the union.[71] There was simply no predicting the consequences once the nation should set forth on that road. As Pierce so famously put it in this fourth annual message, "Extremes beget extremes."[72] Once the moderate path was forsaken, once polarizing speech was allowed, further division was not only possible, but inevitable.

Another external threat came from "foreigners" and foreign influences. This threat took several forms, ranging from the dangers of foreign powers establishing beachheads on American soil to the risk of entangling ourselves in foreign wars. The most frightening scenario was one in which these foreigners incited American Indians against settlers on the frontier. In his third annual message, for example, Pierce announced that "information has recently been received that the peace of the settlements in the Territories of Oregon and Washington is disturbed by hostilities on the part of the Indians, with indications of extensive combinations of a hostile character among the tribes in that quarter, the more serious in their possible effect by reason of the undetermined foreign interests existing in those Territories."[73] Such incitement was a continuing source of fear.

The fear of foreign enemies inciting American Indians against the United States was at least as old as the Declaration of Independence,[74] and the fear of being contaminated by foreign ideas was equally old.[75] These fears were exacerbated as both the nation and its immigrant population grew. As more and more immigrants arrived, concern over their ability to assimilate increased. And as that concern grew, so too did the pressure for measures to both restrict immigration and encourage assimilation of recent immigrants. "The first settlers of a new country," Buchanan said in his veto of the Homestead Act, "are a most meritorious class. They brave the dangers of savage warfare, suffer the privations of a frontier life, and with the hand of toil bring the wilderness into cultivation. The 'old settlers,' as they are everywhere called, are public benefactors."[76] They had learned the lessons from the land that Jefferson and Jackson hoped they would learn. Cultivating the land served, in Gerstle's words, the nation's disciplinary project of rendering "people" into "citizens," and the right sort of citizens at that. The new settlers, on the other hand, styled as "foreigners" by Buchanan, were a different sort—they sought an unfair advantage through bills such as the Homestead Act, they had not learned the correct lessons from the land, and they pressed for advantages that would throw the union out of balance. They endangered the governing coalition by threatening its delicate balance of political compromises among groups.

Expansion created tensions between two conflicting notions of who was entitled to populate and control the new territory. This conflict, and the assumptions that grounded it, was clearly elaborated in the platform and oratory of the Know-Nothings. The Know-Nothings were the nation's first national nativist party. Nativism of the sort that they espoused seemed to be "a complex web of nationalism, xenophobia, ethnocentrism, and racism," but in the nineteenth century, the word *nativism* most often "connoted anti-immigrant sentiment."[77] This sentiment, difficult to explain in a nation controlled by immigrants and their descendants, became more understandable from the viewpoint of protecting cultural dominance and, with it, the political dominance of the governing coalition.

When access to land—and thus citizenship—became widely available, male immigrants from nearly every European country gained access to the political system. Those who had themselves recently acquired these privileges, and who had effected broad changes in their favor through the use of this access, were both loath to share their entitlements and afraid of the consequences such sharing might bring. Thus, they wanted access to land and to the political system restricted to those newcomers who shared their culture and their material interests, or at least restricted to those who could be taught to do so. The ideology of citizenship and the parameters of inclusion both served the material interests of the governing coalition.

The Know-Nothings sought to realign the interests of that coalition in accordance with how they understood the changes in the nation could best be accommodated, preserving some aspects of the national hierarchies while shifting others in ways that would secure their political ascendancy. Consequently, African Americans, whose immigration was involuntary and whose interests were assumed to be necessarily inimical to the interests of those who enslaved them, were to be forever excluded.[78] Catholics, whose adherence to a religious hierarchy was assumed to prevent the adoption of a democratic political ethos, threatened the regime and had to be disenfranchised.[79] The "Slave Power," in its economic competition with poor whites and political domination of the federal government, was considered too much like the antidemocratic Catholics and thus was also a source of deep suspicion.[80] Unskilled and impoverished laborers were assumed to be too hungry for material stability to have the independence necessary for a place at the national table, and were seen as threats to national stability.[81] Interestingly, while hardly advocates for African American civil rights or inclusion, Know-Nothings were strongly antislavery, and they built their national presence on opposition to slavery as much as on opposition to immigration.[82] It was this aspect of the party that allowed it to serve as something of a way station between the Whigs, the Free-Soilers, and the Republicans, as these groups struggled to forge political coalitions capable of winning national elections and governing a nation based on a new ideological understanding of itself.

Unlike Know-Nothings, Free-Soilers did not advocate a clear and explicit policy of racial, religious, and ethnic exclusion. They did want the territories kept free of slavery, but within that advocacy was a clear contempt of slave labor and fear of free African-American labor. The choice was not, as one restrictionist put it, "whether black men are to be made free . . . but whether white men are to remain free."[83] The debate over expansion, like the debate over abolition, was not a debate about the potential and position of African Americans as much as it was a debate about the position and power of white men. African Americans, even in the most liberal understanding of the time, were considered to lack agency and served as political catalysts, but not as functioning political actors. As actors, they remained politically invisible, however much their existence as slaves threatened the national balance of interests and thus national stability.

There were other internal threats to stability as well, indications that even among those who shared the outer accouterments of temperate citizenship, uncontrolled passions could lead to exclusion. By far the most threatening of these insiders-become-outsiders were the abolitionists. Abolitionists were almost entirely to blame, in the views of these presidents, for the problems in Kansas. In his third annual message, while discussing yet another outbreak of violence, Pierce said,

> In the Territory of Kansas have been acts prejudicial to good order, but as yet none have occurred under circumstances to justify the interposition of the Federal Executive. That could only be in case of obstruction to Federal law or of organized resistance to Territorial law, assuming the character of insurrection, which, if it should occur, it would be my duty

promptly to overcome and suppress. I cherish the hope, however, that the occurrence of any such untoward event will be prevented by the sound sense of the people of the Territory, who by its organic law, possessing the right to determine their own domestic institutions, are entitled while deporting themselves peacefully to the free exercise of that right, and must be protected in the enjoyment of it without interference on the part of citizens of any of the States.[84]

These presidents attained political power at the federal level at least partially through the commitment that they would not use it, as this quotation indicated. Domestic matters were best left up to the states. There was no need for a singular, unified approach to most political matters, but respect for local law would lead to the solution to local problems. Only violence of a magnitude indicating outright insurrection could justify federal intervention.

Popular sovereignty could work only if the people of the territories could be trusted to make their own decisions—if they had appropriate democratic temperance—and if they were allowed to make those decisions free from the influence of "outside agitators." It was thus on the peg of popular sovereignty that these presidents hung their hopes for the continuance of the union in its old form and protecting its original provisions and institutions, including slavery. As Buchanan put it in his inaugural, "The whole Territorial question being thus settled on the principle of popular sovereignty—a principle as ancient as free government itself—everything of a practical nature has been decided. No other question remains for adjustment, because all agree that under the Constitution slavery in the States is beyond the reach of any human power except that of the respective States themselves wherein it exists. May we not then, hope that the long agitation on this subject is approaching its end, and that the geographical parties to which it has given birth, so much dreaded by the Father of His Country, will speedily become extinct?"[85] Buchanan put the question of institutional arrangements—of how political differences were to be resolved—off the table. They were beyond debate because they themselves formed the basis for free government. Altering the institutional arrangements on which his governing coalition's power was predicated became an act against the principle of free government. Buchanan thus claimed agreement where none existed. What exactly the Constitution protected was precisely at issue, but it was beyond the scope of debate.

For these presidents, abolitionists were refusing to honor the terms of the original union and were recklessly threatening that union. In fact, their agitation was, according to Buchanan, "productive of no positive good to any human being and . . . the prolific source of great evils to the master, the slave, and to the whole country. It has alienated and estranged the people of the sister States from each other, and has even seriously endangered the very existence of the Union."[86] Because the union was good for all its members, threatening the union had to be bad for everyone. Stability meant stasis, and stasis required silence on matters that were certain to prove divisive. Silence should be enforced by both citizens and the states.

The states that harbored abolitionists, and thus also harbored dissension, were also responsible for the actions of their citizens. Thus the actions of individual citizens became identified with the actions of states, and the danger to the union became one of state, not merely individual action. As Pierce put it in his third annual message,

> It has been matter [sic] of painful regret to see States conspicuous for their services in founding this Republic and equally sharing its advantages disregard their constitutional obligations to it. Although conscious of their inability to heal admitted and palpable social evils of their own, and which are completely within their jurisdiction, they engage in the offensive and hopeless undertaking of reforming the domestic institutions of other states, wholly beyond their control and authority. In the vain pursuit of ends by them entirely unattainable, and which they may not legally attempt to compass, they peril the very existence of the Constitution and all the countless benefits which it has conferred.[87]

According to their theory of government, the federal government existed primarily to protect the rights and prerogatives of the states. Those states, then, as this quotation indicated, also owed some duty to the federal government. The states had local control; they thus also had the responsibility to control their local citizens. States, according to Pierce, should look to their own issues—controlling abolitionists—rather than to the domestic arrangements of other states—like slavery. Because these presidents understood states as the constitutive units of the national government, the states were also considered responsible for disciplining their own citizens. Just as these presidents sought to diffuse power, they also diffused responsibility. If the states accepted the power, but failed to act responsibly, they failed in their duty to the Constitution and endangered the union that was their primary protector.

In John Brown, the defenders of slavery saw all their nightmares realized. Buchanan understood this well. By 1860, terrified of the consequences that slaves were now "inspired . . . with vague notions of freedom" and expecting Lincoln's election to lead to slave revolts, as "a sense of security no longer exists around the family altar," Southerners, in the view of these presidents, were being driven to extreme measures.[88] There was thus a real urgency in stopping the activities of abolitionists and the states that supported their subversive activities. The greater the threat to the union, the more important it became to return to the past, to preserve the status quo, because any change would alter the ideological understanding of national identity and the structural arrangements that stemmed from it. Such changes in the nature of union could only destroy the union.

A similar urgency motivated arguments against the Mormons, who had to be subdued because, in their intemperance, they represented the forces of tyranny and despotism. Like American Indians, Mormons occupied a position both inside and outside the United States. As Buchanan put it in his proclamation on the Mormons in 1858, "You have settled upon territory which lies, geographically, in the heart of the union. The land you live upon was purchased by the United States and paid for out of their Treasury; the proprietary right and title to it is in them, and not in you. Utah is bounded on every side by States and Territories whose people are true to the union. It is absurd to believe that they will or can permit you to erect in their very midst a government of your very own, not only independent of the authority which they all acknowledge, but hostile to them and their interests."[89] The nation could not endure within its borders an alternative understanding of citizenship, an alternative political culture that carried with it alternative political hierarchies. Like American Indians, the Mormons were contained in and thus controlled by the United States. And like American Indians, Mormons remained outside the American polity. Their differences were both the necessary cause and the full justification for their exclusion.

In detailing the threat posed by the Mormons in general and Brigham Young in particular, Buchanan said, "there no longer remains any government in Utah but the despotism of Brigham Young."[90] Buchanan took pains to point out that it was their offensive behavior and consequent determination to extend their tyrannical government, not their religious convictions, that rendered them outsiders in the American polity: "With the religious opinions of the Mormons, as long as they remained mere opinions, however deplorable in themselves and revolting to the moral and religious sentiments of all Christendom, I had no right to interfere. Actions alone, when in violation of the Constitution and laws of the United States, become the legitimate subjects for the jurisdiction of the civil magistrate."[91] Implicitly denying the importance of civic nationalism, Buchanan argued that mere opinions were not cause for exclusion. One could remain within the polity and hold different opinions. Actions alone were cause for exclusion. Holding opinions would be tolerated. Acting on those opinions could not be, for then the alternatives would be instantiated and threatened the majority culture; the disciplinary project would have failed. Immigrants, Mormons, American Indians, could all *believe* as they wished, but they would never really be citizens. Should they continue to *act* as immigrants, Mormons, or American Indians, however, they would not even be allowed to remain physically inside the polity and they exposed themselves to potentially harsh disciplines. Thus, it was necessary to claim that Young and his followers were in a "state of open rebellion" and were determined to exclude those who disagreed with them. This exclusion, however parallel to Buchanan's position on popular sovereignty and slavery in the states, was not to be tolerated.

Buchanan characterized the Mormons in the same terms used to describe abolitionists, referring to their "frenzied fanaticism"[92] as the ultimate source of the threat they posed to the nation. Buchanan could offer no alternative except to meet such a threat with overwhelming force, since "this is the first rebellion which has existed in our Territories, and humanity itself requires that we should put it down in such a manner that it shall be the last. . . . We ought to go there with such an imposing force as to convince these deluded people that resistance would be vain, and thus spare the effusion of blood. We can in this matter best convince them that we are their friends and not their enemies."[93] As potential citizens, the Mormons had to be convinced of the error of their ways. Otherwise, rebellion might become widespread, and defiance of the national order endemic.

The claim that this was the first rebellion was, of course, historically inaccurate, but ideological justification, not factual accuracy, was the aim. It could also serve as a warning: should the abolitionists succeed in inciting a rebellion, then they, too, would be subjected to overwhelming force of arms. If one convinced "friends" through such force, the threat to potential enemies was clear. The Mormons were both politically visible and politically problematic. Because they were politically problematic, they had to be dealt with in ways that would not only solve the immediate problem, but also provide political instruction for others. Like American Indians, they served as an important counterexample of citizenship, of where following the wrong path could lead the nation.

Also like American Indians, Mormons forfeited their ability to reason. Their exclusion was not a matter of willful incapacity, but of choice. Their lack of rationality, however explained, meant that they could not be "good" citizens. As Buchanan's proclamation had it, "Whereas the Territory of Utah was settled by certain emigrants from the States and from foreign countries who have for several years past manifested a spirit of insubordination to the Constitution and laws of the United States. The great mass of those settlers, acting under the influence of leaders to whom they seem to have surrendered their judgment, refuse to be controlled by any other authority."[94] Remember Jackson's strictures on American Indians, who had forsaken reason and preferred the life of bodily satisfaction, who were misled by scurrilous advisers and could thus never make good citizens, and who had to be removed from the polity. Much the same analysis pertained here, for the Mormons were somehow "foreign"; they lived under Young's thrall and existed in a state of rebellion against the Constitution. They lacked the capacity for citizenship in a democratic polity.

Although American Indians and Mormons were willfully destructive, citizens could also threaten the polity through lapses in judgment or unbridled enthusiasm. These people misread the national ethos and, instead of proceeding with the caution and temperance vital to the national interest, allowed their enthusiasm for the national cause to lead them astray. Like abolitionists, although possessed of more worthy motives, they endangered the union. As Fillmore put it in his third annual message, "We live in an age of progress, and ours is emphatically a nation of progress. . . . The whole country is full of enterprise."[95] He was describing the Jacksonian nation, the nation of the frontiersman. But he was also describing the danger that this understanding of national identity posed for the nation in this political context, for this spirit had to be controlled:

> It is not strange, however much it may be regretted, that such an exuberance of enterprise should cause some individuals to mistake change for progress and the invasion of the rights of others for national prowess and glory. The former are constantly agitating for some change in the organic law, or urging new and untried theories of human rights. The latter are ever ready to engage in any wild crusade against a neighboring people, regardless of the justice of the enterprise and without looking at the fatal consequences to ourselves and to the cause of popular government. . . . These reprehensible aggressions but retard the true progress of our nation and tarnish its fair fame.[96]

That which was "new and untried" was less to be trusted than that which had gone before. The union of the founders was the union upon which they should still depend. Of course, it was also the union upon which the political coalition that had brought these presidents to power depended, and it was this vision of union that demanded a specific balance among the various interests contending for power. Balance meant resisting change in favor of stability; it meant that the risks of altering "organic law" were far greater than the risks of political stasis.

Thus, in their enthusiasm for what they deemed to be "American" principles, these people risked upsetting the balance on which the American polity depended. Pierce agreed with this characterization. In a proclamation on the subject, he called such adventurers "derogatory to our character and . . . threatening to our tranquility,"

and exhorted "all good citizens, as they regard our national character, as they respect our laws or the laws of nations, as they value the
blessings of peace and the welfare of their country, to discounte-
nance and by all lawful means prevent such criminal enterprises."[97]
He asked them to demand political stasis and forgo political change.
Buchanan went even further, claiming that there was a right way—
and thus by implication also a wrong way—to acquire land. In his
inaugural he said, "It is our glory that whilst other nations have
extended their dominions by the sword we have never acquired any
territory except by fair purchase, or, as in the case of Texas, by the
voluntary determination of a brave, kindred, and independent people
to blend their destinies with our own."[98] This adventurous pioneer
valorized by Jackson, through his enthusiasm, now threatened the
nation whose growth he had previously fostered.

This ideologically satisfactory if less than completely accurate
understanding of national history here served the goal of defending
national imperialism, so long as it was carried out under the direction of the national government. Controlled, balanced, managed
change was more productive of national stability than was the rock-
eting, individualistic, adventurous change of Jackson. These presidents, charged with maintaining the national balance, were vigilant
in the defense of their principles, careful in how the various interests
were managed.

Fillmore in fact did not rhetorically distinguish between abolitionists and adventurers. Both threatened the nation, and neither had
the proper respect for stability understood as political stasis. In both
cases, there was a confidence in the new, the untried, the unbounded frontier that was inconsistent with democratic prudence, embodied in the national Constitution. In his third annual message Fillmore said, "Our Constitution, though not perfect, is doubtless the
best that ever was formed. Therefore, let every proposition to change
it be well weighed and, if found beneficial, cautiously adopted. . . .
Thus shall conservatism and progress blend their harmonious action
in preserving the form and spirit of the Constitution and at the same
time carry forward the great improvements of the country with a
rapidity and energy which freemen only can display."[99] "Freemen"
here meant not only the status of not being enslaved, but also a certain capacity for freedom; the ability to restrain oneself such that
other restraints—ranging from chattel slavery to the restrictions of a

strong government—were not necessary. Freedom meant a commitment to the Constitution and the union of the founders that would result in the preservation of the prevailing hierarchies, the ideological understanding of national identity that supported them, and the power of the governing coalition of interests that both served.

There was no implicit fear of Manifest Destiny here, but there was a stricture on the ways in which that destiny was to be accomplished. Americans prospered because they had the capacity for appropriate citizenship. They merited an empire because they would spread that capacity. Restraining themselves, they also had to restrain those who failed to exhibit that capacity; a restraint best accomplished through exclusion. The disciplinary project that Gerstle identified in the twentieth century clearly had its roots long before. As Pierce put it in his inaugural:

> With an experience thus suggestive and cheering, the policy of my Administration will not be controlled by any timid forebodings of evil from expansion. Indeed, it is not to be disguised that our attitude as a nation and our position on the globe render the acquisition of certain possessions not within our jurisdiction eminently important for our protection, if not in the future essential for the preservation of the rights of commerce and the peace of the world. Should they be obtained, it will be through no grasping spirit, but with a view to obvious national interest and security, and in a manner entirely consistent with the strictest observance of national faith.[100]

The issue was thus not merely the ends, but also the means; democracy is, after all, as much about process and motive as it is about outcome. And it is only about participation to the extent that participation serves correct process and outcomes. But, as Smith notes, the state is not a neutral arbiter among interests, but an entity whose structures are determinative of political outcomes.[101] By the end of the decade, these presidents had essentially excluded the majority of those legally entitled to citizenship. Not only were groups such as American Indians and slaves excluded, but so were Mormons, abolitionists, many immigrants, anyone with a passionate belief about slavery or an understanding of the nation's founding that differed from that of these presidents and practically everyone else. It came to the point where accepting union almost inevitably meant accepting one's own exclusion from it. It is no wonder that membership in the Democratic party contracted throughout the decade. Relying on the calcification of the nation's politics in service to the vision of the founders became increasingly difficult to manage and increasingly unsatisfactory to many of the nation's varied interests. It finally became impossible.

These presidents saw themselves as the heirs of the founders. Politically, they were actually the heirs of Andrew Jackson, for the political coalition that he forged was the coalition that brought them to power. They could only accept that power on the condition that they not wield it, however, for they governed on the premise that the federal government had no role to play in issues of "domestic" interest. Their political problem was maintaining the power of a political coalition that was already fracturing along new lines created by the dynamic union crafted by the founders and articulated by Andrew Jackson.

In protecting Jackson's coalition, they had to forsake Jackson's model of citizenship in favor of a less adventurous, less passionate, more temperate and settled model. Any change was regarded with suspicion, and any alteration in the national ideology, political structures, or identity was regarded with trepidation. The union was deemed so fragile that anything other than stasis endangered it. Those who vied for national power by advocating changes in national ideology, political structures, or identity were dangerous and had to be overtly excluded. Citizenship and invisibility were placed in the service of balance until balance could no longer be maintained on those terms and the nation went to war with itself.

Conclusion

In the antebellum United States, as in other historical periods, controversy over the nature of the regime was carried out in the larger context of who was to be granted the status of "citizenship."[102] And in the antebellum United States, as in other historical periods, the conception of citizenship was simultaneously inclusive and exclusive, a duality that was reflected in the two founding documents, the Declaration of Independence and the Constitution, as well as the midpoint between them, the Articles of Confederation.

Just as the Declaration made liberty and equality part of the national mission, the Constitution made the institution of slavery a national problem. Because slavery was a "domestic institution" regulated by state law, it posed both a moral problem and political dilemma. For the elimination of slavery required either separate action by each slaveholding state or a national constitutional amendment. Neither course was likely, and neither was easily accomplished. But those who advocated the abolition of slavery became, however unwillingly, also advocates of a strong national government whose action was necessary to preserve the founders' ideals of equality. So, too, did advocates of slavery ask for a strong national government—in demanding the rigid enforcement of the Fugitive Slave Law, slaveholders were also demanding national enforcement, which required the action of a national government and which would serve, however perversely, the framers' ideals of individual liberty.

Both slaveholders and abolitionists shared a firm belief in the inherent rightness of their position, as well as a belief that all local actions now had national implications. Both sides in the impending conflict were thus engaged in a process of self-conscious nation building, which depended on balancing the claims of different, and sometimes competing, interests. At the core of this process were the requirements and privileges of citizenship.

Chief among the requirements was the ability to reason. Perceived as lacking this ability, most American Indians, all African Americans, all women, all Asians, the Irish, and Southern Europeans were disqualified, either directly and visibly or indirectly and invisibly, albeit for different reasons. Also excluded were those who gave in to their passions. Abolitionists, Mormons, and adventurers were all understood as threats to the union, whose citizenship status was viewed as questionable.

In keeping with the conservative mandate of the presidency, these presidents sought to preserve an existing order and therefore also an existing set of institutions (slavery) and governmental structures (a confederal system) that were already outmoded. It proved impossible for them to either stop time or delay any longer the consequences of its passage. The organization of a continental empire was increasingly demanding the presence of a strong central government, even as these presidents argued and acted against such structure. In its turn, centralized administration demands consistency among its constituent parts. By placing itself outside these processes by defending and perpetuating slavery, the South retarded not only its own growth and development, but that of the nation as well. This impediment could not be tolerated in a nation that has always placed growth and development at the center of its self-understanding. The South had a difficult argument to make.

But Southerners had three consecutive presidents—none of them Southerners but all concerned with the preservation of an increasingly fragile union—to make that argument for them. Each in turn based that argument on the common ground that all enfranchised citizens could share: faith in the founders, trust in their capacity to reason (and doubt in that of others), and fidelity to hierarchies that enshrined that faith, trust, and doubt. These presidents thus argued for the systematic exclusion of specific categories of persons in the hope that such exclusion would foster the political stasis their vision of union demanded. Even as others argued against the increasingly entrenched South, they accepted the presidentially proffered terms of debate and the increasingly rigid hierarchies, for those hierarchies served their purposes as well.

The Civil War tested the boundaries of exclusion and, for a time, altered them, along with the terms of national debates over inclusion and exclusion. But all too soon, change would threaten, the old fears would resurface. And again, it was the president who would set the terms of the debate.

3 / The Business of Government during the Democratic Interregnum of Grover Cleveland, 1885–1889

Wall Street owns the country.
—Mary Ellen Lease, quoted in Howard Zinn,
A People's History of the United States

AMONG the lessons of the Civil War, the fragility of order was one that politicians in the United States found particularly resonant. In a nation whose founders were concerned with the preservation of social order amid changing social circumstances, the need to maintain that order and to balance it with change was a paramount concern. After the war, balance and the preservation of order, charges laid on the president,[1] were increasingly difficult. Rapid social and economic change and the increasing visibility of groups pressing their claims for inclusion complicated the president's task of conserving the union. As labor, women, and other groups organized, their ability to become politically problematic increased, thus adding to the demands on the political system. Industrialization and urbanization led to a decline in the importance of personal networks, both social and economic, and to an increase in the importance of standardization, exemplified in the widespread adoption among managers of the principles of Taylorism.[2] Even time itself was standardized during these years.[3] This period stands at a nexus between moments when balancing expansion and incorporation with the needs of stability and order and moments when the president's most pressing concern in this area involved the limits and parameters of citizenship. Cleveland's presidency represented a moment when expansion, order, and issues of citizenship were all concerns. It was also a pivotal point in the journey many groups were making from political invisibility to being politically problematic and differentiated or politically included.

In terms of defining citizenship and granting inclusion in the national polity, these changes meant that there could be no more reliance on traits of character or even on behavior, for these matters were increasingly difficult to discern in an ever more mobile population. Reputation was a less than reliable guide, and its previous surrogates were also, in these times of unsettled hierarchies, inconsistent barometers of the virtues necessary for a republican citizenry. Indeed, the concept of "virtue" as a requirement for citizenship was itself changed and weakened, for "value" was coming to displace it as a measure of capacity for citizenship. Rogers M. Smith calls this "the age of the militant WASP,"[4] because it was a time when new immigrants, women, labor, and other groups were vocally demanding a share of the privileges enjoyed by white male Protestants. The coalition that brought Cleveland to power, however, did not represent these excluded groups and thus worked to maintain the existing power structures and political processes and the ideology that sustained them both.

Cleveland had to balance the demands made on the government by the newly developing sectors of the economy with the demands of the old. Consciously or not, he did so in ways that legitimated persistent ascriptive hierarchies, encouraged the disciplinary project of assimilating citizens, and naturalized continuing economic stratifications. Rather than relying on images of the frontier, as Jefferson, Jackson, and the presidents of the 1850s had, Cleveland instead used urban metaphors, reflecting the strength of his political coalition in the Eastern cities and among those who looked to the city for its political heroes. In using the metaphors of business, Cleveland applied the generally accepted inequalities inherent in capitalism to politics and thus also rendered certain political exclusions invisible by shifting the rationales for inclusion from an overt focus on race or other ascriptive traits to economic productivity.

Throughout these years, money remained the one reliable measure of individual worth.[5] The organic metaphors of the body politic took on new meaning as they were imbued with mechanistic and scientific overtones, changing the national view of how natural civic processes should work and emphasizing the need for standardization.[6] During the Gilded Age, money was how Americans measured success, enterprise, independence, manliness, and character.[7] Money was to Cleveland's polity what land was to Jackson's and temperance was to Fillmore, Pierce, and Buchanan's. Having money meant that one, quite simply, had value. Individuals were evaluated by the amount of money they earned, controlled, spent, and amassed. Making money was widely considered to be the patriotic duty of all Americans, and the most contentious issues of the day involved how much money various segments of society—laborers, capitalists, immigrants, African Americans, and women—were worth.

The processes of government were increasingly understood in the language of business and the developing credo of modernized business practices. Standardization—of government through the civil service, and of labor through increased mechanization—became increasingly important. Gone or going was the importance of individual reputation and achievement as understood by the framers. Gone also was the urgent need for land to fuel the expansion of the market economy, as experienced during the Jacksonian era. The nation was growing again, but it was economic development rather than physical expansion; the issues of the day concerned access to the capitalist system rather than access to land. Increasingly, all citizens were measured by the same single standard, exemplified by the dollar sign, which signified "American" both at home and abroad.

These processes were clearly, if implicitly, outlined in Cleveland's rhetoric: in his application of the language of business to government, in his understanding of good citizens as good workers, his preference for a standardized citizenry exemplified in his concern over both concentrated power and the threats of wide dispersion, and finally in his idealization of the civil service model as an exemplar of citizenship. In delineating the model citizen in a newly industrialized economy, Cleveland relied on both the overtly exclusionist language of balance and the more subtly exclusionary language of citizenship.

Industrial Government

During the Gilded Age, the union of the founders was viewed less as a compact and more as a contract. The founders, although still revered, no longer formed the fulcrum on which the union was balanced. Allegiance to the nation was still understood in largely racialized terms—the inclusive ideals of the founders remained restricted to white male Protestants who shared specific sets of cultural norms—and the benefits of that allegiance were understood in both economic and philosophical terms. Ideology was understood in material terms, as economic benefits were more important than emotional ones for retaining the union. The Constitution had less of its sacred meaning, and more meaning as an agreement between parties for the benefit of both.

Thus, the nation was less a sacred union (although that understanding never entirely leaves us) and more a pragmatic form of economic organization. Cleveland did not change nor did he demean the task of the presidency to preserve the national order. Rather, the terms in which he represented the nature of that task reflected the language of capitalism that was increasingly applied to the public sector during these years. The benefits of the constitutional contract, however, would not be equally available to all.

But this notion of union was not entirely self-interested, nor was it entirely selfish. For Cleveland, membership in the political community—citizenship—meant a commitment to the "general welfare," not to one's individual preferences.[8] An appropriate balance among the nation's competing interests would be achieved by a reification of the common good (which became identified with policies that favored Cleveland's coalition). In many ways, this was similar to the common good as FDR would later come to understand it. It was, as Smith notes, a use of democratic rhetoric to advance the capitalist interests that had brought Cleveland to power.[9] Aware of his coalition's tenuous hold on national power, Cleveland, like many other presidents, argued that his policies actually represented the national interest, not merely parochial interests. In his 1885 inaugural, he said:

> The large variety of diverse and competing interests subject to Federal control, persistently seeking the recognition of their claims, need give us no fear that "the greatest good to the greatest number" will fail to be accomplished if in the halls of national legislation that spirit of amity and mutual concession shall prevail in which the Constitution had its

birth. If this involves the surrender or postponement of private interests and the abandonment of local advantages, compensation will be found in the assurance that the common interest subserved and the general welfare advanced.[10]

For all practical purposes, the Civil War ended the argument between the states and the federal government over which would have controlling power. The governmental philosophy and the institutional arrangements favored by Pierce, Fillmore, and Buchanan, like the political coalition that brought them to power, were now irretrievably gone. The federal government now had a different sort of balancing problem. It derived different institutional arrangements—such as the creation of the career civil service—to manage that balancing problem, and different sorts of ideological justifications to legitimate those arrangements. For Cleveland, that meant, as the preceding quotation indicated, a stress on the harmony of interests in general, an emphasis on the need to place the common interest above private or local ones when any conflict arose, and an optimism about the capacity of the system, now a century old, to manage the increasing complexities of the national polity.

The variety of interests that presidents in the 1850s found so threatening no longer imperiled the republic because in this understanding of government there was no principle worth the creation of conflict, no principle that could not be reduced to "private interest" or "local advantages." Relying on an interpretation of national history that ignored the contention surrounding the birth of both the Constitution and the first party system, Cleveland argued that the Constitution was less a document that enunciated certain immutable principles that should be strictly followed, and more a document that outlined certain procedures for the process of compromise, such that the business of government could continue unimpeded. As Cleveland put it in his inaugural, "The people demand reform in the administration of the Government and the application of business principles to public affairs."[11] Government would henceforth be seen as analogous to business and would be expected to manage itself according to the best business principles. "Good government," according to Grover Cleveland in his second annual message, "and especially the government of which every American citizen boasts, has for its objects the protection of every person within its care in the greatest liberty consistent with the good order of society and his perfect security in the enjoyment of his earnings with the least possible diminution for public needs."[12] "Good" government was now explicitly defined as that government most likely to foster national prosperity and protect its citizens' enjoyment of that prosperity.

True to their Enlightenment heritage, many Americans of this generation glorified progress and technology, and considered the laws of progress universal.[13] According to this understanding, civilization had advanced (evolved) technologically to the point where humans could become efficient; they could plan the path of their development. To most efficiently follow this path required some degree of standardization. For civilization to progress required change. For change to proceed according to scientific principles required standardization. Taylor, one of the exemplars of the age, was an ardent advocate of scientific management. In the uses made of Taylor by elites and managers, all these principles were revealed. They would come to fruition at the mass level only with Woodrow Wilson and the experiences of World War I.

They were equally clear in the use made of Darwin. Darwin, of course, focused on change, on sequences of cause and effect, which made his ideas particularly attractive to many Americans at the end of the nineteenth century. Because Darwin's evidence came from the natural world, its application to politics and economics lent those processes a certain aura of inevitability and reinforced the idea that it was not government's place to meddle with them.[14] The equation of natural law and character served to legitimate social, political, and economic hierarchies in a world where old justifications had disappeared. As Jackson had used historical inevitability to legitimate his political preferences, and as the presidents of the 1850s had used historical destiny to legitimate theirs, for Cleveland, balance was achieved by the correct (scientific) management of social forces.[15]

Cleveland's rhetoric was thus consistent with the prevailing ideology of his time. As he put it in his first annual message:

The laws of progress are vital and organic, and we must be conscious of that irresistible tide of commercial expansion which, as the concomitant of our active civilization, day by day, is being urged onward by those increasing facilities of

production, transportation, and communication to which
steam and electricity have given birth; but our duty in the
present instructs us to address ourselves mainly to the development of the vast resources of great area committed to our
charge and to the cultivation of the arts of peace within our
own borders, though jealously alert in preventing the American hemisphere from being involved in the political problems and complications of distant governments.[16]

Substitute Jackson's "Providence" for Cleveland's "laws of
progress" and much the same argument was being made in both
cases. Both Jackson and Cleveland relied on arguments concerning
irresistible forces to remove agency and to legitimate their policy
choices. Both Jackson and Cleveland assumed that the path American civilization was taking was the only correct path for civilization
in general. Both Jackson and Cleveland also relied on natural metaphors—tides, birth, and death—and on travel metaphors—paths and
roads—to make their cases, and to linguistically tie the conscious
choices of government to the natural progress of nature and man.
Jackson and Cleveland thus differed from Fillmore, Pierce, and
Buchanan in that those presidents sought to freeze time and create a
static union. Stasis could not serve the needs of Cleveland or Jackson,
nor could it serve the needs of their governing coalitions. Both needed dynamic unions and dynamic senses of national identity to allow
for the expansion of economic interests.

Yet unlike Jackson, whose coalition rested on the incorporation
of previously excluded Protestant white males and whose dynamic
union thus required the creation of new elites, Cleveland's required
limited expansion—mainly through the inclusion of immigrant
groups—and a strong disciplinary project aimed at rendering those
immigrants into American citizens. He needed to standardize those
immigrants, make them useful as workers in an industrialized economy that required flexible management at the top, but a ready supply of workers below. He needed a dynamic union like Jackson's and
a socially static union like that of the 1850s.

Even though technology had changed, and despite the changes of
industrialization, the political obligations and problems of the nation
remained the same as they had been in the 1830s and 1850s: develop economically while avoiding the taint of European politics, and

maintain supremacy in the hemisphere. Because the obligations and problems remained static, the implication was that the elites appointed to fulfill those obligations and cope with those problems should likewise remain static. Through this mechanism, various exclusions would be legitimated and an appropriate balance between the interests of the people and the national interest in orderly development could be maintained.

As in the preceding example, the metaphors used to discuss this understanding of government were either organic or mechanical (or both). In either case, they implied that each person, each part, had a role and that the whole functioned best when those roles were understood and maintained by all. If balance was the product of natural forces, then it was best maintained by aligning human action with those forces. As we saw in the case of Andrew Jackson, and as we will see in Woodrow Wilson's language, these metaphors removed agency. In this formulation, the "decay" of "weaker" civilizations had nothing to do with the actions of Americans or the American government but was the product of historical inevitability.

This claim of historical inevitability blurred the distinctions between public and private spheres. This change was an important one in American politics, one that needed to be justified ideologically as well as rhetorically. Where economics had previously been considered outside the province of the national government and, indeed, by encouraging faction, dangerous to the survival of government, the economy increasingly was becoming the business of government. In an 1886 Communication to the House and Senate, Cleveland said, "Under our form of government the value of labor as an element of national prosperity should be distinctly recognized and the welfare of the laboring man should be regarded as especially entitled to legislative care. In a country which offers to all its citizens the highest attainment of social and political distinction its workingmen cannot be justly or safely considered as irrevocably consigned to the limits of a class and entitled to no attention and allowed no protest against neglect."[17] The government now had an explicit interest in the "welfare of the working man" that went beyond ensuring that the economy was prosperous. Social Darwinism and the principles of scientific management were united in urging that the government had a role in what had been the private province of the workplace. Workers were citizens and citizens were workers; all were entitled to

the belief that they could improve their station in life through diligence and care. It was the government's job to act as a watchdog on
industry to best protect that entitlement.

Citizens as Workers

When the language of business was applied to government, the
metaphor for "citizens" became "workers." Citizenship during the
Gilded Age was about money, as it was about land during the Age of
Jackson and about temperance before the Civil War. Citizens were
loyal to the government not because it was the government of the
founders, nor because of any sacred obligation—those bonds had
been substantially weakened in the carnage of the 1860s and were
not yet remythologized in a generation that could not remember for
itself the blood and death of the war. Citizens-as-workers honored
the government because through it, their rights to self-advancement
were protected. This continued the removal of dangerous passions
from government and placed politics on a more pragmatic, professional, even businesslike plane. In keeping with the demands of a
recently reunified nation, Cleveland thus defined politics not as a
contentious arena in which warring interests did battle, but as a
process of negotiating practical compromises among those interests.
Self-interested civic mindedness became a marker of a rational republican citizen. Cleveland spoke in his inaugural of the need to compromise "private interests" and "local advantages," but he also spoke
of the reward for this behavior as "compensation."[18] Civic duty was
thus rendered into the language of commerce.

It was during the Gilded Age that many of the myths associated
with the American dream were born. During this time, national prosperity finally and irrevocably trumped national virtue as the measure for judging the state of the union. It was during these years that
the rags-to-riches success story attained national popularity. It was
not a coincidence that in these stories, an enterprising but poor
young man made good through a combination of luck and hard work,
and it was not surprising that "making good" was defined in exclusively material rather than moral terms. The age's robber barons also
often flaunted their rise from humble beginnings to positions of
wealth and power. Equally often, these tales were based on things

other than fact.[19] Undoubtedly, some of the great fortunes of the Gilded Age were based on corruption as others were founded in talent and fortuitous circumstances. Most probably, there were elements of all three in most. But this was not how they were contemporaneously portrayed. Instead, throughout the popular culture of the time, the path to greatness was seen as an economic, not a moral endeavor.[20]

The late 1800s was a time of both standardization and of hyperindividualism. The terms *workers* and *citizens* were becoming interchangeable,[21] and, not coincidentally, individuals with the wherewithal to do so were increasingly determined to demonstrate their individual imprimatur. This dynamic could not be more clearly illustrated than in the life of Theodore Roosevelt during these years.[22] Roosevelt was a particularly interesting case, for he sought to counter the ease and luxury available to his class with strictures on the necessity of a strenuous life, as the only life able to forge a proper sort of citizen. In Roosevelt there were strong echoes of Jackson's adventurous frontiersman.[23] He saw in this active, frontier life the same virtue that Jackson had—men learned the lessons of citizenship through encounters with what they considered hostile forces such as nature and American Indians.

Most Americans, however, were unlike Roosevelt in that they were members of the "toiling classes," and for them, the emphasis was less on the rights of citizenship and the promise of individualism than on the duties attendant on them as citizens. Chief among these was the duty to the economy—consumption. As Cleveland put it in his second annual message:

> We congratulate ourselves that there is among us no laboring class fixed within unyielding bounds and doomed under all conditions to the inexorable fate of daily toil. We recognize in labor a chief factor in the wealth of the Republic, and we treat those who have it in their keeping as citizens entitled to the most careful regard and thoughtful attention. This regard and attention should be awarded them, not only because labor is the capital of our workingmen, justly entitled to its share of Government favor, but for the further and not less important reason that the laboring man, surrounded by his family in his humble home, as a consumer is vitally

interested in all that cheapens the cost of living and enables him to bring within his domestic circle additional comforts and advantages.[24]

The wealth of the republic was the important value. As contributors, laborers also should be beneficiaries—that is, they should be able to amass some measure of material gain. The nation's project of turning "people" into "citizens" was not without reward—one could achieve some level of material comfort if one behaved in suitable ways. Citizens were both workers and consumers.

Laborers were important as producers of wealth and as consumers of products, not merely as citizens or inhabitants of the nation. They held, it appeared, little intrinsic interest for the government. But as contributors to the economy, they were worthy of government protection and notice. Because they made an economic contribution, workers were entitled to government protection. That protection allowed them to fulfill their patriotic duty to the economy and to "bring within his domestic circle additional comforts and advantages." As both citizens and workers, then, average Americans were valued to the extent that they could contribute to the nation; that contribution was understood almost exclusively as economic.

Under Jefferson, the valorized, prototypical American citizen was the yeoman farmer, quietly working his subsistence farm and exemplifying ideal citizenship through his independence and thrift. For Jackson, that farmer had become a backwoodsman, a hardy pioneer whose adventurous spirit expanded an enterprising nation and its market economy. By the 1850s, the spirit of adventure was creating some problems of stability for the nation, and it needed to be restrained, rendered more temperate and cautious. In Cleveland's industrialized age, the enterprising energy was displayed in the expansion of an industrialized economy. Wage earners, once politically powerless and despised for their lack of independence, were now politically visible, if somewhat problematic and in need of discipline. Capitalists were valorized as the new pioneers; workers were praised for their ability to contribute to that greater endeavor. Again from Cleveland's second annual message:

Those who toil for daily wages are beginning to understand that capital, though sometimes vaunting its importance and clamoring for the protection and favor of the Government, is dull and sluggish till, touched by the magical hand of labor, it springs into activity, furnishing an occasion for federal taxation and gaining the value which enables it to bear its burden. And the laboring man is thoughtfully inquiring whether in these circumstances, and considering the tribute he consistently pays into the public Treasury as he supplies his daily wants, he receives his fair share of advantages.[25]

Given plaudits for providing the "magical hand" to capital, labor was apparently the hero of the capitalist tale. But that heroism had to function within clear limitations. Workers were demanding equality, not on the basis of shared citizenship rights or an equal devotion to the universalized principles of the nation, but because without them, capital languished. Political entitlement followed economic contribution. The contribution made by workers was to the national economy; their rights as citizens were to be protected through a more equitable tax policy. Citizens were workers, and those who did not work were de facto excluded from the polity. Balance and citizenship were thus inextricably connected. But for citizens and workers to be completely identical in an industrialized economy, there had to be some degree of standardization.

Standardized Citizens

Citizens were thus encouraged to have no strong ties that would differentiate among them. In particular, they were to have no strong partisan loyalties and no sectional prejudices. In his inaugural, Cleveland noted that his election had occurred "amid the din of party strife" but argued as well that "the best results in the operation of government wherein every citizen has a share largely depend upon a limitation of purely partisan zeal and effort and a correct appreciation of the time when the heat of the partisan should be merged in the patriotism of the citizen."[26] Certainly, this call for moderation of divisive attitudes was understandable. In the first place, this was an inaugural, and unifying appeals are predictable elements of the genre.[27] Furthermore, Cleveland was a Democratic president in a country that thought of itself as largely Republican. The muting of partisanship was crucial to his ability to govern. Finally, the "sectional prejudices" that harkened back to the war could only continue to divide a nation that needed to understand itself as somehow whole. Presidents in this strongly differentiated nation have ever called for unity. Those calls become stronger when the reasons for union seem weakest. The point here is less that Cleveland felt the need to ask for unity and more about the sort of unity he requested. In keeping with the pervading spirit of Taylorism among managers and other elites in the 1880s, Cleveland's unity was based on a citizenry of standardized workers.[28]

Cleveland thus needed the dynamic union of Jefferson and Jackson to allow for and encourage economic growth, which depended in part on the inclusion of immigrant workers, women, and African Americans into the labor pool. But as these groups' economic power grew, their potential political power grew as well, and their opposition to capitalistic power intensified. In party strife, Cleveland saw also strife between labor and capital, between agricultural and industrial interests, and so on. Like the presidents of the 1850s, Cleveland also needed a static union, one in which the given hierarchies could be accepted and managed so that the nation would not become unbalanced. Responsive both to the interests of his governing coalition and to the need to manage the nation as a whole, Cleveland derived a standardized view of national unity and national identity.

Cleveland's unity required that all participants in the polity knew and respected their various places in the overall scheme of things. It also required a balance among the different components. Because it encapsulates much of Cleveland's rhetoric on this subject, his second annual message is worth quoting at length:

> But after all has been done by the passage of laws, either Federal or State, to relieve a situation full of solicitude, much more remains to be accomplished by the reinstatement and cultivation of a true American sentiment which recognizes the equality of American citizenship. This, in the light of our traditions, and in loyalty to the spirit of our institutions, would teach that a hearty cooperation on the part of all interests is the surest path to national greatness and the happiness of all our people; that capital should, in recognition of

brotherhood of our citizenship and in a spirit of American fairness, generously accord to labor its just compensation and consideration, and that contented labor is capital's best protection and faithful ally. It would teach, too, that the diverse situations of our people are inseparable from our civilization; that every citizen should in his sphere be a contributor to the general good; that capital does not necessarily tend to the oppression of labor, and that violent disturbances and disorders alienate from their promoters true American sympathy and kindly feeling. [29]

Rather than the democratic virtues of an idealized yeomanry or the careful temperance of the antebellum citizen, good citizens in the Gilded Age were cooperative citizens. They understood their individual roles, trusted others to faithfully execute their assigned functions, and worked appropriately within their roles to bring about the best result for the whole. The organic union would thrive if its members understood their mutual dependence and self-interest; if each respected their place and that of others; and if all contributed—in their various ways—to the general good. This process rested on acceptance of one's "natural" place, on an ethic that emphasized standardization, and resulted in money as a measure of citizen value.

Because Cleveland understood the union to be an organic or mechanized whole, its nature was to function smoothly. That smooth operation, however, could be interrupted by a corruption of natural processes. As with Jackson, Cleveland understood correct political action to be aligned with the requirements of natural forces. Like Jackson, he argued for the necessity of making correct choices. In Cleveland's representation, poor choices were the result of some sort of corruption of understanding.

For Cleveland, there were two main sources of this corruption: concentration of power, either in monopolies of capitalists or in labor unions; and harmful or "unnatural" contagions, brought by elements such as foreign immigrants, African Americans, women, and striking workers, the immorality of people like the Mormons, or the recalcitrance of the willfully wild, like American Indians. The cures for these corruptive influences were all the same: standardization of citizens along the patterns of Americanization, assimilation, and the creed of republican virtue. The exemplar of such standardization was the federal civil service, designed to eliminate corruption in government and provide rational, standardized public affairs.

This formulation illuminates the processes of attaining some measure of visibility by many groups. Labor was more organized during this period and much more powerful. Women were becoming an important, if ancillary aspect of the national economy. Immigration, stemmed by the Civil War, was again on the rise. And the frontier continued to be part of the fuel that animated the national economic machine. As members of these groups began to organize and press their demands on government, their sheer numbers and influence over matters of governmental concern meant that they could not simply be erased. They were, to one degree or another, politically visible. For those who were marginalized, being politically visible also meant being labeled as politically problematic. One way in which the politically problematic could be brought into the polity was through a sort of rhetorical discipline: members of these groups were divided into "good" and "bad" representatives, with the "good" held up as models of appropriate attitudes and behavior and the "bad" as counterexamples of citizenship. This rhetorical discipline allowed the president to manage the tensions between inclusion and exclusion, to patrol the borders of citizenship through language, rhetorically defining who was—and who wasn't—a "real" American, and to contribute to what Gerstle styles the "disciplinary project of citizenship" wherein "people" are rendered into "citizens" suitable for the American democracy.

CONCENTRATED POWER

The most worrying source of corruption was one that existed in direct contradiction to the historical emphasis on republican virtue: the concentration of power among major industrialists. For Jefferson and Jackson, virtue was concentrated among small landowners, whose values reflected the lessons of the land—commercial interests were perhaps necessary, but among them were no models of republican citizenship. For Fillmore, Pierce, and Buchanan, republican virtue was made clear in the example of the founders, and was temperate. They valorized a Jeffersonian vision of agricultural virtue. By the Gilded Age, however, the frontier was less of a source of new wealth and increasingly a stable part of an industrial republic. Capital and capitalists were the heroes of the time, and the amassing of wealth the marker of success.

Great wealth was indeed amassed.[30] As Phillip Armour, the meat-packing tycoon, told Congress: "We are here to make money. I wish I could make more."[31] The addition of "more" was something of a hallmark of the age, for wealth and its display became the most visible markers of the importance of a capitalistic economy in the United States. The problem presented by these industrialists was less the fact of wealth and power—there was a long tradition of concentrated wealth in the United States—and more the sense that those in power now were less motivated by the collective public interest than they were by individual greed. The belief in these baser motives was heightened by the increasing evidence of the unequal distribution of wealth.[32] Wealth per se was not seen as problematic. Wealth unattached to any notion of republican virtue understood as "civic responsibility" was problematic. Thus the owners of great fortunes also became great philanthropists, and the power of wealth was to some extent diffused in the glow of charity.

The wealth and philanthropy rested on the ideological foundation of individualism. The ability to enact the individualist creed, however, was restricted to a very few. Ideologically, those in power argued that the new economy meant that everyone found a place consistent with their natural abilities. The ideological wheel came back around at this point: failure to achieve was individual and based on flawed character, not the product of a flawed system. There were just enough rags to riches stories to fuel the ideological claim that such success was possible for anyone with the drive, initiative, and good fortune to find opportunities and follow them tenaciously.

This understanding was widespread, even though arguably that system was stacked against workers. While claiming neutrality, official governmental policy often seemed to favor the capitalists rather than labor, especially in actions that sanctioned the use of force—sometimes even the United States military and militias—to control workers and protestors, and interpreting laws such as the Sherman Act in ways that seemed to serve the interests of owners rather than of workers.[33] For proponents of this understanding of American economic history, capital could not have made the gains it did relative to labor without the support of courts and the national legislature.[34]

Even the president recognized the awesome power of capital and understood that this power did not unambiguously serve the national interest. In his fourth annual message, for example, Cleveland said:

> We discover that the fortunes realized by our manufacturers are no longer solely the reward of sturdy industry and enlightened foresight, but that they result from the discriminating favor of the Government and are largely built upon undue exactions from the masses of our people . . . . as we view the achievements of aggregated capital, we discover the existence of trusts, combinations, and monopolies, while the citizen is struggling far in the rear or is trampled to death beneath an iron heel. Corporations, which should be the carefully restrained creatures of the law and servants of the people, are fast becoming the people's masters.[35]

For Cleveland, the state was supposed to function as a neutral umpire, balancing various economic interests to produce the common good. When one set of interests was enjoying too much governmental bounty, the balance needed to be corrected. When the set of interests that brought Cleveland to power were on the losing side of that balance, the need to redress the balance became all the more important. Cleveland's constituents were not the large capitalists, but the smaller enterprises, on whom demands of labor and competition from larger concerns fell the most bluntly. In protecting them, he could also make gains for labor without damaging the overall balance of economic interests on which national prosperity was understood to depend.

Finding the concentration of wealth to be at the root of the problem, Cleveland argued against such concentration, whether it was in the guise of ownership of factories or of land: "Laws which were intended for the 'common benefit' have been perverted so that large quantities of land are vesting in single ownerships. . . . It is not for 'the common benefit of the United States' that a large area of the public lands should be acquired, directly or through fraud, in the hands of a single individual."[36] It was not the ownership per se, but unbalanced ownership (especially when garnered through the "perversion" of laws and fraud) that gave undue advantage to capital and thus upset the balance of the whole. That imbalance was the real problem. Cleveland continued:

> The existing situation is injurious to the health of our entire body politic. It stifles in those for whose benefit it is permitted all patriotic love of country, and substitutes in its place selfish greed and grasping avarice. Devotion to American citizenship for its own sake and not for what it can accomplish as a motive to our nation's advancement and the happiness of all our people is displaced by the assumption that the Government, instead of being the embodiment of equality, is but an instrumentality through which especial and individual advantages are to be gained.[37]

Note the use of the "body politic," a functioning organic whole. Note also that for that organic whole to be healthy, for the spirit of patriotism to flourish, a balance was required—selfishness undermined the ideological belief that everyone could prosper. In undermining that belief, faith in the nation itself was undermined. The democratic creed of equality reinforced and conflicted with notions of civic republicanism, for citizens had to believe that their place in the system would be rewarded for the system itself to survive. Prosperity depended on balancing and moderating capitalistic greed.

The problem of monopoly came full circle: it endangered the individual, and through the individual the polity. Endangering the polity, it also endangered the individual. Not least among the threats of such selfish behavior were the consequences of imbalance—communism and other forms of disorder.[38] Some capitalists, in seeking the imbalance of unfair economic advantages, were ceasing to be cooperative citizens. They therefore had to be reformed and balance restored. This allowed Cleveland to protect the hierarchies that had brought him to power while also mitigating some of their worse excesses.

In defending class hierarchies, Cleveland also argued that the disciplinary project of nation building was not to be class based, but equally applied. For the workers, finding themselves thus "mastered," by "corporations, combinations, and monopolies," were also finding themselves unhappy about it. Cleveland went on to argue: "We find the wealth and luxury of our cities mingled with poverty and wretchedness and unrenumerative toil. A crowded and constantly increasing urban population suggests the impoverishment of rural sections and discontent with agricultural pursuits. The farmer's son, not satisfied with his father's simple and laborious life, joins the eager chase for easily acquired wealth."[39] In this, the "farmer's son," that exemplar of republican virtue, had been corrupted by the search for material gain. The corruption was not the product of the individual search for wealth, however. It was the result of imbalances in the cooperative nature of the national capitalistic enterprise. If balance could be restored to the system, and cooperation to the hearts of those involved in it, individual discontent could be ameliorated.

Cleveland's balance protected the existing hierarchies but allowed also for limited inclusion within those hierarchies. "Good" members of the groups who were gaining some political visibility would be accepted, if not welcomed into Cleveland's polity. "Bad" members of those groups would be subject to discipline, differentiated, and excluded. But even those able to win some degree of acceptance were admitted into the polity on conditional terms. They had to accept and obey the existing institutional structures, political arrangements, and their concomitant hierarchies. Maintaining the balance of interests that brought him to power meant that Cleveland also maintained stable hierarchies of power and privilege.

To put this in terms of Cleveland's example, then, it was also true that the farmer's son was highly unlikely to find wealth. He was, however, very likely to find himself as a wageworker in some factory, in some city. He was also likely to feel discontented and dissatisfied with his lot, and was consequently likely to organize in order to improve it. But to be a good citizen, such efforts to improve his situation had to be cooperative (as the national government understood cooperation) and had to recognize and respect the hierarchical order of the economy and of the polity. Cleveland's rhetoric provided ideological explication for the institutional structures and political arrangements that brought him to power. That rhetoric helped to define the parameters of citizenship and to justify exclusion even while coexisting with and contributing to the arguments members of excluded groups were making to advocate their inclusion.

According to Cleveland's understanding of relationships in the national polity, labor unions were in their own way as threatening to the polity as were the great monopolies and for the same reason. They failed to perceive the "true" interests of the class they claimed to represent and sought to aggrandize their members above their just deserts. They sought to upset the national balance. Like capitalists, workers could be differentiated and subject to presidential discipline. In a proclamation to the House and Senate, Cleveland said, "While the real interests of labor are not promoted by a resort to threats and violent manifestations, and while those who, under the pretext of an advocacy of the claims of labor, wantonly attack the rights of capital and for selfish purposes or love of disorder sow seeds of violence and discontent should neither be encouraged nor conciliated."[40] Workers were due their fair share, according to Cleveland, and many of the workers' demands were the result of "grasping and heedless exactions of employers and the alleged discrimination in favor of capital as an object of governmental attention."[41] But unions and the violence associated with them were also threatening, and those who participated in the unrest were damaging the polity.

Cleveland recognized that governmental authority to intervene in labor disputes was limited by law and custom, but recognizing also the dangers behind the labor unrest, he sought means—arbitration, the appointment of a labor commission—through which government could help resolve these matters and prevent the recurrence of such violence.[42] Cleveland, like Fillmore, Pierce, and Buchanan, had to maintain some sense of national stability among what appeared to be constant threats to national survival. Unlike those presidents, however, Cleveland's response to those threats was to offer some limited inclusion to "good" workers in the hopes of stemming the tide of radicalism that characterized those workers who clearly should not be included in the national polity. Like Jackson, he sought expansion and inclusion as a way of protecting certain hierarchies.

For Cleveland, then, both labor and capital threatened the health of the republic through excessive greed and improperly balanced demands. Balance and a recognition of mutual interests were considered essential to a smoothly functioning body politic. Excessive demands, by either labor or capitalists, would result in a lessening of patriotism, an abatement of commitment to the national contract that had so far resulted in increased opportunity and prosperity for all parties to it. The national body politic was held together by adherence to the national contract in the form of the Constitution. Respecting its hierarchies while promoting limited inclusion among those who would be subject to its discipline was one way of maintaining political equilibrium. That body politic, however smoothly functioning internally, however, was also subject to assaults on its health from without.

WIDELY DISPERSED THREATS

In addition to balancing the interests of those who were clearly members of the polity, Cleveland also had to defend the political arrangements and institutional structures of the polity from those who were defined as "outsiders" to that polity and who, in this era as in others, served as uniformly negative examples of citizenship.[43] The processes of becoming politically visible served Cleveland's task of preserving the national balance as well as created obstacles for that task. Some laborers, regardless of whether they were unionized, were despised. Often black, often Irish or of other "suspect" immigrant stock, laborers who lacked "habits of punctuality or industry"[44] were guilty of behavior that differed from the well-regulated and standardized ways required by an industrializing economy, and were thus rhetorically excluded from that economy and from the polity that supported it. In his inaugural, of all places, Cleveland stated that "the laws should be rigidly enforced which prohibit the immigration of a servile class to compete with American labor, with no intention of acquiring citizenship, and bringing with them and retaining habits and customs repugnant to our civilization."[45] This rare intrusion of policy into an inaugural address showed the enormous tensions between "American" workers and "immigrant" workers, as well as those between labor and capital. Indeed, union activity and the strikes that proceeded from it led to increased tension among workers, as employers used recent immigrants, who badly needed work and who were often from different nations and spoke different languages from those of unionized workers, as strikebreakers.[46]

The economy demanded the presence of such workers. Racialized notions of national identity repelled the possibility that they be included as citizens. Workers were themselves becoming more politically visible and thus were subject to greater degrees of differentiation, as those acceptable for inclusion were divided from those who were not. Rhetorically delimiting citizens in such instances involved a murky realm where those who constituted the included and the overtly excluded were clearly defined, but between them lay a netherworld of those who could, at any given moment, be part of either group, and whose status was thus always insecure, always unclear. Among these people, boundaries became all the more important, small gradients of inclusion all the more precious, and the need to maintain the hierarchies all the more significant.

This was especially true when politics met race and class. Immigrants were also more likely to be members of socialist, communist, or anarchist organizations and parties,[47] a fact that became increasingly important after the Haymarket bombing on May 4, 1886, which exacerbated the national fear of radicalism in general and of anarchism in particular.[48] The connection between "foreign ideas" such as anarchism, and "foreigners" further deepened the tension between older and more recent immigrant workers. Second- and third-generation immigrant workers hoped to better their economic positions—if not in their generation, then in their children's. Part of their antagonism toward more recent immigrants was undoubtedly due to a sense that the gains they had so far made remained tenuous and could be easily imperiled by identification with "radical" and "disruptive," much less violent, activities. They thus had to distance themselves from newer immigrants to preserve their own precarious status.

Thus, the national hierarchies were maintained from below as well as from above, as those who were groping their way toward political acceptance were subject to the national disciplinary project. They often internalized the strictures of the national culture and were adamant about policing the boundaries of national identity. These were the immigrants who chided their children for not being "American" enough and who aspired to a version of the American dream that meant a different, "more American" life for their descendants than the ones they had personally been able to enjoy. They saw the threats to their aspirations in those more foreign than they, not in the government who sought to standardize their behavior and beliefs. In this, they were doing the work of assimilation from outside the polity but from inside their various groups.

But it was the president who both reflected the national culture and set the terms of national inclusion. Cleveland made a distinction, as noted earlier, between American workers and a "servile class."

Through their very servility, the opposite of the manliness that was every American's birthright and patriotic duty, these immigrants demonstrated their incapacity for inclusion in the polity. Just as yeoman farmers were presumed to have the capacity for self-control, Jackson's adventurous frontiersmen were expected to exercise their passion for independence in the service of national growth, and citizens of the antebellum United States were admonished to demonstrate that capacity through temperate behavior in hopes of national preservation, during the Gilded Age, manliness and the manly virtues—the virtues of "good workers" were understood also as signifiers of good citizenship.

Thus, any terms that disqualified one as "manly" also indicated diminished capacity for inclusion in the polity. Such unworthy inhabitants were tacitly considered outsiders regardless of their legal status. As outsiders, they served usefully as scapegoats. In his first annual message, discussing the violence surrounding Chinese immigration, for instance, Cleveland noted that it was both motivated by "race prejudice" and perpetrated by the "lawlessness of men not citizens of the United States."[49] Cleveland implied here that "native" American workers were neither racist nor prone to violence, and the presence of these undesirable elements was the result of foreign contamination. Far from recognizing anything approaching class solidarity, in Cleveland's rhetoric "American" workers were not like "those foreigners." Rather than promulgating class distinctions, this rhetoric instead fragmented workers—the more fragmented and separate they were, the less likely they were as a class to upset the national balance through concerted action. Lack of class solidarity facilitated the disciplinary project of nation building, encouraging workers to assimilate individually rather than demand rights collectively.

It did this at least in part through encouraging members of excluded groups to commit to the nation by disciplining other, less "American" members of their own group. By pitting classes against one another in direct economic competition, the ideological work of nation building was accomplished more easily. Certain segments of a class would be excluded and the rest could be safely absorbed, for they were unlikely to challenge the hierarchies on which the system itself was based. By encouraging a specific, ideological conception of nationhood, those who aspired to it would also, by definition, be rejecting other possible definitions. What Gerstle calls the

"Rooseveltian nation" was being formed rhetorically, even at this early date, and while Roosevelt himself was only intermittently on the national stage.

As workers became politically visible, they also became increasingly politically problematic. In response, Cleveland encouraged the differentiation of workers and thus allowed some to be absorbed and others to be overtly excluded. This reflects the rhetorical nature of the nation's disciplinary project of citizenship. In keeping with the needs of this project and the president's rhetorical role within it, Cleveland also differentiated between those immigrants who came to the United States seeking citizenship, those "good" immigrants who readily adapted to their new culture and who quickly became "Americanized," and those more suspicious immigrants, who arrived looking for short-term economic gain and who sought to retain all or part of their old culture either as permanent residents or as temporary workers. He pressed for laws regulating such suspicious immigrants, based on the "admitted right of a government to prevent the influx of elements hostile to its internal peace and security."[50] The president was asking the nation to codify its exclusionary practices into law. In his first annual message, he endorsed the disciplinary project of citizenship, saying, "The privileges and franchise of American citizenship should be granted with care, and extended to those only who intend in good faith to assume its duties and responsibilities when attaining its privileges and benefits. It should be withheld from those who merely go through the forms of naturalization with the intent of escaping the duties of their original allegiance without taking upon themselves those of their new status, or who may acquire the rights of American citizenship for no other than a hostile purpose toward their original governments."[51]

As immigrants became more and more necessary to the nation's economy, as they arrived in increasing numbers, and as they began to organize, they also became more politically visible—and more politically problematic, asserting certain rights and privileges that they had heretofore gone without. For Cleveland, the problem became one of civic nationalism. As Woodrow Wilson would later assert with increased insistence, immigrants had to decide: they were either members of the American community or they were members of their resident cultures. They could not be both. As they became visible, they were pushed to the margins of visibility or offered the chance to become incorporated—visible as Americans to the extent that they were willing to surrender their ethnic identities.

Unincorporated citizens posed an additional problem: "The rights which spring from domicile in the United States, especially when coupled with a declaration of intention to become a citizen, are worthy of definition by statute. The stranger coming hither with intent to remain, establishing his residence in our midst, contributing to the general welfare, and by his voluntary act declaring his purpose to assume the responsibilities of citizenship, thereby gains an inchoate status which legislation may properly define."[52] The presence of immigrants occupying "inchoate status" was disturbing to a nation insisting on increased standardization. In such a polity, liminality was itself a threat to national ideology, for it meant additional difficulties in patrolling the borders of citizenship, additional trouble in determining who was, and who was not, a member of the national polity. Citizenship was once again put in the service of protecting the prevailing national balance of interests preferred and protected by the governing coalition.

The moral of these strictures on immigrants was that those untrustworthy immigrants-not-citizens endangered national reputation precipitated strikes, became unreasonably excited, and were prone to violence. Clearly, they must be excluded from the national polity, for their contagion was dangerous. The government was justified in its harsh measures against them. This exclusion, like other exclusions premised on balance, was very visible—it was argued for, and was an explicit aspect of national policy. Unlike the subtler forms of exclusion that take hold when balance is less of a question and presidents increasingly shift to issues of citizenship, this exclusion was mandatory, and the justifications for it unabashed. For the nation's disciplinary project to function, visible and harsh exclusionary measures were required for their targets to serve appropriately as negative models.

In his first annual message, Cleveland noted the use of such harsh measures, detailing the cavalry sent against unruly American Indians, troops sent to the aid of American Indians whose land was being encroached upon, and then he said, almost as an afterthought, that "troops were also sent to Rock Springs, in Wyoming Territory, after the massacre of Chinese there, to prevent further disturbance, and afterwards to Seattle, in Washington territory, to avert a threatened attack. . . . In both cases, the mere presence of the troops had the desired effect."[53] No American citizens were apparently fired upon by American troops, but note the casual way in which the president discussed deploying those troops to quell domestic strife in the name of social order and economic stability.

Violence and the threat of violence were also disturbing to the middle and upper classes because it reminded the wealthy that the poor existed—and that they existed in miserable conditions. Consequently, the poor themselves were delegitimized as Americans began to make systematic comparisons between the "respectable" or "deserving" poor and the "undeserving" or "rough" poor.[54] These distinctions, of course, dated back to the English poor laws, but systematic use in presidential rhetoric was not readily discernible until this period. As the nation industrialized and urbanized, the poor were becoming increasingly visible and increasingly politically problematic. They were also subject to increased differentiation—those who were acceptable as citizens were separated rhetorically from those who were less acceptable, and more likely to be excluded.

The ideologically driven assumption that individuals were responsible for their economic fates, and that those fates were thus indicators of talent and character, led many educated Americans, at least in the eyes of one European, to despise the poor as such.[55] Believing in the possibilities of upward mobility, Americans had little sympathy for those who suffered downward mobility or for those who never had a chance to rise. They did not believe that public funds should be used to support the indolent or to give the poor a head start on the upward path.[56] The political visibility of "the poor" went hand in hand with their rhetorical differentiation. Reformers were apt to help the deserving poor, to reinforce hierarchy through charitable activities. The less deserving poor they were apt to castigate and exclude from policy and thus from the polity.

Cleveland himself made distinctions between different classes of "the poor," who now entered American presidential rhetoric and American politics. Consistent with how other groups fared as they moved from invisibility to limited visibility and differentiation to partial incorporation, "the poor" became the subject of public policies as a distinct category of Americans, some of whom were more acceptable than others. Cleveland made the distinction clear in his first annual message:

The so-called debtor class, for whose benefit the continued compulsory coinage of silver is insisted upon, are not dishonest because they are in debt, and they should not be suspected of a desire to jeopardize the financial safety of the country in order that they may cancel their present debts. Nor should it be forgotten that it is not the rich nor the moneylender alone that must submit to such a readjustment, enforced by the Government and their debtors. The pittance of the widow and the orphan and the incomes of helpless beneficiaries of all kinds would be disastrously reduced. The depositors in savings banks and in other institutions which hold in trust the savings of the poor, when their little accumulations are scaled down to meet the new order of things, would in their distress painfully realize the delusion of the promise made to them that plentiful money would improve their condition.[57]

Recognizing distinctions present in America's British common law heritage, Cleveland relied here on the chasm between the "deserving" and the "undeserving" poor. There were now several kinds of poor workers, two of which were equally dependent, easily fooled by facile promises, therefore "unmanly" and unsuitable for real inclusion. There were first the honest, working, manly poor, who were neither dishonest nor easily fooled. The second class were the dishonest poor, and the third, the unfortunate poor, the "widow and the orphan and the . . . helpless." The first deserved respect, the second contempt, and the third charitable compassion. Such differentiation was characteristic of how groups were styled in presidential rhetoric as they approached political visibility. As more groups argued for political inclusion, and as issues of citizenship took on a more important and also more nuanced role in American politics, such differentiation would become all the more common.

The helpless poor should be remembered at moments of thanksgiving,[58] but they did not need governmental assistance because "the lesson should be constantly enforced that though the people support the Government, the Government should not support the people. . . . The friendliness and charity of our countrymen can always be relied upon to relieve their fellow-citizens in misfortune. . . . Federal aid in such cases encourages the expectation of paternal care on the part of the Government and weakens the sturdiness of our national character, while it prevents the indulgence among our own people of that kindly sentiment and conduct which strengthens the bonds of common brotherhood."[59] The helpless poor were politically visible but should not remain so. They were inappropriate subjects for governmental policy and should be removed from the public sight as a matter most suited to private attention. That erasure served national stability. The deserving poor represented a threat to the polity—through pity, citizens could be unmanned and tempted to give over to the government their responsibilities with devastating effects for the national character. Balance and citizenship were thus interwoven, and what served the one would characterize the other. In a polity where value was connected to money, the poor were likely to be seen as less worthy as subjects of public policy than the nonpoor.

Such a simple rule, however, could not completely address the visibility of the poor, for they were too politically visible to be completely erased. So there was yet another layer of differentiation that did the political work of muting the policy needs of the poor and keeping structural questions of how and why there was poverty off the national agenda. Unlike the honest or unfortunate poor, the dishonest poor were those who would try hardest to reap unmerited governmental largesse. During his first term Cleveland vetoed numerous individual pension bills, for instance, citing the claims of the honest pensioners versus those of people importuning the government for personal and unearned advantage: "I can not believe that the vast peaceful army of Union soldiers, who, having contentedly resumed their places in the ordinary avocations of life, cherish as sacred the memory of patriotic service, or who, having been disabled by the casualties of war, justly regard the present pension roll on which appear their names as a roll of honor, desire at this time and in the present exigency to be confounded with those who through such a bill as this are willing to be objects of simple charity and to gain a place upon the pension roll through alleged dependence."[60] Union soldiers, here typifying good citizens, were not, according to Cleveland, willing to leave the ranks of the honorably working to join the legions of the dishonest poor. Their manliness literally was not worth the price. Citizenship, virtue, and money were neatly connected as markers of one another. The ideology of citizenship and civic duty did the political work of maintaining power and privilege.

For Cleveland, individual pension bills exemplified the results of a system of individual networks and personal relationships.[61] They also exemplified for him the problems with those networks and relationships as a basis for governmental decisions. He preferred a single bill, clearly stating a universal standard for government pensions: "I am thoroughly convinced that the interests of the public would be better protected if fewer private bills were passed relieving officials, upon slight and sentimental grounds, from their pecuniary responsibilities."[62] Sentiment was all well and good, but it was not a fit foundation for government. Governmental responsibility for Cleveland was confined to the setting of standards and rules equally applied to all citizens, and specifically excluded consideration of individualized circumstances, no matter how sad. In vetoing yet another pension bill, he said, "But I can not forget that age and poverty do not themselves justify gifts of public money, and it seems to me that the according of pensions is a serious business which ought to be regulated by principle and reason, though these may well be tempered with much liberality."[63] If the poor were truly deserving of governmental assistance, they would not ask for it, thus obviating the need to assist anyone. "The poor" were characterized in global terms and then subdivided. Each subdivision had a political purpose and did some of the political work of keeping issues related to poverty in an industrialized nation off the national agenda in favor of issues related to work and working conditions.

Even fellow members of the deserving poor were cast against one another, and various categories of laborers, encouraged to behave cooperatively for the good of the whole, but also in competition for scarce resources, were often at odds. Union leaders railed against contract laborers, for instance. In uncertain economic times, such labor was an unbridled threat to the livelihoods of union laborers, and the hostility shown to contract laborers indicated widespread awareness and resentment of that fact.[64] Differentiation helped to keep coalitions of those likely to oppose the government from forming and also helped stigmatize the issues of economic equality, allowing the government to focus on issues of work and working conditions.

Not only were members of the working class pitted against one another in economic competition, but they were also competitors for inclusion in the polity.[65] The influx of immigrants from an increasingly broad array of nations further fragmented the laboring classes.[66] And thus labor as a whole was impeded in its ability to act cohesively. National loyalty trumped class loyalty, and allegiance to the national cooperative was used to prevent other cooperative allegiances.[67] As laborers became more politically visible, the government responded with some policies aimed at some of workers' concerns; the focus was always on the workers. Differentiating between workers and the poor, and then between kinds of workers and categories of poverty, increasingly atomized, divided, and paralyzed those who fell into any of these boxes. Some could become incorporated, but at the expense of others. Inclusion was a competitive business in the businesslike polity.

The process of moving from invisibility to inclusion played out in one way for the poor and laborers. African Americans during this period had another set of experiences, another position on the continuum. Finally visible, but as yet undifferentiated, their exclusion was justified by characterizations of them as inimical to the national order, characterizations that applied to the group as a whole. Technically, black Americans were now included in the polity as equal citizens, but that inclusion became increasingly tenuous in the last quarter of the nineteenth century. During the 1880s, for instance, the number of lynchings in the country increased dramatically.[68] This most violent of ways of enforcing a singular standard of behavior was supplemented by other means as well. Systematic disenfranchisement, growing segregation in all areas of life, and the denial of educational and economic opportunities all advanced a standardized understanding of African Americans as belonging to a lowly, if not the lowest, rung on the American ladder, with no real chance to rise. Competition with white labor—even immigrant white labor—was prevented by law, force, or the threat of violence.[69] In one of his very rare explicit comments on African Americans, and this in his inaugural, Cleveland said,

> In the administration of a government pledged to do equal and exact justice to all men there should be no pretext for anxiety touching the protection of freedmen in the rights or the security in the enjoyment of their privileges under the Constitution and its amendments. All discussion as to their

fitness for the public place accorded to them as American citizens is idle and unprofitable except as it suggests the necessity for their improvement. The fact that they are citizens entitles them to all the rights due to that relation and charges them with all its duties, obligations, and responsibilities.[70]

As one of the principles guiding his administration, Cleveland thus articulated an equal place for African Americans. He clearly and explicitly argued for their inclusion on the basis of a civic nationalist understanding of the meanings of "citizen" and "nation," and the relationship of the one to the other. In none of his policies, however, was he actually guided by those principles. He did nothing to protect or "to improve" blacks. Finally citizens, they were once again politically marginalized, if not politically invisible.

Cleveland used the rhetoric of civic nationalism set within a context of racial hierarchy. As so often in history, presidents enable the inclusive topoi rhetorically while maintaining inaction, a feat made possible by disenfranchised groups' relative political invisibility and lack of power. Cleveland could on the one hand agree that all had equal rights. Driven by unquestioned and unquestionable ideological presuppositions and his institutional need to protect the national balance (understood as protecting the interests of his governing coalition), he could also fail to act to ensure the protection of those rights. Indeed, given his political context, he could even fail to recognize any need for such action.

He did, however, have to address African-American audiences. Although lacking enough political power to demand change, they had attained enough visibility to merit some rhetorical accommodation. Given the political exigencies of the time, they were accommodated through the organic metaphors of the common good. African Americans in this formulation best served both themselves and the body politic by understanding their place and its inevitability, and by remaining in it without protest. In Booker T. Washington's often-quoted phrase, "In all things social we can be as separate as the fingers, yet as one hand in all things essential to mutual progress."[71] This rhetoric, consistent as it was with the political preferences of those in power, with the organic metaphors in which that power was often discussed, and with the notion that progress was both inevitable and, despite requisite hierarchies, natural, thus found wide resonance throughout the nation. Blacks could be both visible and invisible. They had a place in the polity, but it was a limited, subordinate place. This was considered neither oppressive nor undemocratic, for each place was equally important, each place served the greater good, just in different ways.

Hierarchy was thus portrayed as equality. Because money served as a signifier for individual worth and for one's value as a citizen, serving cooperatively in one's appropriate place became the means for equal treatment. Because no part of the body politic could be rightly understood as having primacy over any other, all places were equal. Hierarchy was thus both naturalized and displayed as equality. The balance of interests required by the governing coalition and the ideological justifications for citizenship thus met and melded and mutually reinforced one another.

All laborers, of whatever race, and in whatever economic sector, faced one fact in common: integration into the national economy was now essential for their economic survival. It was increasingly difficult to live a largely self-sufficient life. Independent farms, for instance, were increasingly becoming commercial farms.[72] Citizens in the pattern of yeoman farmers were relinquishing the self-discipline of the agricultural life to the discipline of the factory.[73] And a different sort of citizenship, based on both production and consumption, came to be valued.[74] The days of independent economic existence were over, and Americans were coming to recognize that fact.

Exchanging a self-reliant life for one of dependence on wages necessitated an ideological shift such that one's attitude toward work rather than the nature of that work became definitive. One analyst saw labor unions as instrumental in this process of ideological change.[75] The attitude of manliness, so important to the late nineteenth century, could be exhibited by a wageworker, so long as he retained the manly attitude toward that work. The manly worker was important ideologically as well, for "the manly worker was the industrial cousin of the republican yeoman, a vigilant spirit unafraid of standing up to boss or foreman."[76] He also probably had a short life as an employed worker. This idealized yeoman worker did not exist any more than the idealized yeoman farmer did, but like the yeoman farmer, the yeoman worker exercised a powerful legitimating ideological force.

The manly worker had the virtues of independence and forthrightness; he was a model of citizenship in an industrialized age. He was vigilant and unafraid and was thus a reasonable choice as heir to the republican traditions of Jefferson and Jackson. The nation could be balanced on his ideological fulcrum, for he was at once "the mass" and thus democratic, and independent, allowing other workers to feel represented by him. He was thus also an ideological force serving the interests of the powerful. As workers became politically visible, specific ideological representation of workers also became valorized and served as an indirect means of educating hopeful citizens into the disciplines of citizenship and a means of differentiating "good" from "bad" workers.

As immigrants became more numerous, more varied, and more visible, they collectively became more politically problematic. Industry needed their labor. As they became citizens, they became politically attractive to political coalitions who could make use of their numbers. But for that to happen without threatening national stability, they had to be rendered into particular sorts of citizens, citizens who would see their interests as coinciding with the interests of existing political coalitions. They had to be made into standardized citizens, taken from their many cultures and made into one sort of political person. The category of "immigrants" was becoming politically visible—and politically problematic. Political and rhetorical differentiation would not be far behind.

Immigrants hailed from many different nations. They also shared their cities and neighborhoods with large numbers of compatriots. They therefore had less reason to "Americanize" as fully or as rapidly as earlier immigrants and were thus viewed as a threat to the established order. They were often useful as scapegoats, their detractors arguing that their allegiance to the nation was uncertain, that they caused trouble for the nation through their jealous mistreatment of others such as the Chinese, and that they were excitable and prone to disruption, thus making them easy targets for the machinations of those who would undermine the nation. Cleveland, charged with maintaining the balance of interests that had brought him to power and responding to the issues posed by the increased visibility of immigrants, made all three of these arguments.

Rather than differentiate among members of the same immigrant group, this rhetoric tended to differentiate between groups, placing them in the national hierarchy based on their racial and ethnic characteristics, which were thought to be synonymous with "character." Racial and civic nationalism thus collided, and civic nationalism was subordinated to racialized notions of national identity.

The Chinese were fast becoming one of the most reviled immigrant groups. Henry George summarized the prejudices against them in 1869: "Their moral standard is as low as their standard for comfort, and though honest in the payment of debts to each other, lying, stealing and false swearing are with Chinamen the venial sins—if sins at all. . . . [They are] as cruel as they are cowardly . . . filthy in their habits . . . [having] a great capacity for secret organizations . . . [and] incapable of understanding our religion, but still less are they capable of understanding our political institutions."[77] The Chinese thus had some visibility but were understood primarily as a problem. They were one undifferentiated mass and served to highlight the differences among other groups rather than being considered potential candidates for political inclusion themselves. They were prevented from being considered potential citizens by their own natures. Like African Americans and Jackson's American Indians, according to the dominant understanding, the Chinese lacked the capacity to be yeoman workers. They were considered unable to learn how to function within the framework of American institutions or understand the morality that underpinned them, and were thus deemed unworthy as citizens. In terms of racial nationalism, they were excluded because of inherent "faults" attributable solely to their race. They were believed to lack the capacity for citizenship.

Still, the Chinese were politically visible, even within the terms of racially ascribed hierarchies. Regardless of their capacity—or lack thereof—as citizens, Cleveland did not sanction violence against "unoffending Chinamen,"[78] and he directed that "all the power of this Government should be extended to maintain the amplest good faith toward China in the treatment of these men, and the inflexible sternness of the law in bringing the wrongdoers to justice should be insisted upon."[79] His sympathy may have been with the Chinese and his wrath directed against the mob, but his interest was certainly centered on avoiding an open breach with the Chinese government. Consequently, his solution to the problem posed by the presence of Chinese workers was exclusionary. The Chinese were to be kept out of the country "for their own good." Congress would soon increase its restrictions on Chinese immigration. They were politically visible but not liable to be included in the polity. Their numbers were therefore to be limited, or they would threaten national stability. Citizenship and arguments concerning balance again went hand in hand.

The Chinese were not the only threat to America's moral life. Another moral threat to the nation came once again from the Mormons, who persisted in living a life that was an abomination to the polity's increasingly prominent and restrictively interpreted Christian principles. Christianity could function in an exclusionary as well as an inclusive way in the national ideology. When used against the Mormons, it was clearly exclusionary, for Mormons provided a clear contraexample of the importance of republican virtue. As Cleveland said in his first annual message, "The strength, the perpetuity, and the destiny of the nation rest upon our homes, established by the law of God, guarded by parental care, regulated by parental authority, and sanctified by parental love. These are not the homes of polygamy."[80] No longer a military threat to the American frontier, Mormons were now an internal threat to the sanctity of American homes. They remained to some degree visible, and, in remaining so pointedly outside the polity in religious matters, they constituted an ideological problem, but a problem that could be used against others who were demanding acceptance into the national polity.

Thus, Cleveland's strictures on Mormons had particular application to women, for disciplining the one was to provide protection for the other. He continued: "The mothers of our land, who rule the nation as they mold the characters and guide the actions of their sons, live according to God's holy ordinances, and each, secure and happy in the exclusive love of the father of her children, sheds the true light of true womanhood, unperverted and unpolluted, upon all within her pure and wholesome family circle."[81] Cleveland thus used the Mormons, examples of poor citizenship, to define "true womanhood" and to discipline women who aspired to complete citizenship in the form of the vote. The polygamy practiced by Mormons threatened the wholesomeness of all republican women, as disease threatened the whole body. The agitation of some women threatened the sanctity of all women's homes. Women had to be protected from such infections. Women, it appeared, also had a clearly defined place in the nation's hierarchy. It was an ideologically revered and carefully controlled subordinate place. That control became more important as women's political status began to change. In this transitional period, women served as important markers for ideologically based attempts to balance and control the nation's citizenship.[82] They were becoming increasingly visible and thus increasingly subject to differentiation and other forms of discipline so that the national balance of interests could be maintained.

For Cleveland, motherhood and conjugal responsibility were the keys to feminine virtue. He could be harsh in decrying their lack. In vetoing still another pension bill, Cleveland gave the following reasons: "Two witnesses indicate that domestic trouble was the cause of the soldier's suicide. Another says that his wife (the beneficiary) was a pretty rough woman—a hard talker—and that the soldier often consulted him about the matter, and said it was hard to live with her. This witness adds that he does not believe that the soldier would have committed suicide if she had not abused him till he could no longer endure it."[83] Unlike the deserving widow, the carping woman had no right to either our compassion or public support. Only through noble suffering and silence—both public and private—were women to be allowed to serve. Their national role was to be kept both limited and subsidiary to that of men (no one appears to have asked the woman, for instance, about the sources of any "domestic trouble"). As in the cases of the other groups who were gaining political visibility during these years, that visibility lent some gains, some policies even, but also meant that the members of these groups would be increasingly differentiated, divided, and disciplined as part of the price of movement toward inclusion.

But that inclusion seemed possible, at least for women. The roles now assigned to women were having to be articulated by presidents rather than being merely assumed. As more women became workers, it became harder to justify their exclusion as citizens, and so a role as subordinate citizens had to be devised and articulated.[84] Women were moving from the category of "the excluded" to one that was more marginal, a change signaled in Cleveland's rhetoric. As in the example of Andrew Jackson and his strictures on American Indians and the earlier examples of African Americans and immigrants under Cleveland, women too had certain character faults ascribed to them that were considered appropriate grounds for exclusion. This exclusion was not the fault of the government but of those who were excluded; in all cases, the agency belonged with the excluded, to whom generalized characteristics could be ascribed and then used as justification for their disenfranchisement. Women were more politically visible but were still not equals and, en masse, were thought to be too moral, too weak, too susceptible, to become full citizens.

The processes leading a group from invisibility to differentiation toward inclusion worked differently for American Indians. Like women, they were still considered susceptible to the machinations of others. Cleveland explicitly paired them with the polygamous Mormons, claiming that they needed to be properly educated for citizenship.[85] Like Mormons, American Indians were on the margins of American life. Yet because of their centrality to the politics of the period (often characterized by the phrase "Indian Wars" and the difficulties of continuing assimilatory and military campaigns concerning them, American Indians were pivotal—and woefully underexamined—in terms of understanding issues of inclusion and exclusion during the Gilded Age. They thus merit considerable attention here.

For Cleveland the "Indian problem" was complicated by the diversity among tribes, but the distinction between "good Indians" and "bad Indians" was nonetheless clear. Non-Indians tended to conflate and confuse the different nations, and, ideologically, the government generally treated them in collective rather than singular form.[86] As in the rhetoric of earlier presidents, "good Indians" were those who assimilated—although for Cleveland, this had a particular meaning, because assimilation was understood less in terms of culture or "civilization" and more in terms of economics. For Cleveland, to be "civilized" meant that American Indians had learned and were practicing a trade. Even more important, it meant that they had given up "tribal ways" and had accepted private property. For Cleveland, then, fostering citizenship meant destroying tribal identities. It meant rendering American Indians invisible, absorbing them into the larger body politic. A "good" American Indian was invisible, indistinguishable from other Americans, one more ethnicity subsumed into the melting pot. He outlined the pertinent history as follows:

> When the existing system was adopted, the Indian race was outside of the limits of organized States and territories and beyond the immediate reach and operation of civilization and all efforts were mainly directed to the maintenance of

friendly relations and the preservation of peace and quiet on the frontier. All this is now changed. There is no such thing as the Indian frontier. Civilization, with the busy hum of industry and the influences of Christianity, surrounds these people at every point. . . . As a race, the Indians are no longer hostile, but may be considered as submissive to the control of the Government. Few of them only are troublesome . . . their life of entire dependence upon Government rations from day to day is no longer defensible. Their inclination, long fostered by a defective system of control, is to cling to the habits and customs of their ancestors and struggle with persistence against the change of life which their altered circumstances press upon them. But barbarism and civilization can not live together.[87]

Recall the history of that vanished frontier as it was articulated by Jefferson and Jackson, how the empty continent awaited "Americans." Cleveland clearly adopted that version of history and articulated it as leading inexorably to the industrialized nation he governed. History was viewed from a further vantage point, but it was the same history, and its articulation served the same ideological ends.

This patently inaccurate but widely accepted version of history demonstrated that, one way or another, tribalism was inimical to the American Indians' best interests and could not withstand the pressure of "civilization." This history also demonstrated why American Indians were doomed to an inferior place even within civilization, for in it they were characterized as the acted upon, never the actors, passive, dependent, controlled, and barbaric. They were thus in all ways not "manly," they could not be yeoman workers. They had to be "trained and civilized," and most of all, they had to be taught to hold private property, for private property, as Cleveland said in his fourth annual message, "proffers opportunity and inducement to that independence of spirit and life which the Indian peculiarly needs, while at the same time the inalienability of title affords security against the risks his inexperience of affairs or weakness of character may expose him to in dealing with others."[88] American Indians were, in this analysis, not like yeoman farmers. They were not really independent, for they could not alienate their land. They remained childlike and in need of protection. By characterizing American

Indians as children, Cleveland furthered the process of rendering them politically invisible. Once feared "savages," then wandering problems, they had become children, wards of the state, with little or no hope of reaching maturity.

This view of American Indians rested on a specific definition of American citizenship: if American Indians were to *be* "Americans," the logic ran, they would have to learn to *act* like Americans. American Indians were to be brought into the American polity through a forced understanding of private property.[89] Just as Jefferson hoped to make them farmers (ignoring the fact that many of them already were) and thus make them Americans, under the programs favored by Cleveland, American Indians were to be made capitalists, and that would, in turn, make them Americans. Their ability to accommodate themselves to the economic system became the marker of their ability to participate in the political system.[90] Citizenship was often offered to tribes in exchange for their land, and they became important examples of the assimilatory disciplinary project of nation building. If the American Indians would vanish, become politically invisible, then they could reemerge, having lost their identity as American Indians but having gained an identity as "American." The price of inclusion would be distinct identity.

The boarding school was another route to "Americanization." This assimilatory process was thought to be inhibited if American Indian children were simultaneously exposed to both their resident cultures and the "American" culture of the schools. Consequently, American Indian children were taken from their families, by force if necessary, and placed in custodial, militarized schools, where they were forced to give up their tribal languages, religions, and cultures in the service of assimilation.[91] The focus of this reeducation process was, in the often-quoted phrase, "to destroy the Indian and save the man." American Indian children learned to speak English, become Christians, hold their own cultures in contempt, and work in specific—and menial—trades.[92] They were to become "Americanized," but to a lowly position from which they were neither expected nor encouraged to rise. They could lose their tribal identities and gain American ones but would never be truly "American." In gaining this limited American identity, they could aspire to some form of limited inclusion, but it would be restricted as it was for other groups discussed here. One important measure of their ability to become part of the polity was their willing acceptance of their lowly place in it.

By far the most egregious examples of "bad Indians" during Cleveland's day were the Apache, especially the Chiracahua, and most especially those who followed Geronimo.[93] As American Indians became subject to differentiation, the Apache in general and Geronimo in particular served as a metonym, sometimes for all American Indian peoples, and sometimes merely for "bad" American Indians. Cleveland thus reserved his harshest and most exclusionary rhetoric for the Apache:

> I am not at all in sympathy with those benevolent but injudicious people who are constantly insisting that these Indians should be returned to their reservation. Their removal was an absolute necessity if the lives and property of citizens upon the frontier are to be regarded by the Government. Their continued restraint at a distance from the scene of their repeated and cruel murders and outrages is still necessary. It is mistaken philanthropy, every way injurious, which prompts the desire to see these savages returned to their old haunts. . . . Experience has proved that they are dangerous and can not be trusted. This is true not only of those who on the warpath have heretofore actually been guilty of atrocious murder, but of their kindred and friends, who, while they remained upon their reservation, furnished aid and comfort to those absent with bloody intent. These prisoners should be treated kindly and kept in restraint far from the locality of their former reservation; they should be subjected to efforts calculated to lead to their improvement and the softening of their savage and cruel instincts, but their return to their old home should be persistently resisted.[94]

As in the rhetoric of previous presidents, when the government sought American Indian land, those American Indians who were on that land became demonized, differentiated, and subject to the harshest disciplines. For Cleveland, all Apache and by extension all western American Indians were thus by definition savage. Anyone who thought differently threatened the nation. Those Apache who remained peacefully in the squalid conditions of their reservation were considered as culpable as those who fought for their freedom and rebelled against the United States government. Their crime was identical to their identity, and they were punished accordingly.[95]

Although the only solution to the problems posed by "bad Indians" was incarceration of all American Indians—either in boarding schools or as prisoners of war—for the rest of Americans, there were less drastic options.[96] In general, the solution to the problems posed by diversity among citizens was standardization. All groups were subject to similar disciplines. As they moved toward limited inclusion, they were differentiated, divided, fragmented into "good" and "bad" metonyms, and thus taught the models of behavior that would lead to inclusion. They were also taught the hierarchies to which they would be subject. Immigrants had to be "Americanized" or excluded; African Americans had to be kept "in their place"; women were confined to the home. Republican virtue had to be instilled in all the "lower orders," and the notion of service had to be reinculcated into the ruling class. The model for all these behaviors was the civil service.

THE CIVIL SERVICE SOLUTION

All the characteristics of Cleveland's industrial government were epitomized in the civil service, established earlier than his presidency but extended and articulated under his administration. The merit system exalted individual achievement within the rubric of standardized workers. The stress on nonpartisanship allowed workers to be "manly" in that their employment was safe from electoral whims. The requirements of the civil service exam and its ostensibly "objective" nature favored "Americanized" workers. The civil service was an important instantiation of the hierarchies and rules under which groups could hope for limited inclusion.

Ideologically, the civil service was in keeping with the theory of government as a contract between government and individual citizens. It meant that competence rather than partisan, sectional, or personal loyalties was the determining factor in employment and that rational and disinterested administration would be the order of the day. Thus, the civil service system did a lot of the political work of stable and balanced government, showing implicitly that government served as a neutral umpire and that its decisions were rational and unprejudiced, as government simply enforced the rules that were fair to all. Loyalty to government came before all else. The civil service system allowed government to devote itself to national prosperity rather than servicing particularized interests.

Finally, governing under ostensibly neutral rules meant that certain classes, interests, and ideologies would be privileged, old hierarchies reinvigorated and protected with no advertisement or accompanying justification, because government "service" was by definition neutral, serving every citizen as equally as every citizen served the state. Standardization made potential citizens invisible as members of discrete groups, as each gave up specificity to become "American." As Cleveland announced in his inaugural, "Every citizen owes to the country a vigilant watch and close scrutiny of its public servants and a fair and reasonable estimate of their fidelity and usefulness. Thus is the people's will impressed upon the whole framework of our civil polity—municipal, State, and Federal; and this is the price of our liberty and the inspiration of our faith in the Republic."[97] Government served "the people," and that service was defined as a neutral referee among disputing interests, arbiter of objective rules. Conserving the nation, from the president's perspective, meant ensuring stability, which generally also meant preserving the existing power relations among social and economic groups. However benignly intended, it meant preserving the status quo, protecting the interests that brought Cleveland to power. Balance and citizenship served one another and were inextricably intertwined.

An important part of government's function involved maintaining balance. First, all branches of government had to remain in their specified spheres: "Contemplation of the grave and responsible functions assigned to the respective branches of the Government under the Constitution will disclose the partitions of power between our respective departments and their necessary independence," Cleveland said in his first annual message, "and also the need for the exercise of all the power entrusted to each in that spirit of comity and cooperation which is essential to the proper fulfillment of the patriotic obligations which rest upon the faithful servants of the people."[98] Government, like the polity, was an organic whole in which each constituent part had a specific—and a restricted—role to play. Wise government policy protected the rights of capital as well as labor, protected all the people according to their station, and enforced the order so necessary to national prosperity. Limited government, although understood differently here than in the 1850s, was still considered the best protector of the people.

Government officials provided an example of appropriate citizenship. This was true for the president, as he insisted in his inaugural: "In the presence of this vast assemblage of my countrymen, I am about to supplement and seal by the oath which I shall take the manifestation of the will of a great and free people. In the exercise of their power and right of self-government, they have committed to one of their fellow citizens a supreme and sacred trust, and he here consecrates himself to their service."[99] By consecrating himself to the national service, Cleveland was both meeting the requirements of the genre and enacting the respect for place and spirit of cooperative service to the whole that he would later ask of all citizens. In humbly assessing himself as merely one among many "fellow citizens," he was also enacting ideals of standardization. Any other citizen, he implied, would do as well. This rhetoric served the nation-building processes observed by Smith and Gerstle: the government was a neutral umpire, and its officials must be dedicated to serving the common good, not the individual good. The president was an important model of that. This rhetoric worked ideologically to frame the government as the servant of the people, transcending the claims of the coalition that brought its members to power. The invisibility of such interests helped reinforce governmental power while ostensibly arguing for its limitation.

He served those processes in other ways as well. Cleveland treated other government workers similarly as models of citizenship, saying in his fourth annual message: "As public servants we shall do our duty well if we constantly guard the rectitude of our intentions, maintain unsullied love of country, and with unselfish purpose strive for the public good."[100] Disinterested cooperative service was the model, and Cleveland was quick to chastise those whom he found violating that model, reminding those who worked in the departments and agencies that he was serious on this subject: "I deem this a proper time to warn all subordinates in the several Departments and office holders under the General Government against the use of their official positions in attempts to control political movements in their localities. Officeholders are the agents of the people, not their masters. Not only is their time and labor due to the

Government, but they should scrupulously avoid in their political action, as well as in the discharge of their official duty, offending by a display of obtrusive partisanship their neighbors who have relations with them as public officials."[101] The political work here was unambiguous. The government was a neutral umpire, and pubic service a disinterested act. Partisanship, as much as sectionalism, indicated personal loyalty, personal preference, personality. It violated the stricture on standardized merit, and it had the potential to disrupt the balanced workings of the national machine.

Continued civil service reform, and all that it meant instrumentally and ideologically, was not easily established. But for Cleveland, upon its success hinged the continued success of the nation.[102] Continued reform was necessary if the United States was to have the government and the citizenry it deserved, for its effects, as we have seen, had as much to do with the composition and nature of the citizenry as with the administration of the government.

Conclusion

Like all other periods in history, the Gilded Age contained contradictions. Its denizens exalted individualism while wholeheartedly stifling individuals who became in many ways standardized parts of the body politic. Machine metaphors mixed with an organic conception of government that was increasingly parsed in the language of business. These metaphors gave an aura of naturalness and inevitability to political policies that were neither and thus reinvigorated hierarchies that had been weakened by the war and its aftermath. The balance that characterized the nation was portrayed as natural, inevitable, and the hierarchies it supported were portrayed in the same way. Citizenship became connected to the recognition and acceptance of one's place in the national hierarchy.

There were racial implications to the economic arguments. Increasingly, "Americans" were those who were "white."[103] "Whiteness" in turn became associated with certain cultural preferences and economic practices. Race, economics, and culture became increasingly identified with one another and increasingly signified identical elements of an individual's place in society and in the polity. The established hierarchies became difficult to challenge, for their aura of inevitability was buttressed by real economic consequences for the rebellious. As various groups worked their way toward limited acceptance into the polity, the models held out for emulation depended on maintaining existing hierarchies, structures of power, and institutional arrangements. For all these groups, increased political visibility made them subject to differentiation and discipline.

The country was awash in the ideology of standardization, and those who did not fit the mold found themselves excluded from full participation in the polity. "Good" workers were those who contributed to the national economy, who knew their place within that economy, and who fulfilled the demands of that place. As the language of business was applied to the government, "good" citizens began to closely resemble "good" workers—they knew and accepted their place in the body politic. In the Gilded Age, we can see the seeds of contemporary conceptions of government and its relationship to the polity.

Yet the criteria that Cleveland established for inclusion—industriousness, cooperation, civic responsibility, fidelity to family and nation—were both instrumental in developing the national economy and emblematic of values associated with civic nationalism rather than racially ascribed hierarchies. Balance, the theme of earlier presidents, and citizenship, which would come to characterize the rhetoric of later presidents on issues of diversity, were closely intertwined during these years. All people, regardless of race, religion, or gender, could argue that they deserved inclusion because of their beliefs and behavior. Although it would have had little effect on Cleveland or on the politics of his day, this rhetoric may have influenced the burgeoning arguments for inclusion of women, American Indians, and others.

The issues of the usefulness of difference and the value of homogeneity were not resolved during the Gilded Age. They would arise again and would prove even more problematic for the polity, because the next time they appeared, it would be in the context of a world war.

4 / Establishing a Transcendent International Order under Woodrow Wilson, 1913–1921

Every man and woman who thinks first of
America should rally to the standards of our life.
—Woodrow Wilson, "An Address to the
Daughters of the American Revolution"

THE AMERICAN polity was no more unified at the end of the Progressive era than it had been in that movement's infancy during the Gilded Age. Evidence of that lack of unity was everywhere: in the burgeoning number of strikes, the episodic race riots, and the placards and protests demanding women's rights. Less organized disruptions were also prevalent; the number of lynchings, for instance, rose throughout the period, as did other forms of vigilantism. These disruptions spawned an awareness of—and concern over—the consequences of the vast social and political differences among Americans. As members of previously disenfranchised and marginal groups such as workers, women, African Americans, and immigrants attained more political visibility and began to press their claims for inclusion, government had to respond. These tensions put more pressure on elites, for they had to form coalitions capable of governing and responding to these demands while preserving stability and balance. As the twentieth century unfolded, the president's interest on matters of diversity would come to be understood as one that involved patrolling the borders of citizenship, rhetorically delimiting who was a "real" American. As the civic nationalist creed came to dominate public discourse, overt exclusion became less politically feasible, and more subtle forms of exclusion came into play.[1]

Wilson responded with a strident insistence on the fundamental unity of all Americans. For Wilson this unity was ideologically driven—the United States was united as a nation by a shared commitment to the principles that the nation stood for and embodied. Equally important, Wilson himself became the sole arbiter and definer of those principles, appropriating for himself ideological as well as institutional power.[2] Relying on the twin tactics of setting forth immutable principles and then universalizing their application, Wilson described a new nation whose parameters were ideologically determined and whose transcendent nature would not just dominate the territorial boundaries of the United States, but have the potential to encompass the entire world.

Wilson's example illustrated how a rhetorically constructed polity based on universal principles could nonetheless also be an exclusionary one. Wilson's use of universal principles, in however limited a fashion, also legitimated them and extended them throughout the polity. He thus facilitated both contemporaneous and later arguments for inclusion based on those principles. Groups that were invisible or admitted into citizenship on a contingent basis during Wilson's years could later make arguments for further inclusion based on Wilsonian rhetoric. That rhetoric raised the hopes of many such groups—women, African Americans, organized labor, many immigrants, and American Indians, for instance—and also dashed those hopes, for the full inclusion that civic nationalism promised was long in coming. This era thus highlights the tensions implicit in the effort to enfranchise and expand the polity without changing too radically its identity (which for many was based on notions of racial nationalism) or upsetting the balance of interests that gave the powerful their positions.

Universal Principles

Through rhetoric that depended on universalizing specific and limited definitions of certain principles and denying the validity of others, Wilson both spoke in the language of civic nationalism and defined what in Burkean terms is a transcendent order[3] that could be applied—

indeed had to be applied—to all peoples, everywhere, all the time. In so doing, he set the stage for the "American Century," as "American" came to have limited and specific meaning both at home and abroad. This order was best understood as "transcendent," because in both its ends and the rhetorical means Wilson used to gain those ends, particulars were subsumed in universals, differences were encompassed within similarities, and exclusions were surrounded and thus masked by apparent inclusions.

In this period, civic notions of nationalism (based on shared principles) and racialized notions of nationalism (the idea that those principles were the heritage of one particular race of people, in this case the Anglo-Saxons) often reinforced one another. As groups, especially immigrant groups, became more assimilated, they were also more likely to be understood as "white," as sharing the national heritage. Other groups, usually American Indians and African Americans, were presumed because of their race to be incapable of sharing and enacting those ideals. Through the ideology of race and nation, inclusive principles could be publicly and unequivocally embraced while certain exclusions were naturalized and maintained. Through an emphasis on citizenship, balance could be maintained.

Governing Principles

Wilson relied on three main principles in delineating his transcendent order. The first was his stress on the importance of political party as a vehicle of policy and as a mechanism of social control. His second tactic was a dependence on the limits of his power as the primary determinant of the limits of inclusion, a reliance that removed agency and made no one individual responsible or accountable for those limits. These two tactics culminated in a third, Wilson's denial of the sort of organic unity that Cleveland had depended on in favor of arguments advocating sameness, what Burke would call consubstantiality.[4]

Where Cleveland and his predecessors had relied on differentiation and division as groups approached inclusion, for Wilson, it became much more important for groups to lose their sense of ethnic identity, to gain inclusion at the price of difference. Partly, this was a response to the sheer number of groups who were seeking citizenship and inclusion into the polity during these years. Better organized, more politically visible, and more vociferous, women, laborers, and immigrants were making more demands on the federal government. They were armed with inclusive rhetoric as well, for the political argot of the day relied on universal principles. The rhetoric of sameness was in part a response to the differences among those groups—they were united in demanding inclusion but in very little else, and the disciplinary project of making "persons" into "citizens" with a shared national identity faced formidable obstacles. Regardless of the motive behind the use of this rhetoric, it masked difference and rendered both the processes of exclusion and those who were excluded invisible.

PARTY AS AN INSTRUMENT OF LEADERSHIP

Unlike many Progressives, Wilson was not only an adherent of party government, but, like Jefferson and Jackson, also a remarkably effective party leader.[5] He believed, with fellow Progressive Herbert Croly, that "the men whose standards are higher must learn to express their better message in a popularly interesting manner."[6] Wilson saw political parties as the instrument for enacting those higher standards into public policy, and persuasion through rhetoric as the means of leadership.[7] He was a believer in the old adage, "the way to lead is to lead.'"[8] In his first inaugural, for example, Wilson said, "The success of a party means little except when the nation is using that party for a large and definite purpose."[9] Note the shift from Jacksonian understandings of party that he made here—the party became the tool of the nation and was legitimate only to the extent that it was used as such by the nation. Jackson was concerned with the problems of governing a nation that was expanding geographically; indeed, the success of his governing coalition was premised on that geographical expansion. The presidents who governed during the 1850s had to manage the consequences of that expansion, and with the national balance precarious, opted for a more restricted understanding of citizenship. Cleveland, in turn, presided over a nation whose growth was largely economic—he had to incorporate and manage a greater diversity of economic interests as well as a growing divide between rural and urban America.

By Wilson's day, industrialization was largely accomplished, although not as widespread as it would be by the end of World War I. The United States had also become a global colonial power, with territories in the Pacific and interests as far away as Asia. So Wilson faced an amalgam of the problems that earlier presidents faced in that he had to combine an imposing array of economic interests and cope with territorial expansion while managing an enormous influx of immigrants. He needed a political organization that could help him in these tasks and that could articulate them in a manner consistent with the nation's ideals and principles such that the project of nation building could be consistent with the growing understanding of civic nationalist principles. For Wilson, that organization was the political party. But for the party to do this work effectively, it had to be understood as dedicated to national, not purely partisan interests.

That national purpose was, for Wilson, clearly one of purification:

> But the evil has come with the good, and much fine gold has been corroded. With riches has come inexcusable waste. . . . We have been proud of our industrial achievements, but we have not hitherto stopped thoughtfully enough to count the human cost, the cost of lives snuffed out, of energies overtaxed and broken, the fearful physical and spiritual cost to the men and women and children upon whom the dead weight and burden of it all has fallen piteously the years through. The groans and agony of it all had not yet reached our ears, the solemn, moving undertone of our life, coming up out of the mines and factories and out of every home where the struggle had its intimate and familiar seat. With the great government went many secret things which we too long delayed to look into and scrutinize with candid, fearless eyes. The great government we loved has too often been made use of for private and selfish purposes, and those who used it had forgotten the people.[10]

The theme of his inaugural was thus best understood as restoration.[11] Wilson framed his union on a vision of the values of the past. As Rogers M. Smith notes, by 1912 the state was committed to helping overcome poverty and powerlessness, and to the proposition that if immigrants assimilated into the "melting pot," they could share in the nation's bounty.[12] Under Wilson, the emphasis shifted away from the urbanized, pro-business stance of his Republican predecessors and toward an equally urban, but more labor-oriented vision appropriate to a Democrat and Progressive. Where Cleveland had sought an urban yeoman worker and attempted to control both capitalists and labor unions, Wilson believed that the capitalists, whose unbridled greed had gotten out of control, were the greater threat to the nation's balance.

Partially, of course, this difference reflected the two presidents' governing coalitions and the historical epochs during which they governed. But it was also a product of differing political philosophies as they played out within those political contexts. Where Cleveland had presided over a nation undergoing the tumultuous transition to an industrialized economy, by Wilson's day that economy—and the social and political structures required for its support—were largely in place. Wilson therefore faced a different set of tasks, different sets of interests that needed to be balanced. International political upheavals seemed to be the order of the day, and maintaining order at home seemed paramount. That could best be done by reconciling the contradictions caused by the presence of hugely profitable economic interests in a polity that prided itself on social and political democracy.[13] These contradictions became clearer as the United States began to globalize its sense of manifest destiny, extending the frontier into the Pacific.[14] For Wilson, these contradictions could best be reconciled through a vision of the national interest that was grounded in the civic nationalist ideals of the past and that could encompass the entire nation in the present. Through the rhetoric of purification, Wilson could reinterpret the founders and provide an ideology of national identity that would protect the interests represented by his governing coalition.

Thus Wilson argued that the great dream of the founders had been corrupted by those more interested in money than in democratic principles. The time to address that corruption and create a deliberative republic had come. "Our duty," Wilson said, "is to cleanse, to reconsider, to restore, to correct the evil without impairing the good, to purify and harmonize every process of our common life without weakening or sentimentalizing it. There has been something crude and heartless and unfeeling in our haste to succeed and be great."[15] But government could not be cleansed without an instrument to do the work. For Wilson, that instrument was the political party.

He argued for nonpartisan party action in his first inaugural, saying that "it is inconceivable that we should do this as partisans,"[16]
and, in a later speech more informally: "Scratch a Democrat or a
Republican, and underneath it is all the same stuff."[17] It was certainly inconceivable that Wilson, who owed his ascension to the White
House primarily to the split in the Republican party, could accomplish much as an unabashed partisan. It is also clear that such rhetoric both suited the nature of inaugurals and allowed Wilson to seize
the moral high ground. Yet he also meant it. Wilson was an ardent
nationalist and a believer in a national mission and a national identity.[18] He believed that both the mission and the identity were nonpartisan, as they were nonsectional, and not based on class. Wilson's
nationalism was grounded in the faith in certain principles, articulated through his religion and his sense of national history. His vision
was also therefore quite personal, and the Democratic party became
both a personal and a national organization, charged with articulating
national principles and protecting national policies. He said, "I am
not interested in a party that is not an embodied program based upon
a set of principles; and our present job is to get the people who believe
in principles to stand shoulder to shoulder and to do things from one
side of this continent to the other."[19] For Wilson there was no contradiction here. His party was based on national principles. Those
principles spoke to the best of the American spirit, and therefore allegiance to his party was nonpartisan and national.[20]

This was important, for it is in this way that party served both
Wilson's need to establish broad principles, and also indirectly and
perhaps unintentionally as a mechanism of social control and for fur-
thering the disciplinary project of making "persons" into "citizens."
His rhetoric served that purpose. Wilson here engaged in the common tactic of presenting a dichotomous choice that clearly favored
his chosen alternative. The principles that Wilson established for his
party were also those that he established for his nation. Anyone who
did not follow those principles was therefore as undemocratic as they
were un-Democratic. They were liable for censure on both counts;
pointing out differences led to factionalization, which was inimical
to the national unity required to purify and cleanse the national government and the polity as a whole.

Consistent with the earlier, Jacksonian model of partisanship,
Wilson had nothing but contempt for those who saw political parties

and a partisan press as means to political power rather than as vehicles of political principle. Speaking to a New Jersey audience on the subject of jury reform, for instance, he said, "And so at last a time has come when men in America look with contempt upon the little game of politics, look with absolute condescension upon the men who go about to establish their own fortunes, to press the interests of their own little circle, to see to it that the things that they are interested in have their pick in the things that are done and in the things that are preferred."[21] By demeaning "politics," Wilson meant to demean a narrow, self-interested view of what politics was—he meant to demean political machines and their urban, often ethnic approach to government. By encouraging a more national, disinterested approach, Wilson could both serve the political interests of his coalition and encourage the specific sort of national growth that would continue to serve those interests.

Because he believed the unfettered greed of capitalism under the Republicans had led to imbalance, balance—both rhetorical and political—needed to be restored. Presaging what would be clear themes in FDR's New Deal rhetoric, Wilson argued that there was no middle ground because principle was involved. One was either for principle, and therefore with Wilson, or against them both. Wilson became the arbiter and voice of principled politics. He said: "I try to put myself in the place of the man who does not know all the things that I know, and ask myself what he would like the policy of the country to be. Not the talkative man, not the partisan man, not the man that remembers first that he is a Republican or a Democrat, or that his parents were German or English, but the man who remembers first that the whole destiny of modern affairs centers largely upon his being American first of all."[22] The prototypical American "man" was also a Wilsonian. Indeed, he was Wilson himself.

Wilson's use of nouns was telling. Like others who shared his political bent, Wilson approved of "the people" in theory (saying, for instance, that "I believe in the ordinary man"[23]) and worried about "the mass" in practice. The fact of corrupt political machines, the violence of labor strikes, and "their disturbing taste for vices" made Progressives and their allies suspicious of the general public.[24] The numbers of those pressing for inclusion was growing, their arguments increasingly based on forms of civic nationalism. For Wilson, who was an ardent advocate of democracy, this posed a problem because citizenship was a privilege, and to merit it, one had to espouse the ideals of the nation. Only certain sorts of people were well suited to do so. He was able to maintain what he considered to be proper boundaries of citizenship—and thus also able to maintain the national balance—by advocating a certain sort of citizenship. For Wilson, proper citizens operated as individual Americans, not as members of classes or groups.

For Wilson as for many of his generation and time, the task of the elite was to lead, that of the mass was to follow. In this, he shared certain ideas of organic union with Grover Cleveland, for both believed that the polity would work best if everyone understood their place and worked their hardest in their assigned sphere without aspiring to leave that sphere. Wilson had a broader idea of spheres than did Cleveland and was more generous about who had the capacity to rise. He argued in 1914, for instance, "They say the Mexicans are not fitted for self-government: and to this I reply that, when properly directed, there is no people not fitted for self-government."[25] The key to democracy was the "proper direction" of the mass. But once properly directed, all people were capable of self-government, none were to be left permanently outside the democratic sphere. Citizenship had to be earned, but it was open to all. It was closed only to those who lacked—or who refused to take—proper direction. Wilson's inclusive language thus contained the possibility for important exclusions.

Wilson constantly spoke of "the idea of America," "the dream of America," and the "heart of America." Wilson told his audiences what America hoped for, who she was, where she had been and where she was going. He defined the nation's causes, complaints, and aspirations. All presidents, of course, do this, but rarely in such ideologically charged terms. Jefferson's nation comprised peaceful yeoman farmers spreading across a continent. Jackson understood his nation as one growing from that and characterized by an adventurous spirit and a need for land. During the 1850s, a more restrained and temperate citizen was required by the turbulent times, and a different sort of turbulence created Cleveland's yeoman worker. Wilson created an individualized and nationalized citizen, and he used this rhetoric to both advocate specific policies and use those policies, delineated through such constitutive rhetoric, to define his audience. As Wilson helped to construct public opinion, he also helped to construct a certain kind of citizen who was amenable to his industrialized and nationalized vision of the nation.

THE LIMITS OF LEADERSHIP

As clear as Wilson was—and he was very clear—on the extent of his definitional power, his understanding of the presidency was also based on recognition of the limits on his political and persuasive power. He understood himself as the "lead horse" and not the coach driver of the national team, and underlying that was recognition of his relationship to the American public and to the institution of the presidency.[26] He saw the presidency as a powerful locus of moral leadership, but that leadership, to remain legitimate, had to remain close to what he understood as the values and mores of the people.

States' rights, for instance, which were at the time as later, pivotal in Democratic party politics, posed one such limit. Supporting state power against encroachment by the federal government was an instinctive policy for Wilson as both a white Southerner and a Democrat. It is thus a bit ironic that it was during his administration that the federal government came to decisively dominate those on the state and local levels. Although he was able to accrue considerable power to both the federal government and the office of its chief executive, Wilson's ability to wield that power to include previously marginalized groups was limited by personal inclination and the realities of governing. He understood citizenship as belonging to individuals alone and not to individuals constituted as members of groups. He was thus disinclined to think of extending citizenship to groups and unlikely to consider group membership as de facto evidence of discrimination.[27]

He argued, for instance, that he was constrained by the political impact of public opinion regarding women's suffrage. No supporter of equal rights for women, he had stereotypical ideas of women that were not uncommon for his time and considered women to be illogical and often unwise.[28] They were, in short, poor candidates for political participation and unlikely to be the sorts of citizens he hoped to encourage. He also considered action regarding women's suffrage to be too far ahead of public opinion, and too far ahead of women's capacities. Early in his presidency, speaking to a delegation from the National Suffrage Convention, he said,

I have not yet presented any legislature my private views on any subject, and I never shall; because I conceive it to be part of the whole process of government that I shall be spokesman for somebody, not for myself. It would be an impertinence. When I speak for myself, I am an individual; when I am spokesman of an organic body, I am a representative. For that reason, you see, I am by my own principles shut out, in the language of the street, from "starting anything." I have to confine myself to those things which have been embodied as promises to the people at an election. That is the strict rule I have set for myself.[29]

He would not espouse inclusion for a group that the mass of general opinion did not support. It was inconsistent with his understanding of the representative nature of his official position and inconsistent with his idea of how a nationalized, ideologically homogeneous polity ought to function.

If such inaction was indeed his "strict rule," it is one he honored more in the breach than in practice. Those breaches were revealing, for they indicated occasions when Wilson's philosophical understanding collided with his philosophical commitment to universal principles. Respect for the limits of public opinion was not his only reason for refusing to act on the question of suffrage, however. He also cited his "conviction that this is a matter for settlement by the states and not the federal government."[30] When asked about the precedent set by the fifteenth amendment's enfranchisement of African Americans, Wilson denied the applicability of the precedent, arguing that a federal amendment in favor of women's suffrage would be tantamount to forcing policy on an unwilling minority, and this he would not do.[31] In common with many political actors, Wilson presented his unwillingness—stemming from personal preferences, an assessment of political reality, his understanding of public opinion, or some combination of these factors—as institutional incapacity.

Just as Jackson had argued that it was beyond his powers to protect American Indians on the frontier in order to better instantiate his policy preferences without accepting ideological or political responsibility for removal, Wilson here chose to frame his preferences as incapacity—the things he did not want to do were beyond his capability. Thus, he could implicitly claim to support women's suffrage personally while denying them the support of his office. Women, visible and powerful enough to create some problems for Wilson, still lacked power to force him to accommodate their interests.

Wilson's governing principles—the party as a vehicle of national action and an expression of national interests—and his understanding of the limits of presidential and thus national action allowed him to craft a particular sort of citizenship. Citizens were individualized rather than members of a particular group and were subject to specific sorts of discipline—patient in the face of exclusion, willing to forgo self-interest for the national interest, and willing to both follow and lead based on their position and the dictates of public opinion. They were citizens who were adapted to an industrial order and well suited to making that order international in scope. Unlike Cleveland's vision of standardized citizens, Wilson relied on citizens who were not only standardized, but functionally identical and identified.

A SINGULAR NATIONAL IDENTITY

Like many other presidents, Wilson insisted that all Americans were fundamentally the same. For Jefferson, Americans served individual interest by allowing for independent farms; for Jackson it was facilitating the nation's burgeoning growth; for Pierce, Fillmore, and Buchanan, it was through the maintenance of the founder's union and political arrangements. For Cleveland, Americans served individual interest by participating in one grand system that would ensure balance and equality. For Wilson, self-interest and national interest did not need to be reconciled through governmental action, for all Americans were acting in one united interest: "It is so obvious that it ought not need to be stated that nothing can be good for the country which is not good for all of the country. Nothing can be for the interest of the country which is not in the interest of everybody. . . . Nobody can be the friend of any class in America in the sense of being the enemy of any other class. You can only be the friend of one class by showing it the lines by which it can accommodate itself to the other class. The lines of help are always the lines of accommodation."[32] Wilson thus extended Cleveland's logic—the logic that described a diversified, industrialized nation and believed that the interests of all Americans were identical—and were identically subject to definition by the president.

Unlike Cleveland's depiction of unity as the result of the smooth ordering of national diversity, however, Wilson did not separate the nation into groups and then reconcile their differing interests. He denied the potency of group identification and thus the relevance of group interests. He said, "We set this nation up, at any rate we professed to set it up, to vindicate the rights of man. We did not name any differences between one race and another. We did not set up any barriers against any particular people."[33] Wilson offered a peculiar reading of the Constitution here, but it was a reading that served a specific end. Like all the warrants based on civic nationalism, this one argued for nationality and inclusion based on universal principles. As a result, however, this rhetoric also placed inclusion in the foreground and erased exclusion. In claiming that no one was ever excluded, slavery and its legacies simply disappeared. In ignoring the property requirement for voting, the importance of class in American history was obliterated. In denying the barriers set up against women and immigrants, their claims against the government for equity also vanished. Those claims could have no legitimacy and thus called for no governmental action if there was never any discrimination. Both the excluded and their exclusion were simply erased.

This was far subtler than the claims that characterized earlier exclusions. The rhetoric of balance was often explicitly and nakedly exclusive. As presidential attention turned to the finer distinctions of citizenship among mobilized and organized groups, the exclusions become more nuanced, for as groups attained more visibility, their exclusion and erasure became more difficult both to justify and to accomplish. Rhetorical exclusions therefore tended to coexist with inclusive rhetoric based on universal principles, and their consequences become more difficult to tease out. But these more subtle exclusions did the same political work as the more blatant forms of exclusion that operated earlier. These forms of exclusion helped presidents and other political actors defend the political coalitions and institutional arrangements that had brought them to power while also allowing for ideological justifications of those coalitions and arrangements such that any exclusions were naturalized and the exclusions themselves were erased.

Those Americans who were left inside the polity after this erasure were not merely united by interest, for Wilson had no allegiance to any interest defined in group terms,[34] but they were substantively identical and identified. They did not exist as members of groups. For Wilson, American citizens were all the same, united and defined by their national identity alone. Wilson said:

> I have never proposed and I never shall propose, that a single class of society shall have a special preference in what ought to be a general partnership. I have again and again insisted that nobody ought to be excluded from the partnership and I have again and again pointed out that the men who carry the heat and burden of the day—on our farms and in our shops and in the dull depths of our mines and in the forests and on the sea—constituted the greater part of our population and were, therefore, among the senior partners in the firm. But the game of politics has never gone in their direction that I have heard.[35]

This rhetoric, demanding that no one be excluded, no one left out, could not be more inclusive, for if no one was left out, then all were included. But he defined membership in economic terms. That is, citizens were not divided by economic interests, and there was no mention of racial interests. Like the framers, Wilson here presumed a homogeneous cultural community, and in that assumption lay an enormous amount of invisible exclusion, for those who did not fit into his cultural community were erased.

In advocating the inclusion of those whose lack of power had been sorely felt, Wilson balanced the interests among his national constituency understood in economic terms. He also erased the claims of those whose causes he could not articulate without losing the support of that constituency, such as African Americans. Once these people were rendered invisible, the argument for an identity of interest among those remaining within the polity became easier to articulate and enact.

As some groups—especially immigrants—sought inclusion, the price paid for that inclusion was ethnic identity. "White" immigrants, unlike women, African Americans, and American Indians, could be more easily absorbed into the body politic, and they could become like everyone else, ideologically and physically indistinguishable. If their only interests were understood economically, then there was no real barrier to inclusion on those terms. They, too, could aspire to be "senior partners." Wilson here took the position of one who not only understood and spoke for, but would also include all the people thus described. Note how he conflated all the particulars in one long list from which "the mass" was constructed. The totality was not greater than the sum of its parts; it was indistinguishable from the sum of its parts. He used the language of civic nationalism with its attendant universalizing claims. That language also supported, intentionally or not, the retention of certain ascriptive hierarchies, for the interests of women, African Americans, those who were considered nonwhite, could not be understood in economic terms alone.[36] They could only be understood in cultural or racialized or gendered terms, and those terms were explicitly deleted from the national vocabulary. Their exclusion did not apparently conflict with Wilson's language of civic nationalism, because they were not openly part of the presidential vocabulary.

Speaking to that most economically oriented of groups, the Chamber of Commerce, Wilson said, "The longer I occupy the office that I now occupy, the more I regret any lines of separation; the more I deplore any feeling that one set of men has one set of interests and another set of men another set of interests; the more I feel the solidarity of the nation—the impossibility of separating one interest from another without misconceiving it; the necessity that we should all understand one another, in order that we may understand ourselves."[37] No difference could be admitted; solidarity required consubstantiality.

Intentionally or not, this worked to the disadvantage of the excluded, for by pointing to examples of repression, they were also guilty of claiming that their interests differed from those of their oppressors. Thus, the excluded themselves, through the act of claiming exclusion, also justified such exclusion, for they were the ones who caused dissension. They misconceived their own interests. If the process of attaining political visibility was also the process of exposing certain facts about a group's past treatment in the polity, then Wilson wanted none of it. Members of groups who had been previously excluded—most notably immigrant groups—could begin to receive some visibility and some inclusion, but to the extent they voiced allegations concerning past discrimination or asked for assistance from the government in addressing past wrongs, they were displaying their unfitness as citizens. As Wilson himself put it when speaking to an Ohio Chamber of Commerce, "So that when I hear Americans begging to be assisted by authority, I wonder where they were born. I wonder how long they have breathed the air of America. I wonder where their papers of spiritual naturalization are."[38] Becoming legally American was one thing; the thing that counted was "spiritual naturalization," which meant that one had integrated oneself into the nation, become invisible. Those who were arguing— sometimes vehemently and sometimes violently—for inclusion, were thus getting the process wrong. Citizenship was not a matter of becoming politically visible, but of allowing oneself to be absorbed by the mass, becoming politically invisible. Those who argued otherwise, even if native born, were not really Americans—they were, in some way, "foreign." Thus, the rhetoric of civic nationalism was part of the disciplinary project of nation building, reinforcing existing hierarchies and labeling those who challenged them as ideological if not actual outsiders.

In advocating a single and singular national identity, Wilson was responding, as had other presidents, to the pressures of unifying a diverse nation, for he claimed that division and unrest were aberrant, the product, not of natural and inevitable tensions, but of, among other things, "the machinations of passionate and malevolent agitators."[39] Just as Washington styled those who fomented and participated in the Whiskey Rebellion as lacking in virtue and contrary to the public welfare, as Fillmore, Pierce, and Buchanan had styled Mormons and abolitionists as deleterious to the nation, and as Cleveland had argued that American Indians were prone to the manipulations of others, Wilson here claimed that those whose interests did not coincide with the national interest as he understood it were working actively against the national interest, not against his interpretation of the national interest. In an identified and identical nation, anyone seeking division was also seeking self-interest, not the national interest.

In addition to responding to similar pressures as had previous presidents—and doing so in much the same way as previous presidents—Wilson was also being consistent with the "extreme nationalism" of the Progressives and their allies.[40] Wilson was "an instinctive nationalist"[41] and insisted on a singular national identity,[42] premised on Christianity and communalism.[43] Both elements of Wilson's nationalism appeared inclusive and yet served to exclude; non-Christians as well as those who did not see themselves in his communalist vision were perforce left out of his union.

Through Christianity, Wilson could further balance the diverse American interests and unify the nation. He considered Christianity "the most vitalizing thing in the world."[44] However interested Wilson may have been in Christianity for its own sake, he invoked it publicly to further his political principles. Speaking before the Young Men's Christian Association, Wilson said: "I wonder if we attach sufficient importance to Christianity as a mere instrumentality in the life of mankind. For one, I am not fond of thinking of Christianity as a means of saving souls. I have always been very impatient of processes and institutions which said that their purpose was to put every man in the way of developing his character. My advice is: Don't think about your character. If you will think about what you ought to do for other people, your character will take care of itself. . . . And that is the lesson of Christianity."[45] In this interpretation of Christianity, right action took precedence over contemplation, and right action, of course, was in accordance with how Wilson defined it.

Wilson here was clearly creating a certain sort of citizen—one who was, most obviously, Christian and who understood and accepted Christian doctrinal notions of what "good character" was. On the one hand, this definition was inclusive, as the love of the Christian God was inclusive. But it was also exclusive, as it not only relegated non-Christians to the margins of national life, but did so in such a way as to make that exclusion natural if not accidental, a by-product of other things, certainly not of an overt intention to exclude.

The political importance of Christianity extended even into his military policies during World War I, when he not only commended the Bible to enlisted personnel,[46] but also recommended the observance of the Sabbath: "The importance for man and beast of the proscribed weekly rest, the sacred rights of Christian soldiers and sailors, a becoming deference to the best sentiments of a Christian people, and a due regard for the Divine Will demand that Sunday labor in the army and navy be reduced to the measure of strict necessity."[47] All people, not merely Christians, needed a day of rest—but that day would be the Christian day, Sunday. The Jewish Sabbath, for instance, was not accorded the same respect. For Wilson, Americans were a

Christian people, and the exclusions that accompanied that definition were rendered as invisible as were Jews, and those of other
denominations. This focus on Christianity was not portrayed as a
choice, but was simply a fact, uttered as if there were no contingen-
cies upon which it depended. Christianity was important because
America served Divine Will, but it was Wilson's interpretation of
that Will that really merited prominence and attention.

That interpretation led directly to his definition of the singular
national identity shared by all Americans. That definition was, in
fact, informed by Providence and was thus placed well beyond argument. "Patriotism," according to Wilson, "is a deeply grounded principle of action which bids every man subordinate his own interests
to the interests of the common weal and to act upon that, though it
be to the point of utter sacrifice of himself and everything that is
involved. I have sometimes thought that there is a sense in which
patriotism in its redeeming quality resembles Christianity."[48] If
patriotism was redemptive, and the model for redemption was the
Christian model, then certain citizens—those most able to understand and to desire to emulate Christ's example of sacrifice—would
be privileged over others. Such rhetoric, while appearing both benign
and inclusive, also instantiated and reinforced the political hierarchies that privileged Christian citizens over those of other faiths.

His definitional power as president was such that the criteria for
"real" Americanism were known to him alone. Speaking to the
Daughters of the American Revolution (DAR) in 1913, he said, "I
would not undertake, at any rate in a single improvised address, to set
up the canons of Americanism, though I think I can tell whether a
man is an American or not when I talk to him."[49] Americanism,
unlike most Christian denominations, did not have clear canons, but
those who were included in the polity, like Wilson, could recognize a
kindred spirit. Americanism could not be determined by looking at
someone—race and gender were thus not elements of Americanism.
Americanism was a matter of ideology and could be displayed through
conversation. It was rational and could be recognized by the rational.

Americanism was not determined by class, profession, or race, or
by anything that militated against a singular national identity. Over
and over, Wilson claimed that there were no interests that divided
Americans;[50] he insisted that all Americans were equals,[51] spiritually identified and identical. Americans were consubstantial, exist-

ing in and for one another. In a memorial address for the men killed at Veracruz, Wilson said,

> Notice how truly these men were of our blood. I mean our American blood, which is not drawn from any one country, which is not drawn from any one stock, which is not drawn from any one language of the modern world; but free men everywhere have sent their sons and their brothers and their daughters in order to make that great compounded nation which consists of all the shared elements and all the best elements of the whole globe. . . .they were Americans, every one of them, and with no difference in their Americanism because of the stock from which they came. They were in a peculiar sense of our blood, and they proved it by showing that they were of our spirit—that no matter what their derivation, no matter where their people came from, they thought and wished and did the things that were American, and the flag under which they served was a flag in which the blood of all mankind is united to make a free nation.[52]

Here, Wilson relied on civic ideals of nationalism. Americans were the products of a melting pot that rendered all Americans identical. Through Christian sacrifice, these men had died for the nation. "Our blood" defined a particular set of people as sharing a national identity and did so in ways that appeared unconditionally inclusive. Sacrificing oneself in war, as Gary Gerstle points out, is one of the dominant topoi of arguments for inclusion. Through such sacrifice, some measure of inclusion can often be obtained. But as the example of the African-American troops who fought at Veracruz indicated, symbolic inclusion may lend some measure of political visibility, but such visibility did not also inevitably mean political inclusion as well.

Inclusion meant acceptance of national norms and the national ideology: "We constantly discipline our fellow citizens by having an opinion about them. That is the sort of discipline we ought now to administer to everybody who is not to the very core of his heart an American. Just have an opinion about him, and let him experience the atmospheric effects of that opinion."[53] Wilson was explicitly encouraging a disciplinary project of citizenship, asking citizens themselves to patrol the borders of citizenship and to discipline those who fell beyond them ideologically. The correct response to such misdirected thinking was not exclusion but redirection. For such discipline to be righteous it had to be confined to the expressing of opinions. Wilson's good citizens were good Christians, and they preferred education to the harsher forms of discipline.

Wilson was in favor of ideological consistency, but he was no believer in intolerance. Wilson spoke out against mob action during the war in the harshest terms. Speaking to the American Federation of Labor, Wilson said: "The mob spirit is displaying itself here and there in this country. I have no sympathy with what some men are saying, but I have no sympathy with the men who take their punishment into their own hands. And I want to say to every man who does join such a mob that I do not recognize him as worthy of the free institutions of the United States. There are some organizations in this country whose object is anarchy and the destruction of the law, but I would not meet their efforts by making myself partner in destroying the law."[54] For Wilson, the mob spirit was the spirit of lawlessness, greed, and untrammeled will. The democratic spirit was obedient to law, self-sacrificing, and was contained by a rational commitment to the common good. Good citizens were not members of mobs but were dedicated, in the early twentieth century as they had been in the antebellum period, to the protection of temperate order.

In Wilson's view, opinions against dissent should be made known, but not violently acted on.[55] A reasonable polity was amenable to being both a balanced polity and a durable one. Unthoughtful or unreasonable demands threatened both the national balance and—given the war—even national survival. Good citizens remained steadfast even in war, and they remembered that which they were fighting for—and against. Wilson's good citizens were willing to sacrifice themselves for their country, but they were not willing to sacrifice their nation's ideals. Ideologically identified and identical, they would brook no dissent, but neither would they suppress it through violent means. The force of public opinion, as Wilson understood it, would be discipline enough.

Yet his demands that all people abide by his creed of Americanism also encouraged that action. He wanted the conformity that mob actions demanded, but he also wanted that action to stop short of violence. In a statement to the American people issued in 1918 he said, "No man who loves America, no man who really cares for her fame and honor and character, or who is truly loyal to her institutions, can justify mob action when the courts of justice are open and the governments of the States and the Nation are ready and able to do their duty. We are at this very moment fighting lawless passion. . . . I can never accept any man as a champion of liberty either for ourselves or for the world who does not reverence and obey the laws of our own beloved land, whose laws we ourselves have made."[56] Here, Wilson sounded remarkably like Fillmore, Pierce, and Buchanan in his disgust for passion and his preference for a temperate citizenry. Wilson had no use for the passion of a Jacksonian citizen if in his (and I use the pronoun advisedly) zeal that citizen would undercut the nation he so passionately sought to defend. Unlike the presidents of the 1850s, however, for whom any deviation became impossible to sustain, Wilson sought an ideologically identified nation where deviation became unlikely and was treated as a cause for education, not exclusion.

Through his use of the principles of nonpartisan party action, an apparent acceptance of the various limits on his power, which served to instantiate that power both politically and rhetorically, and the combination of the two into an advocacy of identified national identity, Wilson established his authority, increased the power of his office, and constructed a polity based on shared fidelity to universal principles. Despite his insistence that all citizens were substantively identical and identified, that polity privileged certain citizens above others, rendered some politically visible and others either marginal or invisible, and maintained specific sets of political and social hierarchies that were justified and naturalized through his ideological understanding of what constituted citizenship.

Universal Precepts

Wilson's use of universals as the best way to understand American citizenship resulted in a hierarchy among citizens.[57] That hierarchy was grounded in his ideological understanding of the nation, and worked to protect the coalition of interests that brought him to power. This understanding was clear in four elements of his rhetoric:

inclusion based on ideology, the use of casual exclusionary language, deferral of some demands, and a shift from the national to the international arena.

INCLUSION

For Wilson, inclusion in the American polity was based on a shared ideology. During his time in office, that shared ideology was challenged by the determined ethnicity of some immigrants, the jingoism of others, and a fear that mixed national loyalties both undermined the country at home and threatened to involve it in dangerous wars abroad. Assigned the task of preserving the nation, Wilson argued that only those who agreed with his definition of Americanism were to have a full share of the polity's bounty. Because of its specificity, Wilson's talk to a group of newly naturalized citizens is worth quoting at length:

> And, while you bring all countries with you, you come with a purpose of leaving all countries behind you—bringing what is best of their spirit, but not looking over your shoulders and seeking to perpetuate what you intended to leave behind in them. . . . It is one thing to love the place where you were born, and it is another thing to dedicate yourself to the place to which you go. You cannot dedicate yourself to America unless you become in every respect and with every purpose of your will thorough Americans. You cannot become thorough Americans if you think of yourselves in groups. A man who thinks of himself as belonging to a particular national group in America has not yet become an American, and the man who goes among you to trade upon your nationality is no worthy son to live under the Stars and Stripes.[58]

He argued here both for a collective national identity and against the retention of past national identities. Americanism was the only identity all its citizens shared; it was the only allegiance in which they could all participate. It was thus the only identity and the only allegiance that they should all hold. Wilson's citizens were American citizens entirely; they were American citizens only.

As part of the disciplinary project of assimilation, his enforcement of unity was increasingly important, as the differences among Americans became the focal points of organized political action. In the face of that division, Wilson claimed unity as he explicitly rejected that diversity and those divisions, even while ostensibly acknowledging them. Speaking before the National Press Club in 1916, he said, "There is a singular variety among our citizenship, a greater deal of variety even than I had anticipated. But, after all, we are steeped in the same atmosphere, we are all surrounded by the same environment, we are all more or less affected by the same traditions, and, moreover, we are finding out anything that has to be worked out among ourselves, and the elements are there to be dealt with at first hand."[59] Wilson harkened back to the national identity of the founders made explicit in the Declaration of Independence—that nationality, peoplehood, was not dependent on government, but on shared history, environment, and experience. For Wilson, American identity assumed that shared history, environment, and experience, and in making that assumption his rhetoric was both inclusive—all Americans were presumed to be part of this sharing—and exclusive— not all Americans did in fact participate in the nation thus described.

Social diversity, for Wilson, was one thing. It may have been inescapable, even desirable, but it did not therefore need to have adverse political consequences. As in the selective definitions of national history and experiences we have seen from other presidents, this description did not appear to be an even remotely accurate picture of the typical immigrant experience during these years. Nor did it describe the experiences of many native-born African Americans, American Indians, Hispanics, and so on. What it did do, however, was to encompass all the members of these groups ideologically, to transform their actual experience into a vast, idealized shared experience, in which all citizens became equal ingredients in the national melting pot. Wilson made this point clear in a speech at the National Service School for Women, also in 1916:

We are beginning to realize how a nation is a unit, and that any individual of it who does not feel the impulse of the whole does not belong to it and does not belong in it. We have heard a great deal about divided allegiance in this country, but, before we discuss any divided allegiance in its political aspect, we ought to let our thought run back to what

were perhaps our divided allegiances in respect to our relations with each other. America had been brought to such a
point of diversification of interest, of occupation, of objects
sought, that she was in danger of losing the consciousness of
her singleness and solidarity. . . . We have all been reminded
with an emphasis which I, for one, thank God—that we are
first of all Americans, and only after that at liberty to seek
out other interest.[60]

Note how this experience was less material than ideological. It
was a matter of consciousness, not of interest. It was less the actions
and more the thoughts of citizens that Wilson sought to assimilate.
This rhetoric was both inclusive and exclusionary. It purported to
include any and all Americans, so long as they agreed to become part
of the national unit, to "feel the impulse of the whole." But it also
excluded, for any divided allegiance, any attempt to be American in
ways that differed from how Wilson understood Americanism, and
marked that person as someone who did not belong.

Wilson was clear about the parameters of citizenship, and he
held up models so that potential citizens could imitate them. In an
address on Commodore John Barry, for instance, Wilson held up
Barry's example of citizenship as one worthy of emulation, saying,
"That is my infallible test of a genuine American—that when he
votes or when he acts or when he fights, his heart and his thought
are nowhere but in the center of the emotions and the purposes and
the policies of the United States."[61] One's heart and thoughts had to
be in the center; even moderate deviations from the mainstream
were inimical and were potential causes for exclusion from the polity. Acts of citizenship—voting and fighting—must be done with the
nation at the center; no regional interest, no ethnic interest, no self-
interest was permitted. Again, this was the language of civic nationalism, but even as such, it had the potential to exclude even as it
included. To have any identity but the one Wilson assigned to Americans was to lose one's identity as American.

In practical terms, this meant that members of the groups who
were seeking political visibility and inclusion were being clearly
instructed on the process of transformation that they would have to
undergo to merit that visibility and inclusion. Thus, one's ethnic
identity had to be sacrificed for a new national identity. A product of

their numbers and political visibility was the chance to become politically invisible as ethnic, and visible only as "American." There is good evidence that many immigrants came to internalize the creed of "Americanism."[62] Such internalization may be one reason why members of so many groups sought to demonstrate that they had "earned" inclusion, often through patriotic service, if not sacrifice during war.[63] Members of these groups often took pains to assure Wilson of their loyalty.[64] Such loyalty, service, and sacrifice seemed to have the desired effect: American Indian veterans were granted citizenship in 1919,[65] and the women's suffrage amendment went into effect in 1920. In both cases the justification included both a need to enact democratic principles as part of the war effort and mention of service during the war. In finally advocating women's suffrage, Wilson said,

> Are we alone to ask and take the utmost that our women can give,—service and sacrifice of every kind,—and still say we do not see what title that gives them to stand by our sides in the guidance of the affairs of their nation and ours? . . . I tell you plainly that this measure which I urge upon you is vital to the winning of the war and to the energies alike of preparation and of battle. And not to the winning of the war only. It is vital to the right solution of the great problems which we must settle and settle immediately, when the war is over.[66]

For Wilson, not only was women's suffrage important to the war effort, but also to the solution of the problems that would face the nation following the Armistice. Through their dedication and sacrifices, women had proven that they were truly American and were thus finally acceptable as American citizens, rather than merely the mothers of citizens. Women—at least white women—had proven themselves worthy of inclusion on the terms Wilson had set out.

Some groups could never adequately assimilate, however, and no amount of service or sacrifice seemed to matter. Anti-Semitism, for instance, was omnipresent during these years, regardless of class or geographical location,[67] and despite attempts by Jewish organizations to manage Jewish immigration in ways that would lessen negative stereotypes, prevent socialism among them, and decrease the concentrations of Jews, all of which were considered fodder for anti-Semitism.[68] Given the Christian nature of Americanism as Wilson enunciated it, indeed, given the Christian bias in national history, it was hard to imagine significant tolerance being shown to those of other faiths, although examples of tolerance generally exceeded the number of examples of its opposite.

Yet as more groups came to the United States, and as members of these groups attained more political visibility, tolerance was developing as one of the values considered essential to civic nationalism. Americans were coming to understand themselves not only as defenders of liberty but also as adherents of a tolerant civic life. That belief in tolerance, possibly a result of the increased numbers and political visibility of those previously considered "foreign," also probably helped members of other groups along the path of visibility.

For Wilson, most immigrants could meet the test of ideological assimilation. Speaking to "various ethnic societies," for instance, he said, "Nothing in this war has been more gratifying than the manner in which our foreign-born citizens and the sons and daughters of the foreign-born, have risen to this greatest of all national emergencies."[69] Despite their foreign birth, these people—sons and daughters—had fully assimilated and had adopted the United States as their only true home and Americanism as their only true identity. Civic nationalism had triumphed over allegiance to their original countries.

Those few who were too insistent on difference to be ideologically complete Americans needed to be excluded by real Americans as they had already excluded themselves. In commemorating Memorial Day during the war, he said, "In some instances—they are not, my fellow countrymen, very numerous—but, in some instances, men have allowed this old ardor of another nationality to overcrow [sic] their ardor for the nationality to which they have given their new and voluntary allegiance."[70] Notice how this exclusion was self-inflicted. If only members of these groups had stopped behaving and identifying as members of groups, they would have been fully and completely included. As with earlier examples of overt exclusion, its subjects were always the agents of their own marginality.

Woodrow Wilson did a great deal to include the previously disenfranchised and to extend the principles of civic nationalism. His ideological understanding of American citizenship, however, also proved to be potentially if not actually exclusionary, as it was based

in a particular formulation of how Americanism was to be understood and enforced. His rhetoric on national identity was, by and
large, based on notions of citizenship rather than balance, for his
concern was less with the geographical incorporation of immigrants
and indigenous peoples, and more with the boundaries of citizenship
as they pertained to the interests, political arrangements, and institutional structures that as president, and as the leader of a particular
political coalition, he was charged with maintaining. The inclusion
of some was part of the story of how he defined citizenship. The
terms under which others were excluded were also important.

EXCLUSION

In addition to facilitating inclusion, Wilson's universalizing rhetoric
could also facilitate the masking and naturalizing of exclusion
through casual exclusionary language. Since his universals purported to include everyone on "equal" terms, the telling of slanted stories, racist epithets, and the use of women as negative examples of
undesirable behavior were not overtly exclusionist. The language of
balance, prominent in earlier times, could be overtly exclusionist,
because so few of its subjects had political visibility or political
power. By the early twentieth century, however, African Americans,
women, and immigrants were more visible, wielded a little more
power, and it became more difficult to differentiate, divide, and
exclude them. The rhetorical mechanisms of exclusion became more
subtle. Such language thus functioned to mask both the exclusion
and its exercise by those in positions of power. This was made possible by the unstated premise that Americans were all the same and
that such stories, epithets, and examples spoke only to trivial differences that lacked political meaning.

The processes that led to increased political visibility were not
uniform, and some groups were more likely to be overtly excluded
than others. As the examples that follow illustrate, during these
years many exclusionary attitudes remained strong—and were
strongly defended. Wilson's language, often more liberal than that of
his contemporaries, was unusual in that few presidents spoke as
bluntly, as publicly, or as often on these issues as did Wilson. However, these stories shared the casual racism of the time and the common tendency to impute specific sorts of characteristics to specific

groups, a tendency that was particularly vicious during these years.[71] The discriminatory and exclusionary nature of this tendency became less obvious to those who were not directly affected by them, legitimated and rendered trivial or invisible as they were by rhetoric like Wilson's.

When a group has visibility but lacks political power, it becomes subject to differentiation, to being categorized based on imputed behavior, characters, and morals. This both set the terms by which that group might one day be included, and justified and explained their present exclusion, for they were "known" to be lacking some trait important for proper citizenship, or possessed another that disqualified them for it. As groups attained some level of political visibility, however, such blunt examples became more difficult, for members of the group had some resources to counter such overt exclusionary claims. So these claims became more subtle, if no less potent, and appeared less in policy statements, and more in casual ways, as illustrative stories, colorful examples, and so on. Wilson, who had a reputation as a raconteur, was especially fond of such rhetoric. Seemingly trivial, it carried potent political messages.

In one of his rare direct communications to American Indians, for instance, Wilson began by calling them "my brothers." He then quoted Thomas Jefferson on the ability of his audience to assimilate. Recalling Jefferson here was also, of course, recalling Jefferson's rather than Jackson's view of American Indians—they could be educated out of savagery and put on a path toward civilization. Having been rendered politically invisible over the last century or so, American Indians could now hope to assimilate into the American polity—at the same price of their ethnic or racial identities.

Wilson then said, "This I say to you again today: but a hundred years has gone by, and we are nearer these great things than hoped for now, much nearer than we were then. Education, agriculture, the trades are the red man's road to white man's civilization today, as they were in the day of Jefferson, and happily you have gone a long way on that road." According to Wilson, Jefferson's assessment of American Indians had been correct, and they were on the path toward renewed visibility and inclusion. Wilson concluded his message with the claim that "the Great White Father now calls you his 'brothers,' not his 'children',"[72] a claim that may have offered some symbolic solace, but as a practical matter did little to alter the power relations between the federal government and its wards. Given the destruction of American Indian communities, the erosion of the American Indian land base, the comparative destitution of American Indian peoples, and the destructive consequences for their religions and cultures in those intervening hundred years, one can only imagine how they understood this great civilizing project.[73] The frontier had officially closed some years earlier, and American Indians were no longer a military or social threat to the United States. They were viewed by some philanthropists as an interesting set of cases in need of benevolent assistance, but were largely considered politically irrelevant and politically invisible. Wilson, like most Americans of his time, gave American Indians very little of his attention.

Like Cleveland's union, Wilson's polity was not premised on the frontier, either as a national or an international construction, and unlike many twentieth-century presidents, he rarely used pioneering metaphors. His polity was industrialized and urbanized, and his preoccupations were with industry and the cities. He was concerned with the closing of the frontier and with what that might mean for the education and absorption of immigrants, but he was not comfortable with and did not use the frontier mythology as his contemporary Theodore Roosevelt was so inclined to do.[74] His few mentions of American Indians were not in the context of the frontier, and except as characters in his casual stories, American Indians were politically invisible to him.

One such story is worth including, for it illustrated the use of casual racism and widely accepted stereotypes of American Indians, as well as the political uses of such racism and stereotyping:

> I heard a story the other day that was ridiculous, but it is worth repeating, because it contains the germ of truth. An Indian was enlisted in the army. He returned to the reservation on a furlough. He was asked what he thought of it. He said, "No much good; too much salute; not much shoot." Then he was asked: "Are you going back?" "Yes." "Well, do you know what you are fighting for?" "Yes, me know; fight to make whole damn world Democratic party." He had evidently misunderstood some innocent sentence of my own. But after all, although there is no party purpose to it, he got it right as far as the word "party," to make the whole world

Democratic in the sense of community of interest and purpose.[75]

Notice that Wilson removed agency: it was not his story, merely
one that "he heard." Furthermore, he disavowed the content of the
story, calling it "ridiculous" and specifically calling his own role
"innocent." Thus he could not be held accountable for its content or
racist slant, for it was neither his nor did he give it any real credibil-
ity—except by telling it. Notice also that American Indians continued to be portrayed as savage others—they were disappointed that
the army required discipline rather than violence. They were childlike in their understanding of the great issues of war and peace, as
well as of the smaller issues like the role and limitations of the
Democratic party. Finally, notice that the American Indians in the
story were speaking what some contemporary American Indians call
"Tonto," a form of English singularly lacking in proper grammar,
that served to point to their inability to truly assimilate—they could
almost be "American," but as their lack of facility with the language
indicated, they weren't really part of the polity, despite their best
efforts.[76] They remained an exotic other. Tellingly, Wilson's story
derived its "humor" from the naive but well-intentioned mistakes of
the American Indians. He here reflected but also naturalized the
views on American Indians prevalent in the early twentieth century
and justified their exclusion without ever making them part of a policy initiative.

Wilson's attitudes toward American Indians were, like those of
many of his contemporaries, full of stereotypes and inaccuracies, yet
there was little overt malice in his treatment of them. Lacking visibility, they also lacked the capacity to engage him. The same could
not be said for African Americans. Wilson's attitudes toward blacks
were of a piece with his time and his region. He was said to respect
"good colored folk but had little sympathy with aggressive ones. At
Princeton [he] had been unwilling to force the issue of a Negro's right
of admission to the university. It seemed to the President that segregation of the races kept embarrassing problems from arising and he
did not comply with repeated pleas from champions of Negro rights
whose support he had sought in the election campaign."[77] Although
unwilling to work for African-American equality, he was also more

liberal than many of his contemporaries. Although unlikely to have dined with Booker T. Washington, as Theodore Roosevelt did, he was also unlikely to have allowed a miscarriage of justice as Brownsville, which Roosevelt perpetrated.[78]

Yet many of his stories had a racial theme, and they were revealing of his attitudes, if not his policies, on race:

> A friend of mine, or rather, in view of the story, I should say an acquaintance of mine, was Chairman of the local campaign committee in one of the Oranges in New Jersey, and on election day towards the end of the day an old colored man came in and stood and shifted and shifted and finally my friend looked up and said: "Well, what do you want?" "Is dis Mr. Annin?" "Yes." "Is you de Chairman of de Republican committee?" "Yes. What do you want?" "Well, Mr. Annin, I think dar is a lot ob dese niggers agoin' to vote de Democratic ticket." He said, "Well, what are you going to do about it?" The darkey said, "I think if I had about two dollars apiece for dem niggers, I could fix em." Annin said, "Look here, what you are proposing is in any case wrong, but when you don't need the votes, it is a crime, and I don't need them."[79]

Notice here how Wilson's language removed agency; again, how it distanced members of an excluded group from the mainstream through the use of dialect. Again, power relations were enacted within the story as if they were natural and inevitable: Annin was the arbiter of morality, albeit a somewhat skewed morality, as he was a Republican, and the African American was portrayed as "shifty," he was kept waiting and treated abruptly, he was there to solicit a minor pecuniary advantage for his fellows, he was dishonest, and he was unnecessary to the powerful. Finally, Wilson again imputed less than worthy characteristics to this group, although in this case, he also added the use of vicious racial and racist epithets. In all these ways, intentionally or not, Wilson legitimated and set as "natural" the exclusion of members of this group.

This story functioned ideologically to locate African Americans in the prevailing political hierarchy. It naturalized their place there, as the previous example naturalized the invisibility of American

Indians. These stories also functioned to explain and justify the marginal place in the political hierarchy of these groups, and functioned also to provide the terms by which these groups could hope to attain some measure of political visibility and perhaps eventual inclusion. American Indians had to give up their savage ways, and African Americans had to develop political maturity and public morality. The widely shared stereotypes reflected in these stories reinforced other ideologically driven assumptions about members of these groups and had a powerful effect on the national self-understanding in terms of who was included in the polity and under what conditions.

These stories were not restricted to members of minority racial groups. Wilson also used women as negative examples and in ways that served to justify and explain exclusionary policies toward them on the federal level while ostensibly illustrating very different points. Asked what his intentions were regarding hostilities between Russia and Japan in 1913, for instance, Wilson responded, "When your neighbors quarrel, let it alone. . . . It is like a friend of mine who saw a man brutally beating his wife and intervened; and then the wife joined the husband and beat him. He then determined to let alone domestic quarrels. It is the irony of fate under the circumstances that that sort of feeling should arise out of a wholly disinterested act."[80] The logic of how hostilities between two foreign nations could be reduced to a "domestic quarrel" was hardly the point. The distancing effects of Wilson's rhetoric again seen here, do not need underlining. Women, in this example, were incapable of recognizing, much less appreciating, the value of disinterested action and turned on their would-be rescuers. There was clearly a moral here for men, if not for nations.

In all these cases, through this rhetoric, Wilson indirectly illustrated and enacted the racial and gender hierarchies that were protected through the processes of American politics. By highlighting stereotypical characteristics and attributing them to entire groups, Wilson legitimated and sanctioned the lowly place of those groups in the national hierarchy. Because these lowly places were depicted as inevitable if not natural, members of these groups were viewed as being unreasonable if and when they demanded change. Patience on their part was required, for neither political nor physical evolution could be hurried.

DEFERRAL

Presidents are charged with preserving the nation; that often entails conservative action and the preservation of existing hierarchies. As groups approached some measure of political visibility and made increasing demands on government, and as the language of that government became more dependent on notions of universal rights and civic nationalism, continued exclusions became more difficult to justify. Yet the political coalitions that brought specific presidents to power rarely had any incentive to stretch the political system and accommodate these new demands. Twentieth-century presidents thus had to walk a difficult line between protecting the political arrangements and institutional structures associated with their political coalitions while not overtly excluding those who could be perceived as legitimately pressing for inclusion. One way of handling this delicate situation, as we have just seen, was by naturalizing exclusion through the use of casual stereotyping. Another way, which would become prominent in the rhetoric of presidents as different as FDR and George H. W. Bush, was by deferring these claims.

As a rhetorical strategy, deferral explicitly puts the onus on the minority group, not on the political system. All citizens are expected to respect the system and accept its limitations. Outright exclusion places some beyond the system; outright inclusion legitimates other demands. Deferral represents a midpoint between these positions. It goes some distance toward legitimating demands, but in claiming systemic incapacity, it also makes those demands appear excessive, immoderate, and thus inappropriate.

Wilson, for instance, argued that patience was required of minorities, that full inclusion had to wait until they, or those who were excluding them, were "ready." Generally, this delay was infinite, as those who had the most to lose by changing the established hierarchies were precisely those whose "readiness" was demanded as a condition for change. This was one way of recognizing that a group's heightened political visibility justified its ability to make claims on government, thus further legitimating that group, while also delaying actual accommodation, thus preserving existing political and institutional arrangements. Speaking on a proposed clause in the League Covenant mandating racial equality, Wilson said:

> The trouble is not that any one of us wishes to deny the
> equality of nations or wishes to deny the principle of just
> treatment of nationals in any nation. The trouble is not with
> our decisions here, but with the discussions that would cer-
> tainly be raised in the Plenary Council if the word suggested
> were introduced into the Covenant. My own interest, let me
> say, is to quiet discussion that raises national differences and
> racial prejudices. I would wish them, particularly at this
> juncture in the history of the relations with one another, to
> be forced as much as possible into the background.[81]

This argument justified deferral on the basis of the need to maintain an international political balance. Wilson adhered to the principles of "equality among nations" and "just treatment of nationals in
any nation" but was unable to force that principle through the Ple-
nary Council. Just as in the earlier discussions of the uses of political incapacity, here it allowed Wilson to lay claim to the principle
while legitimating its (very real) limitations in practice. In trying to
get controversial issues of inclusion off the public agenda, in this
case so that those issues would not delay or prevent the ratification
of the League Covenant, Wilson was also postponing that inclusion,
perhaps indefinitely. Political exigencies would allow voice only to
those who were already always in agreement. Other issues, labeled
"divisive," were rendered invisible.

Deferral both legitimated a group and served to render it less visible. Here, as was often the case with FDR, a group's political visibility was highlighted, and symbolic favors would follow. The president would, for instance, meet with them or speak with them or
send his wife to them, but no actual policy would then result.
Members of groups that had attained enough political visibility to
merit such symbolic treatment were then stymied, because they
lacked the political power to bargain for policy. Symbolic inclusion
preceded political effectiveness.

But for the time being, Wilson used the plea for patience with
equal finesse at home, although personal attitudes as well as political exigencies were probably equally responsible for this tendency. In
response to a group asking his assistance in ending discrimination
and "Jim Crowism," for instance, Wilson replied:

I am very much obliged for your generous address. You have certainly interpreted my intentions correctly, but every man is surrounded by all sorts of limitations of which I am impatiently aware, and you may certainly be sure that everything in my power to accomplish justice will be accomplished. We all have to be patient with one another. Human nature doesn't make giant strides in a single generation. It is not as careful of our faults as we would wish that it were, and I have a very modest estimate of my own power to hasten the process, but you may be sure that everything I can do will be accomplished, and I thank you very much for your audience and wish you God speed.[82]

This argument went hand in hand with his claims that he lacked efficacy, as noted earlier. According to this argument, neither government as a whole nor Wilson in particular had the power to change human nature. By behaving themselves and waiting patiently, change might come—in its own time. But change would not be hurried by any action of Wilson, the government, or—most important—members of excluded groups. Thus, further pressure on the government would not result in the desired policy but might, in fact, threaten its achievement by illustrating the group's lack of understanding of the political process and thus their unsuitability for inclusion.

This approach also suited Wilson's view that government would be beholden to no special interest, but only to the public interest. The public interest would best be served by those already included in the nation; their demands on government were not new and had only to be restrained and restored to a proper balance. He was reluctant to add new demands. In this, Wilson disappointed many of the reformers who had helped bring him to power,[83] which in small ways threatened to harm his political coalition. But on this matter, Wilson's personal preferences, political instincts, and governmental philosophy all pointed in the same direction: deferral of new demands on governmental largesse.

Yet, during these years the conditions under which these people were to wait so patiently worsened. "Plagued by unemployment, the poor were inadequately fed, clad, and sheltered. 'My people do not live in America, they live underneath America,' declared a Ruthenian priest in Yonkers, New York. 'America does not begin till a man is a workingman, till he is earning two dollars a day. A laborer cannot afford to be an American.'"[84] This identification of citizenship with work, a carryover from the Gilded Age, remained a powerful ideological force during Wilson's years and into Franklin Roosevelt's, limiting the potential of even the most inclusive rhetoric. The poor, differentiated and divided under Cleveland, lacked the political capacity to make unified demands on the government, and those demands were thus comparatively easy to defer, especially as the press of business from other, more visible groups also increased. And as the war loomed, such demands were easy to style as petty and selfish.

It was on these grounds that Wilson objected to labor unions, which did not exemplify the patience that Wilson argued was required but, in his view, instead engaged in strikes and tended toward violence if their demands were not met. Although Wilson believed that genuine improvement in working conditions were needed and he was a consistent advocate for labor, he did not necessarily believe that union activity was the best means to that end.[85] Speaking at the dedication of a new American Federation of Labor building, for instance, he said, "The trouble in a great many of the labor contests we have had, my fellow citizens, as you will bear me out in saying, is that one side or the other side did not wish to sit down and talk it over, and that the great difficulty in the settlement of a great many labor disputes has been difficulty of getting candid and dispassionate conference with regard to the points at issue."[86] That is, labor disputes brought disruption and accentuated difference rather than relying on the reasonableness that was crucial to his understanding of Americanism. Such disputes threatened the national balance and should be avoided. Those who engaged in such disputes were not worthy of inclusion. Since disruption was the focus, the national balance was at issue. As always when balance stands at the center of debate, more overt exclusionary language can be—and in this case was—invoked.

Wilson could justifiably claim that he was on the side of the workers, and he both spoke and acted on their behalf, saying in a speech before Congress on tariff reform early in his presidency that "we must abolish everything that bears even the semblance of privilege or any kind of artificial advantage,"[87] and, "It is our business to make sure that they are genuine remedies" for the problems of working folk.[88] But he was concerned about the unions as vehicles for action, fearing that they were neither restrained nor easily restrainable. In 1918, for instance, he felt compelled to remind laborers that "the war can be lost in America as well as on the fields of France, and ill-considered or unjustified interruptions of the essential labor of the country may make it impossible to win."[89] Losing the national balance could, at least in time of war, threaten the survival of the nation. Workers had attained sufficient political visibility and sufficient political power to merit the president's attention and to be rewarded with specific political policies, such as improvements in working conditions. But Wilson, like Cleveland, understood labor unions as the vehicle for political action to be of dubious political value, because they threatened the national balance. The harsher language of overt exclusion could be used against them.

Like labor unions, immigrants and immigration continued to be a source of social tension. Fifteen million immigrants entered the United States between 1900 and 1915, condensing into those years the growth that the nation experienced in the previous forty years and accounting for nearly one-third of the nation's growth.[90] The diversity among them and the number of immigrants led to the vocalization of both antiurban and racist concerns, as people warned of the dangers of "Balkanizing" the United States.[91] Americans were ambivalent about immigrants and immigration, and they—like Wilson— objected to their tendency to refuse assimilation. "Let us think of America before we think of Europe"[92] was his constant refrain. For those who did not, Wilson had harsh words, saying, in his 1915 annual message, "Such creatures of passion, disloyalty, and anarchy must be crushed out. They are not many, but they are infinitely malignant, and the hand of our power should close over them at once."[93] According to Wilson, loyalty to the home country was equal to disloyalty to the United States and should be treated accordingly.

The language of citizenship, generally inclusive in appearance with any exclusionary elements muted, was here quite obviously exclusionary. This indicated the importance Wilson attached to rendering the numerous immigrant "persons" into "citizens," and how dangerous he considered unassimilated immigrants. They not only brought foreign mores and habits into the nation's cities, they not only fomented strikes and advocated foreign theories of government like communism and socialism, but they also threatened the national cohesion, the sense of the nation as identical and identified, that was basic to Wilson's definition of national identity. Rather than accepting Wilson's understanding that immigrants should disappear as members of ethnic groups and become only Americans, these unassimilated immigrants offered a potential national identity that was an amalgam of various loyalties and identities.

The tensions caused by fear of the consequences of these various loyalties were more than rhetorical. In 1915, the Ku Klux Klan was re-formed in Stone Mountain, Georgia, just one year after the lynching in Atlanta of Leo Frank.[94] The religious biases of the Frank case joined with the already virulent racism of the period. It was not an easy, or safe, time to be a member of a minority group in the United States. Wilson offered an understanding of citizenship that was, with all its limitations, far more inclusive than other contemporaneous alternatives.

Still, as we have seen, Wilson was no advocate of civil rights. In this, he was very much a (white) man of his times, region, and political party. The national government, for instance, was significantly more segregated as a result of his administration.[95] In addition, immigration became more restricted on his watch, and he has been called "probably the most racist president" of the twentieth century.[96] He denied, for instance, that segregation was in any way discriminatory. Speaking to a group of African-American leaders as part of a "dialogue," he said, "Now, what makes it look like discrimination is that the colored people are in the minority as compared to the white employees. Any minority looks as if it were discriminated against. But suppose that the Negroes were in the majority in the departments in the clerkships and this segregation occurred? Then it would look like discrimination against the whites, because it is always the minority that is discriminated against, whereas the discrimination may not be intended against anybody, but for the benefit of both."[97] African Americans had attained some measure of political visibility and, under the Republicans, had also made some limited political advances—enough that they could argue for government jobs and begin to develop a middle class. That visibility and political power—however limited—allowed them a platform on which demands for further inclusion could be based. Wilson thus felt obligated to meet with representatives of black communities and to acknowledge their claims. However, he did not feel obligated to accommodate those claims or even to legitimate them. African Americans had not yet reached that level of political visibility or political power. At a point between political invisibility and political power, they were subject to the rhetoric of deferral.

Deferral operated to protect and legitimate both the status quo and the nation's universal principles. The claim to balance and fairness implicit in this quotation, for example, allowed Wilson to tolerate discriminatory and prejudicial policies and directives while distancing himself from their effects. The claim to be acting on a universal principle justified the unequal application of that principle. Note also that the claim that there was no intent served as a surrogate for "therefore it wasn't really discrimination." For any policy or action to be discriminatory in this formulation, there also had to be discriminatory intent. In this analysis, if good people meaning no harm engaged in policy that hurt others, there was no real harm because none was intended. Thus, to warrant a change in policy, that policy had to be shown to be unfair in both intention and result. Such ideological claims reinforced and legitimated the prevailing structures of power and the political positions of Wilson's coalition. Democrats owed little or nothing to African-American voters, and they yielded them nothing in terms of political policy.

In addition, through this sort of language Wilson indirectly illustrated and enacted the racial and gender hierarchies that were protected through the processes of American politics. By highlighting undesirable characteristics and attributing them to entire groups, the lowly place of those groups in the national hierarchy was legitimated, naturalized, and implicitly sanctioned. Because these lowly places were depicted as inevitable if not natural, members of these groups were viewed as unreasonable if they demanded change. They had gained some measure of political visibility and political power but not yet enough to make demands on the government. Such rhetoric proved to be yet another way through which Wilson could silence his critics and establish himself as the sole national spokesperson.

What Wilson did for the presidency on the domestic stage he would also do for it in the international arena. Under Wilson's stewardship, not only did the presidency come to dominate national political conversations but, in the person of the president, the United States also became a major participant in world affairs, especially in Europe. He did as little to affect international hierarchies as he had done to change domestic hierarchies. He used universals in both arenas—as in his claim, cited earlier, on the equality of all nations—but he well understood that all nations were not, in fact, equal. His concern was that his notion of world justice be enacted and that the moral voice of the United States not be neglected. He was thwarted in both of these ambitions in the short term, but in the long term, the United States became not just the beacon of liberty, as in the Pilgrim's vision, but a force for establishing its vision of liberty around the globe.

INTERNATIONALIZING AMERICA

The result of Wilson's universalizing rhetoric was the transference of the national to the international arena through an insistence on a national unity that was based on an unstated premise of shared American economic interests. His emphasis on unity in turn occluded all difference. All Americans became the same American, driven to erase internal differences in the face of external exigencies. This transcendent understanding of America and its role in the world was defended through the use of specific historical examples and a particular view of shared national history. Like Jefferson, Jackson, and all presidents since, Wilson took a specific view of American national history, one that lacked nuance and served specific ideological ends, legitimating specific sets of institutional structures and political arrangements, and justifying particular sets of inclusions and exclusions. Because of the way this worked to unify the image of America on the international stage, it also functioned to demand unity of all Americans on the national stage as well.

Wilson's historical examples amount to a narrative of identification that, again in Burke's words, served "to cloak the state of division" as it asserted national unity.[98] Its workings were simple: first, Wilson argued that all citizens were equally Americans. When the focus shifted from the hierarchies within the nation to the hierarchies between nations, even those Americans who were most marginal within the nation became privileged. Wilson's foreign policy, according to one of his biographers, "bred chauvinism," intentionally or not.[99] Thus, even those most oppressed by domestic hierarchies were privileged members of an international regime. By exerting American influence—and sometimes American force—abroad,

American presidents following Wilson could also sometimes defuse claims for inclusion at home.

Wilson's historical narratives began with the national experience and then expanded and extrapolated into the international realm. Like Jackson's use of Jefferson, and Fillmore, Pierce, and Buchanan's use of the frontier myth, Wilson relied on valorized past presidents and myths to legitimate action in the present. Just as Jackson altered Jefferson's vision to accommodate his own, and the presidents of the 1850s altered Jackson's to suit the ideological needs of their time, Wilson also adapted the past to suit the needs of his present.

For Wilson all Americans shared a history of greatness. There was little recognition of the nation's humble beginnings, little notice of its geopolitical insignificance for much of its history, little attention to its rather recent emergence as a colonial or world power. Discussing his Latin American policy in Mobile, Alabama, in 1913, for instance, Wilson said, "This is not America because it is rich. This is not America because it has set up for a great population great opportunities of material prosperity. America is a name which sounds in the ears of men everywhere as a synonym with individual opportunity because a synonym of individual liberty. . . . The nation that loves liberty truly sets every man free to do his best, and that means the release of all the splendid energies of a great people who think for themselves. A nation of employees cannot be free any more than a nation of employers can be."[100] Wilson adopted the legacy of the Puritans and their wish to establish a "shining city on a hill" as the national mission; it was an ideological mission, not one of territorial conquest. Its accuracy was dubious; its ideological work, however, was clear. America, for Wilson, was founded on liberty; that value was one he sought to internationalize.

The rather abrupt introduction of employers and employees notwithstanding, Wilson insisted that material greatness was based on moral greatness. As he said to the DAR that same year, "We established an independent nation in order that men might enjoy a new kind of happiness and a new kind of dignity, that kind which a man has when he respects every other man's and woman's individuality as he respects his own, when he is not willing to shut the door of privilege in the face of anyone."[101] Again, the focus was not on equality but on liberty. Americans were, above all, a free people. That freedom was predicated on individualism, on individual rights, not on rights as members of groups. Thus, discrimination based on group membership was rendered invisible. All American interests were united in the mission of internationalizing American moral virtue understood as liberty, which led to material prosperity.

Second, Wilson believed that democracy was simply the best, most advanced, effective, and humane form of government ever devised.[102] He argued for his foreign policy in ways that seemed to imply that he would use the same principles in dealing with minorities at home as he would with other nations abroad. For instance, in speaking on Latin American policy, he said, "Interest does not tie nations together; it sometimes separates them. But sympathy and understanding does [sic] unite them, and I believe that the new route that is just about to be opened, while we physically cut the two continents asunder, we spiritually unite them. It is a spiritual union that we seek."[103] As this example indicated, Wilson used much the same language in both the domestic and international arenas, and strove for much the same effect in both. Of course, this also meant that the hierarchies he took as natural at home were also likely to be instantiated in foreign affairs as well. However, just as he believed that all Americans had the capacity for eventual citizenship, he also believed that all peoples had that capacity, if properly educated first.[104]

Speaking on the issue of what to do with Hawaii, Puerto Rico, and the Philippines, for example, Wilson said, "Such territories, once regarded as mere possessions, are no longer to be selfishly exploited; they are part of the domain of public conscience, of serviceable and enlightened statesmanship. We must administer them for the people who live in them, and with the same sense of responsibility to them as toward our own people in our domestic affairs."[105] This, for the time, quite liberal stance, had at least two implications. To an international audience, he was claiming that the United States would be as democratic abroad as it was at home. To a national audience, the implication was that people at home would be accorded the same rights as were minorities abroad. Wilson's internationalization of the American order thus had domestic as well as international consequences, for he enabled those who felt excluded in either realm to argue on the basis of such clearly articulated universal principles for inclusion. He also encouraged a confluence between international and national politics, such that they could come to reinforce one another and events around the world could have important consequences for political action at home, something that the more isolationist understanding of America would have precluded.

Wilson was clear about his belief that the United States had a mission to perform in the international arena. Unlike the previous presidents studied here, who had largely restricted their sense of mission to domestic arenas, Wilson prefigured twentieth-century presidents who tended toward a more international understanding of America's mission and manifest destiny.[106] Wilson's rhetoric on China illustrated that mission's moralism, paternalism, and ethnocentricity, elements that have long been part of presidential rhetoric on international affairs:

> The government of the United States is not only willing, but earnestly desirous, of aiding the great Chinese people in every way that is consistent with their untrammeled development and its own immemorial principles. The awakening of the people of China to a consciousness of their possibilities under free government is the most significant, if not the most momentous event of our generation. With this movement and aspiration the American people are in profound sympathy. They certainly wish to participate, and participate very generously, in opening to the Chinese and to the use of the world the almost untouched and perhaps unrivaled resources of China.[107]

This rhetoric recalls Jefferson, Jackson, and even Cleveland's opinions about American Indians. In all cases there was an explicit assumption of American cultural and political superiority, a sense of obligation stemming from that presumed superiority, and an expectation that all other peoples strive, however unknowingly, to be Americans, or just like them. It was probably not coincidental that in all cases there was also a clear recognition of the vast resources controlled by those inferior peoples and that in "civilizing" them, Americans could also gain access to those resources. Thus, Wilson would do for China as he would do for culturally deficient minorities at home: help them to become "civilized" so that they could better participate in the transcendent international order.

That order was based on universalized "American" principles: "The interesting and inspiring thing about America, gentlemen, is that she asks nothing for herself except what she has a right to ask for humanity itself. We want no nation's property. We wish to question no nation's honor. We wish to stand selfishly in the way in the development of no nation. We want nothing that we cannot get by our own legitimate example. And, standing for these things, it is not pretension on our part to say that we are privileged to stand for what every nation would wish to stand for, and speak for those things which all humanity must desire."[108] The principles that motivated the United States were also those that motivated the world. America represented the world: "America has been made up out of the nations of the world and is the friend of the nations of the world."[109] In representing America, Wilson thus represented the world, and the circle was complete.

Just as Wilson approached the task of governing the diverse and industrialized United States by rendering all Americans identical and identified, erasing differences even as newly organized groups attained some political visibility and political effectiveness, he approached the tasks of world governance through a specific understanding of citizenship. He spoke in universals, which meant that all people, and all peoples, were potentially included. But those universals were, paradoxically, culturally specific to Western Europe and the dominant culture of the United States. Just as Wilson erased domestic differences—and some domestic groups—while privileging others through his use of universals at home, he also erased some cultures and privileged others through his use of universals in the international realm. When America came to represent the world, those who were most like Wilson's vision of America were more centrally placed than were those who tended to least resemble that vision.

As these examples indicated, rhetorically, even before the excesses of the war, American foreign policy under Wilson had an evangelistic quality.[110] This evangelistic quality has, of course, been present since before the founding and is present today. Speaking to the DAR in 1915, for instance, he said, "America has a cause which is not confined to the American continent. It is the cause of humanity itself."[111] In Wilson's public speech, as in that of most presidents, Americans were united in opposition to the primitive or warlike Other, and joined together to provide an example of civilization for the world to envy and emulate. Wilson, however, following Theodore Roosevelt, was willing to globalize the frontier. He said, "I mean the development of constitutional liberty in the world. Human rights, national integrity, and opportunity as against material interests—that, ladies and gentlemen, is the issue which we now have to face."[112] Civilization, understood not just as liberty but as constitutional liberty, and as the forces of principle, stood opposed to material interests. Americans spoke for and represented an idealized form of politics, not seeking material possessions but only to enlighten the world. Ideologically, American interests thus expressed as civilization's interests, and as principled interests, encompassed the interests of the world.

In addition, moving to the international arena meant that Wilson maintained national hierarchies while simultaneously rendering them invisible. In a Detroit luncheon address Wilson said, "the spirit of the United States is an international spirit, if we conceive it right. This is not the home of any particular race of men. This is not the home of any particular set of political traditions. This is a home, the doors of which have been opened from the first to mankind—to everybody who loved liberty, to everybody whose ideal was equality of opportunity, to everybody whose heart was moved by the fundamental instincts and sympathies of humanity."[113] Again, in this formulation, Wilson rendered all Americans ideologically identical and identified. Americans may have come from all regions of the world but, upon becoming Americans, were all subsumed into one ideological whole. That whole, having come from the world, was also representative of the world.

Wilson's use of universals in this manner was not restricted to this single case. On September 15, 1919, for instance, at a luncheon address in Portland, Oregon, Wilson said, "You must not forget that America is made up out of the world and there is hardly a race of any influence in the world, hardly a Caucasian race, that has not scores of hundreds, and sometimes millions, of people living in America with whom they are in correspondence, from whom they receive subtle suggestions of what is going on in American life, and the ideals of American life."[114] Note the progression of terms here, the use of what Burke called "ultimate terms." Burke noted that when elements were placed in a dialectical tension with one another, both voices spoke, indeed, they "jangled." When, on the other hand, competing voices were placed in "a *hierarchy* or *sequence*, or *evaluative series*, so that, in some way, we went by a fixed and reasoned progression from one thing to another, the members of the entire group being arranged, *developmentally*, with relation to one another."[115] Ideologically, this privileged the last in the series, the one that is most developmentally complete. Thus, through Wilson's use of ultimate terms, "the world" became "a race of any influence in the world," which became "a Caucasian race," and "the world" was reduced to "Caucasians." It was, of course, this ideological dynamic that allowed us, not once, but twice, to declare what were primarily European wars to be world wars. It was also a logic that helped to cement racial hierarchies into the twentieth-century definition of "Americanism," as some ethnic and racial group traditions became formally devalued as others were formally privileged.

Wilson's use of universals was a powerful legitimating tool. It legitimated the claims for inclusion by many newly visible groups, and it also legitimated the accommodations, deferrals, and denials of those claims. When applied to the international arena, these universals enabled protection of hierarchies at home while also instantiating and extending them abroad. Yet at the same time, by so visibly connecting the national to the international realm, these universals would become powerful topoi for arguments against American oppression at home as well as American imperialism abroad.

Wilson's rhetoric indicated just how complicated the business of managing the nation had become. The often overtly exclusionary rhetoric of balance had largely given way to the language of citizenship, which tended to be both inclusive and, often, subtly exclusive as well. In trying to render increasing numbers of politically visible persons into citizens, Wilson crafted an ideologically based definition of national identity that would continue to resonate both nationally and internationally long after his presidency.

Conclusion

Insofar as "modern" presidents are also "rhetorical" presidents, Wilson was a pivotal case in the development of the institution.[116] His use of nonpartisan party leadership, focus on the limits of his power, and the claim to an ideologically driven national consensus enabled him to silence his critics and assume a position as the sole arbiter of national values. This rhetoric, which allowed for the inclusion of some through demonstration of a commitment to civic nationalism, also excluded others through casual racism and acceptance of ascriptive hierarchies. It also contained implications for the international order through universalizing the American experience of the world.[117]

As one of the important precursors to the rhetorical presidency, Wilson's public communication helped him establish the definitional primacy of the office and assisted him in formulating it as the powerful rhetorical institution it has become. His construction of the American people as unified ideologically despite racial and ethnic differences was among the most powerful—and powerfully consequential—elements of his rhetoric. Wilson was, although dubious about the ascribed characteristics of certain racial, religious, and ethnic groups, also more accepting of those groups than previous presidents and certainly more accepting than his contemporaries. The idea that members of these groups had the potential to be included as full Americans was itself important. This capacity was not extended to all—African Americans in particular were disadvantaged by his treatment of them and of their concerns.

Wilson's rhetoric was full of the contradictions of his time: inclusive and racist, moralistic and strategic, conforming and visionary. He created certain conditions for inclusion in the polity that, imperfectly applied in both his day and in ours, nonetheless facilitated arguments for more evenly applied notions of citizenship. Some of those arguments were already being made, and others would be articulated in the context of the Great Depression.

5 / Balancing the Nation: Brokering FDR's Economic Union, 1932–1940

> It is the problem of Government to harmonize
> the interests of these groups which are often
> divergent and opposing, to harmonize them in
> order to guarantee security and good for as many
> of their individual members as may be possible.
> The science of politics, indeed, may properly
> be said to be in large part the science of the
> adjustment of conflicting group interests.
> —Franklin D. Roosevelt

WOODROW WILSON gave us an internationally transcendent union based on universal principles and an ideological definition of "Americanism" and citizenship. Roosevelt, something of a disciple of Wilson, expanded both the meaning of those principles and the number of groups that were legitimated by them, although he did little to alter the stratification of the national hierarchies, for in many ways, Wilson's governing coalition was also FDR's. Both needed to maintain Democratic preeminence in the "Solid South," both needed to protect Democratic interests in the urban North, and both saw great possibilities in the agricultural West.

Roosevelt, of course, changed and expanded the Democratic party, and the New Deal coalition remains an important part of the Democratic party even now. That coalition was based on the incorporation of new groups into politics and on the extension of inclusion to some who were already politically visible but who remained largely on the

margins. For Roosevelt, group membership was a legitimate compo-
nent of self-identification, and he worried a good deal less about
"hyphenated Americans" than had Wilson. Roosevelt expanded the
idea of citizenship and increasingly opened its borders, especially to
white immigrants from Europe. He was more interested in economic than in ethnic identification, and inclusion in his republic would
be on those terms.

Governing a nation where industrialization was an accepted fact
of life, and where large numbers of immigrants had been successful-
ly disciplined into citizenship and incorporated into the polity,
Roosevelt had fewer of the fears of fragmentation than had Wilson.
His polity was a bit more like the nation in the 1850s, in that serious economic troubles threatened the fabric of union and nation. His
polity was quite unlike the union of the 1850s, however, for the rifts
were neither regional nor sectional, but national. And to these
national problems he proposed national solutions. For Roosevelt,
like Wilson, but unlike Fillmore, Pierce, and Buchanan, "progress"
was all-important, change a given, and a strong national government
was to be the progenitor and protector of both. A strong national government meant for Roosevelt also a generally inclusive regime, one
in which group interests could be legitimated, brokered, and mediated, and the national interest therefore protected.

Citizenship was the overriding interest. The issues of balance
that Roosevelt faced had less to do with maintaining the nation's ideological structure in the face of geographic expansion and the incorporation of "foreign" peoples, and more to do with maintaining that
ideology in the face of the challenges posed by socialism, communism, and the economic crisis at home. Because of the overwhelming nature of that crisis, Roosevelt's understanding of citizenship
was also largely economic. The threatened instability of the regime
meant that those who were politically visible enough to make
demands on the federal government had to be in some way accommodated, for any further disruption, any more instability, and the
national balance could be tipped, and the nation might fall. These
very real concerns meant that for Roosevelt, citizenship and balance
were intimately connected.

Under FDR, the national hierarchies were not stable and based
on race or other ascriptive traits. No single group of citizens was singled out by Roosevelt for valorization, epitomizing national virtue.

Instead, the position of each group was fluid; a group might move up or down the ladder of presidential attention, political status, and policy. Maintaining the whole—the nation—was more important to Roosevelt than was appeasing any single one of its parts.[1] The goal always was to preserve the social order—if moving a group up or down the social hierarchy helped to maintain the larger cohesion of the whole, then that was an acceptable price as far as Roosevelt was concerned. In the face of internal breakdown and external threats, Roosevelt could claim to have preserved capitalism and democracy. In so doing, he also helped to define social justice in economic terms and, while legitimating group membership as "American," provided a template that made demands by groups somewhat less legitimate. By co-opting and excluding, deflecting, and deferring those demands, Roosevelt kept firm control over the final definition of economic and thus social justice.

Roosevelt thus maintained the national balance by managing citizenship, but not through the rigid discipline characteristic of Wilson. He opened the doors of the American polity comparatively widely and then orchestrated the relationships among groups, and between groups and the national government, in such a way that members of groups could be accommodated and their allegiance to the state could be kept secure.

Roosevelt's vision of the nation, and of the role and nature of citizens within that nation, was rooted in the pluralist political tradition, which required flexible leadership such that the president could juggle the various claims on the national government. He accomplished this juggling act through rhetoric that stressed the co-option, or denial, deflection, or deferral, of these interests. This rhetoric is clearly illustrated in his metaphors of community.

A Pluralist in the White House

Roosevelt scholar George McJimsey notes that Roosevelt's conception of leadership was a pluralistic one, that he saw politics as an arena of competing group interests, and that the government's job was arbitrating among those interests.[2] Unlike Wilson, Roosevelt did not argue that all Americans were identical and identified. Unlike Cleveland, he did not conceive of them as different parts of an organic whole. Where Jackson sought stability in growth, and the presidents of the 1850s sought it in stasis, Roosevelt sought national stability and balance through fluid relationships among Americans. As one might expect from a president who gave rise to a new coalition, a new alignment of political and institutional interests, Roosevelt, like Jackson, sought movement and he created a dynamic union. Like Jackson, he sought to reshape some hierarchies while maintaining others. Unlike Jackson, he would do this not on the basis of establishing a new set of hierarchies, but by placing all of them in flux, by brokering interests and allowing groups to understand that their place was negotiable. In so doing, he maintained both the overall set of hierarchies and opened up the polity for demands for (further) inclusion. He gave even groups that remained excluded or marginalized important topoi through which their place in the order could be eventually challenged and changed.

America, for Roosevelt, was not a fixed society with stable hierarchies and lasting group and national interests. It was instead a process. In a radio address on "Brotherhood Day" in 1936, for example, he said, "I do not look upon these United States as a finished product. We are still in the making."[3] The unfinished nature of the union meant that its hierarchies, its terms of citizenship and inclusion, were contestable. For Roosevelt, citizenship was premised as much on the future as on the present. It was promise as well as performance, and what looked chaotic was really the product of imperfect vision.[4] In his first inaugural address he declared that "the basic thought that guides these specific means is not narrowly nationalistic. It is the insistence, as a first consideration, upon the interdependence of various elements in and parts of the United States."[5] For Roosevelt, the nation was, as it had been for Cleveland and Wilson, interdependent, but for Roosevelt the terms of that interdependence were fluid, not rigid. They were not narrowly nationalistic.

Pluralism was in Roosevelt's day what progressivism had been in Wilson's, a way of understanding how democracy, born in small agricultural republics, could possibly work in a geographically expansive, industrialized one.[6] The pluralists argued for a group-based understanding of democracy and believed that all groups met on equal ground in the policy process, with government acting as a neutral umpire. Out of group conflict came the national interest.

Roosevelt's union was inchoate, always in motion, always developing. Maintaining the national balance thus required constant adjustment, and a constant mediation between powerful forces defending the established forces and less powerful, but equally persistent challenges to that order. Roosevelt's interest in and ability to effect change in the relative positions of groups or to overcome existing distinctions was, given the rigidity of social, political, and economic institutions, limited at best.[7] What he could do was effect change by bringing group demands into a manageable equilibrium, where some previously delegitimated groups (such as labor or European immigrants) found that at least some of their concerns could command a hearing. In a speech to veterans he said,

> Some people who visit us from other lands across the seas find it difficult to credit the fact that a Nation sprung from many sources, a Nation one hundred and thirty million strong, a Nation stretching three thousand miles from east to west, is, in all the great essentials of its civilization, a homogeneous whole; for not only do we speak one language, not only are the customs and habits of our people essentially similar in every part of the country, but we have given repeated proof on many occasions, and especially in recent years, that we are willing to forego sectional advantage where such advantage can be obtained only by one part of the country at the expense of the country as a whole.[8]

Seeing the nation as homogeneous made it possible to believe in a common good, for if Americans were all the same, then finding a common interest among them became easier than if they had been recognized as possessing diverse or competing interests. In reducing those interests to "customs and habits," Roosevelt, like Wilson before him, erased all those who differed in either. Rhetoric that seemed to include through amplification was also potentially exclusionary.

Through such amplification, Roosevelt gave voice to the multitude of Americans; as Walt Whitman earlier described each individual as a "leaf of grass," now Roosevelt seemed to include all Americans—at least all those from common European stock. In this rhetoric, that which separated Americans was trivialized. Americans were connected "in all the great essentials." The consequent erasure of those who were not part of American homogeneity, however, was also implied, if not necessarily intended. The ideology such rhetoric conveyed was important, no less so because it was widely shared at the time. Americans were not "a homogenous whole" in many important respects, but by envisioning a horizontal equilibrium among groups, FDR's language choices both fostered and masked the actual vertical stratification of those groups.

So many groups now had so much political visibility and were now so willing, as constituent members of groups, to make demands on government, that government had to make some accommodations. Overt acts of exclusion, while not as difficult as they would eventually become, were, for most of those considered to be "white," at least, difficult. Yet government lacked both the will and the capacity to accommodate all these group interests. Roosevelt responded by summoning some of the will, increasing some of government's capacities, and managing group interests on a contingent and constantly shifting basis.

As a good Wilsonian, he argued that he alone had a national perspective. He alone could see the big picture. He alone could see things not from a partisan, but "from the American point of view."[9] He alone had both the institutional position and the institutional power to manage the various group demands in ways that would actively serve the national interest, which Roosevelt understood as reflected in its ability to support the "human personality." In greeting attendees at a national conference on social work in 1936, for instance, he said,

> Many of us are accustomed to appealing for the cause of humanity. Let us remember that humanity is not society; humanity is just plain folks. Some of our so-called leaders have made the mistake of looking upon men and women as economic and social units. . . . In matters of social welfare we should keep sight of the fact that we are not dealing with "units," "individuals," or with "economic men." We are dealing with persons. Human personality is something sacred. It enjoys the light of reason and liberty. It grows by rising above material things and wedding itself to spiritual ideals. Our social order is worthy of human beings only in so far as it recognizes the inherent value of human personality. . . . We cannot be satisfied with any other form of society in which human personality is submerged.[10]

This depiction of the democratic ethos served to include—as all humans were sacred, they all deserved certain things from a just government—yet by elevating the spiritual above the material, it also excluded those who shared a different view of the sacred, of human personality, of spirituality.

It also rendered material issues secondary. If government was to represent the social order, and if its focus was on "human personality," then encouraging human economic and political equality was not necessarily the task of government. Government, for FDR, became a great protector of the "human personality," which was reasonable and spiritual and in need of liberty. Good government would not stop at the protection of liberty but would also nurture the reasonable and spiritual aspects of human nature as well. Any lesser endeavor was not worthy of democratic governments. In this, he greatly expanded the role and purpose of the American government.

At least in part because of the power that accrued to Roosevelt through this understanding of his role, FDR was subjected to extremely heavy criticism for encouraging elitism and class rivalry, and advocating policies that worked to the detriment of both the free enterprise system and the Constitution.[11] He was also accused of threatening individual freedom.[12] These criticisms were all the more ironic since Roosevelt credited himself—as did many of his supporters—with saving capitalism rather than undermining it,[13] and he was a constant supporter of individual freedoms, the definition of which he would enlarge a good deal. He may not have approved of all capitalists, but he certainly approved of capitalism, which he equated with opportunity and freedom. As he told the DAR in 1938, "The spirit of opportunity is the kind of spirit that has led us as a nation— not as a small group but as a nation—to meet the very great problems of the past."[14] It was to that spirit that he looked to meet the problems of the present and future as well. Roosevelt's speech was overtly inclusive, and it relied on many of the universals that those familiar with Wilson's speech would recognize. In the same way that they worked in Wilson's speech, these universals helped Roosevelt to both enable the topoi of democratic inclusion and mask the extent of exclusions still present in the American system. His language and his government were nonetheless more inclusive than Wilson's had been.

As part of his effort to save capitalism, for instance, FDR made it clear that as far as he and his administration were concerned, all the poor constituted the "deserving poor." Given the quiescence among Americans and the tendency among the unemployed to blame themselves rather than the system[15] this attitude was especially important. As Harry Hopkins put it,

Of all of the outrageous things that were done to American people, treating these people like outcasts. Behind that is a moral philosophy, if anyone is poor, it's because something is wrong with them. Give them just as little relief as possible so you won't encourage them. They want those unemployed to walk up timidly and knock on the door and why should they? They are American citizens like the rest of us. It is no fault of their own that they are out of work, and it is the business of society to take care of them. It shouldn't be done as an act of degradation. I made up my mind early in this game that relief was a matter of right and not a matter of charity.[16]

This understanding of the relationship between government and the people relied heavily on universals, in which all American citizens were somehow the same, were somehow deserving. The willingness of Roosevelt and the members of his administration to see the poor and unemployed as mainstream members of the polity rather than as outcasts probably did more than anything else to explain why these people developed so passionate a personal commitment to the president and to the programs he managed.

As the twentieth century continued, and as economic conditions worsened, Roosevelt governed a polity in which increasing numbers of increasingly well-organized groups, legitimated by the universalistic rhetoric of presidents like Wilson, made increasing demands on a government that lacked both the will and the capacity to respond to all of them equally. Roosevelt, relying on pluralistic governmental philosophies, understood his role as manager of both the national interest and the national diversity. He approached this task through the creation of a certain sort of citizen—constituted on the basis of group membership and willing to be flexible on the timing and nature of governmental accommodations to their group.

Juggling Interests

For Roosevelt, the essence of the presidency was juggling and balancing various group interests. Roosevelt used three primary strategies to accomplish that task. Each was connected to and reflective of his approach to citizenship. His first tactic was one of limited co-option combined with overt exclusion. This rhetoric used universals and relied on the language of tolerance. The implication was that all politically visible groups had been included, and there was room in the nation for everyone. The second involved deferral, in which he legitimated both the group and their demands, but asked for patience in accomplishing those demands. His third tactic was deflection, which legitimated the group but pushed their demands to the margins. Through these three tactics, Roosevelt thus absorbed, to different degrees, certain interests and the members of certain groups, including them politically in the administration and rhetorically as members of the national polity. Their inclusion, however, was premised on the exclusion and marginalization of others. Essentially powerless at the onset of the Depression, they remained so throughout the 1930s. The more politically visible a group, the more likely it was that the group would receive some accommodation; the less politically visible, the more likely were deflection, deferral, or denial of claims to inclusion.

CO-OPTION

When early presidents adopted universal claims, as had the founders, those claims were implicitly understood as applying mainly to members of certain classes and certain social groups. By the twentieth century, those claims had become ever more widely applied as various groups used them as the basis for their arguments for inclusion. By the 1930s, although balance was again a national preoccupation, the rhetoric of balance had to be placed in the increasingly inclusive understanding of citizenship. That gave Roosevelt both opportunities as a leader of a broad coalition and problems in that all members of that coalition would expect something from government in return for their support of its titular head.

Roosevelt's social order, while clearly more open than that of his predecessors, was still stratified. Through rhetoric that stressed limited co-option, Roosevelt legitimated groups within a hierarchy through application of universal principles, silenced those that didn't fit and rendered them invisible, scapegoated opponents, and relied on the language of tolerance, forbearance, and fair play, assuming that all were equal contestants on a level playing field. He thus legitimated the overarching order even while allowing for (minor) adjustments within that order, for it was potentially open to anyone who could muster the resources to participate.[17] This openness, restrictive though it was, sent an important symbolic message that the United States had become more authentically democratic. The New Deal both offered real gains to members of previously excluded groups and extended the rhetoric of civic nationalism to encompass a broader array of citizens.

Labor, for instance, only partially visible and often subject to differentiation and division under Cleveland and Wilson, was increasingly brought under Roosevelt's aegis and was largely invigorated by the New Deal. In understanding himself as an important figure in orchestrating balance between labor and capital, he also gave labor legitimacy as an interest equal to capital on the presidential scales.[18] Further, FDR believed that labor had rights—and that the protection of the national order demanded the protection of those rights. Labor was now fully politically visible and was considered a constituent part of the Roosevelt coalition. As such it had the power to push Roosevelt and his understanding of citizenship further to the left than he might otherwise have gone.[19] The inclusion of labor allowed Roosevelt to foster a different sense of citizenship, one in which the mass of workers was accepted and valorized. As the nation both democratized and dealt with the Depression, this sense of belonging may well have helped balance the nation. Citizenship and balance, as so often in the nation's history, served one another.

The creation and protection of Roosevelt's coalition thus meant that labor and capital were to be treated as at least symbolically equal and that the state was now overtly involved in the protection of labor's rights. In 1933, shortly after taking office, Roosevelt made both of these commitments clear. Upon signing the National Industrial Recovery Act, he said, "Its goal is the assurance of a reasonable profit to industry and living wages for labor with the elimination of piratical methods and practices which have not only harassed honest business but also contributed to the ills of labor."[20] Note that capital and not labor was subject to differentiation here. There was a distinction between "honest business," which would support Roosevelt's policy, and "piratical" business. The old hierarchies had shifted, if only infinitesimally. Yet business did not have to fear great change, for Roosevelt's view of economic justice was that capital got "a reasonable profit," and labor "a living wage." Both of them received protection from "piratical practices," and the outcome was therefore fair. All labor could reasonably expect was "the wages of decent living."[21] The protection of their right to this wage—as well as the determination of exactly how much constituted a "decent living"— was not up to laborers themselves but could be safely left in the hands of the president. The old hierarchies had shifted to accommodate labor but had not shifted so far as to favor it.

In listing the purposes and foundations of his recovery plan in a 1933 Fireside Chat, for example, he said, "The workers in this country have rights under this law which cannot be taken from them, and no one will be permitted to whittle them away but, on the other hand, no aggression is now necessary to attain those rights. The whole country will be united to get them for you."[22] "The whole country," that was, in the person of Roosevelt himself. He would defend their rights—so long as labor remained responsible in the exercise of those rights. The White House would not support aggressive behavior that sought more than workers were entitled to. "Good" labor would follow the president's lead and would accept what he could broker for them, just as "good" business would accept the president's role in negotiations and would come to a reasonable accommodation. Consistent with his pluralist understanding of government and his role in it, Roosevelt would manage the conflict of interests between labor and capital so that the conflict remained minimally contentious, and the national interest would be served. Labor, as a negotiating partner with business, an ally in the national balance rather than a threat to it, had been brought into the government's fold. It was both politically visible and politically powerful.

It was not more powerful than business, however. Despite the fulminations of his opponents, Roosevelt had no intention of supporting anything resembling a redistribution of national wealth. To that, labor was decidedly not entitled:

We have, however, a clear mandate from the people, that

Americans must forswear that conception of the old acquisition of wealth which, through excessive profits, creates
undue power over private affairs and, to our misfortune, over
public affairs as well. In building toward this end we do not
destroy ambition, nor do we seek to divide our wealth into
equal shares on stated occasions. We continue to recognize
the greater ability of some to earn more than others. But we
do assert that the ambition of the individual to obtain for
him and his a proper security, a reasonable leisure, and a
decent living throughout life, is an ambition to be preferred
to the appetite for great wealth and great power.[23]

Management, like some workers, would be protected in their
right to "earn more than others," and there would be no policies sug-
gesting "equal shares" of "our wealth." No one would be allowed
"excessive profits," and moderation in demands from both capital
and labor would rule the day. Responsible laborers would understand
and respect the rights of management, and would be respected in
turn. Indeed, in showing moderation, labor became a model of virtue
that those in business would do well to emulate. Labor had become
both visible and powerful enough politically, central enough to
Roosevelt's governing coalition, that it could be valorized and held
up as a model of citizenship for those aspiring to inclusion.

Because he had a view of labor that entitled them to just so much
and no more, and consistent with his role as protector of an orderly
society, FDR, like other presidents, understood strikes and collective
action as "aggression," and was as intolerant of the destructive capacities of such aggression as he was of business's "piratical" tendencies.
Regardless of his personal views, he supported the passage of the
Wagner Act in 1935, which revitalized organized labor.[24] It did not,
however, end labor disputes but seemed instead to fuel them.[25] In
1937, autoworkers in Flint, Michigan, invented a new tactic: the sit-
down strike, with devastatingly effective results.[26] When a settlement was reached, labor was the clear victor. Unions were henceforth both legitimate and powerful. And although only a few scholars actually argue that Roosevelt's policies directly led to strikes,[27]
it is true that "with growing unionism came a rash of strikes."[28]

The inclusion and partial co-option of labor was thus something
of a double-edged sword, for although Roosevelt could plausibly argue

that supporting rather than opposing the government was in labor's interest, the support of labor led to heightened political visibility and gave their demands heightened legitimacy. Not all laborers, and not all labor unions, saw their interest in the way that Roosevelt did, but enough of them did so that fears of a labor-based revolution were never realized in the United States.

But as militancy along with the strikes and organizational activity associated with it grew, labor became more of a troublesome issue, as the number of those strikes reached frightening proportions.[29] In response, FDR increasingly differentiated between "good" labor and "bad" labor. Through such differentiation, he could divide labor, maintain cordial relations with those important to his governing coalition, and hope to discipline the rest into a proper—Rooseveltian—understanding of their place in the national order.

Good labor included those groups that would work with FDR— and do so on his terms. "The overwhelming majority of the workers understand," he told the American Federation of Labor at the Samuel Gompers Memorial in 1933, "as do the overwhelming majority of the employers of the country, that this is no time to seek special privilege, undue advantage, or personal gain, because of the fact of a crisis. Like the duly constituted officials of your Government, we must put and are putting unselfish patriotism first."[30] Again, by illustrating moderation and proper patriotism, laborers proved themselves model citizens of an industrial democracy. As he would do consistently, Roosevelt here cited numbers as both justification and goal. Because he had a majority, he was a legitimate leader and could speak for labor in its best interest. His legitimacy conferred legitimacy on those who supported him and delegitimated those who opposed him. More politically visible and more politically powerful under Roosevelt than they had been before, labor was still subject to discipline, and their continued inclusion was predicated on their continued cooperation.

Just as the model laborers were those who exemplified moderation in their demands and willingness to compromise at the president's direction, "bad" labor included those—and there were more and more of them as the 1930s progressed—who engaged in strikes, or even in lobbying. Worried about a 1936 dispute between management and laborers in the railroad industry, Roosevelt said, "What disturbs me is the apparent inability of the managements and the men to cooperate in working out such common problems. Issues which ought to be settled by friendly negotiation are being fought out in the battle grounds of Congress and the courts. Legislation has its place. Often it has been necessary for the welfare of labor or capital or both, but it is a remedy to be taken with great caution or it may prove worse than the disease."[31] Any expression of an "undue" demand, and any effort to have that demand met—whether by violence or legislation—was to be condemned. Labor had been co-opted, but only in a limited fashion. Its demands would be met in the same limited fashion. Politically visible and possessing political power, neither was assurance that the government would obey labor's will or alter the national hierarchies around labor.

Instead, Roosevelt argued that all Americans were fundamentally equal and were equally beholden to the same universal principles. In a 1936 Fireside Chat he said, "We refuse to regard those who work with hand or brain as different from or inferior to those who live from their property. We insist that labor is entitled to as much respect as property. But our workers with hand and brain deserve more than respect for their labor. They deserve practical protection in the opportunity to use their labor at a return adequate to support them at a decent and constantly rising standard of living, and to accumulate a margin of security against the inevitable vicissitudes of life."[32] Thus, all workers had the right to attempt the American dream—to improve their material status as a result of hard work and systemic opportunity. All Americans were workers as they had been at least since Cleveland's day, and because of the ideological importance Americans attached to work, they were all treated as workers, even in the face of massive unemployment. The actual work was not the issue; the commitment to work was the marker of citizenship. Through work, the American dream of rising prosperity could be attained. As it had been in the 1880s, good workers were also good consumers who were also good citizens.

As a case in point, Roosevelt often referred to "the" immigrant experience. Generally speaking, FDR rarely mentioned ethnic groups as ethnic groups (rather than as workers, for instance), and when he did, it was to praise them, often in ways that would become more common as the century progressed, for their ability to represent "American" values.[33] Like all inclusive rhetoric based on such glossing of difference, it was inclusive and exclusive simultaneously, for it set limits on the differences that were allowed among citizens and erased the political meaning of those differences, which nonetheless marginalized members of these groups and lowered their position in the national hierarchy.[34]

When FDR mentioned ethnicity, it was generally in speeches to immigrants, which, as in the case of the poor generally, mattered a great deal because these workers were among those hit hardest by the Depression.[35] Roosevelt offered these workers rhetorical legitimacy, assuring them that despite their economic woes, they were included in the national polity. They were not treated as causes of the nation's economic problems as had been the case so often in the past, but were acknowledged as among its most helpless victims. Politically visible, they were less likely to become scapegoats and more likely to be offered some degree of governmental attention.

In one of his more poetic moments, Roosevelt said,

> The night is falling and the spirit of other days, too, broods over the scene. Andrew Jackson looks down upon us from his prancing steed, and the four corners of the square in which we are gathered around a gaily lit Christmas tree are guarded by the figures of intrepid leaders of the Revolutionary War— Von Steuben, the German; Kosiusko, the Pole; and Lafayette and Rochambeau from the shores of France. This is in keeping with the universal spirit of the festival we are celebrating; for we who stand here among our guardians out of the past and from far shores are, I suppose, as diverse in blood and origin as are the uncounted millions throughout the land to whom these words go out tonight.[36]

It is hard to imagine a more eloquent claim to national unity— at least for those who traced their ancestry to Christian Europe.[37] Again, note the exclusive properties of rhetoric that was clearly intended to be inclusive. Through such rhetoric, he symbolically co-opted members of previously marginalized immigrant groups, especially those from Eastern Europe into the polity, for the rhetoric of co-option depicts members of its target groups as already fully included and places that inclusion beyond question and beyond debate. Through such co-optive strategies, FDR led the movement of the disenfranchised into the Democratic coalition. He provided a sense of belonging to many previously disenfranchised groups: labor, Jews, African Americans, Catholics, and immigrant groups all flocked to the New Deal coalition.[38] Through such rhetorical acceptance, members of these groups found also a measure of political visibility and political power.

Roosevelt thus created a sense of national unity that ratified key elements of the existing order while expanding it to accommodate the most assimilated members of previously invisible groups. Those who were most able to participate in the system were rendered more visible through it. Others were simply forgotten, ignored. The continued exclusion of their less assimilated, less educated, less Americanized compatriots went on less visibly. That this rhetoric and the inclusion it authorized were politically possible was a testament to the success of the nation's disciplinary project of turning "people" into "citizens."

That project had been so successful, in fact, that although more assimilated immigrants were more likely to profit from inclusion, ostensibly, immigrants did not even have to assimilate in order to find acceptance. In a brief address celebrating Maryland's tercentenary, Roosevelt said, "Lord Baltimore and his colonists sought in their charter liberty not alone for members of the expedition, but for all later comers as well. It is a good thing to demand liberty for ourselves and for those who agree with us, but it is a better thing and a rarer thing to give liberty to those who do not agree with us."[39] Although this rhetoric purported to include all immigrants, it was a bit more exclusive than it at first appeared, for "we" were those who tolerated "them," the ones who disagreed with "us." And Roosevelt did reserve a special place for those immigrants who brought with them values he deemed central to American democracy—values from Europe:

Men everywhere throughout Europe—your ancestors and mine—had suffered from the imperfect and often unjust Governments of their home land, and they were driven by deep desire to find not alone security, but also enlarged opportunity for themselves and their children. It is true that the new population flowing into our lands was a mixed population, differing often in language, in external customs and in habits of thought. But in one thing they were alike. They shared a deep purpose to rid themselves forever of the jealousies, the prejudices, the intrigues and the violence, whether internal or external, that disturbed their lives on the other side of the ocean. Yes, they sought a life that was less fettered by the exploitations of selfish men, set up under Governments that were not free. They sought a wider opportunity for the average man.[40]

Note how Wilsonian Roosevelt was here. He took the widely differing experiences of a wide variety of people and peoples, who came to the United States for a wide variety of reasons, and out of those many experiences, peoples, and reasons, he made one narrative. He created a nation out of a vast amalgam of difference. In so doing, he erased the political meaning of those differing experiences, and made of them a new meaning. The price of inclusion, for immigrants as for labor and for other groups, was to surrender difference, become invisible, and be absorbed into the nation.

In such passages, Roosevelt wrote "the" story of America—this was the American dream, personified by a European immigrant. "Surface" differences of culture, habit, and thought were not as important as the "deep similarities," the shared commitment to a single set of values and goals, all reducible to material prosperity—all equal to living in a capitalist democracy. He was assuming that the default "American" identity was that of the assimilated descendent of a white, European immigrant. This is how he framed his appeal for the election of liberals during his "purge" in 1938: "Look over the rest of the names on the ballot next Tuesday. Pick those who are known for their experience and their liberalism. Pick them for what they have done, and not just for what they say they might do. And one last important word: Pick them without regard to race, color, or creed. Some of them may have come of the earliest colonial stock; some of them may have been brought here as children to escape the tyrannies of the Old World. But remember that all of them are good American citizens now."[41] Note who is included in this group as acceptable. European immigrants were clearly welcome in FDR's coalition. Note also who was rendered invisible by their absence: Hispanics, African Americans, and women notable among them. Although he said that candidates should be picked "without regard to race, color, or creed," all of his examples were of white male European immigrant "stock."

The inclusive language, and very probably the inclusive intent, was immediately modulated by the limited examples that followed, and once again, the exclusionary potential of inclusive language was revealed.

Consistent with that inclusive intent, and with potentially exclusive results, Roosevelt also spoke for, summarized, and glorified "the" immigrant experience. Celebrating the fiftieth anniversary of the Statue of Liberty, he said, "It has not been sufficiently emphasized in the teaching of our history, that the overwhelming majority of those who came from the Nations of the Old World to our American shores were not the laggards, not the timorous, not the failures. They were men and women who had the supreme courage to strike out for themselves, to abandon language and relatives, to start at the bottom without influence, without money, and without knowledge of life in a very young civilization."[42] Roosevelt's union was a dynamic union that would have been, in this sense at least, recognizable to Andrew Jackson. It was a union of courageous, adventurous souls who were willing to forge a new world, to make new beginnings. This dynamism may well have related, in Roosevelt's case as in Jackson's, to the particular requirements of those who create new political regimes.[43] As Jackson's dynamic union had allowed him to enfranchise the vast majority of white males over the age of twenty-one, Roosevelt was, through an implicit reliance on the frontier myth, in rhetoric couched in its terms, to include previously marginalized and disenfranchised immigrants. Rhetorically, they were now the center of the nation. They had gained both visibility and power, and were no longer attached to the nation; they now vanished within it.

All these courageous people remained bound by a single event, for they were central to Roosevelt's conception of citizenry, and that event would be constitutive of the national identity: "The realization that we are all bound together by hope of a common past has helped us to build upon this continent a unity unapproached in any similar area or population in the whole world. For all our millions of square miles, for all our millions of people, there is a unity in language and speech, in law and economics, in education and in general purpose, which nowhere finds its match."[44] Regardless of the timing of their immigration, all Americans were depicted as sharing a common past. They were equally heirs of the founders no matter how recently their tenure in the nation had begun. The "common heritage" that for the founders had been the key to inclusion was now shared by all white European immigrants.

Note however that this inclusive claim also had exclusive elements. Those who did not share the common past, common values, or common experiences, those who were, for whatever reason, unwilling to share in this fiction, were not merely delegitimated, they were erased. That common past was Roosevelt's mythology, as it had been Jackson, Fillmore, Pierce, Buchanan, Cleveland, and Wilson's. Acceptance of its ideological terms meant at least some inclusion into the polity; denial of those claims led to exclusion. The disciplinary project of citizenship was, for these immigrants, no longer about race; it had become one of ideology. Yet inclusion came at a price, for one could become politically visible only by adopting the identity and culture of mainstream Americans, by becoming ethnically and culturally invisible. There was a singular common future, and as president, FDR, like Wilson before him, was the one who enunciated its shape for all Americans.

Immigrants were not the only group within the New Deal's inclusive reach. Women were also largely co-opted by the New Deal, even though it incorporated and enacted "maternalist" values, which assumed both women's dependence on men and the centrality of child rearing to their lives.[45] In so doing, the New Deal reified those assumptions into law and social law.[46] In general, New Deal policies were congruent with and did little to challenge the nation's cultural politics on matters of gender. Those politics were not easy on women. Working women were the first to lose their jobs, and pressure was brought to bear on others to let men have the available work. Roosevelt, as women themselves admitted, made no special appeals to women, other than the appointment of Frances Perkins to his Cabinet, but "he saw no interests that were not their interests and by this simple act he testified to his belief that whatever has to do with the general welfare be it the problems of children, or of economics are the common concern of both men and women."[47] *Not* treating women as if their interests were special, *not* offering policies especially for them became in this analysis a strength, not a sign that women were being ignored. The rhetoric of co-option implies that a given group, in this case women, was already fully included and needed no "special" attention. They were citizens, just like everyone else. Women had become politically visible and politically powerful enough to merit the extension of the suffrage to them; they now became invisible again, vanished into the mass of citizenry.

Many groups, as this analysis showed, had become more politically visible and were in the process of vanishing again as they became incorporated into the governing coalition. Members of previously marginalized or excluded groups were now able to enter the mass citizenry, assimilate, and disappear into it. They could still enjoy cultural ethnicity—their festivals, their foods, the outer trappings of their cultures were increasingly thought to add flavor to the brew of the melting pot. But the process of melting remained important. The limited co-option these groups faced was contingent. And examples of groups still exposed to harsher discipline in the national project of creating citizens were not hard to find.

EXCLUSION

As president Roosevelt spoke more often to more groups and on a wider selection of topics than had any previous president, his silences were all the more interesting. FDR spoke to audiences constituted as economic entities, as voting blocs, and as having regional and political identities. In thus speaking, he ratified and legitimated these various identities. There were, however, clear limits. He did not, in the first two terms, speak to Asian-American groups. He did not visit American Indian reservations. He did not spend time in Hispanic communities, and he did not open the doors of the White House to African Americans. These groups remained relatively politically invisible and relatively politically powerless. Despite their contributions to his electoral coalition, they were not invited to be part of his governing coalition.

But their electoral significance did not go entirely unnoticed, and some of the conditions that would help them gain some measure of political visibility were set in motion. Unlike previous presidents, for instance, Roosevelt did not single these groups out as negative examples of citizenship, nor did he characterize them as savage, wild, and troublesome. On them, he was merely silent. Amid the plethora of words that constructed the New Deal, these people and their concerns were absent. Doubtless unintentionally, still, they were rendered less legitimate than others by their absence, literally, without a word being said.

Others found exclusion to be the flip side of co-option as a result of more positive rhetorical action on the part of the president. Through his attacks on big business, for instance, Roosevelt made it appear that he was on the workers' side. He did so at a price that would only further endear him to those workers—he incurred the wrath of business. Under Roosevelt, making money became a marker, not of virtue, but of its (as least potential) lack.[48] The business classes thus resented him for threatening to displace the order that had been ordained by Grover Cleveland and left essentially in place ever since.

Some groups were thus made to regret their political visibility, for Roosevelt would use them, in a completely undifferentiated and abstract manner, to illustrate negative points about citizenship.[49] He pointed no fingers at identifiable people or groups, but could treat his critics harshly. Groups and individuals whose self-interest did not give way to the national interest in the way and at the time Roosevelt thought that they should, for instance, were open to severe criticism, which usually took the form of ridicule or name calling.[50] In his fourth Fireside Chat he displayed his talent for such rhetoric saying, "At the bottom of most cases of criticism and obstruction we have found some selfish interest, some private ax to grind. Ninety percent of complaints come from misconception. . . . It is also true that among the chiselers to whom I have referred, there are not only big chiselers but also petty chiselers who seek to make undue profit on untrue statements."[51] His critics were thus selfish, only interested in private interests, leaving the public good to suffer, mistaken and petty at best and dishonest at worst.

Roosevelt insisted that he was open to criticism yet was hard in his responses when he was criticized. Legitimating his critics was not the Roosevelt way. He called them "modern Tories,"[52] "Doubting Thomases,"[53] most famously, perhaps, "economic royalists,"[54] and assorted other names. He used adjectives like "selfish," "unprincipled," and "cynical" to describe them. He undermined their status, he questioned their motives, and he rendered them caricatures of principled arguments, as in this example from a 1936 Florida address: "Continued growth is the only evidence that we have of life. Yet growth and progress invariably and inevitably are opposed—opposed at every step, opposed bitterly and falsely and blindly."[55] Thus described, these were not people with legitimate concerns, with honest differences on governmental and political philosophies. These were people whose every argument, however apparently plausible, had to be dismissed as unworthy of the American people's attention.

These people, however, were not part of identifiable racial, ethnic, religious, or other sorts of groups. To the extent that they had a collective identity, it was an economic class, or a set of economic interests. Roosevelt demonized most brutally only those who were already included well inside the polity. His coalition, like Andrew Jackson's, was premised on the inclusion of the previously marginalized, and those inside the polity were his political enemies, not those who remained excluded.

All of FDR's co-optive strategies, and their companion exclusion, took place within a rhetorical and ideological structure that assumed all interests were equal and that they all had an equal chance on a level playing field. This included some interests and some groups while erasing the exclusion of others. There were also other forms of exclusion, which, when put in the language of citizenship, tended to be subtle rather than overtly exclusionary. One such example was deferral, which operated in many ways like Wilson's calls for patience on the part of excluded or marginalized minorities. Wilson asked that those who were marginalized or excluded learn the parameters of appropriate citizenship and then work their way up from invisibility through differentiation and division to inclusion—which would entail a return to invisibility as the members of the group were incorporated into the polity. For FDR, the process was much the same, although it rested on slightly different assumptions. FDR was, as we have seen, less preoccupied with the elimination of ethnic identities. Roosevelt, like most presidents, assumed the inherent fairness of American democracy; he also assumed its inherent capacity for inclusion. Rather than arguing that groups needed to exercise patience while they readied themselves for inclusion, he argued that everyone was already included. The demands of some interests simply had to wait a bit before being fulfilled. In his role as presidential broker, FDR argued that all demands would be met as soon as they reached the top of the national agenda. Because no one interest was favored, no one should complain when they were simply being deferred rather than denied. When everyone played by the same set of rules, it was only reasonable to ask that all players wait their turn.

DEFERRAL

Roosevelt's nation was ostensibly equal but implicitly hierarchical. At any given moment, the claims of some groups were considered more vital to the national interest than were those of others. Because Roosevelt understood the task of balancing these interests as a process, some claims had to be deferred until they were on the verge of erupting and disturbing the balance or until such time as their fulfillment was identical with that national balance. This meant that at any given moment Roosevelt was occupied with deferring some group claims and group demands. Deferral of demands reinforced democratic ideologies of fairness and majority rule. It relied on the assumption that all players had equal access to equal resources and the belief that they would be given approximately equal opportunities to avail themselves of those resources and opportunities. Often, these assumptions were not borne out politically no matter how useful they were rhetorically, but that undermined only the tactic's accuracy, not its ideological power. Unlike co-option, which presupposed complete inclusion, deferral offered a group political legitimacy but asked for patience concerning the fulfillment of their political goals. The group demands were explicitly laid against the system's stability, and the group was asked to defer their goals in the interest of maintaining that stability. FDR's use of deferral as a potentially inclusive yet also exclusionary tactic was amply demonstrated by the New Deal experiences of many African Americans.

FDR's relationship with and attitude toward African Americans was constrained and dominated by his political dependence on the "Solid South" and thus on the white supremacist ideology that controlled politics there. The South was vitally important to FDR's electoral success. It was also therefore a powerful constraint on his political agenda.[56] Keeping the loyalty of the South was integral to FDR's continued political viability,[57] especially given the power of Republicans in the Northeast and the fickle nature of the Progressive coalition in the West.[58] The importance of this relationship did not mean that it was always a smooth one. The need for federal dollars in the South collided with fear of federal power—especially in the area of civil rights,[59] and the alliance was an uneasy one at best.

At least as far as civil rights were concerned, white supremacists—either Northern or Southern—had little to fear from FDR.[60]

He refused to support antilynching legislation, refused to meet with the International Labor Defense about Scottsboro, and refused in general to put any of his political muscle behind any issues that could be associated with civil rights in a political sense, counseling patience instead of providing action. Roosevelt saw economic issues as central; social and political questions were secondary. This was particularly true on issues involving race.[61] In fact, the Roosevelt administration would have been in clear philosophical agreement with Ralph Bunche when he declared that "the so-called Negro problem in America is only incidentally a racial one. Many of its roots go deeper than race and are themselves embedded in the fundamental problems of economic conflict and distress which afflict the entire society."[62] Like members of other groups, blacks were considered only to the extent that their problems fit into the New Deal economic framework. "Social" problems like segregation and lynching were not the president's concern. At least one analyst, for instance, argued that the influence of the South created a welfare state as a structure designed to support claims of entitlement by whites rather than becoming a legitimately inclusive system based on need, such as FDR would have preferred.[63] This stress on economic definitions of group problems legitimated African Americans and their demands—they were poor, and poverty was the issue—while postponing the fulfillment of those legitimate demands.

Civil rights policies during the New Deal need to be understood as economic policies. The two were one and the same, an identification that muted the racial elements of nationalism during these years.[64] Civil rights issues that were not amenable to economic solutions were off the Roosevelt agenda. Although limiting in some respects, this was still important. There was good evidence that the Depression was particularly hard on blacks, as was most famously documented in detail by Gunnar Myrdal.[65] Racial justice would have been important; economic help kept people from starving. And although the two were not mutually exclusive, Roosevelt acted as though they were. Blacks were visible enough to merit some attention from government but not so visible that they would have specific programs dedicated to their economic interests.

Unlike his wife, Roosevelt was very much a (white) person of his time on racial matters. He followed segregationist practices in his own administration—members of the black press, for instance, began requesting permission to attend White House press conferences as early as 1933, yet the color line remained unbroken for eleven years.[66] He also took no public position on the Scottsboro case, arguably the most important racial case of his early administration. Roosevelt wanted African-American support, but any symbolic or material gain that he offered to them threatened his support among white Southerners, the bedrock of the national Democratic party. He would not be the last president to find himself in this particular dilemma, as the white South would exercise a disproportionate influence on national policies concerning race and civil rights throughout the twentieth century.

In keeping with the history of presidential rhetoric as well as the temper of his times, Roosevelt's rhetoric concerning African Americans was paternalistic at best. He congratulated African Americans on the progress they had made in the previous seventy years on the anniversary of the Emancipation Proclamation but neglected to congratulate the nation for the progress it had made. Thus, intentionally or not, he separated "Negroes" and "the nation" through his silence, again demonstrating the exclusionary capacity of rhetoric meant to be inclusive.[67] Like Wilson, Roosevelt implied that "the nation" was a complete entity and that those who would be part of it had to do the hard work of making citizens of themselves. Because the country was no longer primarily an agricultural nation, potential citizens were no longer able to learn the lessons of citizenship from the land; yet those lessons still had to be learned, and participation would be deferred pending that learning.

Seeing the advances that African Americans had made in both political visibility and political power, Roosevelt was hopeful that "they" would continue the good work of progress, noting in 1935 that "it is truly remarkable, the things which the Negro people have accomplished within living memory. . . . It is my hope and belief that the Negro, inspired by the achievements of the race to date, will go forward to even greater things in the years to come."[68] Such an understanding was based on the very real improvements for African Americans. Yet it also tended to erase the differences between them and their white fellow citizens, and naturalized the lower place of blacks in the national hierarchy. African Americans still had far to go, it was clear, before they could participate fully as "real" Americans.

In another example of the same dynamic, Roosevelt was similarly pleased to congratulate blacks on their progress as a race (again rather than discussing the issue of racial progress in the United States) and referred to them as integral to the nation in his yearly greetings to the National Association for the Advancement of Colored People (NAACP), but also reminded them of their obligations: "As an integral group in our American democracy we look to you to uphold its ideals, to help carry its burdens, and to partake of its blessings."[69] There was considerably more upholding and carrying during these years than there was partaking. As with many groups having attained some visibility and some political power, blacks were still being disciplined, reminded that citizenship was a privilege and that it brought with it obligations. These obligations had to be accepted before the granting of full citizenship.

If pressed, as he was at one press conference, FDR would talk about race relations, but in the most positive ways he could, accurately noting that things had indeed improved. He said, for instance, that there was more racial tolerance in the nation than "ten or twenty years ago. I think, in other words, that it would be harder to start a movement based on racial intolerance today than it would have been ten or twenty years ago. I still think it can be done. It is always a possibility, but I think we are wiser and there is less sectionalism. I think we have learned a lot."[70] In other words, racial matters were largely Southern matters, and as Southerners became more like the rest of the nation, the problems currently associated with the South would disappear. Of course, lynching, Klan membership, and racism were not limited to the South, but to the extent that it could be understood as a "sectional" problem, it could be contained rhetorically. Arguing that there is "less sectionalism" clearly made racism sectional and disciplined white Southerners while also claiming that the nation as a whole was headed in the right direction. White Southerners, also subject to national discipline, would be more fully American as they relieved themselves of the burdens of their racism. Both blacks and white Southerners had work to do before they were fully admitted into the polity.

In addition, by speaking positively on racial matters, Roosevelt redirected the issue. By not speaking about the problems of African Americans in the North, he erased them and left Northern blacks voiceless. In another example of such redirection, when he spoke at Tuskegee, for instance, he neglected to mention civil rights at all.[71]

Consistent with his task of preserving the national order, Roosevelt, like most presidents, argued for incremental rather than dramatic change whenever possible. Blacks were to some degree politically visible. They were also politically problematic, and as such, were subject to differentiation, division, and erasure. "Negroes" became "Southerners," and the racism and segregation that they faced in the Northern cities became subordinated to their image as rural Southerners. By making all blacks the same, difference was both reinforced, for urban blacks were encouraged ideologically to despise their Southern counterparts, and erased, for Northern blacks became invisible politically even as—perhaps partially because—they were beginning to feel some political power.

Still, the political gains were real, if limited. FDR forbade discrimination in New Deal programs, but most of them were designed to allow so much administrative latitude that de facto discrimination often went unreported if not unnoticed.[72] He also formed an important ex officio body, which became known as the "Black Cabinet." The Black Cabinet brought African Americans into the administration, gave them some voice in racial policy, and demonstrated to all African Americans that their interests were taken seriously. Even here, it is worth noting that there was no minority representation in the actual Cabinet, and the influence of Black Cabinet "secretaries" was largely if not exclusively confined to explicitly racial policy. Because they could expect at least some economic gain from the New Deal, and because their options were so very limited, it made sense for African Americans to support the New Deal despite the deferral of many of their important interests.[73] Their limited political visibility and political power could garner them only so much in terms of policy.

In the case of African Americans, who had limited political visibility, deferral could operate in a less than subtle fashion. Other groups, who had more political visibility and less of the onus of racism, posed a slightly different problem, although in both cases, the rationale for deferral rested on the same ideological ground: the system was inherently fair, and if groups were willing to wait their turn, they would be accommodated. "Fairness" thus became a powerful ideological tool in defending the practices of deferral.

Roosevelt was able to defer African Americans' demands rather brusquely, and he reserved claims to fairness for the more politically visible and economically powerful groups. In his fourth Fireside Chat, for example, he said,

> In every step which your Government is taking we are think-ing in terms of the average of you—in the old words, "the greatest good for the greatest number"—we, as reasonable people, cannot expect to bring definite benefits to every per-son or to every occupation or business, or industry or agri-culture. In the same way no reasonable person can expect that in this short space of time . . . that every locality in every one of the forty-eight States of the country, could share equally and simultaneously in the trend to better times. The whole picture however—the average of the whole territory from coast to coast . . . shows to any person willing to look, facts and action of which you and I can be proud.[74]

As with Cleveland's argument that each part profited only when the whole profited and that the profit of one part was identical to the profit of the other parts, and in Wilson's request for patience based on every group's responsibility to respect the whole, in this case, FDR argued that "reasonable" people would subordinate their imme-diate claims to the nation's long-term interest. This is precisely how deferral operates—legitimating the group, but postponing fulfillment of their goals in favor of maintaining systemic stability. "Fairness" was thus about the entire country and about a process that looked at the country holistically. Ideologically, the emphasis on "the aver-age" worked to render the default "American" identity equivalent to the "average" American—the white, middle-class male American. Deviations from that norm, deviations from the "average," were deviations that meant marginalization, whether or not it was intend-ed to do so.

Like Cleveland's speech that urged a national organic unity and Wilson's rhetoric that rendered all Americans identical and identi-fied, this language did important ideological work in the creation of national unity. By focusing on the nation as a whole, FDR encour-aged the developing sense of national identity. By stressing the fair-ness of the national system, he encouraged loyalty to it on both self-interested grounds and because of shared belief in key values (fair-ness) best rendered at the national level. This understanding of national identity served both the needs of nation building and regime maintenance during times of massive economic dislocation.

FDR got considerable mileage from this rhetoric, although he could also modify it on occasion. For Roosevelt, fairness could be about outcome as well as about process, where outcome was defined as social or economic justice, giving to citizens what they most needed. In his 1937 annual message, he said, "It is not enough that the wheels turn. They must carry us in the direction of a greater satisfaction in life for the average man. The deeper purpose of democratic government is to assist as many of its citizens as possible, especially those who need it most, to improve their conditions of life, to retain all personal liberty which does not adversely affect their neighbors, and to pursue the happiness which comes with security and an opportunity for recreation and culture."[75] Note the nationalizing function of such rhetoric, which united the nation in the interests of the "average man" and "as many of its citizens as possible." The constraints and limits on possibility were not made clear but needed no underlining as the Depression lingered. The government would do what it could for as many people as it could. If you were one of those still suffering, at least you shared the knowledge that the government was doing all it could.

"Need" here was defined as opportunity, not as result, and was defined as a matter of group benefit, not individual assistance. Speaking to state directors of the National Emergency Council in 1934, Roosevelt said, "We know the human factor which enters so largely into this picture. We are trying to apply it to all groups needing aid and assistance and not merely to just a few scattered or favored groups."[76] The government assumed the obligation for helping its citizens, at least in the mass. Individual and group-based exceptions were erased. The rhetoric of citizenship held more subtle exclusions than had the rhetoric of balance.

This reliance on group identification and numerical criteria worked to his ideological advantage, for he could restrict access to the system and thus ensure balance while touting the system's essential fairness (in which he deeply believed). Over time, all legitimate needs would be satisfied, all reasonable demands met. The task he faced more urgently was to procure the necessary amount of time for the system to do its work. To procure that time, he had to create a specific sort of citizen, one who was willing to wait his or her turn, who would moderate demands on the system and support that system consistently until it had the time to accommodate all reasonable demands. Through the ideological appeal of such rhetoric, FDR rendered a dynamic union also a stable one.

In explaining his approach to governing, in 1938 he said, "We are engaged, today, as you know—not just the Government in Washington, but groups of citizens everywhere—in reviewing all kinds of human relationships, and in making those reviews we are asking an old question in a new form. We are saying, 'Is this practice, is this custom, something which is being done at the expense of the many?' And the many are the neighbors. In a national sense the many, the neighbors, are the people of the United States as a whole. Nationally, we must think of them as a whole and not just by sections or by States."[77] He relied on "an old question" in making this argument—that is, he claimed to be using an old standard, not changing the standard, itself a powerful appeal to stability. But in using the national, not the sectional or regional standard, he was reinforcing a Wilsonian sense of nationality, one that was based not on primarily local allegiances and identities, but on national, "American" ones. By using the standard of "the average" and "the whole," Roosevelt was able to claim success as a result of his plans for recovery and to mitigate criticism that those plans had not been effective enough. Those who were still waiting their turn at least had the solace of knowing that their patience was contributing to the national interest.

Here, Roosevelt combined a dynamic, nationally oriented union, such as the one favored by Andrew Jackson, with the more staid, temperate unions of the 1850s and 1880s. Given the depth and intensity of the national crisis, Roosevelt could not favor stasis, even if he was so disposed. Action, activity, movement, and growth were more amenable to him personally and to the political requirements of his time as well. This dynamism allowed him to speak in terms of growth and movement and change, thus involving even those who economic lives were stagnant in a sense of motivating purpose. Deferral allowed him to accommodate those he could without overtly excluding others.

But those exclusions were there. The underprivileged were not the only ones whose interests were deferred. Those whom FDR considered "overprivileged" were also likely to be placed on the national waiting list.[78] Roosevelt, as has often been noted, had something of a cyclical understanding of history, in which the preferences of the many alternated with the demands of the elite.[79] For some of his critics, this view led to rhetoric and policy that were tantamount to class warfare.[80] The rhetoric could indeed be pretty extreme. In one instance, Roosevelt likened himself to one of his heroes, Andrew Jackson:

> I need not describe the dismay that the election of Jackson excited—and honestly excited—in the hearts of the hitherto elect, or the widespread apprehension that it aroused among the so-called guardian groups of the Republic. Groups such as those have never fully disappeared from American political life, but it will never be possible for any length of time for any group of the American people, either by reason of wealth or learning or economic power, to retain any mandate, any permanent authority to arrogate to itself the political control of American life. This heritage, my friends, we owe to Jacksonian democracy—the American doctrine that entrusts the general welfare to no one group or class, but dedicates itself to the end that the American people shall not be thwarted in their high purpose to remain the custodians of their own destiny.[81]

Roosevelt here used Jackson as the same sort of ideological warrant that Jackson had found in Jefferson's example. He selectively interpreted the past to legitimate the ideological premises and political policies of the present. Jackson here became the hero of inclusion, who opened the doors of the polity wide and thus spoke for everyone. The important historical context was lost—the specific and limited definition of who got included as part of "everyone" was subsumed into the notion that inclusion in this historical moment was implied in the more limited inclusion of the past. This sort of historical simplification did important ideological work for Roosevelt as it does today, establishing the nation on a trajectory of increased democratization and erasing the more exclusionary aspects or rendering them irrelevant in the more important context of increased inclusion.

This quotation revealed other important themes as well, especially for the creation of a specific model of "good" citizenship. In contrast to the "overprivileged" stood the "good neighbor," a concept FDR first applied to foreign policy and then applied to domestic policy as well. The good neighbor was not only able but willing to accept temporary sacrifice on behalf of his fellow citizens, because, "a democracy, the right kind of democracy, is bound together by the ties of neighborliness."[82] This was union based not on organic unity or ideological identification but on neighborliness—on a nationwide web of geographical communities of free peoples voluntarily associated with one another. Good citizens were good neighbors. The good neighbor recognized that "the herculean task of the United States government today is to take care that its citizens have the necessities of life. We are seeking honestly and honorably to do this, irrespective of class or group."[83] Good neighborhoods relied on equal access to "the necessities of life." There could be no special privilege if all groups were to be equal partners in the national democracy. All groups, according to this pluralist model, were equally politically visible, equally politically powerful. Because this rhetoric singled out no one group or set of groups, in keeping with the language of citizenship, it also appeared inclusive. But because it also erased the very real differences among groups, it also reinforced and naturalized existing hierarchies.

Roosevelt also argued that war—both in terms of the actual European war and the metaphorical war on the Depression—required unity, and all "true" Americans would be willing to put their own personal and petty self-interest temporarily aside in the interest of the greater good.[84] Early in his first term he said, "It is a mistake to assume that the virtues of war differ essentially from the virtues of peace. All life is a battle against the forces of nature, against the mistakes and human limitations of man, against the forces of selfishness and inertia, of laziness and fear. These are the enemies with whom we never conclude an armistice."[85] Roosevelt thus assumed that all life was a battle and that Americans were united in waging war against "the forces of nature, against the mistakes and human limitations of man," against the forces of "selfishness and inertia, of laziness and fear." In that unity, there would be no differentiation. By denying difference, Roosevelt both included and subtly excluded.

Wars demanded a specific kind of unity, and FDR was neither

slow nor shy in calling for national unity in the face of the national crises, unity based on the principles and practices of war. As he said in his first inaugural,

> If I read the temper of our people correctly, we now realize as we have never realized before our interdependence on each other; that we cannot merely take but must give as well; that if we are to go forward, we must move as a trained and loyal army willing to sacrifice for the good of a common discipline, because without such discipline no progress is made, no leadership becomes effective. We are, I know, ready and willing to submit our lives and property to such discipline, because it makes possible a leadership which aims at a larger good.[86]

The nation was not only united but also interdependent. As with Cleveland's claim to organic unity and Wilson's argument in favor of national ideological sameness, this was the inclusive language of civic nationalism. As with all uses of the war metaphor, it was also language that overtly called for discipline and national unity. Intolerant of difference, exception, and disagreement, any such calls also were exclusionary. The call was for submission to his vision of the national good as much as it was for inclusion. Inclusion was predicated on submission.

In summoning war rhetoric, Roosevelt also underlined his premise that the "enemy" was fear, and the correct response was therefore "courage." Much as Jackson's dynamic union was premised on the actions of adventurous pioneers, Roosevelt constituted his dynamic union on the basis of courageous and united citizens, submissive to the disciplines of war. It also meant that people needed to expect some level of deprivation to continue until the battle against the economic crisis had met with "unconditional surrender." Group demands that could not be co-opted or excluded were therefore likely to be deferred. Such deferral was justified by the discipline required by war and the implication that all needs would eventually be met in this protracted situation. Those who were politically visible were likely to be moved to the top of the priority list; those who were not visible were deferred.

Sounding more like Cleveland with his stress on organic unity than Wilson with his sense of identification among all Americans, Roosevelt's claim that some groups had to have their demands temporarily denied was based on the interdependence of all groups and the need to find balance among them. Rather than opposing "the many" to "the few," to deny the legitimacy of some claims, this argument fragmented "the many" and through amplification complicated any one group's claims. By pressing their claims too hard, even "the many" could cause the structures of recovery and reform to lose their delicate balance. In forcing that imbalance, "the many" became as destructive of order and progress as "the few." He cataloged those who would force such an imbalance in 1933: "There are the perfectly natural problems of selfish individuals . . . there are hot-heads . . . there are insidious voices seeking to instill methods or principles which are wholly foreign to the American form of democratic government," there are employers who "shudder at anything new. . . . who think in terms of cents instead of human lives."[87] No matter what the motivation or need, any imbalance was dangerous to the system as a whole and could not be tolerated.

It was not, perhaps, surprising that those who were most often asked to defer their demands were those groups that lacked numbers, organization, or resources—it was, in fact, generally those groups that lay most often at the bottom of the national hierarchy. Fluid as that hierarchy may have been at its upper reaches, the ordering of groups at the bottom remained more consistent than not. In this period as in others, political visibility was associated with political power. Previously excluded or marginalized groups were subject to deferral as they were subject to differentiation or erasure.

Still, more and more groups were increasingly politically visible. Because FDR treated them as economic rather than as racial-, ethnic-, or gender-based identities, members of these groups were both enabled in their movement toward increased viability and impeded in that movement. They were enabled because they were free of overt stigmatizing at the hands of the president. He rarely used specific groups as negative examples of citizenship and focused on behavior rather than ethnicity or race as a justification for deferral or exclusion. But they were also impeded. Refusal to recognize the key interests of ethnic and racial groups rendered those interests less visible politically, and members of those groups became subject to other, more subtle forms of exclusion.

DEFLECTION

Some groups lacked even the ability to get their demands on the presidential agenda long enough to be deferred. These tended to be the smallest and weakest of the competing groups, those least likely to be able to upset the national social order through protest or disruption, or those whose demands, were they to be acted on, would unbalance that order. The less politically visible a group was, the more likely it was to lack political power, and the more likely its members were part of the electoral but not governing coalition. They were thus more subject to the national discipline. Groups that were important enough to merit some symbolic attention but not important enough to merit deferral—not politically visible or powerful enough to get their demands, however tentatively, on the national agenda—were often subject to deflection. Deflection did important ideological work, as in its relatively subtle exclusions it also overtly maintained the appearance of a fair and just system. The rhetoric of deflection operated to legitimate the existence of a given group but not that group's political demands. To the extent that the group had legitimacy in fact, that legitimacy was based on erasing any political demands. Deflection thus implicitly acknowledged a group's burgeoning political visibility without also recognizing its right to make demands on the political system.

Groups whose demands created unbearable or unacceptable tensions for FDR's governing coalition often found those demands deflected onto the person of his wife.[88] So important was Eleanor Roosevelt that Alice Longworth Roosevelt called FDR "two-thirds mush and one-third Eleanor."[89] It was a long way, however, from Eleanor's ear to the president's desk. More than one group left the White House feeling as if their concerns had been heard; that feeling would be the only result of their time there.

FDR deflected still other concerns onto the executive bureaucracy. In 1933, for example, he appointed reformer John Collier as Commissioner of Indian Affairs, giving him broad discretion in designing and administering policy.[90] Collier, long an activist on American Indian issues, was so progressive that he could forthrightly state that "we find the Indians, in all the basic forces and forms of life, human beings like ourselves."[91] Reflective of general attitudes toward American Indians in the 1930s, Collier's policy was more enlightened than such quotations appeared. He was strongly influenced by the ideas published in 1928 as the Merriam Report. The report, widely circulated, argued that "the economic base of traditional culture had been destroyed by the encroaching white civilization."[92] Collier thus reasoned that the key to economic revitalization in Indian Country was cultural revitalization. American Indians, previously encouraged to assimilate and become culturally invisible, were now encouraged to use their cultural distinctiveness as a commodity through which they could become members of the national economy and thus members of the nation.

To that end, Collier and his allies advocated the 1934 Wheeler-Howard Act, also called the Indian Reorganization Act (IRA) and the Indian New Deal.[93] Its most important elements were the return of "surplus" American Indian land and the ending of the policy of allotment in severalty, both of which helped to end the erosion of the American Indian land base.[94] The IRA also provided for the establishment of tribal governments. Collier shifted educational policy away from culturally disruptive boarding schools to a policy of day schooling, allowing American Indian children to remain at home. The goal was still assimilation, but the assault on American Indian culture was at least slightly abated.[95] American Indian peoples were partially politically visible and were, as ever, defined as politically problematic. The goal of governmental policies remained American Indian invisibility through absorption into the "American" polity.

These policies were intended to help reestablish American Indian cultures, but toward nontraditional ends. Cultures were revived not for intrinsic reasons but for profit. American Indian cultures, in the material forms of basketry, ceramics, rugs, and so on, as well as dance and religion, were commodified by governmental policies. The selling of culture in itself created issues concerning authenticity and cultural appropriation that remain important today.[96] It is not clear that what was revived for non–American Indian consumption was more than tangentially related to the cultures as they had existed before the devastation of previous governmental policies. The notion that culture had commercial value was an idea that did much to undermine the integrity of the cultures thus commodified and retailed.

American Indian nations were not able to revive traditional governmental forms under the IRA—the IRA was intended to facilitate assimilation, not to preserve American Indian differences. Rather than restoring their indigenous forms of government, American Indians were instead required to meet the expectations of national policymakers, which meant that the new American Indian constitutions strongly resembled those of the various states and the federal government, and sat uneasily with indigenous traditions.[97] The problems set in motion by the tensions between traditional forms and tribal governments under the IRA became some of the most contentious in contemporary history.[98]

For Roosevelt, who lacked Collier's zeal and interest in American Indians if not his paternalism toward them, American Indians were all but invisible. He spoke of them only in a particular ideological context, and to them not at all. In his only national statement on American Indians, made endorsing the Wheeler-Howard bill, his paternalism was clear: "We can and should, without further delay, extend to the Indian the fundamental rights of political liberty and local self-government and the opportunities of education and economic assistance that they require in order to attain a wholesome American life. This is but the obligation of honor of a powerful Nation toward a people living among us and dependent upon our protection."[99] Note the use of the singular: "the Indian." All American Indians were subsumed into one category, all differences among them rendered politically invisible. The more invisible they were at any given moment, the more they were subject to such rhetorical erasure.

From Roosevelt's rhetorical treatment of American Indians here, it would be hard to know that they were U.S. citizens and had been since the 1920s. They were, to him, still "foreign," although weak and dependent. For Roosevelt, the government had to assume the burden of its wards. After that statement, they vanished as the subject of presidential concern and reappeared only as characters in his story of American history. They lacked the numbers, organizational skill, and resources to be among the groups whose interests were brokered in Washington. Like members of other disenfranchised groups, American Indians' interests were deflected and they themselves were silenced and rendered invisible.

Invisible they may have been; patronized they certainly were. But these were not outcomes caused by malice or genocidal ambitions. Quite the reverse. They were outcomes all but mandated by the New

Deal's ideological emphasis on the economy. During these years, at least, for Roosevelt, pleas for social justice were identical to pleas for economic justice. Economic equality was the bedrock on which political equality was built, and was the foundation, as such, for social equality as well. Having done what he could for American Indian economic development and political advancement, Roosevelt was uninterested in them. They were neither part of his governing nor his electoral coalition, and he had no incentive to formulate further policy on their behalf.

As the example of American Indians indicated, groups that lacked political visibility were likely to be subject to further exclusion. He did a great deal to assist those who were marginally visible—immigrants from Europe, labor, and the poor being the most obvious examples. He also legitimated to some degree the demands of those who continued at the margins of visibility, mainly those who were defined as groups based on their economic interests. But for those whose important definitions were racial or ethnic—Jews, African Americans, and American Indians—Roosevelt did little. Under his administration they saw some signs of economic improvement, but little in the way of social acceptance. Such social acceptance was not, in Roosevelt's eyes, part of the New Deal. He did a great deal to advance the tenets of civic nationalism, but those efforts were complicated by the still powerful ideological undercurrents of racial nationalism, still strong and largely unquestioned.

THE LANGUAGE OF COMMUNITY

Within this ideological context, two prominent themes in Roosevelt's rhetoric revealed his definition of the polity—and indirectly, who was to be included within it and excluded from it. The themes of religion and its place in the world and of the pioneers and their place in American history melded into an ideological premise that justified both Roosevelt's position as interpreter for the polity and his definition of the right sort of citizen for that polity. Largely inclusive, they also resulted in the exclusion of some groups from that polity.

Roosevelt's Religion

When questioned about his personal ideology, Roosevelt famously responded, "I am a Christian and a Democrat. That is all."[100] He certainly stressed the values and importance of Christianity in the national history: "We cannot read the history of our rise and development as a Nation, without reckoning with the place the Bible has occupied in shaping the advances of the Republic. Its teaching, as has been widely suggested, is ploughed into the very heart of the race."[101] For Roosevelt, as for most presidents, the United States was predominantly a Christian nation, built on the foundation of belief in a Christian God. And for Roosevelt as for Wilson before him, this inclusive language was also exclusionary, erasing as it did the contributions and the presence of non-Christians.

Roosevelt believed that shared spiritual values assisted in community stability and thus social stability. Speaking extemporaneously at a Hyde Park church in 1933, Roosevelt said, "It is not only the spirit of these times, but it seems to me that it is fundamentally a matter of common sense, that in our religious worship we should work together instead of flying off on different tangents and different angles, pulling apart instead of pulling together as a unified whole. During these latter years there has been a splendid change for the better in this regard."[102] Religion was thus intrinsically useful in terms of one's individual soul, and socially useful as a unifying force.[103] By constructing "good" citizens as religious, Roosevelt used citizenship to serve the national balance and promote national stability.

Roosevelt also used Christianity to legitimate his own policy preferences. Greeting a group of visiting ministers in 1938, he defined his policies thus: "We call what we have been doing 'human security' and 'social justice.' In the last analysis all of these terms can be described by one word, and that is Christianity."[104] By labeling his policies Christianity in action, Roosevelt both reinforced the Christian nature of his polity and legitimated those policies—criticizing the policies became at least potentially an unchristian act. The polity and the policies reinforced and supported one another in rhetoric that both included and excluded.

In another example, Roosevelt stressed the moral value of work as a way to get some groups to defer their own demands. In a 1937 radio address he argued that unemployment was not evidence of moral failure but a sign of the need for national compassion and assistance: "There is danger that we may be blinded by the welcome light of returning prosperity to the very real need that still exists for a considerable part of our population. We must not forget that there are people who are still hungry, their children under-nourished; that rags are the clothing of many of our countrymen and miserable shacks or crowded city tenements their only home."[105] Roosevelt was asking those who had been helped by his policies to remember those still in need of help; he was asking them to behave as good religious citizens.

Unemployment was not a sign of poor moral character.[106] The absence of work was, however, deleterious to one's morals. As he said to the Civilian Works Administration Conference in 1933, "When any man or woman goes on a dole, something happens to them mentally, and the quicker they are taken off the dole the better it is for them for the rest of their lives."[107] To maintain a moral citizenry, Roosevelt had to maintain a working citizenry. As it had been at least since Grover Cleveland's time, good workers were good citizens and good citizens were good workers. The two were ideologically connected, and their relationship assumed, not cause for debate. As land had once taught the lessons of citizenship, now work, generically defined, would fulfill that ideological function. Work thus had benefits for body as well as soul, for the individual as well as the community. Although necessary, relief benefited no one; work benefited everyone and provided spiritual solace and community security.

Roosevelt's Pioneer

Roosevelt personified this conception of the individual within the community in the image of the pioneer. One of his favorite analogies, it probably appeared more often than any other during these years.[108] For Roosevelt, it not only harkened back to Jefferson and Jackson, but also accomplished for him some of the political work that the frontier myth had been doing since the 1800s in terms of justifying and legitimating ideas about the nature of the polity and its citizens. In a 1934 address in Green Bay, Wisconsin, for example, he said, "Yes, we are but carrying forward the fundamentals behind the pioneering spirit of the fathers when we apply the pioneering methods to the better use of cast land and water resources—what God has given to us to use as trustees not only for ourselves but for future generations."[109] "God," "the fathers," and the pioneers thus nicely melded together in one seamless version of national history. The "empty" continent was given to Americans by God. Americans proved worthy of it through brave efforts to conquer the "wilderness" and spread civilization. All those who participated in this were equally included members of a society that faced different challenges with the same spirit—the spirit of the pioneer. As Wilson had made all members of his polity the ideological heirs of the founders, so too did Roosevelt make all Americans, recent immigrant or not, the ideological heirs of the pioneers. The pioneer myth melded and meshed with the immigrant myth and the notion of the national melting pot so that all Americans, regardless of their national origin, were united as the heirs of the founders and the pioneers. All Americans became archetypal Americans.[110]

Like previous presidents, Roosevelt had a particular ideological understanding of the frontier and the pioneers who inhabited it. Roosevelt's pioneer was not, as Jackson's had been, a recalcitrant individualist. Roosevelt's pioneers, like the citizens of Roosevelt's polity, were interdependent. They held to the essential values of neighborliness and community spirit. As he said in an address at Washington College in 1933, "It is true that the pioneer was an individualist; but, at the same time, there was in the pioneer a spirit of cooperation and understanding of the need of building up, not a class, but a whole community. It was that spirit that made possible these United States themselves, and it is the understanding of that spirit which made our first president's name revered above that of any other American in our history."[111] Rather than the staid and quiet yeoman farmer of Jefferson, recalled as well in the 1850s, Roosevelt's pioneer was, like Jackson's adventurous backwoodsman, the hero of a dynamic union. But that union was built not by individual initiative alone, but by individual initiative backed by the solid cooperation of neighborliness. Roosevelt invoked individual self-reliance combined with compassionate communitarianism. He evoked the existing understanding of the frontier myth in the service of his new understanding of the dynamic union of his own day.

Roosevelt seemingly never tired of drawing parallels between the experiences of the pioneers and those of the Americans caught in the economic crisis. The same uniquely American virtues were required from both sets of citizens.[112] In 1935, in Fremont, Nebraska, he said, "We all know the heroic story of the pioneers. We know the hardships and the troubles that they suffered. If ever we need a national demonstration that the pioneering spirit that originally settled this country still lives, unshaken and undiminished, the farmers of

America have proved it in the years through which we have just passed. I well realize the suffering and the desolation of those years. I know the faith and hope, the patience and courage you have shown. For this I applaud you; for this I extend the thanks of the Nation to the farmers of the Nation."[113] Roosevelt here combined Jefferson's yeoman farmer with Jackson's adventurous pioneer. Both embodied endurance, courage, and dedication to the task of nation building. Both suffered but through their suffering created the nation. They both embodied the spirit of American pioneers and were thus valuable models of citizenship for all Americans; indeed they had become all Americans, or rather, through their privation and Roosevelt's rhetoric, all Americans had become them.

On the surface, this rhetoric could not be more inclusive. These virtues were not, however, inclusive of all Americans. In dedicating a national park on, ironically enough, what was once American Indian land, Roosevelt once again invoked the pioneer:

> Today we no longer face Indians and hard and lonely struggles with nature—but today we have grown soft in many ways. If we are to survive, we cannot be soft in a world in which there are dangers that threaten Americans—dangers far more deadly than were those the frontiersmen had to face. . . . The arrow, the tomahawk, and the scalping knife have been replaced by the airplane, the tank, and the machine gun. Their threat is as close to us today as was the threat to the frontiersman when hostile Indians were lurking on the other side of the gap.[114]

Although this rhetoric served to unite those Americans who could see themselves, however improbably, as the heirs of the pioneers, this version of our national history underlined the political invisibility of American Indians as contemporary American citizens. They surely were not immigrants. They certainly did not participate as willing partners in the settlement of the West. Indeed, in this formulation, they were a prime cause that the settlement was as dangerous as it was.

One result of the widespread acceptance of this myth was that American Indians lost their place as actual three-dimensional persons worthy of presidential attention. They henceforth became historical caricatures, supporting an ideology based on the settlement of the frontier without being allowed real participation. The experience of the immigrant pioneer became flattened and homogenized in FDR's narrative. Similarly, the experiences of American Indians became flattened as well. They were no longer actors on the historical stage, so they were rendered into props instead.[115] American Indians were consigned to political invisibility in presidential pubic rhetoric, from whence they would only occasionally resurface.

The pioneering metaphor was ideologically potent, especially when combined with religious overtones, as was the case in Roosevelt's rhetoric. In telling "the" story of the immigrant who became the pioneer, Roosevelt told "the" story of America—he erased its violence, acquisitiveness, and exclusion, and rendered American history as powerfully democratic and powerfully inclusive.[116]

Just as the civil service proved a workable model of democracy for Cleveland, the neighborly and communitarian frontier summarized a good bit of Roosevelt's rhetoric on issues of national diversity. All Americans became the ideological heirs of the pioneers; they all shared the same story. Much as the founders presumed all Americans to be culturally homogeneous, and Wilson sought to create national ideological identification, Roosevelt took the great cultural heterogeneity of America in the 1930s and rendered it culturally and ideologically singular. Powerfully inclusive, this also had some exclusionary overtones, as those who were erased from this shared national history were those who were still considered to be inadequate citizens on racial grounds. Civic nationalism had made great headway; it was supported, however, by sustained, racially based exclusions and ascriptive hierarchies.

Conclusion

For Roosevelt, the fact of national economic interdependence was the key to national unity. Americans were united because the actions of one American affected all Americans. Citizens were seen collectively as members of economically defined groups. Those groups were legitimate sources of self-identification. Their places in society were roughly equal and equally deserving of celebration, so long as the proper balances among them were respected and maintained. For

Roosevelt, democracy was about the entire nation, not about a single part of it, and it was about the long term. Rhetorically, he considered any group by definition motivated primarily by short-term interests, and those interests could be accommodated, co-opted, excluded, deferred, deflected, or sacrificed as the occasion demanded. The president, with his national perspective, was the broker who mediated group demands, a task that required constant, delicate adjustment.

Because only the president could determine the relative legitimacy of any group's interest at any given moment, group membership was considered more inherently allowable than were group demands for economic benefit or social, political, or economic power. Roosevelt's claim to be concerned with "social justice," however honestly offered, was also disarming—it was just true enough to provide evidence for the claim that it was always true. For reasons that had as much to do with political possibility as with personal preference, Roosevelt was a great deal more concerned with discrimination in hiring and its effect on the national economy than he was with lynching or Jim Crow laws. Yet he did offer members of previously disenfranchised and excluded groups both economic benefits and the promise of full inclusion.

But when social justice was defined as economic well-being, something important was overlooked, for community life was not reducible to economics. And when the president, charged with nation building and maintenance and thus the spokesperson for the nation's hierarchical structures, became the definer of when that justice was achieved, definitional power was far removed from the underprivileged, rendering them voiceless and invisible, objects of governmental attention, not participants in government.

Earlier presidents argued paternalistically from their position atop the national hierarchy and were spokesmen for the benefits of those hierarchies. Roosevelt assumed a position as spokesman for those whose place was at the bottom of the national hierarchy, in an ideological move that placed the "common man" atop the rhetorical order while leaving the political, social, and economic orders largely untouched. When "millions of working-class Americans came to see Roosevelt not simply as their president but as their special advocate, even their personal friend,"[117] there were implications for both the workers and the system.

It is important to note, as Gary Gerstle does, that the New Deal legitimated the use of civic nationalism to challenge the existing national hierarchies.[118] Although Roosevelt's use of this rhetoric had both inclusive and exclusionary consequences, that use established important topoi that the marginalized would later use to challenge the powerful. Intentionally or not, FDR's vision of civic nationalism helped to establish a language for future protest that, when combined with the experiences of World War II, would unsettle the national hierarchies in ways he could not have predicted nor would have necessarily endorsed.

The apparent fluidity of the social order, the ability of members of some groups and for some groups in their entirety to move up in that order, had the triple effect of delegitimating group demands as coming from an entire group, of reinforcing the individualist dynamic and blaming the poor for their own plight, and of defining the American dream in economic, not political nor social, terms. The national success story became "the" story of the American immigrant who, through individual effort, made use of the economic opportunity proffered by the system and managed to achieve reasonable, if not spectacular economic success and social acceptance.

The consequences of these three effects would become apparent in the 1950s, when the population spread into the suburbs and the citizenry, defined as consumers, were themselves commodified and then contained.

6 / Citizenship Contained: Domesticating God, Family, and Country during the Eisenhower Years

> Problems were not lacking; what seems to
> have distinguished the period is the way they
> are dealt with. The characteristic response
> was to dampen and deflate them, rather than
> dramatizing or inflaming the issues, to check
> them and move them toward peaceable
> resolution, to confine and reduce their
> emotional impact on our people.
> —Andrew J. Goodpaster, "Foreword," in
> *Eisenhower: A Centenary Assessment*

MANY OF the achievements of the 1950s, associated with Eisenhower's cheery placidity, were negative, and consisted of keeping potentially divisive issues off the national agenda, preventing social upheavals, and foreclosing public arguments. The cold war, named during the Truman administration and enunciated under Eisenhower's, became a powerful force for restoring social order. "Containment" was its governing metaphor.[1] As the union of the 1850s had been faced with the threat of internal disintegration, Eisenhower's union faced the threat of external annihilation. The response in both cases was the creation of a stable, temperate, contained citizenry. Eisenhower's union was even more diverse, more inclusive, and potentially more fractious than the union of the 1850s, however, and the challenges of uniting it rhetorically were commensurably more difficult.

Eisenhower rooted his rhetoric in a specific understanding of American political traditions, and like Roosevelt, melded those traditions with contemporaneous politics to create an ideologically persuasive version of the national history and the national present that justified action in the past as well as the present. Because Washington, Jefferson, Jackson, and Lincoln (to use four of Eisenhower's favorite examples) used the word "equality," for example, Eisenhower could argue that "equality" had always been the basis of our politics. These presidents would have meant something vastly different by that word than did Eisenhower and his contemporaries, but that fact was made negligible. For Eisenhower, all "true" Americans adhered to the same set of values, played out in the same ways. All "true" Americans were the heirs of a seamless political tradition, linear descendants of a singular philosophy exemplified by Washington, Jefferson, Jackson, and Lincoln. Just as all presidents use specific and selective interpretations of the founding and the American national identity, Eisenhower rested his selective interpretation both on that mythologized past and on the political exigencies of his present. The result was a specific definition of what it meant to be American, which included some, excluded others, and exerted powerful ideological force throughout his time in office and into the present.[2]

Specifically, Eisenhower crafted a coherent if not circular narrative that explained the mission of the United States in the cold war and also, if unintentionally, implied domestication of its citizens. That narrative first placed the cold war in a world-historical context that both claimed for the Americans the blessing of Almighty God and, on a more mundane level, internationalized American domestic politics. American political leaders since before the founding had incorporated an evangelistic quality to the American mission. Eisenhower's rhetoric followed in that tradition and explicitly recalled the language of both Wilson and Roosevelt, who had applied that quality to the exigencies of international political action.

Once the context had been established and the position of the United States suitably blessed, Eisenhower articulated the ways in which the nation's status as the exemplar of democracy could be maintained. Connecting domestic necessities to foreign policy by containing the activities of the national government, Eisenhower also implied that certain kinds of containment at home would also serve the American mission abroad. That containment in turn promoted a stable, orderly progress, which then functioned to contain and control the American citizenry. Certain citizens were valorized as examples of international and domestic democratic citizenship while others were left on the margins, their progress toward increased political visibility and political power slowed by the needs of a static union. Such containment, couched in the universals characteristic of the language of citizenship, was inclusive but was also burdened by the more subtle forms of exclusion associated with that rhetoric.

The narrative thus came full circle—a contained citizenry was unified and identified as one people, under God, serving and served by a limited and contained government. Only such a citizenry could accept and fulfill America's mission. Becoming spiritually sound meant that Americans could freely enjoy their material success, which was given meaning and purpose by its spiritual and moral grounding. Material gain was associated with moral superiority. American prosperity was both a weapon in the cold war and a sign of God's favor in that war. By conflating world history, American history, and the cold war into one unified narrative, Eisenhower helped to establish an ideology of American identity that would continue its hold on the American imagination throughout the cold war.

Containing Citizens

Four elements of Eisenhower's public speech allowed him to rhetorically contain American citizens: his use of the cold war as an all-encompassing context, his insistence on a limited government and on placing potentially political issues into the private and away from the public sphere, and his treatment of all American citizens as fundamentally identical.

THE COLD WAR AS CONTEXT

For Eisenhower, the cold war was not merely a duel of wills and power between the United States and the Soviet Union, but was a battle for the future of the world. In his 1955 State of the Union Address, for example, he described the cold war as an apocalyptic battle: "It is not a struggle merely of economic theories, or of forms of government, or of military power. At issue is the true nature of man. . . . It is therefore, a struggle which goes to the roots of the human spirit, and its shadow falls across the long sweep of man's destiny. This prize, so precious, so fraught with ultimate meaning, is the true object of the contending forces of the world."[3] For Eisenhower, the battle over the "true nature of man" was one that pitted voluntary self-restraint, faith in a Christian God, and a lawful order against the selfishness, godlessness, and instability posed by the Soviet Union. Given the nature of the battle and the fact that both sides had the capacity to destroy the world, for Eisenhower this struggle was best understood as "apocalypse management."[4]

The struggle was constant. The cold war represented the latest battle in humanity's constant fight against the forces of darkness and the essential selfishness of human nature. The cold war was only one act in the drama of humanity's struggle against evil, only the latest of the challenges to human morality represented by America, both ideologically and materially. Americans represented the highest ideals of humanity, but to adequately represent those ideals the United States was called on to act as well as to believe. Early in his first inaugural address, for example, he asked, "How far have we come in man's long pilgrimage from darkness toward the light?"[5] The answer could only be provided in the actions of America and of American citizens. By American actions, the world would know Americans as the chosen, the faithful, the carriers of the torch of freedom.

Eisenhower thus constructed a specific sort of citizen: religious, stable, faithful to the ideals of the founders—as those ideals were construed by Eisenhower—and they were put in a context that understood national history on a clear trajectory from their day to his. Eisenhower's citizens were, like the citizens of the 1850s, heirs to a dynamic union but denizens of a stable one whose ideological justification came from the necessity of preserving the past as much as participating in the future.

This was clear in his first inaugural, where he argued that in the contest between the United States and the Soviet Union, "freedom is pitted against slavery; lightness against the dark."[6] The choices were clear—good citizens were on the side of the light, and any action that contributed to darkness could bring eternal darkness on the entire world. Eisenhower's citizens had a profound moral duty and made profound moral choices. Those choices could not be isolationist, for they influenced and affected the moral life—indeed the material life—of the world.

The United States could not, in good conscience, think only of its own interest, any more than good Christians could think only of their own souls. As he put it in his 1957 State of the Union Address, "Our pledged word, our enlightened self-interest, our character as a Nation commit us to a high role in world affairs: a role of vigorous leadership, ready strength, sympathetic understanding."[7] This language revealed a direct line between Wilson and Eisenhower, between World War I and the cold war. Eisenhower argued that to fulfill its destiny and be rewarded with the kingdom of Heaven, the United States had to think internationally; its citizens had to think of themselves as missionaries. They had the by now traditional American obligation of going forth and multiplying American territories and spreading the American ideology around the world, a burden that had become more urgent than ever.

This missionary obligation was laid on all citizens, whether residing at home or actively traveling or working abroad. Speaking to the Union of Carpenters and Joiners in 1956, for instance, he said, "Your whole-hearted support is assurance of success; your indifference, a guarantee of failure. More than that, you can most persuasively proclaim this mission to the world. And the world will listen. For though you speak with an authentic American voice, whose accent reflects all the working places of America, you speak, too, in international tones—worker to worker. Above all, in the struggle between the cause of freedom and cause of communism, you are the living proof that Marx was wrong."[8] Wilson had rendered all American citizens identical and identified in their global moral mission. Eisenhower unified and united them in a similar mission, equally global, but by his tenure in office labor had become so thoroughly Americanized, so politically visible and politically powerful that it had ceased to be politically problematic. Differences between management and labor could be accepted and even used as a unifying rather than a divisive element in his public speech.

To the U.S. Chamber of Commerce he said, "So I say: as this country was born in the self-sacrifice of its patriots, in their determination to work together, in their respect for one another—if we apply these principles today to ourselves at home, and to our tackling of our relationships with our friends abroad, we can dispel fear from our minds, and we can, as we achieve success, lead happy and full lives in perfect serenity and security."[9] Note here his use of the founding generation, those self-sacrificing patriots who worked together cooperatively and were respectful of differences. This was not the story of the founding as we have come to know it, full of strife, dissension, contesting interests, and competing philosophies of government. This was the story of the founding as it was ideologically useful to the pantheon of presidents who sought to make that historical moment the bedrock of a sense of nationhood that would permit them to govern, to preside over a nation that was both peaceful and prosperous. For Eisenhower, the peace that all true Americans wanted was a peace of shared moral values and cooperation, a peace that would hold among nations as among individuals. Like Wilson, Eisenhower's peace was to be a Pax Americana, a product of American will and promotion of American ideology.

World War II and its aftermath had done even more than World War I and Wilson to internationalize the American mission. "There can be no enduring peace for any nation," Eisenhower insisted in his speech accepting the 1956 Republican nomination for president, "while other nations suffer privation, oppression, and a sense of injustice and despair."[10] Eisenhower, like Wilson, offered the United States as the synecdoche of the world and often argued that the United States did not stand alone, but both symbolically stood for and actually stood with the "free world." In a 1953 press conference, for example, he said, "Our whole policy is based on this theory: no single free nation can live alone in the world. We have got to have friends. Those friends have got to be tied to you, in some form or another. But we have to have that unity in basic purposes that comes from a recognition of common interests."[11] The free world was connected both by ideological identity and by material interest. Eisenhower, a political pragmatist in many ways, was less interested in the nature of the bond than he was in its endurance. Because the free nations shared certain values, they were all targets of communism. It was thus only prudent that they stand united, ideologically as well as militarily.[12]

This understanding of international unity reflected his dichotomous understanding of the world, and also what historian H. W. Brands called Eisenhower's "almost unthinking" anticommunism.[13] That anticommunism may have been reflexive, but it was also grounded in a particular understanding of the nature of communist thought. For Eisenhower, democracy promoted individual freedom, and communism rejected it. While democracy fostered the common good through the protection of individual rights, communism sacrificed those rights in favor of an abstract notion of what constituted the common good.[14] As Eisenhower himself put it in one of his diary entries, "On the one side lies slavery, preceded possibly by a momentary independence, as in the case of Czechoslovakia. On the other side lies possibly a slower and more orderly process toward independence but with the certainty that it will then be healthy and sound."[15] This reflected much of Eisenhower's thinking on the cold war. All nations wanted the same things—development in the Western model. There were two paths to that development, one that led to slavery, the other to democracy. The latter choice was harder, slower, and more painful. It was also more certain.

Just as Jefferson and Jackson and their successors saw all nations and all peoples on the same trajectory of development, with some nations and some peoples further along than others and thus obligated to help those who were further back, Eisenhower understood all nations as essentially identical in their goals and desires, because human destiny was shared, not dependent on cultural expression. This understanding was in many ways profoundly inclusive, for it argued that no matter how different others may have been, they were not so different that they did not share the common destiny of humanity. It could also be profoundly exclusionary, however, for it also implied that culture was not determinative of collective goals and desires. Some cultures were more supportive of shared human goals and desires than others, and a hierarchy was established and subtly maintained. Because America led the world, its culture was, as we have seen, most reflective of the light. It provided the model for others to follow.

America was the model, but again much like Wilson, Eisenhower argued consistently for national self-determination and against cultural imperialism. The exclusionary power of the language of citizenship, couched in universals, was far subtler than the overtly exclusionary argot of balance. He understood the "free world" as united by shared values and argued that respect for one another was crucial to those values. Speaking before the Organization of American States, for instance, he said that "the code that governs our union is founded upon the most deeply held moral convictions . . . ours is an historic and meaningful unity. It has been—for our whole continent—an honest and productive unity. It can be—for other areas of the world—a prophetic and inspiring unity. For it is triumphant testimony, before all the world, that peace and trust and friendship can rule the conduct of all nations, large and small, who will respect the life and dignity of each other. . . . We are custodians of a way of life that can be instructive for all mankind."[16] This argument was grounded in a specific ideological understanding of the American past and the American mission. It was a characterization of U.S. relations with its neighbors to the South that none of those neighbors would recognize unambiguously, because it ignored the number of American-sponsored incursions, invasions, and outright wars fought with those neighbors for the control of territory and resources. It ignored the divisions that remained between the United States and those neighbors on many matters of importance to both, and it ignored the American military presence in many of those countries, as well as the power of American influence over them. But ideologically, it was a powerful statement of the American world-historical view, and it served to justify American action.

This understanding of the world had clear consequences at home and abroad. First, this sense of context meant that for Eisenhower, international politics and concerns dominated the purely domestic. "There is nothing that takes place at home of any great importance—if it is a difficult problem, at least, that is not caused by or at least colored by some foreign consideration,"[17] he said in 1956. There was, in fact, no real distinction between the two as he told a Republican audience that same year, "because, you see, today there is no problem that is simply foreign or domestic."[18] For example, Eisenhower saw civil rights through the lens of the cold war and dealt with the issues involved only when the damage to the American image abroad reached crisis proportions.[19] In another example, reflecting on the accomplishments of his administration, Eisenhower said, "The stature of our leadership in the free world has increased through the past three years because we have made more progress than ever before in a similar period to assure our citizens equality in justice, in opportunity and in civil rights. We must expand this effort on every front. We must strive to have every person judged and measured by what he is, rather than by his color, race, or religion."[20] His unwillingness to separate one set of issues from another could not be clearer.

It also could not be more important for the construction of his missionary, Christian, and contained citizenship. He legitimated American ideals not through static conditions—that is, they were not to be judged by the actual material conditions under which minorities in the United States were living—but by the extent of progress that had been made. Given the dismal past endured by African Americans, progress was both clear and irrefutable. And as Eisenhower formed the standard of judgment around distance from that past as opposed to distance from the ideal, American progress—and its relatively slow pace—was legitimated, justified, and made into evidence for American ideals, not evidence for their absence or American hypocrisy. Incremental change and stable progress toward those ideals were mandated; change that threatened American stability threatened the stability of the world, and was thus deplored.

The cold war as context allowed for the creation of a specific sort of contained citizen, one whose selfish demands were subordinated to the internationalized ideological battle with the Soviets for the destiny of humanity. The stakes were high, justifying whatever price American citizens would be called on to pay. But the rewards were great, and proper action would mean progress in the eternal struggle of light against dark. In that struggle, the citizens were the real combatants; government had a more limited role. "Good" Americans, through voluntary self-restraint, provided examples of model citizenship. Good government was also contained and limited government.

THAT WHICH GOVERNS LEAST

Just as Eisenhower understood a contained citizenry as operating with an ideologically based international context, that same context mandated an equally contained government. Eisenhower argued for clear limitations on the sphere of both governmental and individual action. Indeed, he saw limits as important both as ends and as means. As ends, limits had intrinsic importance; a lack of boundaries was itself threatening and dangerous. Limits implied self-restraint and voluntary self-control; their absence implied the destructive power of selfishness run amok. In his first inaugural, for example, he noted, "The promise of this life is imperiled by the very genius that has made it possible. Nations amass wealth. Labor sweats to create and turns out devices to level not only mountains but also cities. Science seems ready to confer upon us, as its final gift, the power to erase human life from this planet."[21] As in the 1850s model of rendering Andrew Jackson's dynamic union static to preserve it against internal dissolution, Eisenhower contained Roosevelt's dynamic union to preserve it against destruction from without. With so few limits imposed on humans externally, they had to impose limits on themselves if they were to survive.

This also meant that, as Gary Gerstle points out, even as the nation's conception of civic nationalism was becoming more (potentially) inclusive, it was also becoming less flexible.[22] Because of the importance of civic nationalism to the cold war, it became a powerful rhetorical legitimator for arguments against racial discrimination, for instance. But because of the limits such nationalism placed on government, expanding the topoi of dissent beyond narrowly understood political rights to issues of economic inequality became even more difficult.[23]

Eisenhower, however, considered limiting government a means of keeping the American people free, and for him, freedom trumped equality. In his 1954 State of the Union Address, he said, "Our government's powers are wisely limited by the Constitution; but quite apart from those limitations, there are things which no government can do or should try to do."[24] Government was limited not just by the Constitution, and not just by historical practice, but by a specific sense of individual development, in which good citizens were produced by doing the hard work of democracy themselves. The hardy yeoman citizen was Eisenhower's model of citizenship, and that model was fostered by a limited government in a contained union.

Instead of replacing individual action, Eisenhower argued, government should provide supportive structures for it. Like Roosevelt and Wilson, Eisenhower relied on the language of citizenship, an individualized language that rendered "persons" into "citizens" on the basis of individual action, not on the basis of group identification. Regarding a governmental role in labor negotiations with management, for instance, Eisenhower said, "Federal labor-management legislation at best can provide only the framework in which free collective bargaining may be conducted. It should impose neither arbitrary restrictions nor heavy-handedness upon a relationship in which good will and sympathetic understanding should be the predominant characteristics."[25] Government provided the framework; good will and sympathy among united citizens who supported the integrity of that framework provided the rest. No issue was so pressing between citizens that active government was necessary. The practice of citizenship was in the practice of self-control, self-mastery, and cooperation. Limiting governmental action—and believing in "good will and sympathetic understanding" between labor and management— was consistent with how Eisenhower understood the requirements of the laws of both God and democracy.

Speaking to a collegiate audience in 1954, he said, "Now what exactly do we mean by these spiritual values? We mean, I think, those characteristics of man that we call ennobling in their effect upon him—courage—imagination—initiative—a sense of decency, of justice, and of right. The faculty of being ready to admit that the limit placed upon our personal rights is that we do not transgress upon similar rights of others. All of which, in a very real sense, is a translation into a political system of a deeply-felt religious faith."[26] Again, like Wilson, Eisenhower unified the nation by referring to shared traits in language that was both powerfully potentially inclusive and exclusionary and which, in Eisenhower's case and unlike Wilson's, also implied contained government as well as contained citizens. Wilson rested some of his persuasive burden on claims of incapacity; Eisenhower justified limited government on ideological grounds. For Eisenhower, government could assist the individual, but its best choice was to stay out of the individual's way.

This was possible because for Eisenhower as for Wilson, "good" citizens were ideologically committed to the national mission and internalized the national discipline. Individuals could—and should— limit themselves through self-discipline and commitment to democracy. As he proclaimed in his 1955 State of the Union Address, "The aspirations of most of our people can best be fulfilled through their own enterprise and initiative, without government interference. This Administration, therefore, follows two simple rules: first, the Federal Government should perform an essential task only when it cannot otherwise be adequately performed; and second, in performing that task, our government must not impair the self-respect, freedom, and incentive of the individual."[27] By constituting the nation as a collection of contained individuals, Eisenhower could delegitimate the group basis of pluralistic politics in favor of a more individuated relationship between citizens and the government. By arguing against selfishness on the one hand and against group identification through an emphasis on individualism on the other, Eisenhower left only the relationship to the national government as the basis for individual participation in national politics. Claims for group rights were contained, as were the members of groups struggling for political visibility. The ideological understanding of the individual as the basis for American political history was a powerful legitimating force.

In this way, government was both doing the right thing by preserving the material existence of the nation and was doing so without endangering the historic character of the American people. In a letter to one member of Congress he said, "For individual Americans, we seek increase in their opportunity to enjoy good health, good schools, good homes; we seek a lessening in their fear of personal disaster and in the impact of hardships beyond their control. In this endeavor, we reject Federal domination over state and community for we seek to strengthen—not to weaken—the historic self-reliance of our people."[28] This historic self-reliance was as accurate—or inaccurate—a depiction of American political life as were Jefferson's yeoman farmer, Jackson's adventurous backwoodsman, Cleveland's yeoman worker, Wilson's identical and identified international citizen, and FDR's neighborly citizen. Eisenhower's yeoman citizen recalled a mythologized past to legitimate contemporaneous political preferences and institutional arrangements. For him, limited government meant expanded opportunities for American citizens, and expanded opportunities were equivalent to the protection of American liberties in an individualized nation.

Because of his stance on limited government, as the progenitor of contained citizenry and thus the basis of individual liberty, Eisenhower defended states' rights, on at least one occasion citing his "indestructible conviction that unless we preserve, in this country, the place of the State government, its traditional place—with the power, the authority, the responsibilities, and the revenues necessary to discharge these responsibilities, then we are not going to have an America as we have known it; we will have some other form of government."[29] Limited federal government, for Eisenhower as for Fillmore, Pierce, and Buchanan, meant the protection of state governments, which meant the protection of individual liberty. Yet, like the presidents of the 1850s, Eisenhower never stopped insisting that states had the obligation to live up to their responsibilities as well: "Each state owes to its inhabitants, to its sister states, and to the Union the obligation to suppress unlawful forces."[30] In ways reminiscent of the 1850s, Eisenhower argued here for state authority rather than federal responsibility, for he preferred civil rights to remain a local issue and argued that federal action would produce more harm than good. Rather than argue for an activist state willing to aggressively defend individual liberty through intervention in the Jim Crow South, for instance, Eisenhower defended limited governmental inaction as the surest defense of individual liberty.

This formulation clearly depended on who was politically visible to Eisenhower and to the members of his political coalition. Southern blacks, part of neither his electoral nor governing coalition, were not visible as individuals whose liberty merited the extreme measures of governmental intervention that would be required to overturn Jim Crow and restructure the politics of the American South. Eisenhower preferred present stability and incremental change as the best guarantors of their liberty. The individual liberty of white Southerners to maintain their local political arrangements and provide national stability for the sets of interests that brought Eisenhower to power was not necessarily more important to Eisenhower, but it was more visible and more ideologically amenable to protection. Some citizens were more easily accommodated by the governing ideology than were others.

SELF-GOVERNING INDIVIDUALS

Democracy demanded discipline, and since freedom demanded limited government, that discipline had to come from individuals. Unlike FDR, Eisenhower conceived of the nation not as a collection of groups, but as a body of unified individuals. In this, he harkened back to Cleveland, for he faced political exigencies that were, in some ways, analogous. Cleveland governed a nation that was in the process of coming to terms with a new industrialized order, in which dislocations were a constant feature of the economic life of the nation. Eisenhower governed a nation that was coming to terms with its new role as an international superpower, dominant politically, economically, and ideologically across the globe. Both regimes were prosperous, and both saw that prosperity as contingent on maintaining specific political arrangements and institutional structures. The stability of those structures and arrangements were paramount and were threatened by economic dislocations and the political power and political visibility of those who were most subject to them—in Cleveland's case capitalists and unions, and in Eisenhower's African Americans and other minorities. Both sought ideologically based ways of unifying the nation. For Cleveland that ideology rested on the notion of organic unity among the groups that constituted the body politic. For Eisenhower, it was a national unity based on a voluntary union of unified—in Wilson's terms, identified—individuals.

In language that ran directly counter to FDR's conception of government, Eisenhower said in a 1956 campaign address that "we are not a Nation of economic pressure groups—although some may attempt to exploit transient differences into lasting conflicts. Rather, we are a Republic of free individuals, each working out his own destiny, each making his own contribution in his own way to the common good. At the same time, in the deepest sense, we are a united people, spiritually joined in a tight loyalty to the great ideals. Therein lies the miracle of America."[31] "Good" citizens refused to compete with any other individual on the basis of group identity. Individual competition for individual success helped the nation; group competition for group benefits impeded the nation's goals. Eisenhower was no broker among economic groups as FDR had been. Instead, Eisenhower replaced FDR's group-based economic conception of national identity with a self-sacrificing, self-disciplined, individualized one. "Freedom has been defined as the opportunity for self-discipline," he said in the first State of the Union Address following his reelection. "Should we fail to discipline ourselves, eventually there will be increasing pressure on government to redress the failure. By that process freedom will step by step disappear."[32] Freedom demanded individualized and individual self-restraint; it demanded a contained, not dynamic union. But this self-restraint was not the temperance of the 1850s, which Pierce, Fillmore, and Buchanan hoped would foster political stasis and preserve their union. For Eisenhower, self-discipline was the discipline of an industrialized nation of free citizens whose energy was harnessed in the service of "progress," which was understood ideologically, in Eisenhower's day as it had been in FDR's, as the goal of the nation.

Individuals therefore had to self-limit their choices so the nation as a whole could move forward. The forward direction was differently conceived under Eisenhower than it had been under Roosevelt, for now it was not just economic progress and development, but also moral growth, development as the instantiation of the light against the darkness. Good citizens understood the connection between the moral and economic imperatives of the national project and worked for the fulfillment of both.

But they did not work alone. Such citizens needed to be created and nourished through education and public discourse so that they could be wise in their choices. As in Wilson's rhetoric, they had to accept the ideological discipline of citizenship so that they would not impede the progress of the nation and the moral development of the world. Speaking in 1953 at the inauguration of the president of the College of William and Mary, Eisenhower said, "It may be necessary, and it is necessary, that we earnestly seek out and uproot any traces of communism at any place where it can affect our national life. But the true way to uproot communism in this country is to understand what freedom means, and thus develop such an impregnable wall, that no thought of communism can enter. In other words, if I may state it in an utterly simple way, I believe this: the true purpose of education is to prepare young men and women for effective citizenship in a free form of government."[33] The lessons of citizenship that Jackson thought were taught by the land were, as had been the case since the development of public schools, now to be taught explicitly, as all inhabitants of the nation were to be schooled in the disciplines of citizenship and prepared for its responsibilities.

This is evidence of an increased emphasis on civic nationalism, for it assumed that everyone was equally able to bear the responsibilities, and thus equally likely to enjoy the privileges, of citizenship. It also had exclusionary potential, however, for it meant that all citizens were subject to the same set of standards and that differences were not to be politically admissible, and thus those who were understood as different faced a more difficult challenge in their attempts to gain increased political visibility and political power. Language intended to serve the nation's balance had implications for citizenship as well.

As Martin J. Medhurst has noted, balance was a keystone of Eisenhower's rhetoric. In keeping with Eisenhower's view of govern-

ment and with his task as the national conservator, balancing interests was for him choosing the middle between extremes, which, for
Medhurst, explained Eisenhower's reluctance to confront McCarthy,
his reticence on civil rights, and his determination to connect the
foreign and domestic spheres.[34] In this reading of Eisenhower, the
issue was one of long-term rather than short-term survival. The
moderate, patient, incremental path was for him also the one most
likely to lead to that survival. Like the presidents of the 1850s,
Eisenhower chose what he understood as preservation, although his
views encompassed more change than did theirs. He wanted progress,
but a stable progress. Only through discipline and balance could the
entire nation achieve stable progress, for real progress was orderly,
where change was controlled and contained.

Accepting the 1956 Republican nomination for president, he
enunciated this belief: "Change based on principle," according to
Eisenhower, "is progress. Constant change without principle becomes
chaos."[35] Balanced progress meant that drastic alterations in the
national hierarchies would be minimized in the name of order. "It is
because we, all of us, hold to these principles that the political
changes accomplished this day do not imply turbulence, upheaval, or
disorder,"[36] he said in his first inaugural, explicitly accepting the
president's conservatory task. Disciplined citizens understood the
principles of self-regulation and self-discipline and were well suited
to the rigors of national discipline. Disciplined citizens were thus
believers in the national myth of progress toward fuller enactment of
the same set of basic ideals and accepted the distance from the past
rather than the distance from the ideal as the appropriate standard of
judgment. They were also temperate citizens, who had faith in the
long-term goal and were willing to wend the slow but certain way
toward it. Their union was balanced, ordered, contained. American
leadership was required in the global frontier as it had been on the
American frontier, to tame the savage heart of the world and bring it
closer to the light and away from the darkness.

But the light was fragile and the forces of darkness inexorable.
Because of the exploitative and opportunistic nature of communism,
Eisenhower prepared the American people for a protracted and difficult war. "The *worst* is atomic war," he said in 1953. "The *best*
would be this: a life of perpetual fear and tension; a burden of arms
draining the wealth and the labor of all peoples; a wasting of strength

that defies the American system or the Soviet system or any system to achieve true abundance and happiness for the peoples of this earth. . . . This is not a way of life at all, in any true sense. Under the cloud of threatening war, it is humanity hanging from a cross of iron."[37] The struggle was not of Eisenhower's choosing, but was forced upon him. Only with the end of that struggle could a united humanity forge a more promising future.

This dedication was especially required from minorities, whose increased political visibility and increased political power were translating into more demands on the federal government. As Wilson had called for patience, and FDR had deferred and deflected these demands, the pressures on the government increased as the demands continued to go unmet. Rather than yielding to that pressure, Eisenhower instead asked for patience in the service of the national mission, the preservation of national stability.

In particular, Eisenhower tended to stress the need for patience to African Americans. To facilitate the orderly if slow progress he associated with democracy, Eisenhower sought to delegitimate protest by black Americans, an attempt exemplified in these comments at a 1958 meeting with African-American leaders (and it is worth noting that by the 1950s, meetings between such leaders and the White House were fairly routine, an important mark of the progress made toward political visibility and political power):

> We must do something about the Constitutional rights of the individual. To my mind, every American, whatever his religion, his color, his race or anything else, would have exactly the same concern for these matters as does any individual who may have felt embarrassment or resentment because those rights have not been properly observed. So it means that every American, if we are to be true to our Constitutional heritage, must have respect for the law. He must know that he is equal before the law. He must have respect for the courts. He must have respect for others. He must make perfectly certain that he can, in every single kind of circumstance, respect himself.[38]

One reading of this passage is that Eisenhower was taking a position that supported desegregation. Yet the laws were themselves so ambiguous at this point that other meanings were possible. Eisenhower was also asking that his audience rise above the slights of law and "embarrassment," that they made sure that they were worthy of respect, no matter how little respect was shown to them. Given a political context in which African Americans lived with the fear of violence, this plea certainly showed little sensitivity to the difficulties inherent in maintaining self-respect in the face of laws and practices that were designed specifically to prevent it. In asking African Americans to respect the rights of those who were oppressing them, and to respect the laws that declared them less than full citizens, Eisenhower was arguing for individual citizens to be "good" citizens, self-governing regardless of provocation.

The fact that he had this particular audience and that they were free to express their dissatisfaction was a sign that African Americans had continued to advance in terms of both political visibility and political power. They were still more often subjects of governmental action than the agents of it, but they were less the passive recipients that previous calls for patience, deflection, and deferral had rendered them. They were becoming increasingly politically problematic and would be subject to efforts to contain them, but they were making themselves increasingly important factors in the national political calculus.

The preceding quotation revealed other things as well. Civilization was, for Eisenhower, associated with order, not with equality; savagery had to do with disorder, not disrespect. Consequently, good citizens respected the requirements of order, accepted the notion that change was both slow and incremental, and continued to work within the system and to wait patiently when the system could not or would not permit more positive action. At a 1956 news conference, Eisenhower said, "If ever there was a time when we must be patient without being complacent, when we must be understanding of other people's deep emotions as well as our own, this is it. Extremists on neither side are going to help this situation, and we can only believe that the good sense, the common sense, of Americans will bring this thing along."[39] He thus placed both those who wanted change and those who most violently resisted it in the same category. In their resistance to incremental change and balanced progress, they were equally threatening to the national order. Eisenhower would not take sides; the middle path was the one he deemed best for national preservation. Good citizens understood this preference for a contained rather than a dynamic union and actively worked to promote it.

Eisenhower understood American democracy as the best hope for humanity, especially in a nuclear age. He also understood democracy as a demanding form of government that tested its citizens severely. This testing was all the more rigorous in the face of an implacable and committed enemy. The best hope for American democracy, and thus the best hope for the world, lay in the creation of a certain sort of world citizen, both domestically and abroad. That citizen would prize liberty in the form of limited government and would merit liberty through self-discipline. This definition of citizenship, created to meet the exigencies of the cold war, also served a vital legitimating function, ideologically reinforcing existing national hierarchies and supporting the interests of the coalition that had brought Eisenhower to power. That same ideology led to the domestication of some issues and rendered them less visible and less politically problematic.

DOMESTICATING ISSUES

Although Eisenhower did not separate domestic and foreign affairs, he domesticated certain issues—he placed them within the context of home and family and therefore outside the arena of government action. This rendered them less politically visible, less politically problematic, and subjected them to a form of discipline that also rendered them less amenable to public concern and political redress. Civil rights was one such issue.

Eisenhower's preference for avoiding extremes meant that he would not take a public moral stance on civil rights, and thus abrogated his leadership role.[40] He explained this abstention in his postpresidential memoirs:

> After the Supreme Court's 1954 ruling, I refused to say whether I either approved or disapproved of it. The Court's judgment was law, I said, and I would abide by it. This determination was one of principle. I believed that if I should express, publicly, either approval or disapproval of a Supreme Court decision in one case, I would be obliged to do so in many, if not in all cases. Inevitably, I would eventually be

drawn into a public statement of disagreement with some
decision, creating a suspicion that my vigor of enforcement
would, in such cases, be in doubt.[41]

Eisenhower understood his office as one with potent persuasive
power, and he was reluctant to use that power except on issues he
considered to be of pressing national concern. Civil rights was not
that order of issue for him. African Americans had neither the national political visibility nor the significance to his electoral and governing coalitions that would merit prompt interventionist action. For
political reasons and because of his personal preferences, in his rhetoric, the issue was better domesticated than nationalized, better contained than acted on.

His rhetoric facilitated such containment through erasure, by
delegitimating any real cause for complaint and individualizing
responses to systemic structures that supported racism. Speaking to an
international audience of orthopedists in 1958, for instance, he said,

> I am convinced, from the top of my head to the bottom of my
> feet, that there is no enmity among people when those peo-
> ple get to know each other. The emotions, the uncontrolled
> prejudices and resentments we sometimes encounter among
> people are normally because of the ignorance of those people
> as to the others—the people against whom they are resentful.
> The more we can spread the doctrine of people being guided
> by normal human aspirations, common objectives in life,
> common values that they treasure among themselves, by
> that much more we will advance the human race, not only
> in its joints and its bones but in its heart and its head and
> above all things in the way it can live in peace, and in oppor-
> tunity of reaching—each individual and each race—its full
> capacities.[42]

This rhetoric was potentially persuasive given the predilections
of whites and the prevailing ideology that supported those prejudices. By claiming that racism could be addressed by "getting to know
one another," Eisenhower reflected the prevailing ideology. In claiming that Americans were all alike under the skin despite, apparently,
differing racial capacities, Eisenhower also indirectly erased any

claim to difference while also underlining the importance of race. What appeared to be an inclusive move also had exclusionary consequences, for those who felt themselves to be different, who were in fact treated differently as a matter of law, were excluded without even being mentioned. Anyone who didn't share his idea of "normal human aspirations," anyone who wanted things other than the American dream as Eisenhower defined it, was simply and quietly erased.[43] Like the claim that there were "extremists" on both sides, Eisenhower here refused to entertain any notion that the moral position could possibly be anywhere but in the middle. This argument, reminiscent of the calls for temperance made by Fillmore, Pierce, and Buchanan, served the same ideological and political ends of rendering a dynamic union into a static, contained union. It operated as a powerful justification for an apparently balanced cultural dominance both at home and abroad.

Eisenhower made this claim to parity often. Simple fairness, he argued, would require that he meet also with members of the Ku Klux Klan if he were to agree to a meeting with black leaders.[44] Eisenhower's logic aside, one might argue that there were values a president could with impunity prize above fairness thus defined but such a view lay outside Eisenhower's vision of citizenship. Eisenhower consequently had less of a presence on civil rights than any other modern president.[45]

He did appoint some African Americans to his administration, although they tended to occupy positions that were more symbolic than substantive.[46] Certainly, Eisenhower's treatment of E. Frederic Morrow, the most prominent black member of his administration, left much to be desired.[47] As Morrow himself put it, "Here, really, is my deepest conflict: I am an appointee in the Administration, with loyalty to the Administration, to the party, and the President, but I am also a Negro who feels very keenly the ills that afflict my race and its efforts to secure in one fell swoop all the privileges and responsibilities of citizenship that have been denied it for three centuries in this country. It is my responsibility to explain to white people how Negroes feel on this matter, and by the same token, explain to Negroes the Administration's attitude."[48] The painful story of the consequences of that conflict was eloquently told and evocative of the entire tone of the administration on civil rights. Certain minimal concessions—usually symbolic—were made, but Morrow himself was constantly humiliated, ignored, and exploited. That he himself realized this and remained committed enough to the value of his endeavor was evidence for the bind in which many of the developing black middle and professional classes found themselves during these years. They were politically visible and politically powerful enough to merit some presidential attention—even in the administration of a relatively indifferent Republican—but they were neither visible nor powerful enough to force specific policies over the resistance, however passive, of that administration.

Morrow understood the root of the problem to be one of distance. In discussing with the attorney general the problems attending the attempted enrollment of Clennon King at the University of Mississippi in 1958, and the administration's lack of response, Morrow said, "I realized, of course, that in the spaciousness of his air-conditioned office it would be difficult for him to visualize the situation of the poor devils who had asked me to try to get them some help."[49] There is a wealth of information in that "of course," for the distance was, even in Morrow's eyes, unbridgeable. The passage from political invisibility to relative visibility, even for those most privileged by the emerging status of African Americans, was painful.

Few people in America were as distant from the problems of the disenfranchised as the president himself. Because the race problem was so endemic and so national, it was also largely invisible, for these tensions had been marginalized and were thus not necessarily amenable to political solutions or the proper subject of presidential energy. As activism on civil rights began to increase, more presidential attention would have to be given to the issues involved, but in the relative quiet of the 1950s, Eisenhower could largely maintain his reticence on racial matters. At least partially, this reticence was attributable to his desire to build Republican strength in the South. He went so far as to refuse to comment on the civil rights plank in the Republican platform, claiming that the issue was too "charged with emotionalism" to merit presidential comment.[50] And, at least partially, it was the result of widely shared fears and attitudes on the race question. Southern resistance to desegregation ranged from arguments concerning the importance of maintaining social order and the sanctity of tradition to outright declamations on racial purity.[51] Certainly, the resurgence of the Klan and the violence associated with it were markers of Southern resistance.[52]

That resistance was pervasive and often played upon the national fear of communism, further complicating the connection between international and domestic politics.[53] Eisenhower stopped short of implying that participants in the civil rights movement had subversive motives, but not of indicating that their position would lend aid and comfort to subversives. Asked his opinion about "Gandhi-like passive resistance demonstrations of Negroes in the South," for instance, he replied, "It's difficult . . . to give a sweeping judgment. Some are unquestionably a proper expression of a conviction of the group which is making them; others probably can be otherwise classified."[54] The motives of those "others" were used by the government—under Eisenhower and later—in attempts to discredit the civil rights movement and its leaders.[55] African Americans were becoming more politically visible and politically powerful. This made them increasingly subject to differentiation.

Thus, containment at home and abroad required also the containment of "extreme" groups and their demands. Civil rights was only the most obvious example. Eisenhower would not denounce citizen councils, nor would he distance himself from the tactics practiced by those opposed to desegregation, nor would he criticize segregationists themselves. He criticized only the results of their activities and tactics and then only when those results included violence.[56] Asked about the issue at a press conference, he said, "No one can deplore violence in this thing more than I do. I think that violence sets us back, well—years. I think the youngsters that are indulging in violence are not being counseled properly at home."[57] Note that those who were "indulging in violence" were styled as "youngsters," with less implied responsibility, fewer inimical effects than if "adults" were involved. Note also that the problem was not one of bitter racism and economic competition. It was one of lacking proper counsel at home. It was thus not an appropriate matter for governmental action, much less intervention. By domesticating and thus containing the issue, Eisenhower also trivialized the problem, even when violence was involved.

Given his worldview and the political exigencies of the cold war, Eisenhower could not admit that any adult Americans were committed racists capable of perpetrating vicious and violent crimes, for that completely contradicted both his stated view of world-historical development and, worse, gave valuable ammunition to the Soviets in the world campaign of persuasion. Constrained by ideology, personal preference, and political reality, Eisenhower had no road but the middle road. Containment and incremental change were the only paths rhetorically open to him.

But, it is important to note, Eisenhower did finally use governmental mechanism to act, even if his commitment was to the preservation of order and the enforcement of court orders rather than to the substance of civil rights.[58] On September 24, 1957, Eisenhower signed Executive Order 10730, federalizing the Arkansas National Guard, beginning a long and tension-filled process of trying to prevent open defiance of the Court's orders and federal authority while insisting that he was not attempting to integrate the nation's schools by force.[59] One thousand paratroopers from the famous 101st Airborne were also sent to Little Rock. In explaining his actions, he framed the situation not in terms of the importance of equality, but in terms of the importance of law and order: "Certain misguided persons, many of them imported into Little Rock by agitators, have insisted upon defying the law and have sought to bring it into disrepute. . . . Mob rule cannot be allowed to override the decisions of our courts."[60] He acted, much as the presidents of the 1850s had, against the "misguided" action of the mob, because for him as for them, the maintenance of order was paramount. In this case, as in the 1850s, the language of balance was less inclusive than the language of citizenship.

Racial matters, like other domestic concerns during the Eisenhower era, were perceived only through the lens of the cold war. In reflecting his understanding of the difference between communism and democracy he reflected also the need for containment both domestically and in foreign affairs. For the reality of those problems, Eisenhower had little public concern, considering them as outside his political province as president. A free society was a self-disciplined society and required a disciplined government, which protected individual freedoms. All American politics were contained within this tight circle.

The domestication of racial issues was a result of Eisenhower's worldview, understanding of national history, and international political imperatives. It resulted in language that worked ideologically to protect the existing sets of political arrangements and political institutions that favored the preferences of his conservative governing coalition. It also created a specific sort of citizen and, in turn, a particular kind of political community.

EQUALLY AMERICANS, INDIVISIBLE

Eisenhower understood the conservatory task of the president as including the fostering of American unity, which was implied in his notion that equality meant equal access to the American system. All groups were to be treated the same; none were to get special privileges. And they all were expected to adopt and reflect the same attitudes, beliefs, and values as all other Americans. Speaking at a Republican fund-raiser in 1953, he said, "In the American design—as we perceive it—each group in our nation has special problems. None has special rights. Each has peculiar needs. None has peculiar privileges. We believe in people, in all the people: laborer and banker, preacher and teacher, doctor, lawyer, farmer, machinist, white collar worker, housewife, miner, artist, merchant, rancher, farm hand, switchman, clerk—all of them. The supreme belief in our society is in the dignity and freedom of the individual. To the respect of that dignity, to the defense of that freedom, all effort is pledged."[61] Note the inclusive and encompassing nature of this list. Note also its tendency to reduce American differences to those of occupation, not of class, status, race, or gender. All of them were distinct individuals, but as in Wilson's transcendent order, they were ultimately all the same. The language functioned in the same way here as it had for Wilson—including, excluding, and masking exclusion through identification. All Americans shared equally in the respect, dignity, and freedom that characterized their compatriots. As they had been in Wilson's international order, Americans in Eisenhower's union were all equal, all protected, and all unified. And indeed, under Eisenhower, many previously marginalized and excluded groups did enjoy more political visibility and more political power than they had previously.

Jews, for example, once reviled in American politics, received special attention from Eisenhower and were exalted for their ability to assimilate and to espouse values that were shared by all Americans. Not only did he often cite Jews as emblematic of the values cherished by all Americans, he also celebrated them as foundational to those values, representing both the story of the American immigrant and the American founders. At a Jewish tercentenary dinner, he spoke in the sorts of platitudes that, by the administration of George H. W. Bush, would be established as one of the staples of politics. He said, "On that day there came to these shores 23 people whose distant ancestors had, through the Old Testament, given new dimensions of meaning to the concepts of freedom and justice, of mercy and righteousness, kindness and understanding—ideas and ideals which were to flower on this continent. They were of a people who had done much to give to Western civilization the principle of human dignity; they came to a land which would flourish beyond all seventeenth century dreams, because it fostered that dignity among its citizens."[62] Formerly excluded, Jews were now included in both the immigrant and the frontier myths. Much as FDR had included other immigrants, this language functioned to both recognize their increased political visibility and power and to encourage the progression of the group into invisibility as they merged with the rest of Americans. They were no longer visibly apart from the American citizenry, but had joined it. Their assimilation was, in Eisenhower's speech at least, complete.

Not all groups made progress along the same path toward visibility. Assimilation was the model employed concerning American Indians, where the goal of federal policy according to the president was "the full integration of our Indian citizens into normal community life."[63] Rather than maintaining the emphasis on revitalizing American Indian cultures that had prevailed during the Roosevelt administration, and to a lesser extent the Truman administration, Eisenhower's American Indian policy stressed integration of American Indians into mainstream American society, which was understood as "normal," and the termination of separate, tribal status.[64] He wanted American Indians to finally disappear, definitively absorbed into the polity. His Commissioner of Indian Affairs, Truman appointee Dillon S. Myer, had previous governmental experience as the official in charge of the relocation and incarceration of Japanese Americans during World War II. Myer believed that reservations were equivalent to concentration camps, administered them as such, and thus believed that American Indians needed to be "freed" from them.[65] Consequently, the goal of the administration's American Indian policy was to eliminate the reservation system, which would thus reduce American Indian dependence and foster assimilation and integration.

"Termination," as the policy came to be called, had immediate and devastating effects, and immeasurably harmed the ability of members of terminated tribes to retain their cultural status once their political status had been so drastically altered. Five American Indian nations (Flathead, Menominee, Klamath, Potawatomie, and Chippewa) as well as numerous bands in California, New York, Texas, and Florida were scheduled for termination, and on June 17, 1954, the tribal status of the Menominee nation was officially terminated. The affected American Indians had literally become politically invisible as American Indians and were legally as well as rhetorically no longer citizens of any nation but the United States.[66]

Theoretically, termination worked with a policy of relocation, which was intended to move American Indians from the reservation to urban areas and which was supposed to provide job training, support while they made the transition, and other forms of assistance. Relocation was supposed to help render previously American Indian "persons" into democratically minded, self-supporting, American "citizens." Such support never materialized, and American Indians subject to relocation frequently found themselves in American Indian ghettoes, facing lives of hardship and despair.[67] Much as the earlier system of incarceration in boarding schools helped to fuel pan-Indian identity and activism, however, the removal of many American Indians into urban environments had a similar result. The unintended consequences of relocation would be felt at Alcatraz and Wounded Knee, as American Indians, politically invisible here, would erupt into political visibility.[68]

Politically invisible, American Indians remained ideologically useful. Like so many presidents before him, Eisenhower used the frontier metaphor, and with it displayed the same ideology of erasing the American Indians' experiences on that frontier in favor of a more ideologically useful version of history—one that did not include war, genocide, and colonization. Dedicating, ironically enough, the laboratories for the National Bureau of Standards (NBS) in Boulder, Colorado, he said, "Here we have a new type of frontier. This spot only a few short decades ago was inhabited by Indians and by buffalo and by, finally, the trappers and the miners. . . . But the frontier days when we could go out and discover new land—new wonders of geography and of nature—has seemed largely in the past."[69] Note the selective view of history here, and the notion of progress and civilization that it entailed. The frontier was always open, and the changes it brought affected everyone equally in the natural progression of history—the American Indians gave way to trappers and miners, who gave way to their modern counterparts. This myth included all Americans as the ideological heirs of the American Indians and the buffalo, of the miner and trappers, and of the scientists who worked within the NBS. It excluded those who did not see themselves in this version of history. Eisenhower thus historicized the experiences of American Indians along with the frontier and thus elided the very real problems they faced. American Indians no longer "really" existed. They were placed in the same category with the buffalo and were deemed as important politically as the buffalo. American Indians, according to this view of history, had vanished with the frontier. They thus also vanished from the American political memory as expressed by its presidents.

What he did not historicize of American Indian experience, Eisenhower romanticized, which operated as a different, more subtle form of erasure. At another dedication, this time of the Hiawatha Bridge in Red Wing, Minnesota, he said,

> I am not thinking of the Hiawatha of that charming legend of Longfellow's poem in which I found such enchantment when I read it as a boy. . . . Today it is the real Indian, Hiawatha, not the poetic legend, that I find so meaningful and whose work seems to me so relevant to the season of history that is now upon us. The American Indian Chief Hiawatha is said to have lived about 400 years ago. But his deeds in the 16th century in what was then Stone Age America, are strikingly reminiscent of the work we are undertaking today. . . . Hiawatha was a founder of a United Nations organization in America. . . . Hiawatha's league failed, though for several generations it was remarkably successful in the achievement of its objectives.[70]

That "the real Indian" did not live in a "stone age" but was a member of an advanced political system, founded a confederacy that did not gently pass away as naturally and inevitably as the phrase "season of history" implied but which continues today, and was certainly in existence in Eisenhower's day, undermined only the truth, not the ideological force or persuasive power, of this argument.[71]

Such an inaccurate yet ideologically satisfying depiction served the interests of the colonizer, as depictions of American Indians had been serving those interests before Jefferson's day and ever since.[72] American Indians were politically invisible enough, politically powerless enough, to make such a recounting of the old ideologies plausible and possible.

These depictions worked to legitimate American colonialism and territorial acquisition in a time when the ways and means of such acquisition were increasingly under international scrutiny and cause for international debate. As had been the case with the American treatment of its African-American citizens, the American conquest of the continent provided the Soviet Union with powerful propaganda tools in the struggle to persuade the hearts and minds of the international audience. Such a mythology masked the brutality of that conquest, simplified its complexities, and justified it as ideologically prior and thus essential to America's contemporaneous position as leader of the free world.

In both of these cases—African Americans, American Indians, and in others as well—"equality" for Eisenhower was defined, as it was defined by most of his contemporaries, as equality of opportunity. Any failure to achieve material prosperity was considered to be the fault of the individual. Individuals were the basic constituents of the democratic system as Eisenhower understood it. They needed to be self-disciplined, self-reliant, and responsible.[73] Chief among those responsibilities was adherence to the will of God.

Eisenhower applied the language of citizenship to all Americans, and in so doing both reinforced the progress that had been made in the inclusion of members of previously disenfranchised groups and masked the continued exclusion and erasure of others. But his use of this language, like Wilson's, enabled members of those groups who were being erased, marginalized, or excluded to make powerful arguments in their own defense. And while the cold war necessitated in some ways Eisenhower's arguments concerning their exclusion, it also opened spaces for them to make those arguments. Eisenhower's use of universals was premised on his understanding of the United States as a Christian nation, and his belief that the future of humanity lay in the acceptance of Christian beliefs and behaviors on an international scale. This set of ideological assumptions was both inclusive and exclusionary.

One Nation, Under God

Although all our presidents have stressed, to one degree or another, the importance of the Christian (Protestant) tradition in American democracy, few did so as often or as insistently as Eisenhower. For Eisenhower, the cold war was legitimated by his understanding of the national mission, which was given to us as a sacred duty by God. As Martin J. Medhurst noted, "The defense of the country and its values, founded upon Judeo-Christian presuppositions, was to Eisenhower a mission of sacred, almost religious nature."[74] For Eisenhower, the fact of atomic power did not undermine the presence or importance of God. Instead, the atomic age was to him evidence for an even greater need for and dependence on religious instruction and faith.[75] So strongly did he feel on this point, for instance, that he had the motto "In God We Trust" added to our national currency. He also began his first inaugural with a prayer, later noting in the first volume of his memoirs, "Religion was one of the thoughts that I had been mulling over for weeks. I did not want my Inaugural Address to be a sermon, by any means; I was not a man of cloth. But there was embedded in me from boyhood . . . a deep faith in the beneficence of the Almighty. I wanted, then, to make this faith clear without creating the impression that I intended, as the political leader of the United States, to avoid my own responsibilities in an effort to pass them on to the Deity. I was seeking a way to point out that we were getting too secular."[76] The danger of becoming "too secular" was that the nation would lose sight of its mission, and thus forgo its ability to fulfill that mission. That mission was, as so many American missions had been, explicitly religious. It was thus also implicitly exclusionary.

AMERICAN MISSIONARIES

Following in the tradition Woodrow Wilson established during World War I, FDR's framing of World War II made American values an important element of postwar domestic politics.[77] The limits of those values—and the political importance of those limits—were made abundantly and tragically clear in the fact of Nazi genocide and the weakness of the Allied response to it,[78] and were underlined in the feeble American reaction to the Hungarian uprising.[79] Despite these events, which highlighted the difficulties of translating American values into political action, belief in the sanctity of the American mission remained. Contained at home, Americans were to be ideological bearers of the gospel abroad.

Their mission was no longer defined in terms of manifest destiny, with its emphasis on territorial acquisition, but harkened back to the Puritan conception of America as the "shining city on a hill," the exemplar of democracy whose light would illumine the world, and as it had been amplified in the justifications for both world wars. In his first inaugural Eisenhower said,

> We are called as a people to give testimony in the sight of the world to our faith that the future shall belong to the free. . . . And so each citizen plays an indispensable role. . . . No person, no home, no community can be beyond the reach of this call. We are summoned to act in wisdom and in conscience, to work with industry, to teach with persuasion, to preach with conviction, to weigh our every deed with care and with compassion. For this truth must be clear before us: whatever America hopes to bring to pass in the world must first come to pass in the heart of America.[80]

All Americans were summoned to give testimony to their faith in democracy as all Christians were summoned to give testimony to their faith in God. The deployment of these democratic disciples was not in the service of imperialism or territorial acquisition of any kind, but was exclusively moral. It was, with its Christian bias, also morally exclusive.

As with all callings, the American mission was not voluntary; the call itself came only from God. One could refuse the calling, as one could turn away from God, but it was not given or refused lightly and was thus the stuff of heavy responsibility. Speaking to the American Advertising Council in 1956, he said, "We must carry not only a material message to the world of what kind of enterprise we have—the kind of system—can do for a people. We must carry those moral values, spiritual values of the worth of man—what he is entitled to as an individual."[81] American prosperity and American principles were the gospel that Americans are obliged to spread. Eisenhower, like Wilson, believed in the American responsibility to establish and maintain an international, moral order based on specific universal principles, which both included and had exclusionary consequences. As he said in his 1957 State of the Union Address, "The appeal of these principles is universal, lighting fires in the souls of men everywhere."[82] All humanity was again reduced to one understanding of the possibilities of humanity—Eisenhower's understanding.

But more was required of citizens than simply the spreading of good news. He put it this way in his second inaugural: "The building of such a peace is a bold and solemn purpose. To proclaim it is easy. To serve it will be hard. And to attain it, we must be aware of its full meaning—and ready to pay its full price."[83] History, for Eisenhower, had shown that Americans were up to the task. The privileges of citizenship brought with them responsibilities, and good citizens were cognizant of both. They were locked in a long twilight struggle for the soul of the world and could not falter in that struggle. Discipline, dedication, sacrifice, and unity were all required.

This conception of the mission associated with the United States was reinforced by the experiences of World War II, and specifically from the way those experiences had been framed in the public imagination. As he said in his first inaugural, "We feel this moral strength because we know we are not helpless prisoners of history. We are free men. We shall remain free, never to be proven guilty of the one capital offense against freedom, a lack of stanch faith."[84] Faith was the free choice of free people, and faith in a Christian God was the bedrock upon which the American commitment to the struggle was premised.

But although the United States was clearly the more moral of the combatants, and "although American policy had to be based upon moral ends, America had to play by the same amoral rules as the opponents."[85] Eisenhower asserted that the object of war was to win and that victory as an end could be separated from the means used to achieve it; that, by definition, in war no means were likely to be ethically acceptable. Victory was the only possible justification. In his 1953 State of the Union Address, he said, "We have learned that the free world cannot indefinitely remain in a posture of paralyzed tension, leaving forever to the aggressor the choice of time and place and means to cause greatest hurt to us at least cost to himself."[86] For Eisenhower, appeasement should never again be an option in either a hot or in a cold war.

Yet in a cold war, where causing death could be avoided, means could be separated from ends—at least in public. Thus, he could authorize a secret government, on the one hand, and still argue publicly that how we did things mattered as much or more than what we actually did.[87] In a 1953 news conference he argued that "we must not destroy what we are attempting to defend."[88] More specifically criticizing the excesses of McCarthy, he said, "But we know that freedom cannot be served by the devices of the tyrant. As it is an ancient truth that freedom cannot be legislated into existence, so it is no less obvious that it cannot be censored into existence. And anyone who acts as if freedom's defenses are to be found in suppression and suspicion and fear confess a doctrine that is alien to America."[89] Except in such indirect ways, Eisenhower, of course, refused to take on McCarthyism or McCarthy directly, although he was reportedly both infuriated at and offended by him.[90] He noted in his diary that "I really believe that nothing will be so effective in combating his particular kind of troublemaking as to ignore him. This he cannot stand."[91] Eisenhower clearly understood the power of silence as a tool of containment. As obnoxious as he personally found McCarthy and however much he deplored his excesses, however, Eisenhower certainly provided little or no public leadership to combat him, either because of personal and political style or because, fundamentally, Eisenhower agreed with McCarthy—at least on the issue of the need to keep communists out of the government.

Eisenhower's goal regarding the threat of communists, like his reaction to other threats to the American polity, was best understood as containment. He went so far as to sign legislation outlawing the Communist party.[92] At least in part, Eisenhower considered communists dangerous because they were godless. After declaring that our two national goals were global peace and an expanding domestic economy in a 1955 luncheon hosted by the Associated Press, Eisenhower said, "The fundamental hazard to the achievement of both objectives is the implacable enmity of godless communism. That hazard becomes the more fearsome as we are guilty of failure among ourselves to seek out and face facts courageously; failure to make sacrifices for the common good; failure to look beyond our selfish interests of the moment; failure to seek long-term betterment for all our citizens."[93] Good citizens were disciplined, domesticated, Christian. They were courageous and willing to make sacrifices. Good citizens would not fail Eisenhower. They had both the material and spiritual wherewithal to succeed in their appointed task.

Americans were missionaries, rejoicing in their spiritual and material bounty, and ready to share both with the world. Communists had only the material goods and could offer the world no spiritual sustenance. They suffered both spiritually and practically because of it. They served as counterexamples of citizenship, showing Americans the perils of material gain without spiritual sustenance. Indeed, because of the American faith in God, its material wealth was both legitimated and given meaning.

THE EARTHLY REWARD

Eisenhower did not understand Americans to be crassly materialistic, although that danger existed. As he told Congress and the American people in 1954, "No government can inoculate its people against the fatal materialism that plagues our age. Happily, our people, though blessed with more material goods than any people in history, have always reserved their first allegiance to the kingdom of the spirit, which is the true source of that freedom we value above all material things."[94] Spirituality, the "kingdom of the spirit" was given primacy in the United States. That spirituality was the root of American liberty, the basis of the idea that individuals possessed inalienable rights as gifts from God. That liberty fostered American prosperity. So American prosperity had spiritual roots and was given meaning by spiritual values.

Because material goods were given meaning by spiritual values, so American consumerism was legitimated. As he said in a nationally broadcast message, "Now, as we first take a look at the strength of America, you and I know that it is the most productive nation on earth, that we are richer, by any standard of comparison, than is any other nation in the world. We know that we have great military strength—economic—intellectual. But I want to call your particular attention to spiritual strength. . . . I want to call your attention to this particular part of the American strength, because without all this, everything else goes by the board."[95] That union of the spiritual and the material was a powerfully comforting one for people who believed in the importance of the former and who were nonetheless apparently fascinated with the latter. It had the potential to be a powerfully inclusive definition of the American polity, for it assumed that all Americans were equally spiritual, equal in the eyes of the state as they were in the eyes of God. But it also erased and disenfranchised those who did not share in these (Judeo) Christian values, for their prosperity was not legitimated by religion and was therefore less legitimate.

The appeal to spiritual values may also have resonated given the unevenness of the economy, which both prospered and seesawed during these years. According to some estimates, more than thirty million Americans, roughly one quarter of the population, lived in poverty throughout the 1950s.[96] Others place the number even higher, by as much as ten to twenty million people.[97] Many of the poor were virtually invisible, residing as they did on farms, in urban ghettoes and barrios, and in rural localities such as Appalachia.[98] Except for the farmers, the poor got little sympathy from Eisenhower, whose own friends ranked among the business elite and whose personal finances were certainly healthy. Seldom did he wear the same suit more than twice.[99] His Cabinet was equally elitist, derisively referred to as consisting of "eight millionaires and a plumber."[100] The plumber was among the first to leave the Cabinet. The millionaires appear to have found the administration more congenial.

For those who—like Eisenhower, his friends, and his Cabinet—could enjoy the economic good times, that prosperity seemed endless and endlessly expansive. The American middle class developed, expanded, and began to exercise political power on a worldwide scale during the decade.[101] It measured itself—and its relationship to others, at home and abroad—in terms of individual and group consumption of goods.[102] Those goods were more widely available, and the promise of "the good life" seemed within reach of those willing to work hard enough to attain it.

As a result, fewer middle-class women worked during these years, and the role of women as political actors was both expanded and reduced. On the one hand, Eisenhower could—and did—speak to women as if they were every bit as educated, intelligent, and interested in policy as men. He often gave speeches in which there was no notice taken, in approach, content, or language, of the fact that his audience consisted largely or entirely of women. On the other hand, he could also be very clear that the proper place for women was in the home, tending the family, and raising the next generation of citizens. Speaking to a national audience of active Republican women in 1955, for instance, he said,

> Personally, in such a problem, in such a purpose, I believe that women are better apostles than men. Men are engrossed in many kinds of activities. They earn the living. They are engaged in business all day, and they are very apt, at times, to lose that great rounded concept of man that women almost always have before them: that he is a spiritual, and an intellectual, and a physical being. He is not merely someone trying to get a higher wage. He wants a higher wage for a purpose, to give greater opportunity in all these fields to their family. Because women think of these things in their process of homemaking, think of men in terms of children and the family, I believe that their influence in spreading the basic doctrines of this kind is more profound than that of men.[103]

This quotation—and its use of both nouns and pronouns—made Eisenhower's view of women's positions during these years clear. They were politically visible and politically active enough to merit routine yearly meetings with the president—one of the few such groups who got such meetings. Yet they were not independent enough to be free of his patronizing stereotypes, as he ascribed to all women attitudes and economic positions that they had never all shared, flattening and erasing the complexities of women's experiences. Women were both included in ways that rendered them full citizens and also excluded from full participation. They were partially visible politically but were not considered to be politically problematic either as potential constituents or as potential opponents.

As the case of women illustrated, good citizens were disciplined, able to look, as Eisenhower did, to the long view. They were Rooseveltian citizens in having this patient capacity and long-range view, and Wilsonian in their ability to premise that patience on spiritual values that unified the entire polity. They were uninterested in territorial gain but sought spiritual benefit, which was the basis for material gain. The values that led to American liberty and prosperity were best found not in the conquest of foreign lands, but at home.

DOMESTICATING CITIZENS

Eisenhower understood America as comprising, in important ways, individuals rather than members of groups defined either economically, racially, or ethnically. But individuals had to somehow be collected into a nation if there was to be collective action, and so Eisenhower also understood America as individuals collected into a whole community of families, and in this he owed something to Roosevelt's notions of "neighborliness" as the force that unified the polity. In introducing one speech, for instance, Eisenhower began, "Tonight, I would like to talk to you as individuals and as American families,"[104] thus revealing the important constituent parts of his view of America. It was not uncommon for him to describe and defend his policies on the grounds of their necessity for the American family, which he connected to good citizenship.[105] "In our own land, it is largely through the family that character is formed. Americans love fair play, bravery, hard work, and believe in human brotherhood because American fathers and mothers, by precept and example, teach these virtues to their children."[106] Jackson had found the lessons of citizenship in the land, and other presidents had located those lessons in other places and in other experiences. For Eisenhower, the lessons of citizenship were learned at home, and the American family was the bedrock of the American polity. During the cold war, in fact, families were both a haven and a key locus of American vulnerability.[107] Protecting the family became intertwined with protecting the state.[108]

Like Wilson, Eisenhower proclaimed his trust in the American public and in American public opinion, always assuming that Americans had access to all the facts and were properly educated.[109] As he said in a meeting of African-American leaders on the subject of racism:

> In such problems as this, there are no revolutionary cures. They are evolutionary. . . . As long as they are human problems—because they are buried in the human heart rather than ones merely to be solved by a sense of logic and of right—we must have patience and forbearance. We must depend more upon better and more profound education than simply the letter of the law. . . . I do not deny laws, for they

are necessary. But I say that laws will never solve problems that have their roots in the human heart and in the human emotions. It is because of this very reason that I am more hopeful that we will, as the years go past, speak to each other only as Americans without any adjectives to describe us as special types of Americans.[110]

This was cultural dominance by default. If Americans were all the same, then those Americans who were different were either not really "American" in some crucial sense, and thus were liable to be excluded, or they were not really different in some crucial sense. Insistence on difference became insistence on exclusion, because if the rigors of domesticity and family life were neglected, the consequences could be dangerous. Ostensibly inclusive rhetoric had exclusionary potential.

Those whose lives lay outside the mainstream were not only "other" but were also a potential threat to the very survival of the nation and the ideals it represented. Middle-class white women, for example, were not expected to work, and middle-class white women became the mediated model for what was proper and desirable, even if it was not possible for most women.[111] It was not merely serendipitous that Richard Nixon's famous "debate" with Soviet Premier Nikita Khrushchev took place in a newly designed and frenetically automated prototype of an American kitchen. Although most American women lived outside these boundaries, they were nonetheless affected by the expectation that those boundaries were the proper ones and that they were consequently, in one form or another, transgressive. Certainly, there was empowerment as well as punishment implicit in such transgression.[112] In terms of the disciplinary project of nation building, the former was more dangerous than the latter and much more likely to be contained through silence. By rendering the experiences of other women invisible, those women—and women's issues generally—could be contained.[113] Women who differed from the norm were rendered politically invisible.

Eisenhower himself was most comfortable in "a world of men. The only genuine relationships he had ever formed with women revolved around role images that he felt comfortable with, specifically those of mother, wife, and secretary."[114] Intentionally or not, the women in his life appear to have been contained through emphasis on role. In the broader society, sexual containment depended on creating and maintaining new systems of sexual inequality while the prevailing ideology of equality required that such structures be suitably masked.

Eisenhower shared the ideology so prevalent throughout his time. According to this model of the white, middle-class woman, women were in charge of the "home front" and were responsible for raising the right kind of citizens as well as providing the right kind of home life for the men, the breadwinners of the family. Through the widespread imposition and acceptance of such gender-based roles, sexuality could be contained, and with it the individual citizens. By containing citizens, the family could be maintained, and success in the cold war against the hydra-headed communist threat could be promoted. McCarthy, in fact, worried as much about "effete" members of the Washington elite and homosexuals in general as about communists.[115] Sexuality, however, as the publication of Alfred Kinsey's books on sexual behavior would amply demonstrate, was neither so easily categorized nor easily controlled, and citizenship involved considerable tension and incipient protest as well as obedience and conformity.[116] Despite the importance of the *Kinsey Report* and the consequences it had for American society, and consistent with both this ideology and his conservatory task as president, Eisenhower continued to treat Americans as if they were rhetorically interchangeable— all white, all middle class, all devout. The middle class had gained respectability, but not the possibility of variety.

Some scholars now consider McCarthyism to have a homophobic element, bearing as it did such strong implications about heteronormativity.[117] Although by no means entirely visible, much less politically visible during these years, gay men were clearly visible to some, and their emergent visibility meant also that they were perceived as a threat—both in terms of national security as potential victims of blackmail and as more direct threats to the established American way of life. Attaining some small measure of political visibility meant also that they were subject to intense governmental scrutiny and the discipline of American society. Gays and lesbians were not yet politically visible but were already subject to differentiation and discipline.

Labor's gains were equally ambiguous. As the first Republican administration in twenty years, Eisenhower's was expected to be sympathetic to business.[118] He more than met expectations, for he was never comfortable with labor or its leaders and had no natural sympathy for them or their work.[119] Like many business leaders, Eisenhower saw labor more as a potential for unrest and imbalance than as a natural constituency. Consequently, management moved to appease organized labor on the one hand while preventing it from developing further on the other.[120] To protect the national balance of interests, labor had to be co-opted, domesticated, contained.

Organized labor did profit from the expanding economy and won both benefits and better wages as a result of the broadly based economic growth.[121] Workers who were not part of preexisting unions fared less well, as laws such as Taft-Hartley militated against the development of new unions. The corruption that accompanied union success and that was widely publicized during the Kefauver hearings also undermined labor, which retained a stronger organizational than ideological presence throughout the 1950s.[122] Postwar changes in the labor force were another factor, as the two fastest-growing segments of labor—white collar workers and women—were generally unenthusiastic about unions.[123] Labor was politically visible but not really politically problematic for Eisenhower. Constituted as unions rather than as individual workers, labor was simply not part of Eisenhower's governing coalition and was thus incidental to his rhetoric.

Although he exalted American labor, he did so in largely ceremonial, platitudinous, and general terms, calling them "the middle class," or "America," and noting their productivity and patriotism.[124] However, he also worried about labor when it was constituted as an organized group, rather than as a collection of autonomous workers. Dedicating the new AFL-CIO building in 1956, he said, "Labor organizations and government alike must serve the individual and not seek to dominate him. People are what count."[125] Those people were best served as individuals, not as members of groups.

In keeping with the interests of his coalition, Eisenhower conceived of the relationship between labor and capital as a partnership.[126] All he asked was that all groups subordinate their collective, specific, and short-term interests to the good of the nation as a whole—and he defined the nature of that "good."[127] For management, this meant acceptance of slightly lower profits. For workers, it meant the acceptance of lower salaries, lower benefits, and a reduced use of the strike as a negotiating tool in exchange for lower inflation.

With labor as with other groups, Eisenhower kept trying to make distinctions between doing something because it was right, and taking some political action to mollify a particular group. Early in his term he noted in his diary his sense of this problem: "Again, we come up against the whole question of the ability of a free government to continue functioning in spite of pressures from inside the body politic, where these pressures are created by immediate self-interest."[128] Thus, in Eisenhower's view, "free" government was government that avoided catering to the self-interest of groups. He was no broker in the model of FDR, mediating among groups in an effort to encourage a dynamic union. Eisenhower's union was contained, and the demands of groups were best contained as well.

Good citizens in Eisenhower's republic were domesticated and disciplined. They were constituted as (white, middle class) families. They learned the lessons of democracy at home and passed them along to the world through example. As in Wilson's republic, Eisenhower's was intended to encompass the world and to provide a light that would lead the world from the godless darkness of communism. Ideologically, all these ideas were, for Eisenhower, implicit in the history of the nation, which had always been leading to this point. He told the national story to the world audience, and its ideological power remains with us today.

NARRATING AMERICA

Eisenhower's rhetoric produced a profoundly nostalgic—and mythologized—view of national identity and national history, a nostalgia that he helped to create even while he was in office. In his 1959 State of the Union Address, for example, Eisenhower said, "As we meet today, in the 170th year of the Republic, our Nation must continue to provide—as all other free governments have had to do throughout history—a satisfactory answer to a question as old as history. It is: Can Government based upon liberty and the God-given rights of man, permanently endure when ceaselessly challenged by a dictatorship, hostile to our mode of life, and controlling an economic and military power of great and growing strength? For us, the answer has always been found, and is still found in the devotion, the vision, the courage, and the fortitude of the American people."[129] The idea that free governments have existed throughout history much less have addressed similar questions is, of course, inaccurate. It is, however, in keeping with the rhetorical forms required by the annual message.[130] His rendering of world history was tailored not to accurately depict world history, but to allow his rendering of American history and contemporaneous American politics to mesh into a seamless whole in which the contemporary challenges became identical and identified with humanity's timeless challenges.

Note, for instance, how world-historical questions became conflated into "our mode of life." This language cannot be attributed to the genre, for it was not restricted to his State of the Union Addresses. This sense of national history as national destiny was not, of course, unique to Eisenhower, and we have seen it operate through every president included in this study. Eisenhower relied here on Lincoln at Gettysburg, who made the question of this nation's survival also the question of whether any democratic nation could survive. Eisenhower accomplished through Lincoln the reconstitution of the American identity around the central question of liberty, understood though the global context of the cold war.

In so doing, Eisenhower did not merely conflate world history with contemporaneous American history; he also conflated all our national history until it was synonymous with the present moment. For instance, there were, throughout Eisenhower's public speech, as in FDR's, both implicit and explicit claims that the United States had always been dedicated to the same ideas and values. The only difference was that Americans were getting better at enacting them. His language at a national conference on civil rights is worth quoting at length:

> There can be no doubt that America has not reached perfection in attaining the lofty ideals laid down for us in our founding documents and in the amendments that have been made to our Constitution. The important thing is that we go ahead, that we make progress. This does not necessarily mean revolution. In my mind it means evolution. . . . We are saying that the concept of equality among men is equality in their opportunities, that we do not deny them that opportunity. I think no one could find complete equality between

any two individuals in the world, if we wanted to take absolute values in all of their spiritual, intellectual, and physical connotations. But we can talk about equality of opportunity, guaranteed to each person in this Nation.[131]

This language both expanded and contracted the idea of equality. Equality was expanded in that it was promoted as a crucial value, with an identical meaning, that has informed all American history. The potential for expansion implicit in this sort of civic nationalism was limited, however, for it was equality in what is not denied, not in what was guaranteed. This sense of world history, and of America's place in it, had profound ideological effects, for Eisenhower as they had for FDR. Through such teleology, for instance, Eisenhower and his successors were permitted to reason backward through American history, erasing, sanitizing, and rewriting the past so that it merged into a single narrative legitimizing present political exigencies. In this view of the United States, its new status as a superpower was not an accident, nor even a consequence of events over which Americans exercised little control. Instead, it was the fulfillment of national destiny, present since before the founding.

Speaking to a group of Republicans in 1957, for instance, he said, "But while our principles have remained unchanged for a hundred years, the problems to which these principles must be applied have changed radically and rapidly."[132] And in Williamsburg, Virginia, a few days later, he claimed that, "Here in Williamsburg, three centuries ago—in nearby Jamestown a half century earlier—lived men and women who cradled this mighty Republic. Devout in faith, their spirit strong, their deeds heroic, they permanently shaped our destiny. As long as this Republic endures, their wisdom and example will inspire our people."[133] Neither of these statements was particularly good history. They were, however, both good examples of the ideology so prevalent at the time and came to dominate the American political culture throughout the cold war.

That ideology was clear throughout Eisenhower's public speech. It relied on a specific and narrow view of American history that served to claim for the United States a natural and inevitable role as leader of the free world, the strongest force for liberty that the world had ever known. That claim may well have been accurate. But in making it, Eisenhower also erased much that contradicted it; he simplified and telescoped American history and made those who were not subject to his inclusion on those terms all the more conscious of their political invisibility and exclusion.

Conclusion

Much of our contemporary understanding of the cold war, of what was the Soviet Union, and a good deal of American history is tinted with the notions of American history as understood by Dwight Eisenhower. That understanding of history, widely shared and disseminated during the 1950s, has had—and continues to have—an important ideological impact on the United States. It dominated and influenced both domestic and international politics throughout the cold war, and our contemporary yearning for the peace and ordered existence of those times strongly influences contemporary conservative thought and political action.[134]

Among the most significant consequences of this ideological impact was the establishment of a culture of fear. That culture made it possible for Americans to turn on each other in order to avoid having anyone turn on them.[135] It was similar to the delegitimating tactics used by other presidents, but its connection to the cold war embedded it deeply into American contemporary national identity. One piece of evidence for this is that when celebrating "the greatest generation," Americans celebrate—and rightly so—the contributions of that generation to victory in World War II, and the sacrifices they made for freedom. In doing so, however, Americans often neglect to remember that in many cases, these were the same people who supported segregation, who fought against minority rights on any number of fronts, and who continued to stand for and with those who would defend the existing and often oppressive ascriptive national hierarchies. Their commitment to freedom was not unbounded but was both contained and specifically focused and directed to external rather than to internal political issues.

Yet another consequence is the way that Americans have accepted the idea that the middle way, as promulgated by Eisenhower, is the best way; that the only moral choice is the middle between two extremes. Although this sort of rhetoric dates at least as far back as the Whig platforms of the 1840s and 1850s, its use in the contemporary era has been consistent since the 1950s. One of the most damning delegitimizing arguments in modern politics—whether it is used against a Barry Goldwater or a George McGovern—is the use of the word "extreme." It remains an appellation Americans mistrust today. Anyone who advocates rapid change—sometimes anyone who advocates change at all—is regarded with deep suspicion. As Eisenhower said, "When sensible Americans—men and women—sit down together to discuss a problem in the hope of achieving a solution that is good for the whole Nation, something sensible comes out. We don't have crackpot ideas. We don't have doctrinaire opinions or solutions."[136] Americans believe in progress, carefully managed, and favor solutions that appeal to the common sense of the middle— "sensible Americans"—and worry about extremes of either the right or the left.

Earlier presidents had established the expectation that presidents would speak on issues of national import. Eisenhower chose to elide that expectation when it did not suit his political ends. He did face criticism for this refusal to speak, but it was never so intense as to force him to change his behavior. Consequently, countless Americans—blacks, suspected communists, gays and lesbians, and others who lived nondomesticated lives in the 1950s—faced lives that were far more difficult and sometimes far more dangerous than they might otherwise have been. Lacking political visibility and political power, members of these groups were not often overtly stigmatized by Eisenhower but were subject instead to the more subtle forms of exclusion associated with the language of citizenship.

Like other presidents, Eisenhower based his claim to unity on the disenfranchisement of those who threatened that unity. American diversity became a threat to American victory in the cold war, while at the same time, the country's often-vaunted tolerance for diversity became an important weapon in the prosecution of that war. As the fissures created by the contradiction widened, so did the disparities and differences in opinion among Americans as to the precise nature of the national identity. In the context of continual international crises, those disparities and differences took on major significance, and the breach between Americans would soon widen into the confrontations of the 1960s and 1970s and then solidify into the nostalgic backlash against such groups that often seems to characterize contemporary politics.

7 / Managing Diversity in a Fragmented Polity: The Post–Cold War World of George H. W. Bush

What Bush represented was more of the same but less. Less open acceptance of bigotry. Less braying insensitivity to the unfortunate. Less grasping and petty corruption. Less celebration of greed and gaucherie. Less indolence and inattention in the Oval Office. Less of a "lone cowboy" style in world affairs. Yet Bush was clear that he considered these matters of style rather than substance.
—Michael Duffy and Dan Goodgame, *Marching in Place: The Status Quo Presidency of George Bush*

IT IS POSSIBLE to read American history as alternating cycles of expansion and contraction, dynamism and stasis. The civil rights movement, for instance, gathered momentum in the years following Eisenhower's term in office, leading to an increased incorporation of previously disenfranchised groups. Women were increasingly part of the workforce and the political process. Many more groups—American Indians, Asian Americans, Hispanic and Latino/Latina Americans, gays and lesbians—took both inspiration and strategy from the civil rights movement and began to insist that they be accorded political visibility and political power. The union became more difficult to maintain on its old terms, but the cold war context seemed to prevent the establishment of new terms.

Issues of citizenship were nationally visible and were hard for any president to ignore. These issues were no longer restricted to questions of who was legally a citizen—although those issues remained important—but also included questions about the appropriate relationship of economic inequality and racism to citizenship, the influences of social behaviors, as well as structural concerns such as the quality of inner-city schools and how to best implement—even whether to implement—Affirmative Action programs. Presidents could no longer argue that America should not incorporate some "persons" as "citizens," except when discussing immigration, an increasingly important topic on the national agenda. They now had to decide in what ways members of these various groups could be incorporated.

By the late 1980s, one of the few things that seemed to be widely accepted was the fragmentation of American life. There were lobbies for minorities, together and separately, lobbies for those who opposed the inclusion of minorities, lobbies for oil interests and the environment, so many lobbies for so many things that it became easy for politicians and pundits to label and dismiss them all equally as "special interests."[1] As the interests of both those who sought to maintain the national hierarchies and those who sought to rearrange them became more organized and vocal, they also became more engaged in public duels with one another, most often in the halls of Congress, but for a time also on the streets, then in the courts, and finally throughout the polity.[2] According to Gary Gerstle, the Rooseveltian nation, founded during the beginning of the century, was in danger of disintegration as the press for civil rights and the Vietnam War had led to such serious fragmentation that the nation could no longer be unified.[3]

George Bush thus came to govern a polity whose very governability was at issue. Elected as Reagan's heir,[4] he was less ideologically divisive a figure,[5] more of a guardian, in Richard Rose's terms, than a leader.[6] Faced with large deficits, committed to a position that restricted his ability to maneuver, and less astute than Reagan politically, Bush found that Reagan was, in nearly all respects, a very hard act to follow.

Bush inherited a fractious polity in which issues of national identity were discussed openly, often, and acrimoniously. In responding to these various pressures, Bush's rhetoric on national diversity and national identity had three important themes: faith in the system as a way to manage change, an explicit preference for the private over the public arena, and the inclusion of various groups based on their ability to exemplify certain specific values, or what I call "celebratory othering."[7] The first two of these worked to defend, naturalize, and legitimate existing institutional arrangements and political hierarchies. They were enabled by the third, for celebratory othering both included others and distanced them. By allowing others to represent Americans, those others were included on the one hand as representative. They were also distanced, however. By representing Americans, they were prevented from actually being considered fully American, and their experiences and histories were erased even as they ostensibly were brought into the national polity.

Unlike deferral and other presidential calls for patience, which legitimate demands while postponing their achievement, celebratory othering implies that its target groups have already been included fully. Although acknowledging a group's political visibility, it has the rather perverse effect of delegitimating its demands by making it appear that a reasonable degree of inclusion has already been attained and that further demands are tantamount to "special rights." It is a way of ostensibly offering inclusion to everyone while also maintaining the existing political hierarchies. This rhetoric—whether used instrumentally or, as was more often the case, ceremonially if not platitudinously—encouraged optimism and quiescence among American citizens while distancing American government from responsibility in social policy. Celebratory othering satisfied a perceived political need to include all Americans, criticize no American overtly, and claim a unity for the nation on the basis of a shared national identity. This rhetoric continues to characterize a considerable amount of presidential rhetoric on national identity.

Bush's Faith in the System

George Bush had the unenviable task of following Ronald Reagan into the Oval Office, but despite Bush's harsh anti-Reagan rhetoric during the 1980 campaign and his generally more moderate politics, by 1988 Bush seemed to have little quarrel with the general tone and content of Reaganism.[8] Stylistically, of course, Bush could not hope to compare with Reagan, and he lacked Reagan's simplified world-view and determination to act on it.[9] He also attained office after a bitter and, according to some, racially charged but otherwise empty campaign that resulted in an unclear mandate.[10] Bush thus entered office with a political legacy of conservatism in a context that was increasingly divided over the direction the country should take on matters of national diversity—matters that were increasingly on the national agenda.

Virtually no group in American politics seemed to be politically invisible, yet every group seemed to feel that it was in the process of being marginalized. Nearly everyone, it seemed during these years, could make a case for being a minority. As the economic opportunities open to Americans seemed to shrink, everyone began to fear disenfranchisement. Their demands on government increased, and the system strained to keep up. Bush's rhetoric was reflective of many of those fears, tensions, and strains, and he sought ways of defending the system. The most prominent of these ways was an explicit defense of it.

DEFENDING THE STATUS QUO

All presidents are conservative, for all presidents are brought to power by a nexus of forces that favor stable institutions and consistency with the past. Presidents normally favor incremental over rapid change. Even by that standard, however, Bush was cautious in comparison with many of his modern counterparts. Caution was both a rhetorical strategy and a preferred approach to life for George Bush, who has always been a supporter of the status quo. This approach also led him to protect the existing system of hierarchies at home and overseas.[11] In both arenas, because of his personal and political preferences about how change should be managed, his actions and rhetoric functioned to maintain and protect the existing structures of power and the accompanying social hierarchies, even when that was not his explicit intent. Speaking at a commencement ceremony in College Station, Texas, shortly after taking office, he said, for example, that "containment worked. Containment worked because our democratic principles and institutions and values are sound and always have been. It worked because our alliances were, and are, strong and because the superiority of free societies and free markets over stagnant socialism is undeniable."[12] This quotation, of course, was about foreign policy, and it reflected, among other things, the continued dominance of Eisenhower's understanding of the cold war and argued for a continuation of the policies favored by Eisenhower. Bush, like Eisenhower before him, believed in containing and managing change, not in being governed by its demands.

A believer in the established ways of doing things, Bush often talked about change and its proper management. Probably the most frequently cited instance is his inaugural, where he referred to change through such gentle metaphors as a page turning and a breeze blowing, and softened its potentially threatening nature by saying, "On days like this we remember that we are all part of a continuum, inescapably connected by the ties that bind."[13] Change for Bush was natural, inevitable, and progressive, not disruptive. Like Eisenhower, Bush believed that change should also be slow, because stability was a key value. Of course, the promise of stability is always an important part of the inaugural itself, and given a president succeeding someone of his own party, any call for change would be moderate at best. However, the multiplicity of examples available indicates that it was not merely fulfillment of a generic requirement but a philosophical orientation as well.

Like Eisenhower, Bush was not threatened by change, because he saw no reason for any change in the American way of doing things. His notion of managing change was additive, not transformational, because he believed that the institutional structures were sound and could be trusted to control change so long as they were not overwhelmed by it. Again speaking on foreign policy, he told the Ohio Chamber of Commerce in 1990, "But in this world of change, one thing is certain: America must be ready. And as excited as I am about the changes moving toward a more peaceful Eastern Europe, America must be strong. And a strong America means not only a strong economy; it still must mean a strong defense, a ready and highly effective defense force. . . . The jury is no longer out. Markets work. Government controls do not work."[14] These policies, advantageous to his governing coalition, were justified in ideological terms as what America needed.

For Bush, the most important task of a president, as for all members of the polity, was preservation. "Prudence," he said, was a president's "first duty."[15] This was especially characteristic of Bush's actions in foreign policy. Noting the impending changes in the international order in a speech to a 1989 Joint Session of Congress, Bush said, "Prudence and common sense dictate that we try to understand the full meaning of the change going on there, review our policies, and proceed with caution."[16] Study, not action, would be the first order of business.

Like Eisenhower, Bush argued that, in part, this caution was so important because of American international responsibilities and the high stakes that accompanied them: "What is at stake," Bush claimed in his 1991 State of the Union Address, "is more than one small country; it is a big idea: a new world order, where diverse nations are drawn together in common cause to achieve the universal aspirations of mankind—peace and security, freedom, and the rule of law. Such is a world worthy of our struggle and worthy of our children's future."[17] With so much at stake, no president could afford to act rashly, especially given the potential benefits of prudent action. In his 1992 State of the Union Address, Bush said, "Much good can come from the prudent use of power. And much good can come of this: A world once divided into two armed camps now recognizes one sole and preeminent power, the United States of America. And they regard this with no dread. . . . They trust us to do what's right."[18] Eisenhower's vision of the battle for the soul of the world had been vindicated, and the world had indeed been saved. Bush argued that this was no time to change the nature of the leadership that had won the cold war, for doing so would lose for American leadership the trust of the world.

Bush attributed the end of the cold war to a long history of presidential prudence, which earned for the United States the trust of the world, and he thus also sought to align himself and his political approach with past presidents. But in Bush's case, at least according to his critics, caution became tantamount to inaction.[19] This caution allowed Bush to forge compromises and create coalitions; it also permitted him to avoid taking a strong stand on many issues of national importance.[20] Instead, Bush, in common with much recent presidential practice, offered a 1991 group of executives a long list of vague bromides he could support:

> And I share that vision, for what is the American dream if it isn't wanting to be part of something larger than ourselves? If it isn't creating a better life for our children than we might have had? If it isn't the freedom to take command of our future? For most people, these aspirations mean enjoying the blessings of good health or having a home to call one's own or raising a family, holding a stake in the community, feeling secure, secure at home or in our neighborhood. But for others, sadly, America has not yet fulfilled the promise of equality of opportunity. We know who they are: They're the hopeless and the homeless, the friendless and the fearful, the unemployed and the underemployed, the ones that can't read, the ones that can't write. They are the ones who don't believe that they will ever share in the American dream. I'm here to tell any American for whom hope lies dormant: We will not forget you. We will not forget those who have not yet shared in the American dream. We must offer them hope. But we must guarantee them opportunity.[21]

Bush offered an expansive version of the American dream—the participation in "something larger than ourselves"—but failed to offer a vision of what that something was. Americans wanted to command the future, but it was unclear to what purpose. The cold war presidents had a clear sense of purpose and a clear justification for nearly every action. At the end of the cold war, domestic issues could once again be justified on their own terms, but those terms had to be defined and defended.

He spoke in compassionate tones but outlined no specific policy. He promised to remember certain previously excluded groups, to offer their members opportunity, but it was not clear how that opportunity was defined nor how it would be offered. Like many other modern presidents, Bush could support a broad range of vague goals intended to garner and maintain political support, but his innate political caution prevented him from making many of them policies, and thus he talked progressively while acting to preserve the status quo.

Bush's faith in the system as a way to manage change offered many of the same ideological enticements that had operated for Eisenhower and were also plausible because they were familiar. Eisenhower had been able to offer reassurance and call for national sacrifice. But Bush operated in a different political context, in which reassurance remained important but calls for sacrifice were unwelcome. His caution did defuse some of the demands on government and did some of the ideological work of constructing a certain sort of citizen, one who would be patient and steady, unwilling to take risks on the national security, and existed more in the past than in the present. Bush's speech was not a simple defense of the status quo, however, but involved rather more complicated rhetorical terrain. Three main premises supported his argument that caution was justified because the system was sound: a stress on preservation, an attempt to lower expectations, and a belief in the system's essential fairness. If these premises were granted, the only sensible approach to governance would be a prudent one.

INTERPRETING HISTORY

Bush has been called a "true conservative, an American Tory."[22] In keeping with that image, he told the Kentucky Fried Chicken convention in 1992, "I'm a conservative, and to me being a conservative means to renew, to reinvigorate what has always made America great, and that is the power of the individual."[23] Bush echoed both Wilson and Eisenhower here, and implied that the key to American greatness would be found in an examination of the American past. This emphasis on the past as a way to understand the present—to preserve that which had *always* made America great, was typical— both of Bush and of presidential rhetoric more generally. Ideologically, it worked to connect the sort of citizen Bush constructed with a version of history that argued that Americans were always that sort of citizen. Bush could therefore render a fractious polity more manageable by uniting it through a shared sense of national destiny.

Bush had a specific rendering of the American past. Again from his 1990 speech to executives:

Some people think of our great country as a nation of rugged individualists alone against the odds. And that is a part of the American tradition, but only a part. There's another tradition, a tradition as old as America itself, as old as the Pilgrims and the Mayflower Compact, as old as the pioneers who settled the West. It's the tradition Tocqueville described more than 150 years ago when he came to America, observed the scenes, and wrote that, "Americans of all ages, all conditions, and all dispositions constantly form associations." That shouldn't surprise us, because the act of association is nothing less than democracy in action: individuals translating common interests into a common cause.[24]

Bush thus grounded the contemporaneous culture in the past traditions of America and saw the contemporary world as the product of a linear development from the Pilgrims.[25] This required less an understanding of American history than an appropriation of that history—Tocqueville's associations were as different from those Bush was addressing as the Pilgrims were from contemporary Americans.

We have seen this tactic before, and it performed the same ideological work here. His rhetoric ostensibly included all Americans—he relied on both the individualist and the communitarian traditions in American culture, for instance, and also referred to the great moments and characters of American history—the Pilgrims and the pioneers. The implicit argument was that Americans could be both individualists and act collectively, that Americans could have group identity through their various associations and still feel most strongly about national identity, the "common cause." It was up to Bush as president to define that common cause; unity was the responsibility of the people. Bush thus legitimated group identification, and this language was potentially quite inclusive.

It also had the potential to exclude, however. Note that his notion of "associations" was Tocquevillian—that is, he relied on a notion of groups as voluntary associations. Groups thus constituted were in the finest traditions of civic nationalism, but also operated to reinforce racial nationalism, for groups that were not voluntary had much less legitimacy. They were not lauded as a constituent part of a healthy democracy. In arguing for voluntarism, for instance, he said, "Today, we look to voluntary fraternalism to lead us back to our roots and away from a debilitating social experiment: Government paternalism with all its mandated benefits designed by some subcommittee on Capital Hill. Before the advent of the modern welfare state, voluntary associations, usually religious or fraternal in character, provided most social services. . . . We need this spirit of voluntarism more than ever in the history of our country."[26] Note the mixture of historical evidence and ideological assumption here. This was less an objective analysis of history than an ideological argument, designed to promote a specific view of national history and, from it, a specific trajectory for national policy, one that would serve the interests of Bush's governing coalition.

As with FDR's attempts to render some issues a matter of private rather than public concern and Eisenhower's efforts to domesticate issues, Bush's interpretation of a shared national history did the ideological work of rendering some things less suitable for the public agenda than others. Just as Cleveland relied on the charitable impulses of Gilded Age citizens, Bush relied on those same impulses in the polity he managed. By making those impulses part of the national heritage, the implicit claim was that government had never been effective as a provider of social services and ought not to have tried to assume that role—it was a "debilitating social experiment." The reliance on voluntarism was not portrayed as a political choice but as the product of an objective and neutral historical lesson.

This line of argumentation clearly served Bush's conservative political goals. In preserving history, Bush also preserved the existing national culture, especially those parts of it that were considered by many social conservatives to be under assault. At the *American Spectator*'s annual dinner in 1990, Bush said: "The values I'm talking about have a home in the family, in our churches, and in our communities. And these institutions are strong, much stronger than the alarmists out there would have us believe. Each of them contributes to our public life, enriches it in ways beyond measure. Each of them makes this nation strong, gives it a sense of purpose and a role in the world. And this is the culture that sustains us, the culture that we must ourselves sustain. And that's our challenge today."[27] These values and these institutions were the ones that were important to Bush's coalition; they buttressed and were buttressed by the political arrangements and institutions favored by members of that coalition. They were the values and institutions of the Eisenhower era.

This was not a culture that he would open to change, to the influences of the many immigrants, workers, and others whose experiences he lauded. This was the dominant culture, and he was pledged to protect its interests. In pledging that protection, Bush was also making it clear—albeit indirectly if not unintentionally—who was included as American and who was left outside the national community. That indirectness was characteristic of the more subtle language of citizenship in the context of what Gerstle sees as the dissolution of the Rooseveltian nation. One way of managing a diverse nation that had lost its faith in civic nationalism was to erase difference by making vague but universal and apparently inclusive nods toward "all Americans." So many groups were so politically visible and were contending so publicly that erasure was accomplished through inclusion on the basis of one set of values, or rules, or norms.

In clarifying national inclusion, Bush also co-opted the history of minority Americans. He adopted their heroes as national heroes, and by placing the national government on their side instead of in opposition to them, took them, their experiences, and their examples out of context. He thus included them in the national history but did so on terms that also excluded them. In speaking of Dr. Martin Luther King, Jr., for instance, Bush first acknowledged the "loneliness of that struggle" and the continuing existence of racism and prejudice, and then said, "He taught us the difference one man can make in a country dedicated to the ideals of brotherhood. He saw an America that was like the welcome table the spiritual speaks of, where all Americans can eat and never be hungry, drink, and never be thirsty. With your continuing commitment and help, we will meet these great challenges and make real the dream of Martin Luther King."[28] In examples like this, the implicit message was that the lessons of King and of others like him had been learned by the majority of Americans. Racism and prejudice continued to exist among only a small minority. The vast majority of Americans (whether or not the spiritual he mentioned restricted Heaven's bounty to one nation alone) needed no further persuasion, no further argumentation or action. All Americans needed was the national commitment—and this, for Bush, was clearly outside the presidential purview. African Americans were included through King; nothing remained for the government to do—any further demands on it were requests for "special rights."

It is important to note that this language also excluded those who were racist and prejudiced. Civic nationalism was the only overt form of nationalism present in the public sphere. Those offering racialized versions of nationalism were generally marginalized or overtly excluded in Bush's rhetoric. The overt language of racism was no longer acceptable. Exclusions were still possible but had to be subtler, as in this example of historical co-option.

This use of historical co-optation facilitated the argument that the nation was headed in the right direction and that all Americans had to do was wait and watch history unfold. The American people needed to take no action, and neither did the government. By using a selective version of history to support his policy preferences, Bush could use the same sort of historical inevitability that we have seen in every president included in this study. Relying on history justified the continuation of certain exclusions as natural and inevitable. The progress that had been made historically justified the continued slow pace of change, and the argument removed agency from contemporary political actors making contemporary political choices and placed the agency onto history itself. Since history was working in its own way and at its own pace to gradually bring all Americans closer to the ideals of the founding, no one should expect too much of the government. It moved at history's behest.

LOWERING EXPECTATIONS

Bush's polity was thus grounded in a specific rendering of the American past, one that fostered key values through limited government. Protecting that system in the present thus required a muting of demands on the system, lest it become overburdened and unable to function properly. Fewer demands for inclusion would thus promote more inclusion in the long run. Lower expectations would make it more possible for the system to meet expectations. Speaking at a commencement ceremony in Michigan, for instance, Bush said, "We don't need another Great Society with huge and ambitious programs administered by the incumbent few. We need a Good Society built upon the deeds of the many, a society that promotes service, selflessness, action."[29] Bush reduced the ambitions of the 1960s to more limited goals, ones he argued were more suitable to the budgetary constraints of the 1980s and 1990s. Like Eisenhower, he wanted a contained union, not a dynamic one, for the contradictions and tensions of his time had to be controlled before they could be managed.

Through such pronouncements, Bush consciously strove to reduce the profile of the presidency within the government and of the president within the national pantheon of celebrities. To another university audience, this one in St. Louis, he said, "Most Americans believe that in the America of the 1990s our challenges must be met in several ways—by government, by thousands upon thousands of other institutions, and by the people themselves working together— or they won't be met at all."[30] Government had a role, but it was, as it had been under Eisenhower, a limited role.

In addition to believing that the role of government was limited, he told a 1989 gathering of the United Negro College Fund, "most Americans . . . believe that government can be an instrument of healing."[31] That healing function existed in tension with the preference for limited government. His reliance on voluntarism was one way that this tension was reconciled, for it was really to places other than government that citizens should look for healing. The first belief (in government's limited role) overrode the second (in government's healing power). Good citizens thus moderated their demands on government and did not look to it first. Good citizens in Bush's republic managed their own concerns.

Bush argued that the impetus for lowered expectations came from the people, who realized that government was only one of many actors in the domestic policy realm. "The strength of democracy," according to President Bush in his 1991 State of the Union Address, "is not in bureaucracy. It is in the people and their communities. . . . We must return to families, communities, counties, cities, States, and institutions of every kind the power to chart their own destiny and the freedom and opportunity provided by strong economic growth. And that's what America is all about."[32] Individualism, community values, and destiny all favored a limited government. Eisenhower wanted to contain the polity during the cold war and offering a limited government helped him to reduce FDR's dynamic union to a more restricted one. After the Great Society, Bush's advocacy of lowered expectations had much the same ideological effect, helping him to construct a more manageable polity. As he said to the Future Farmers of America in 1989, "Our task now is to build upon that spirit, the spirit of 'America can,' not 'Washington must.'"[33] If government was supposed to do less, and the president was less responsible for the nation's social policy, Bush could construct a specific sort of citizen, one who expected less from the government.

Bush's call for lowered expectations functioned in similar ideological ways to the arguments of earlier presidents to reduce pressures on the federal government, slow the pace of change, and protect the existing political arrangements and institutional structures. It implied the creation of a specific sort of citizen, one who was already included and should be satisfied with the status quo. This argument was sustained and reinforced by a rhetorical reliance upon rules and process, which worked in similar ways to calls for patience and deferral and implied that since the system was fair, it would function as a neutral umpire, and all demands would be treated equally, according to the agreed-upon processes of democratic decision making.

RULES AND PROCESS

Dedication to rules and process meant that Bush would accomplish his more aggressive political ends through inaction. Because the system as a whole was considered fair, then its decisions were also fair. The lack of a lengthy domestic agenda intensified the competition to get on that agenda. The issues that did not make it onto that agenda were probably also those that did not serve the goals of his governing coalition. Rather than actively deny action, however, a reliance on rules and process meant that the de facto result was inaction but that the agency for that "decision" was displaced. No one was responsible; it was the result of a fair process. This reliance on rules and process did the same political work for Bush as similar rhetoric had for Wilson and FDR; it enabled him to make political choices without seeming to make any such choices. Inaction was the rule and not the exception. Bush's claims to fairness and decency were expressed in ideological terms—terms that were widely shared by his audiences. These terms included the use of ideological language and a critique of partisanship by political actors other than himself.

Playing Fair. George Bush, by most accounts, is a sincerely decent man.[34] For him, the rules of decency, honor, and fair play are deeply important. As president, he argued that they were deeply embedded in the American character. In a typical statement, he said:

> And that's why, with all the flash and the fluff in the world today, there's something we can't afford to lose sight of, something deceptively simple: It's who we are that makes this nation what it is. You know—we all know—democracy is more than the machinery of government, more than just a system of checks and balances, clashing interests. More than anything else, democracy depends on the decency of its people. And I am convinced that there is in this country a deep reservoir of democratic decency—a respect for others, a sense of responsibility, a solid recognition that values matter. This reservoir of decency is there for us to draw on to renew our dedication to the fundamental ideals of a free government.[35]

Citizens in Bush's nation were decent citizens. They were Roosevelt's good neighbors. They respected others, assumed responsibility for their actions, and upheld American values. They were citizens of Gerstle's Rooseveltian nation, who honored civic nationalist principles. This rhetoric, which appeared so inclusive, also had exclusionary implications, however. A subtle kind of exclusion was grounded in claims to such decency, in the argument that courtesy was more important than policy, in the belief that good people could not knowingly damage others. Bush claimed that the nation was committed to civic nationalism, through and through. By arguing that such principles were widely—even universally—accepted, Bush ignored the ways in which they were not accepted, not acted on, and the damage to American minorities that was thereby done.

For Bush, civility was not just a personal value; it was a national value, the very bedrock of American democracy, and the bedrock of the democracies the United States sought to create and support around the world. As he said to the United Nations Security Council in 1992, "The will of the majority must never degenerate into the whim of the majority. This fundamental principle transcends all borders. Human dignity, the inalienable rights of man, these are not the possessions of the state. They're universal. In Asia, in Africa, the United Nations must stand with those who seek greater freedom and democracy. And that is my deep belief; that is the belief of the

American people. And it's the belief that breathes life into the great principle of the universal declaration of human rights."[36] This language, so reminiscent of Woodrow Wilson, accomplished the same ideological functions for Bush: the stress on universals both included and subtly excluded by reducing all human desires to American desires—as the president understood and articulated those desires. The United States was willing to support democracies, especially when they resembled democracy as it was defined, articulated, and practiced in the United States.

Bush often cited the American commitment to process as a way of arguing for his policies. During the Tower nomination imbroglio, for instance, he said, "Americans, whatever their policies—and I'll bet you agree with this—and whatever their politics, are committed to the concept of fair play and are committed to decency."[37] In democratic politics, of course, the key debates center around questions of what constitutes fairness, and how fair play is to be determined. Everyone may well have been for "fair play," and there could well have been a plethora of different interpretations of what exactly that meant. But only one definition had constitutive power. Ideologically, this argument did important political work for Bush. Fair play was used to support processes that Bush understood as "neutral" but that indirectly and implicitly conveyed his political preferences into policy.

This had important implications for citizenship, because the government did not, in fact, act as neutral umpire, and the rules of the political game always advantage some players over others. By arguing that the rules were fair, and the judgment even, those people whose interests were already part of the standard routine of government were kept there, and those whose interests were excluded were kept there as well. Fairness understood as existing process always advantages the already advantaged.

Bush's commitment to "playing fair," for instance, did not translate into an unequivocal support for civil rights.[38] Bush always claimed to be a supporter of civil rights in general, but before his presidency there was little evidence for any specific support.[39] His advocacy of the Americans with Disabilities Act as a civil rights measure, however, should not go unnoticed here, and it is important to note that in 1991 he finally signed a Civil Rights Act. Nonetheless, his initial veto of the 1990–1991 Civil Rights Act signaled to many observers the weakness of any commitment to civil rights within the Bush administration.[40] Defending that veto via his history on civil rights, he said, "I have long stood for civil rights. I think anybody in public life knows that I have long stood for civil rights. But I just don't think its fair to sign a bill that will result in quotas. The day I vetoed that bill I attached to it a civil rights bill challenging all these proponents of civil rights. Pass a real civil rights bill. And they didn't even permit the House and Senate to vote on it because they wanted to try and embarrass the President. I am for civil rights and I am against quotas."[41] African Americans, both politically visible and not without political power during the Bush administration, were also politically problematic for Bush. He used differentiation—he was for civil rights and against civil rights defined as quotas—to enunciate an argument that implied a lowered expectation for government and a reliance on the private sphere. Civil rights were a positive good, but they did not require this specific government action. Bush used the rhetoric of fair play to accomplish this differentiation both from political principle and from a need to render the issue manageable in ways that would serve the interests of his governing and electoral coalitions.

Bush further explained his stance by focusing on civil rights as an economic issue, much as FDR had done. "Civil rights," he said in his 1991 State of the Union Address, "are also crucial to protecting economic opportunity. Every one of us has a responsibility to speak out against racism, bigotry, and hate. We will continue our vigorous enforcement of existing statutes, and I will again press the Congress to strengthen the laws against employment discrimination without resorting to the use of unfair practices."[42] Using strongly civic nationalist language, Bush argued that the civil rights bill meant quotas, and quotas constituted "unfairness." Yet Bush made little explanatory headway. The nation had come a long way since FDR was president, and arguments that worked for him were no longer effective for other presidents—especially not contemporary Republican presidents, bearing as they do the burden of suspicion on civil rights matters in general. It didn't help Bush that the issue of a civil rights bill dragged on and on, and thus became associated with a plethora of other political events and presidential actions.

Bush's problems in this regard extended also to civil rights in the international order. Whereas Wilson and Eisenhower had used the international arena to forge certain sorts of widespread ideological consensus at home, Bush's support for international human rights was criticized as being no more consistent and principled than was his support for domestic civil rights. Again, the political context had changed, and the polity had become more fractious, more internationalized, more difficult to manage. Bush argued before the Council of the Americas in 1989 that "my administration will work to build a new partnership for the Americas, a partnership built on mutual respect and mutual responsibilities. And we seek a partnership rooted in common commitment to democratic rule. The battle for democracy is far from over. The institutions of free government are still fragile and in need of support. Our battlefield is the broad middle ground of democracy and popular government; our fight, against the enemies of freedom on the extreme right and on the extreme left."[43] Just as Eisenhower had made similar statements about the U.S. relationship with Latin America—and had relied on similar inaccuracies—Bush's claims here had similar ideological effects. He used the metaphor of partnership, with its implied equality, to underpin a view of the relationship that was mutual and based on shared values. The inequality of the relationship, like the importance of culture and cultural understandings of democracy, was erased. The argument supported the middle ground, against extremes of either side. For Bush, as for Eisenhower, the middle ground was the turf on which manageable politics were conducted. Here as elsewhere, Bush preferred the prudent path, the middle path. But the existing policy of American government had a force and a trajectory of its own, and despite Bush's rhetoric, his actions remained consistent with that force and its trajectory. The potentially inclusive rhetoric masked the more subtle assertion of power in the international arena as at home.

Latin America was not the only example. He condemned the massacre in Tiananmen Square, for instance, in the strongest terms: "During the past few days, elements of the Chinese Army have been brutally suppressing popular and peaceful demonstrations in China. ... The United States cannot condone the violent attacks and cannot ignore the consequences for our relationship with China, which has been built on a foundation of broad support by the American people."[44] But even before he ended the statement, he backed away from his own harsh tone: "This is not the time for an emotional response, but for a reasoned, careful action that takes into account both our long-term interests and a recognition of a complex internal situation in China. . . . The process of democratization of Communist societies will not be a smooth one, and we must react to setbacks in a way which stimulates rather than stifles progress toward open and representative systems."[45] Unsurprisingly, his relations with the Chinese government remained cordial.[46] In this respect, of course, Bush was following a time-honored pattern of presidential behavior. As with the rest of his presidency, he was aware of political complexities if not always willing or able to convey those complexities to the public. As a result his policies were often unclear and always cautious. The rhetoric of citizenship contained more subtle exclusions than the rhetoric of balance, whether in the national or international realm.

As these examples indicated, both internationally and nationally, his stress on rules and process with its accompanying plea for civility implied that it was unmannerly, if not downright rude, to question the status quo. "The American people know fairness when they see it," he told reporters tartly in 1991.[47] Fairness and procedure were important to this president, and in preserving them, he also preserved much of the status quo, for those rules were not politically neutral, regardless of the prevalent ideological claim to the contrary. Other potent ideological claims and political exclusions could be found in his specific language choices.

Ideological Language. If decency was required for a functioning polity, and the preservation of the polity was the overriding goal of the president, certain ideological positions followed, such as an emphasis on fairness and process, and a preference for the "middle ground" as synonymous with the "correct ground." This emphasis led to a reliance on certain rhetorical forms, which carried with them exclusionary images and ideas while maintaining distance from that exclusion. This language reflected, whether intentionally or reflexively, the understanding and acceptance of a particular vocabulary that emanated from a shared ideology. It thus supported a rhetoric that helped to legitimate and reinforce the political arrangements and institutions that advantaged Bush's governing coalition.

George Bush did set a compassionate and inclusive tone. As he told a group of high-school students in 1989, "I've learned, for

instance, that we are not black and white, rural and urban, the privileged and the poor. We are . . . Americans. And I've learned that any
definition of a successful life insists that we help those for whom the
American dream seems like an impossible dream. And I have learned
that for different generations this help may take different forms, for
conditions vary, challenges change. And yet what does not, must
not, change is our capacity—responsibility—to assist society at
large."[48] For Bush, as for presidents at least since Wilson, Americans
were all fundamentally the same. They could all be equally served by
the same policies. The same policies that served the specific interests of Bush's governing coalition could also be understood to serve
the mass public as well. Sharing these interests and policies, Bush's
citizens were both responsible and compassionate. Indeed, they saw
compassion as one of their responsibilities.

He could be equally compassionate in discussing specific policies as general attitudes. At the *American Spectator*'s annual dinner,
he said,

> Take an issue like homelessness. There is no condition more
> repugnant to the democratic values and the dignity of the
> individual and there's no problem more susceptible to mis-
> understanding. . . . And in some ways, our difficulty in deal-
> ing with homelessness begins with the label, a label that
> tells us what the homeless lack is homes. But the problem is
> far more complex—more complex because the real problem
> of homelessness is not one-dimensional. . . . If our policy
> towards the homeless doesn't treat these causes, if it doesn't
> combine the basic need for shelter with other support serv-
> ices that reach the real reasons for homelessness, all the best
> intentions in the world won't get the homeless off the street
> once and for all and back into society.[49]

This quotation brings Roosevelt's compassion toward and inclusion of the poor most readily to mind. The difference was that Roosevelt saw it as the government's responsibility to assist the poor, for
government action was important to his efforts to build a dynamic
union. Bush understood the private citizen as the locus for action,
preferring, like Cleveland and Eisenhower, the construction of a
more restrained, manageable union. Bush therefore offered little in

the way of policy directed at those he addressed so compassionate-ly.[50] But the tone and the willingness to speak on issues like home-lessness did provide some legitimacy to the concerns of the less pow-erful, and offered legitimacy that they had previously lacked. The homeless were politically visible and politically problematic, but they were widely perceived as lacking agency and were far more like-ly to be the subjects of governmental discourse than the agents of it. They lacked significant political power.

Yet even with this compassion, Bush's acceptance of certain mainstream ideological positions led to rhetoric containing implicit assumptions. The clearest example of this language in operation was Willie Horton, who appeared (for the first time in life as "Willie") in campaign ads during the 1988 presidential election and whose shad-ow never quite left the Bush White House.[51] As late as 1991, Bush was having to defend himself on charges of racism during the cam-paign, charges that he tried to dismiss as "part of the liberal litany,"[52] as if using the liberal brush to tar his critics would cause them to consider him less motivated by stereotypes. And indeed, the questions did not go away because Willie Horton was not a singular example of this tendency.[53] African Americans were politically visi-ble and politically problematic. They remained subject to some forms of differentiation, as in the case of Willie Horton. But as Horton's example also indicated, this differentiation would not go unchal-lenged in the public arena; such differentiation thus operated most effectively through ideological language. The political context had changed a great deal, and exclusions had to be more subtle to go uncontested. Other, more ideologically contained examples occurred more often in his speech.

The most encompassing of these examples was "security." Bush used "security" in the domestic context as a way of arguing that middle-class people needed to feel safe—and what threatened them was left up to the listener. Speaking to an audience of law enforce-ment professionals in 1989, Bush said, "A secure community is the right of every American."[54] "Security" functioned as part of an enthymeme, and race, poverty, and other unmentionable threats were the unspoken connectors in the syllogism. In an international-ly televised address on our national drug control strategy that same year he said, for example, "And while illegal drug use is found in every community, no where is it worse than in our public housing projects. You know, the poor have never had it easy in this world. But in the past, they weren't mugged on the way home from work by crack gangs. And their children didn't have to dodge bullets on the way to school."[55] This language was potentially inclusive, for "safety" was understood as the right of all citizens. But it was also potentially exclusionary. Those who lived in public housing were subject to the ideological consequences of presidential differentiation.

His solution to these dangers was not to improve the housing conditions for the poor, not to sponsor gun control laws. His solution was to enforce drug laws, which had a disproportionate impact on the black and the poor. The connection between illegal drugs, poverty, and the threat to security was clear, if implicit. In making the poor the subject here, he both included them as part of the national community and offered them up as a warning: If Americans did not act quickly, all neighborhoods would suffer the same pathologies as these neighborhoods. The "us" and the "them," while implicit, were nevertheless potentially powerful components of this rhetoric. As always, the language of citizenship had implications for balance but contained more subtle exclusions.

Given the context of security, as in this example, another powerful, although less subtle, example was drugs. Certainly drug use continued to be a major concern throughout the Bush years.[56] As a result, Bush's drug policy received a fair amount of administrative attention, including one infamous speech complete with a bag of crack cocaine as a prop.[57] At an international conference on drug enforcement, for instance, Bush noted that drugs represented an enormous threat to the established order: "Drug addiction does not discriminate against a person because of race, religion, or financial status. It is the great equalizer, sharing sons and daughters of the rich, the poor, the middle class. Sometimes the opposite occurs, and kingpins are reduced to paupers."[58] It was possible to understand this as an example of Bush arguing for united action against a scourge that threatened all Americans equally, as inclusive rhetoric. But drugs did not affect all Americans equally. The black, the poor, those without economic, social, or political power, were more likely to suffer the most daunting effects of drugs. So another way to read this was that Bush was seeking to mobilize the middle class against "those people" who used and sold drugs in order to protect their communities from becoming "like theirs." African Americans had attained a great deal of political visibility but not a commensurate degree of political power. Black communities were thus subject to messages of differentiation and division, and individual African Americans were still available as both positive and, more frequently, negative models of citizenship.

In another example, Bush's use of "rural" and "urban" functioned, however implicitly and unintentionally, as ideological markers for the "good" and "bad" communities in the United States:

> In many respects, let's face it, urban America offers a bleak picture: an inner city in crisis. And there is too much crime, too much crack, too many drop outs, too much despair, too little economic opportunity, too little advancement, and— the bottom line—too little hope. But there's something else that's true about our inner cities, something we can't overlook, something the Urban League has worked tirelessly to strengthen; and that's a core community that is simply too strong to succumb, a community where there is too much faith, too much pride, too strong a sense of family not to fight back—whatever the challenge, whatever the odds.[59]

The inner cities were the sites of national pathologies: crime and crack, dropouts, despair, and lack of opportunity. The denizens of these places remained strong, but the places were nonetheless dreadful. Such rhetoric implied that "we" should help "them," but Bush also seemed to be arguing that "they" were doing just fine without government help—they had that core community to fall back on. In keeping with his political ideology and his conception of the proper role of government and the presidency, Bush's diagnosis of the troubles plaguing the inner city didn't take notice of the structural and economic contributions to those troubles, and made the social problems identified with the inner city unique to it. It was a matter of localized or individualized concern, and not a matter that was attributable to, and thus the responsibility of, the government.[60]

What applied to the urban dwellers in general applied also the nation's poor—who were, of course, largely presumed to be on welfare and living in the inner city. The poor, like the homeless, were politically visible but not politically powerful. They remained problematic and were subject to differentiation. In a 1992 radio address on welfare reform, for instance, Bush said,

> After years of trying to help those who are in need, we have found that too often, our assistance does not help people out of poverty; it traps them there. It's not just that people stopped caring; it's that the system stopped working. We want a welfare system that breaks the cycle of dependency before dignity is destroyed and before poverty becomes a family legacy. But today we must face this fact: Our system has failed. . . . We must balance America's heart with our responsibility to the taxpayers who underwrite governmental assistance. . . . Those who receive Government assistance have certain responsibilities: the responsibility to seek work or get education and training that will help them get a job and the responsibility to get their lives in order. That means establishing lifestyles that will enable them to fulfill their potential, not destroy it.[61]

The poor here were not the deserving poor of Cleveland's union, nor the mass poor of FDR's union, but a differentiated poor—largely an African-American poor. They were the subjects of failed government policies and the victims of failed programs. They were not actors with agency but subjects of the agency of others. Americans could potentially have helped the poor (who at some unspecified time "stopped caring" and thus Americans had to act for them and in their name) out of the welfare system by reforming it, making sure that tax dollars were safe and that the irresponsible and disorderly "lifestyle" of welfare dependency was ended. "We know," the president told the Knights of Columbus, "that our welfare system has literally destroyed the concept of personal responsibility, tearing families apart, with no incentives for people to work and save and improve."[62] Social, not factual, knowledge was contained here. The ideological assumptions implicit in this rhetoric were powerful legitimating forces for Bush's fractious union, mandating less governmental responsibility, making the poor responsible for their own condition, and protecting the extant national hierarchies. The urban poor were, in Bush's language, negative examples of manageable citizens. They were not responsible, they wanted governmental aid, and they were subjects, not agents.

Unlike urban America, rural America was emblematic of America's virtues, not its pathologies. In remarks addressed to a group of Midwestern farmers—an important part of Bush's political base—he said, "Rural America is a model of strength on social issues that are vital to our future. Thank God that family and family values remain so important to agricultural America."[63] Urban residents excited American compassion; rural residents excited American respect. Rural Americans were repositories of that which Americans held most dear: "Farm families embody what's good in America. They express it in the way they live and the diligence that they apply to their craft. The spirit of rural America is found in family entrepreneurs running their own businesses; farm and ranch families willing to reach across the fence to help a neighbor, wives, husbands, children pitching in as a team to reap nature's harvest."[64] Like Jefferson's romanticized yeoman farmer, the farmers of Bush's union were romanticized examples of good citizenship. They were diligent, entrepreneurial, independent, and neighborly. The farmers of Bush's union were composites of all the good farmers of Jefferson, Jackson, Wilson, FDR, and Eisenhower.

The differentiation between rural and urban was of course racially loaded. Note for instance the use of "crack" instead of "cocaine," widely considered a dividing line in black versus white drug use; certainly it was a dividing line in terms of economic and social class. It is possible to read this rhetoric as conflating race and class, race and drugs, race and "security," such that the message of exclusion was unstated but clear.[65] African Americans were politically visible and politically problematic. Lacking political power commensurate to their visibility, they were subjected to differentiation. Because of their visibility and degree of political power, that differentiation would be subject to challenge and debate when it was too heavy handed, and tended to proceed within the parameters of widely accepted cultural assumptions, through the use of ideologically based language.

The most explicit example of this phenomenon was in his discourse following the trial of the officers accused of beating Rodney King and the violence that erupted after the verdicts.[66] The officers involved and their supporters cited reverse racism and argued that "of all of the victims of the violence, Rodney King was not one of them . . . Rodney King was the least victimized of all."[67] Perhaps befitting the nation's chief law enforcement officer, Bush's concern was with the maintenance of order above all else: "Yesterday's verdict in the Los Angeles police case has left us all with a deep sense of personal frustration and anguish. Yet it is important that we respect the law. . . . I call upon all citizens to be calm and abide by the law."[68] Consistent with his political beliefs, Bush argued that order was based in the responsibilities of citizens, not of the government: "There are some principles of law and of behavior that should be repeated in these circumstances. First, we must maintain a respect for our legal system and a demand for law and order. Second, we have a right to expect a police force that protects our citizens and behaves in a responsible manner. Third, in the American conscience there is no room for bigotry and racism. And fourth, we have responsibilities as citizens of this democracy."[69]

Note that "we must" have law and order but that Americans only had a "right to expect" a protective police force. Racism was wrong, and the responsibilities of citizens were paramount. Obedience was required of citizens; justice was not required of government. Bush later came out in favor of national prayer and healing,[70] but King remains an icon of victimization, and the civil unrest that followed the verdict in the trial of those accused of beating him remains a contentious issue.[71] At the time, that unrest garnered significant international media attention, for it was the first incident of its kind since 1968 and one of the most deadly ever.[72] In the wake of the violence, the pronouncements issued from the White House were controversial at best, as when presidential press secretary Marlin Fitzwater claimed that the riots were "the result of the Great Society programs of the 1960s and 1970s."[73] But in the main, Bush did not seem to give Los Angeles much attention. In this, he was not alone—not one of the three presidential candidates announced any sort of policy or program aimed at the prevention of such violence in the future.[74] There was thus no context requiring any policy, and so Los Angeles, unlike King, never acquired a meaning beyond the specific event.

In this, Los Angeles was an ideal example of how ideological language functions. Framing, along with the silence of both incumbent and aspiring political leaders, made the "issue" of Los Angeles—the uneven policing practices in this nation, the accusations of police brutality, the fear of the "urban element"—vanish. The ideology still operates. As much a product of a very real faith in the American civic nationalist traditions as anything else, such rhetoric still functioned to displace the equally real issues that undergird such events from the public agenda, rendering them invisible.[75]

Nonpolitical Politics

Lacking an ambitious political agenda of his own, Bush critiqued those who had such agendas. For Bush, as for most sitting officials, policy disagreements were more appealing in the abstract than in practice, and it was very easy, and very common, for him, as for all presidents, to accuse those with whom he had policy disagreements of being "merely partisan." In this respect, Bush would seem to most clearly echo Woodrow Wilson, but his polity was both more open and thus more fractious than Wilson's, and it was considerably more difficult for Bush to argue that his party represented the whole of America.

One of Bush's favorite ways of undermining the motives of his opponents was to criticize their experience in Washington. This criticism fell more gracefully from the lips of ostensible outsider Reagan than from consummate insider Bush, but Bush used the tactic often, if not eloquently. Phrases such as "But for too long, the Nation's business in Washington has been conducted as if . . . basic rules do not apply,"[76] which he used in a 1990 nationally televised address on the federal budget agreement, functioned more to stigmatize the fact of disagreement than to help resolve it. Such stigmatization has become a staple of presidential politics. Like many a chief executive, Bush often attempted to make "Washington" a surrogate for "partisan," and "partisan" a surrogate for "unprincipled." In the fractious polity in which he governed, when so many groups had so much political visibility, it was difficult to label specific groups directly as poor examples of citizenship. One response, as we have seen, was the use of ideologically grounded differentiation. Another was this form of stigmatization. Both functioned to delegitimate opposition without engaging it.

On at least one occasion, Bush took this rhetoric to another level, not just arguing against the Democrats but also accusing those who disagreed with him of "political correctness." Speaking at the University of Michigan's 1991 graduation, he said:

The freedom to speak one's mind—that may be the most fundamental and deeply revered of all our liberties. Americans, to debate, to say what we think—because you see, it separates good ideas from bad. It defines and cultivates the diversity upon which our national greatness rests. It tears off the blinders of ignorance and prejudice and lets us move on to greater things. . . . What began as a crusade for civility has soured into a cause of conflict and even censorship. . . . We all should be alarmed at the rise of intolerance in our land and by the growing tendency to use intimidation rather than reason in settling disputes.[77]

Bush here criticized no one group, per se, but an ideology, which Bush defined as the antithesis of free speech, that most American of values. Presumably, then, those who espoused any form of "political correctness," or minority inclusion on minority terms, were guilty of undermining the foundation of American political life. They had become that which they claim to most deplore—unreasonable and prone to intimidation. Such labeling on the president's part, undoubtedly offered in good faith, functioned to foreclose precisely the sort of debate he was ostensibly celebrating. It implied an ideological formation of a specific sort of citizen, one who was civil but did not seek to enforce that civility; one who cultivated diversity on specific terms; above all one who was tolerant. This would also lead to the sort of citizen who demanded little change from government, a good citizen for turning a fractious union into a more manageable one.

The most painful example of claiming that political differences were best understood as "merely partisan" or "purely political" centered on issues of race, for African Americans were the most politically visible and the most politically powerful of the racially defined American minorities, and the most able to contest differentiation and division. In this case, the claim that political differences were "simply partisan" involved the considerable controversy over the nomination of Clarence Thomas to the United States Supreme Court.

In June 1991, Justice Thurgood Marshall retired from his seat on the U.S. Supreme Court. An icon in the civil rights movement and a hero to much of liberal America,[78] Marshall was also the only African American on the Court and his retirement presented both a challenge and an opportunity to the president. It became a nightmare for him. Instead of improving his relations with black Americans, Bush's handling of Thomas's nomination alienated them further. Instead of a powerful conservative or important moderate voice on the Court, he got instead a controversial justice. Many conservatives supported Thomas, although others objected to his possibly "checkered moral past."[79] Many women were dismayed that those in power seemed to take charges of sexual harassment so lightly, and moderates were disappointed that Bush had not found a more conciliatory choice.[80]

But Bush's defense of Thomas was not based on any factors that were of concern to these groups. He argued that race had nothing to do with Thomas's nomination, calling him "the best person for this position" and a "model for all Americans."[81] When asked if the nomination was a "quota," Bush replied:

> I don't see even an appearance of inconsistency because what I did is look for the best man. And Clarence Thomas' name was high on the list when the previous nominee went forth, Judge Souter, Mr. Justice Souter now. And so, I don't accept that at all. The fact that he is black and a minority has nothing to do with this in the sense that he is the best qualified at this time . . . so Clarence Thomas, seasoned now by more experience on the bench, fits my description of the best man at the right time, or the best person at the right time because women were considered as well. . . . I don't feel that I had to nominate a black American at this time for the Court.[82]

Bush's politics forced him into a weak argumentative position here. The sheer number of ways he felt compelled to defend himself on "charges" of nominating Thomas because of his race was astonishing. Because African Americans were politically problematic, it was politically important for Bush to argue that the Thomas nomination was based on individual merit rather than on the imperative of maintaining a "black" seat on the Supreme Court. But as the constellation of issues surrounding affirmative action were so contentious, there was no good strategy for him as political necessity collided with widely perceived political reality, and left him no good rhetorical choices.

In the time-honored style of presidents on the defensive, Bush often replied to criticism of his nominee by questioning the motives of his critics rather than by addressing the content of the criticism: "On the Thomas nomination now, there is a kind of flurry of outrage and predictable smearing of the man. But if people get to see him, they get to know his record, they get to know his background—I have this feeling this country is strongly behind him. And it is not just the—I think it's also in the minority community. The survey yesterday showed that, strong support for Judge Thomas in the black community. This is a good thing. I think that's a very good thing."[83] By citing the support of African Americans, Bush hoped to deflect some of the criticism by liberals, for African-American support of Thomas would substantially weaken the Democratic opposition to the nominee. This deflection became more difficult after Anita Hill's allegations were made public. During the entire fiasco that the Thomas hearings had become, Bush never publicly wavered in his support for or belief in his nominee, who was, of course, finally confirmed by the Senate.

Like Wilson—and like Ronald Reagan—Bush interpreted political differences as "merely partisan" and argued that these differences were therefore illegitimate. Unable to overtly differentiate and divide groups who were increasingly politically visible and vocal, such indirect means helped him to mute (but not silence completely) his critics and create a more manageable union. This suited his political as well as his personal preferences and allowed him to expand the private at the expense of the public arena.

The Private Arena and the Public Order

A moderate conservative like Eisenhower, and like Eisenhower seeking a more contained and manageable union in every issue area that did not explicitly involve foreign policy, George Bush preferred private to public action. Bush was a firm supporter of states' rights, and like Reagan, sought to lessen Washington's influence over policy in a wide variety of domestic matters.[84] He supported returning programs to the states and, as we have seen, in many cases also supported lessening Washington's influence over policy in favor of the private arena. For Bush, as he told the U.S. Chamber of Commerce in 1991, "The simple truth is this: Democracy and the freedoms it enshrines can never be the gift of government."[85] They were instead most properly understood as the province of the private sector. In relying on the private arena, Bush's rhetoric functioned to individuate both virtue and exclusion, used voluntarism to make the government less responsible for continued inequality, reconciled individualism with community, and set the frame for minorities as representatives but not members of the nation. Voluntarism came naturally to Bush and gave him a way to extend his personal preferences into policy.[86]

On education, for instance, he said, "You want to ensure that parents, not bureaucrats, decide how to care for America's children. And Wyomingites don't want to expand the budget of the bureaucracy, you want to expand the horizons of our kids."[87] By positing a world in which the horizons of children existed in diametric opposition to governmental bureaucracies and their budgets, Bush was also constructing a world in which government was unlikely to be the appropriate response to a national domestic problem. This rhetoric thus implied a certain sort of citizen, of an ideological piece with his other rhetoric. Good citizens in Bush's republic were independent of government help, enterprising, and personally involved in the administration of their own affairs. They did not abrogate their domestic responsibilities to government. As with Eisenhower's domestication of issues to create a contained citizenry, Bush's preference for the private sphere did the ideological work of creating a more manageable union.

Voluntarism individuated virtue, as well as its lack, and maintained existing hierarchies while reconciling the tensions between the individual and the community. In his 1991 State of the Union Address, the president said: "We all have something to give. So, if you know how to read, find someone who can't. If you've got a hammer, find a nail. If you're not hungry, not lonely, not in trouble, seek out someone who is. Join the community of conscience. Do the hard work of freedom. And that will define the state of our Union. Since the birth of our nation, 'We the People' has been the source of our strength. What government can do alone is limited, but the potential of the American people knows no limits."[88] This rhetoric helped to render the private sphere the preferred sphere, created good citizens as responsible and caring citizens, and meant that private, not public action was the answer to whatever problems America faced. It helped to construct a manageable union, a "community of conscience."

This rhetoric blurred disparate and unequal things into a single mass. It also blurred the potential solutions to those things. Loneliness was not necessarily the province of government action; hunger, at least potentially, was. In this construction of voluntarism, Bush made loneliness and hunger equal and equally amenable to private, not public solutions. The hungry, like the lonely, should not look to government but to that community of conscience of good citizens for aid. In making the hungry the virtual equivalent of the lonely, in making them ineligible for government aid, Bush also rendered them less politically visible, for they were the subject of private, not public action, and thus should be privately, not publicly visible. Ideologically, this rhetoric supported the preferences of his governing coalition. It rendered their interests visible while denying visibility to those interests that served their opponents' political agendas.

Bush's rhetoric also individuated virtue. In accepting the nomination for the presidency at the 1992 Republican National Convention, Bush said, "We believe that now the world looks more like America, it's time for America to look more like herself. And so we offer a philosophy that puts faith in the individual, not the bureaucracy; a philosophy that empowers people to do their best; so America can be at its best."[89] America's moral worth depended on the individual's, the individual's moral worth could not depend on the nation's. Individual Americans were not good because the nation was good. The nation was good because its citizens were good. This meant that individual Americans did not benefit from equitable or compassionate policy. Americans benefited only by participating in equitable or compassionate actions on an individual basis. And as individual Americans would thereby improve their individual moral tone, the nation's morality would also be elevated. For Bush, as for Eisenhower, citizenship was a privilege, and it brought with it some responsibilities. Good citizens accepted those responsibilities and helped to make the nation both more moral and through that morality, more manageable.

Above all, good citizens shared his commitment to family and to God. "I believe that family and faith represent the moral compass of the Nation,"[90] Bush told a Joint Session of Congress in 1989. He often argued that they were the strength of the nation as well. Like the good citizens in Wilson's transcendent international union, in FDR's neighborly union, and in Eisenhower's contained union, good citizens in Bush's manageable union shared his commitment to religious values, which both characterized the nation and undergirded its commitment to voluntarism. Certainly both the political rise of the religious right on the one hand and the increasing secularization of the nation on the other were seen as important facts in the national civic life at the end of the twentieth century.[91]

For Bush, the importance of religion was unquestioned and unquestionable. "We believe America is special because of fidelity to God. We have not forgotten that we are one Nation under God, and that's an important thing to point out on July 4th."[92] Bush thus equated religious faith with all that was good in America. It was associated with family, community, enterprise, and tolerance, with neighborhood and fellowship, and with the nation's revered past. This rhetoric, like previous presidential uses of religion, was both inclusive and exclusive. Non-Christians were thereby disconnected from the nation's strength, from its families, communities, and values. The language of citizenship, here as elsewhere, was more subtly, but just as insistently, potentially exclusionary as the language of balance.

For Bush, Americans were free in part because they were blessed by God, and his use of religion had both inclusive and exclusionary potential. Bush often expressed his own faith and encouraged others to practice theirs. "Prayer," he said at one National Prayer Breakfast, "has a place not only in the life of every American but also in the life of our Nation, for we are truly one Nation under God."[93] Religion formed an important part of his rhetoric on values, and he celebrated groups for their devotion to a Christian God: "Your good works and your faith and your beliefs are an inspiration to this country," he told the National Baptist Convention. "And it was the first American Baptists in Rhode Island who led the campaign for religious tolerance. And it was the Baptists who played an important role in securing our freedom of religion in the American Constitution. And it was the Baptists who, as pioneers, built sturdy new churches on the empty prairies and the plains of the West."[94] This rhetoric appears ecumenical, but it is only ecumenical as that term is understood by the mainstream American religious traditions—as inclusive of all Judeo-Christian religions. Practitioners of faiths derived from other

traditions—Buddhists, Muslims, American Indians, for example—
were at least potentially excluded. God underwrote the American
mission and sanctioned this view of American history, making both
a matter of holy destiny fulfilled rather than of ambiguous political
choices individually chosen. For Bush, without God as he understood
Him, there could be no freedom. Even ignoring—as most Americans
did—the exclusionary effects of this prose on those whose religious
beliefs (or lack thereof) were not encompassed by this characterization, the president was essentially stating that those who failed to
worship God also failed in their support for American freedom. Freedom, Bush's most central value, depended on religion, specifically
defined.

Bush's stress on voluntarism, which was associated with religious faith and compassion, thus functioned to maintain political
and social hierarchies. As two Bush biographers note, noblesse oblige
functions both to protect the status quo and to allow donors to feel
better about themselves.[95] Individuals did not have to worry about
an inequitable structure of power if they were "giving back." This
rhetoric thus accomplished some important ideological work for
Bush, helping to stave off challenges to the existing set of political
arrangements and institutions by labeling those who preferred those
arrangements and occupied positions of power within those institutions as not only benign, but beneficial to the republic. Voluntarism
thus contributed to Bush's rendering of a fractious union into a more
manageable one.

In addition to individuating virtue (good citizens were volunteers
who had a common faith, did not look to the government to solve
their problems, and were patriotic and respectful of the nation and
its citizens), Bush's rhetoric on voluntarism individuated exclusion.
His rhetoric on welfare reform, quoted earlier, was a case in point.
There were also others. "Some," the president said in a 1992 Independence Day address, "regard principles as disposable, like TV dinners, but they couldn't be more wrong."[96] Bush's negative examples
of citizenship included those who thrived in the "welfare lifestyle"
and those who lacked religious faith and commitment to the nation's
spirit in the way that he understood it. In a political environment
that discouraged the public naming of groups as negative examples
of citizenship, a context that permitted the demonizing of some attitudes but not of the people who held them, the national ideology

that fostered Bush's manageable union rested on the fact that these people were faceless and nameless, an inchoate other. Like "welfare cheats," Americans knew that "they" existed but did not need to elaborate on "them" in too much detail.

Reflecting this implicit imperative, Bush discussed negative examples of citizenship this way: "A nation in which half of our youth is ignorant of geography, in which drugs are rampant, in which a substantial proportion of the population knows little hope—such a nation will not long remain competitive. And in the final analysis, improving our schools, driving out drugs, and bringing hope and opportunity to those who need it most—these are issues of our national well-being, even our national identity."[97] Intentionally or not, Bush thus removed agency—from both the good citizens and the government—and made no one responsible for the examples of negative citizenship. It is one more way his public speech resulted in a privatizing of the public arena and individuation of the private arena.

The individuation of the private arena authorized in Bush's public rhetoric meant that government had much less responsibility for continued inequality and injustice.[98] He was fond of the "points of light" metaphor and used it consistently in domestic policy addresses. If the nation wanted something accomplished in social policy, this rhetoric implied, it was up to the nation to do it. Rather than include groups through policy action, Bush, like many a contemporary president, settled for rhetorical inclusion through values.

Representing Our Values:
The Language of Celebratory Othering

As more groups became politically visible and began to wield increasing political power, the demands on the national government also increased and became much harder to deflect, defer, or ignore. Members of those groups could not be easily stigmatized or differentiated and disposed of rhetorically. They could not be accommodated, however, because that would have required fundamental changes in the political system and structures of power, and presidents are conservative actors within a conservative political system. So more subtle forms of managing these groups and these demands came increasingly into play. These forms were often apparently inclusive and thus served to legitimate these groups and their participation in national politics, but also contained subtle exclusions, which helped to manage that participation.

Those who were previously defined as outside the mainstream were welcomed into that mainstream with rhetoric that has been increasingly practiced by presidents and has by now become something of an art form. Bush relied heavily on "American values" in his public speech, which he used as a way of including those who are otherwise somehow foreign or alien to him—and therefore to America.[99] Early in his term, at an Associated Press business luncheon, he discussed those values at length:

> The first step in every initiative that I've undertaken is to square our action with enduring American principles. Whatever the problem, we can count on public support so long as our policy and principles share a common root. And these principles are: freedom for individuals, for nations—self-determinations and democracy; fairness—equal standards, equal opportunity—a chance for each of us to achieve and make our way on our own merits; strength—in international affairs strength our allies can count on and our adversaries must respect—and at home, strength and a sense of self-confidence in carrying forward our nation's work; excellence—the underlying goal of the collective efforts that we undertake, and accountability for the work we do; and in the workings of government and the private sector that lies beyond its limits.[100]

Bush thus claimed that all his actions were principled, that the principles in question were "enduring" and were rooted in national traditions and history. This rhetorical move, as we have seen, had a powerful legitimating function. The key value for Bush was freedom, not equality, and was rooted in work and the private sector. All American values were rooted in private property, which for Bush, as for the founders and all presidents since, meant both security and order. Bush sought a citizenship based on principles that would create a manageable union out of his current rather fractious polity.

At the University of Michigan he said, "Free enterprise . . . lets one person's fortune become everyone's gain. This system built upon the foundation of private property, harnesses our powerful instincts for creativity. It gives everyone an interest in shared prosperity, in freedom, in respect."[101] Private property, then, was the foundation for all American society. This meant that those without such property were definitionally marginalized and that those who had more private property were more important contributors to the nation, better citizens. To the extent that "one person's fortune becomes everyone's gain," those with greater fortunes were contributing to the nation and those without were merely free riders, gaining without contributing.

As he put it at the Electronics Industry Association's Government–Industry 1989 dinner, "A more ennobling life can mean many things, it means education and opportunity. It means a nation of responsive citizens not only willing but eager to share, and it means the economic development which makes this sharing possible. For prosperity depends on growth, and growth depends on freedom. My friends, the freedom to dare, to risk, to defy the odds forms the heart of free enterprise, just as free enterprise is central to the American dream."[102] Bush's citizens were willing to share, but good citizens first and foremost possessed the wherewithal to share. Private property and free enterprise, key elements in the national ideology, thus represented a bulwark against social chaos.

For Bush, as for most conservatives, freedom was the highest national value, but equality, understood as equality of opportunity, was also important. As he told the American Association of University Women in 1989, "In America today there is no greater imperative, moral or practical, than providing equal opportunity to every man, woman, and child. And this means equal opportunity in housing and jobs, and flexibility and parental choice in child care and education. And it means equal protection from hostile elements, whether criminal or environmental, and equal opportunity in service and community action, whether through public, private, or nonprofit organizations."[103] Although he was opposed to quotas—defined as governmentally mandated programs that set numerical targets—he could support the principle of equal opportunity, which carried no targets, had no specific mandates, and was entirely voluntary. Equal opportunity thus understood was consistent with Bush's personal preferences as well as with the political arrangements that best suited his governing coalition.

In arguing for equality of opportunity, and reflecting rhetorical forms present at least since Eisenhower, Bush connected the national to the international, declaring before the National Governor's Association that "America cannot continue to lead the world if we lag in providing opportunity at home."[104] This reliance on opportunity, reflective of the national ideology, functioned to individuate poverty by implicitly claiming that all the government had to do was provide the opportunity; it was up to the individual to take advantage of it. Bush's rhetoric thus slighted structural factors that may have prevented some individuals from sharing equally in that opportunity. Poverty became the fault of the individual, not the consequence of the national economic, social, and political structures. Consistent with conservative ideology, this line of argument depoliticized poverty and made it less a matter of governmental concern. The overtly inclusive nature of promoting "equality of opportunity" was also loaded with exclusionary elements.

Equal opportunity, especially when understood as economic opportunity—and its apparent absence for many Americans—was an issue throughout the Bush years. Labor began to reorganize, if not to reinvigorate, itself in the early 1990s. Labor had been politically visible as a part of the Democratic coalition since the New Deal, but the Republicans had begun to make inroads, as the "Reagan Democrats" indicated. Potentially part of Bush's electoral coalition, labor received some time and attention from the president. Bush told a 1989 meeting of the AFL-CIO,

> Labor has been an enduring force for freedom, at times a lonely cry in the wilderness, at times the conductor of a thundering chorus, rejecting all forms of totalitarianism, Fascist and Communist alike. With each passing year, through the labor movement, freedom is finding its voice. You understand that democracy rests not on cold marble and pieces of paper but on institutions freely formed, fully free. . . . You and I—look, I know that we have differences, but those differences are a sign of democratic life, a way of life that demands respect for differences and respects an honest opinion as much as it respects an honest day's work.[105]

Rather than posing a danger to democracy, as in the rhetoric of so many previous presidents, by 1989 labor was the defender of democracy, the model of citizenship. Labor was politically visible, but not particularly problematic. Labor thus merited some attention and support but was not a significant enough part of Bush's governing coalition to merit policy shifts in its direction. Bush, like many a president before him, was prone to giving labor ceremonial recognition but not necessarily policy support.

In a typical example, he said, "We rest on Labor Day in order to reflect upon all our Nation owes to its workers, the 'doers of deeds,' whose noble dreams and diligent efforts have shaped our homes, towns, and schools—indeed, our way of life."[106] But, as is typical in ceremonial address, no specifics about how this gratitude ought to manifest itself were forthcoming. Instead, the president seemed more interested in the economic structure than in the workers who maintained it: "Today we also give thanks—not only for the American worker but also for the strength of our Nation's economy."[107] The worker and the economy were subsumed into one another, and the individual became indistinguishable from the structure. Agency was removed from governmental policy, and the issues of class vanished into a vague celebration of the American hierarchy: "On this Labor Day, we take special pride in the rights and opportunities that our system of government and innate sense of fairness ensure all American workers. As long as we cherish these rights and opportunities that are uniquely ours, this Nation will continue to be blessed with prosperity and progress."[108] The responsibility for individual and collective prosperity thus belonged to the individual, not to the system, but the credit belonged to the system, not to the individual.

In other ways as well, class remained an important issue throughout the period.[109] According to one conservative historian, "America in the 1990s was essentially a middle-class country, in which over 60 percent owned their own homes, 20 percent owned stock (though only half more than $10,000), 77 percent had completed high school, 30 percent had four years in college, and the largest single group, 44 percent, were in professional, technical, and administrative jobs. The true blue-collar working class was only 33 percent and shrinking fast, the remainder, 23 percent, being in service and farming."[110] It was a testament to the power of conservatism that with only 10 percent of the nation actively participating in the stock market, 70 percent of citizens failing to attend colleges or universities, and the num-

ber of blue collar workers shrinking because of a rise in unemployment not a rise in higher status jobs, that these facts were presented
as data for the strength of the middle class.

The Bush administration vaunted the unparalleled opportunities
available to those in the middle classes. Yet those opportunities
seemed ever more elusive to the less privileged Americans, and the
growing gap between rich and poor was increasingly obvious.[111]
Policies such as the bailout of the savings and loan industry (which
increased the federal deficit by $50 billion over three years[112]) served
to underline the widespread belief that Bush cared more for the
wealthy than for the middle class or the poor. By 1991, as the reces-
sion deepened and the economic hard times began to affect the middle class, pressure on the federal government increased. Bush's lack
of response, although consistent with both his personality and his
policy goals, proved fatal to his popularity and ultimately to his
chances for reelection.[113] The fractious polity contained too many
groups who were too politically visible and too politically powerful
to tolerate the feeling of being ignored by the president. Bush's union
was not easily managed.

Despite the criticisms of his elitism and inability to understand
the working classes, Bush never faltered in support for one group:
America's disabled. The Americans with Disabilities Act (ADA) was
"an unprecedented piece of legislation."[114] The ADA was the subject of Bush's most impassioned defense of civil rights: "The quest
for civil rights is not a zero-sum game. It shouldn't mean advancing
some at the expense of others. The quest for civil rights is a quest for
individual rights and equal opportunity. And it's a crusade to throw
open the doors of opportunity and tear down the walls of bigotry.
The ADA works because it calls upon the best in the American people, and then Americans respond."[115] The ADA exemplified Bush's
belief in the essential decency of Americans, in the importance of
freedom and opportunity, and in the understanding that if the government made it possible for people to enter America's mainstream,
that was exactly where they would go. Because of the American
commitment to this shared history of freedom, opportunity, and
independence, it was possible to welcome members of all groups into
the American mainstream, so long as they could be used to exemplify those values. Again, the rhetoric that seemed to include also
had exclusionary potential.

Nowhere was this more clear than in his rhetoric addressed to minority audiences. Bush, possibly because of his problems on racial questions, spoke relatively often to African-American audiences and in celebration of "black" events. In all these occasions, he worked to show that "Black history is, in fact, America's history."[116] His narrative of "the black experience" was a fairly traditional one: "Despite first slavery and then segregation, African Americans have overcome seemingly insurmountable odds to be at the cutting edge of change in American society. From the winning of independence—when Crispus Attucks gave his life in the Boston Massacre and Benjamin Banneker helped draw the plans for our nation's capital—to the present day, black Americans have played a vital role in the development of the United States."[117] This narrative reflected rather than created the national ideology. It glossed over much of the pain and sorrow of the early history, and nearly all the struggle since. It selected certain African Americans who contributed to mainstream historical events and celebrated them as if they also represented mainstream black experiences. Crispus Attucks and Benjamin Banneker were important because they were present at events that were important to mainstream history. Few Americans could name the white people who were killed in Boston or the white man who designed the Capitol, because for them, it was the event, not the individuals present at it that mattered. The fact that African Americans were present at these events included them as equal actors in historical events at times when their exclusion was specific and largely uncontested. To discuss "their" contributions to "American" history was to both include and underline their continued exclusion. This use of minorities in representational roles constituted the language of celebratory othering.

African Americans were not the only groups Bush treated this way. American Jews, for example, reminded us "that the enduring spirit of liberty can never be crushed by the cruel hand of tyranny and enslavement."[118] The Irish "have long demonstrated a capacity for hard work, as well as a strong penchant for full, spirited, and upright living."[119] Hispanics and Latinos/Latinas were given credit for a history that "arose out of risk and romance"[120] cherishing the values of "discipline, caring, patriotism, love of God."[121] All these groups were celebrated in interchangeable ways. Ethnic pride was emphasized, and the content of ethnic identification was trivialized.

Americans with an Asian-Pacific background were also exemplary of the American way, with little or no mention, in their case, of discrimination, past or present. Their unique history was all but erased, rendered into vague terms and related to mainstream values: "America has embarked on a new chapter, a chapter of healing. Your Asian-American community shows us how to begin. . . . You remind this Nation that the Asian-American values, freedom, family, self-determination, and opportunity, are treasures of this land and the goals of our people."[122] In this example, Asian-Pacific Americans were not fully part of the nation. Instead they served as reminders to it. Resting on equal parts vacuity and stereotyping, this formulation perfectly reflected the prevailing national ideology and included while also maintaining the hierarchies of exclusion.

In keeping with prevalent stereotypes about American Indians, they too came in for their share of celebratory othering, in their case, as prototypical environmentalists.[123] Speaking, not to American Indians themselves, but at the centennial of Spokane, Washington, in 1989, the president said, "You see, I think many of us are beginning to understand something that Native Americans understood long before we got here. When it comes to preservation of our precious environment, there's a connection between the smallest individual action and wide-spread global consequences. No words convey that better than a legendary speech given in the 1800s by an Indian chief named Seattle."[124] Never mind that Chief Seattle never actually gave that "legendary speech,"[125] or that because of long-established government policy American Indian reservations had been repositories of some of America's most toxic waste for years.[126] In failing to understand—or to even feel an obligation to understand—the actual experience of American Indians, celebratory othering became an exclusive strategy even as it ostensibly included, for it offered inclusion on the basis of a myth, or a mistaken belief, or a romantic notion of a group, not on the basis of a right, entitlement, or simple fact. It was one way of managing the plethora of politically powerful and politically visible groups.

In a more general example, Bush summed up "the" American experience: "The American adventure has always had the capacity to inspire others and to astonish the world: the voyages of Columbus, the taming of a continent, the invention of flight. America's democracy is the world's greatest experiment that continues to unleash the creative energy of the world's most diverse population. It's what took

American pioneers to the Moon and back. It's what will take you as far as your dreams can soar."[127] In this narrative, all immigrants were the same immigrants, with the same experiences, and revealed the same celebratory things about America.

This was an extension of FDR's appropriation of the frontier and immigrant myths to buttress support for his understanding of the polity as united by a shared historical past. Bush united the polity, as he united past and present, under the umbrella of shared values that had "always" characterized the polity. Historically inaccurate as such renditions were, they nonetheless exerted ideological force and helped him to create rhetorically a united, manageable polity out of the fractious one he inherited.

Like many other contemporary presidents, Bush tended to include by listing. "Men, women, immigrants, Americans of every kind" was a typical locution that pointed to the importance of political visibility.[128] Members of these groups were politically visible and politically indistinct; they had vanished into the mass of Americans. Absent the sort of insensitivity made famous by Reagan's Interior Secretary James Watt, this sort of listing offended no one, ostensibly included everyone, and cost nothing. But note that its use conflated different experiences of different groups and put all experiences of all groups into the terms and experiences of the mainstream.

One good example of this came from his remarks at the annual meeting of Association Executives in 1991, where he said, "The story of America has been the story of opportunity. Throughout our history, we've pioneered the frontiers of liberty for all humanity. . . . The story of opportunity in America is the story of Thomas Paine and Frederick Douglass, Clara Barton, the Wright Brothers, Rosa Parks."[129] Of course, the experiences of the people in this group were simply not condensable to one story without rendering those experiences meaningless. There was here not one story but many stories, and each of them highlighted something different about the nation and its history. This listing seemed to provide common ground but did not. It ignored the possibility that truly common ground may not be the ground determined by the dominant culture and its attendant hierarchies.

To his credit, Bush spoke out against racism and in favor of diversity. During the Gulf War, for instance, he said, "But I want to take this opportunity to tell you something that bothers me because I've heard from some and then I've read accounts that suggest Arab-Americans in this country, because of the conflict abroad, are being discriminated against, and it's causing pain in families in this country. And there is no room for discrimination against anybody in the United States of America."[130] Even in time of war, this president would not condone discrimination. It was a private matter, a matter of individual conscience and not one requiring governmental action, but in the arena he considered appropriate, he did speak out forcefully and often.

His statements against racism, prejudice, and bigotry were not confined to situations resulting from military conflict but formed a consistent pattern in his discussions to and about minority groups. In a typical example, he said, "Discrimination, whether on the basis of race, national origin, sex, religion, or disability, is worse than wrong. It's an evil that strikes at the very heart of the American ideal."[131] Bush backed up these words with some action: he put minorities in his Cabinet, including two Hispanics (Lauro Cavazos and Manuel Lujan) and the controversial African American Louis Sullivan. Arguably, this reflected more the representative nature of the Cabinet and its utility as a way of providing some symbolic representation to politically visible minorities than the preferences of the Bush administration. But Bush also appointed minorities to posts with less representative functions, such as Colin Powell as Chair of the Joint Chiefs of Staff.[132]

These actions revealed the increased levels of political visibility and political power of these groups. But as they coexisted with the language of celebratory othering, the limits of that visibility and power were also made clear. Celebratory othering was a distortion of American history as well as of the American present. In Bush's rhetoric, this distortion was clear even when he was ostensibly correcting the historical record. In the middle of the Gulf War, for instance, Bush took the occasion of Black History Month to celebrate the Tuskegee Airmen: "And they never received the credit, they never received the credit they deserve for their devoted patriotism, for their vision, and their sacrifices . . . for two centuries, black soldiers have established a record of pride in the face of incredible obstacles."[133] This rhetoric made it appear that now credit was being given, that race relations and discrimination were no longer a problem in the American military. All that was safely in the past. We could talk about past discrimination. Current discriminatory practices were erased. Language that thus purported to include, that no doubt was honestly thought to include, nonetheless had exclusionary elements as well, for the inclusion in this case seemed predicated on a willingness to forget or at least ignore the past. The ideological service that such amnesia would do is obvious, for it would mean that nothing in the present structures would bear the taint of past actions. The system would in fact be vindicated. It had overcome any discriminatory actions and leveled the playing field. It had triumphed over racism and was enacting the American values that had always been with us.

Because of such exemplars, this sort of complimentary exclusion individuated and separated those who still felt excluded, telling them—intentionally or not—that their experience of exclusion was wrong or somehow misguided, that they were the ones who did not understand. Upon signing a proclamation designating an Asian-Pacific Heritage Month in 1990, Bush said, "Look at the scope of America's demographic change. Cambodian, Laotian, Vietnamese neighborhoods flourish just across the Potomac River. The minaret of a mosque rises over the skyline of a Dallas suburb. The student body of a school in Southern California is made up almost entirely of Hmong children. Pacific Islanders have enriched the culture and heritage of Orange County. Filipinos have called America home since the first son of the Philippines arrived on these shores in 1763."[134] It was a testament to the greatness of America that minority communities existed so close to the nation's seat of power. They could almost aspire to one day come even closer to that power, maybe even to share in it. If they still felt excluded, it was not because they were pushed to the margins of American life. It was because they did not see their proximity to its center.

This particular approach to managing the tensions caused by the increased political visibility and political power of so many different groups, and the conservative nature of the institutions that had to find a way to accommodate or contain the demands made by these groups, worked ideologically to appear to include while also excluding. It appeared to open the system while also restricting access to it. It individuated exclusion and also contributed to an impoverished political rhetoric. As two of Bush's biographers put it, "Under Bush . . . the bully pulpit has been gelded into a platform for right-minded, mushy sentiments—for better schools, against illegal drugs—while taking care not to say anything disagreeable."[135] The unwillingness to offend has not led to a more inclusive politics, but to a falsely civil civic order. In celebrating the contributions to our democracy, in marking them out as exemplary of our values, this language also erased the very real exclusion of these groups and marked their experiences as somehow dishonorable and dishonoring of the nation. In the very act of attempting to include, such language also implicitly excluded.

Conclusion

All these rhetorical manifestations—faith in the system as a way to manage change, an emphasis on process, a preference for the private rather than the public arena, and allowing "them" to represent "America" in clearly delineated and demarcated ways—functioned, intentionally or not, to gloss over the exclusion of many groups from the national mainstream even while claiming to celebrate their admission into the heart of American culture. "They" were extraordinary exemplars of "America," for they overcame prejudice and discrimination and exemplified the nation's most deeply held values. This rhetoric ignored the fact that "they" were often still exposed to individual prejudice and continued to face the insidious effects of institutionalized discrimination. By placing their trials in the past and their success in the present, it became all too easy to claim that any further claims for justice were simply demands for special treatment, not for equality.

In exonerating the system without critically examining how that system functioned to exclude and include, this rhetoric precluded any real debate about the real issues that plagued the nation. The political system was the great beneficiary of this sort of rhetoric. In making these issues a matter of individual behavior and individual political attitudes, the system was vindicated. Members of both the right and the left saw its exclusionary effects as products of individual ill will. It thus served to contain the nation, to make the fractious polity a more manageable union.

This rhetoric absolutely suited the national interest of the American nation on the world stage and was a powerful legitimating ideological force. Those who controlled our national texts were able to maintain one definition of national identity, because the national ideology on identity that had been emerging since the founding was, while flexible enough to be adapted over time, also immensely powerful. This is an issue for presidential rhetoric in the contemporary age and is one that transcends the presidency of George H. W. Bush.

Conclusion: Choosing Our National Identity

> To conceive American history as the story of
> freedom alone is to present only half the story.
> Freedom is inseparable from power—the power
> to acquire and exclude, but also the power to
> rise up and participate.
> —John Patrick Diggins, *On Hallowed Ground:
> Abraham Lincoln and the Foundations of
> American History*

> We won't die secret deaths anymore. The world
> only spins forward. We will be citizens. The
> time has come.
> —Tony Kushner, *Angels in America: A Gay
> Fantasia on National Themes*

THIS analysis has presented seven snapshots of different moments in
time, different instances when national identity was contested, when
presidents, using the language of their ideological eras, reflected
these ideologies in their rhetoric and helped to constitute national
identity in terms appropriate to those ideologies. Our president, even
now, is doing exactly the same thing, in ways that are difficult to
fathom but that have consequences we can as yet poorly determine.
It is, however, important to try. A brief look at our history may help
in that effort.

Themes in Presidential Articulations of National Identity

The presidency, as scholars too numerous to list have noted, is a conservative institution. Presidents seek to preserve the existing political structures while also attempting to craft enough change to maintain their political coalitions and secure their places in history.[1] This study has provided evidence for this understanding of the institution. Presidents are firmly embedded in the ideologies of their times. They generally articulate those ideas having the broadest acceptance, and their constitutive efforts are geared toward conserving existing political orders rather than rearranging those orders to adapt to changing circumstances.

Presidents do not, in most cases, probably accomplish the constitutive ends addressed here either consciously or intentionally. In the main, the presidential focus is on the instrumental tasks of policy formation, coalition building, and ceremonial duties rather than on the implications of their speech in terms of national identity. Nonetheless, that speech does have constitutive consequences that can be considered through examination of the themes of balance, visibility, tensions between conceptions of civic and racial nationalism as they have played out historically, and the processes of rhetorical inclusion, as groups emerge into political visibility, become differentiated, and the terms for their eventual (if often incomplete) inclusion are set.

Presidents who governed early in the nation's history were understandably preoccupied with balance, with preserving and extending the union geographically. They tended to use restrictive definitions of citizenship to aid in that balancing effort. The language of balance was often overtly and explicitly exclusionary. Presidents in the late nineteenth and early twentieth century governed a nation that added comparatively little to its geographical boundaries, but added enormously to its internal diversity and international ideological reach. These presidents thus were concerned with citizenship. Its language was overtly inclusive yet often contained subtle exclusionary elements as well. Throughout American history, different groups varied in their degree of political visibility and political power. Those themes were woven through presidential treatments of both balance and citizenship.

BALANCING THE NATIONAL INTEREST

The United States has always been a complex nation, facing elements that work against a consensual national identity as well as those that support it. Presidents, charged with preserving national order, have focused on these centrifugal as well as centripetal forces, and have sought balance among them.

For Andrew Jackson, for instance, the challenge was to balance the demands of a burgeoning market economy with the principles of the founders' republic as he understood them. He accomplished this balance through an idealization of the pioneer, who symbolized both the yeoman farmer of Jefferson and the spirit of entrepreneurial enterprise required by the developing economic order. As a result, ownership of land became an important marker of political entitlement, and those without land, as well as those deemed to make insufficient or inappropriate use of it, were excluded—both politically and geographically—from the polity.

By the 1850s, the tensions between the new market economy and the political and economic order endorsed by the founders had nearly reached the breaking point. The three presidents of this period relied on the founding as a source of legitimacy that they hoped would preserve the system, frozen in time. In conditions so fraught, any change, development, or adaptation to the contemporary environment was a potential threat to the union itself. These presidents sought a balance in which the best outcome was immobility. Immobility proved impossible, and so too for a time did union.

For Grover Cleveland, a transitional president who contended with issues of both balance and citizenship, and who managed the government during its postwar industrialization, immobility was neither possible nor desirable. The era was characterized by movement—from rural to urban areas, from farms to factories, from Europe to the United States. Rather than advocate political stasis, Cleveland instead had to find ways to channel the forces impelling rapid change. He did so through the rational and unemotional language of business in which organization, efficiency, and service to the whole allowed more Americans to find a place of some kind in the new order. Those who could not exemplify those characteristics were marginalized or excluded.

The contentment people found in those varied places was ephemeral, however, and various groups began to organize themselves as competing interests rather than as constituent parts of a mechanized or organic whole. Woodrow Wilson attempted to balance these competing interests through rhetoric that offered a vision of a transcendent order, which silenced his critics and afforded him a position as sole arbiter of the national ideals. Those who agreed with Wilson were included in the hierarchical polity, as the terms of civic nationalism both challenged and reinforced racial and other ascriptive hierarchies.

Franklin D. Roosevelt, who eventually inherited that position, made the most of it as he attempted to balance class-based and ethnic identities in a time of serious economic distress. He did so through practices of exclusion, deferral, and deflection, which allowed him to broker a series of policy and symbolic initiatives aimed at preserving the national order in difficult times. Although increasing numbers of ethnic groups were included, racial hierarchies were very much a part of the order endorsed by FDR.

Dwight Eisenhower governed during one of the most placid periods in recent history. He deserved considerable credit for that placidity, however, for he also governed during potentially tumultuous times. Eisenhower managed potentially difficult clashes among national interests by containing them, by restricting national politics and the national agenda, and under the rubric of civic nationalism, many continuing exclusions were rendered invisible.

By 1988, that containment was no longer possible. The social unrest of the 1960s and 1970s, the dislocating aftermath of Vietnam, the contentious politics and fiscal deficits that followed Ronald Reagan into office, and the end of the cold war opened the national agenda to various groups in ways that no one could have predicted. Bush's approach to balancing these groups reflected the ideology of the contemporary age: policies that sustained the status quo and a ceremonial obeisance to various groups that appeared inclusive while masking continued exclusions.

In all these cases, the presidents sought to preserve the political structures and alignments that had brought them to power. In every case, those political alignments and structures faced real pressures from changing circumstances, highlighting the difficulty of the president's task of managing the national balance.

CITIZENSHIP

Gary Gerstle insightfully analyzed the tensions between civic nationalism (inclusion in the polity based on a shared commitment to certain ideals) and racial nationalism (exclusion from the polity premised on certain ascribed characteristics).[2] Both kinds of nationalism remain important in the nation, sometimes challenging, sometimes reinforcing one another.

The Jacksonian era was a complicated amalgam of racial and civic nationalism, for it was both the age of the "common man" and a time when American Indians were exterminated and removed, when African Americans were unashamedly enslaved, and when the promise of democracy seemed open to all yet available to only a few. Jackson himself embodied many of the contradictions of his age: a virulent Indian hater who adopted an American Indian son, a child of poverty himself who grew up to make several fortunes, a slaveholder who espoused democratic ideals and who developed the Democratic party to fight for them. Despite his own limited application of those ideals, Jackson helped to make them a lasting part of the national self-understanding, continued the founders' legacies into his own time, and forged a legacy of his own that would last far beyond that time.

That legacy seemed in doubt a mere two decades later, however, as civic nationalism calcified and racial nationalism became the sine qua non of union. The three presidents of the 1850s fossilized the founders in their search for political stability and justified the elaborate structure of racial and ethnic hierarchies that the political exigencies of preserving the union demanded.

Those hierarchies remained largely in place during the Gilded Age, despite the intervening war and the changes it brought. Grover Cleveland, charged with preserving the national order during a time of rapid change, did so through rhetoric that functioned to legitimate those hierarchies as "natural," even beneficial to the whole. At the same time, the emphasis on work as the criteria for citizenship opened the possibility of inclusion to groups who had previously been excluded.

In many cases, that possibility became reality under Woodrow Wilson, as American Indians were granted citizenship and women earned the suffrage. Wilson, a strong proponent of hierarchy, still advocated civic nationalism on a broader scale than had any previous president, an advocacy that despite his own limited willingness to include others, would help legitimate the demands of the marginalized in later years.

Basing his electoral coalition in large part on those previously marginalized citizens, Roosevelt brought more groups into the mainstream of American politics than ever before. Previously stigmatized ethnic groups were valorized and welcomed into the economic union, and civic nationalism was one of the pillars of his reassuring New Deal rhetoric. Political exigencies required the existence of continued racial stratification, however, and FDR did little about that stratification unless it could be understood in economic terms.

Before the members of those groups could exert too much influence, however, war intervened. World war had become cold war, and the demands of those groups were contained in obeisance to the demands of that new war. Domestic conflict—and its absence— became a weapon in the international contest, and domestic groups were rendered minor players in that greater game. The language of civic nationalism, as Gerstle points out, was integral to that greater game.

And the ideals expressed through that language were, according to the first George Bush, integral to our victory in it. By the time of his administration, the language of racial nationalism would not— probably could not—be spoken publicly by any sitting president. No political actor could advocate the exclusion of any group based on ascribed characteristics without raising a storm of (often vituperative) protest. Through rhetoric that relied on faith in the system as a way to manage change, a preference for the private sphere, and the language of celebratory othering, Bush hoped to render the fractious polity he inherited more manageable.

ISSUES OF VISIBILITY AND ERASURE

Each president valorized some groups and erased others' claims. In most cases, this was less the product of malignant ill will than of the assumptions that the prevailing ideologies rendered "natural" if not inevitable. Presidential discourse both reflected and shaped these ideologies.

This dynamic is evident in the rhetoric of Andrew Jackson. Certainly, throughout the Jacksonian era, many interests were rendered invisible by national consensus. Women and African Americans, to cite the two most prominent examples, had no rights to the national agenda during these years. Their exclusion was considered natural and was naturalized by their absence from political speech. American Indians, on the other hand, were both visible and visibly reviled. They were contrasted to the hardy American pioneer, whose virtues were deemed emblematic of the new republic.

Those farmers were still valorized in the 1850s, but in slightly different terms. Rather than the exuberant woodsmen of Jackson, the ideal farmer and citizen of the 1850s was tempered and temperate. Those who differed from this ideal by displaying passionate attachment (to anything other than the union itself) were dismissed or denigrated. Both positive and negative examples of citizenship were highly visible in the presidential rhetoric of the period, but the objects of the most intense passion—the slaves themselves—were visible only as objects of others' discourse and as property. As individuals, they were invisible.

By the Gilded Age, although property remained an important consideration, humans were no longer counted as chattel. Citizens in this new order were included to the extent that they could be understood as workers, which meant that those whose work was not valued were politically invisible—women certainly fit this category, as did some immigrants and some unionized workers. Good citizens were good workers, and good workers made for good citizens.

For Wilson, the citizenry expanded, as did the importance of silencing the opposition that came along with that expansion. He wanted to control the national agenda, and to do so on his own terms. Adherents to the American creed were, in general, acceptable as citizens, but they were also consequently absorbed into that mass, and their individuality was rendered invisible.

During the 1930s, issues that could not be understood in economic terms did not trouble the national government. Increasing numbers of ethnic groups and others were included and legitimated, but their noneconomic concerns were delayed or deflected. Groups were constituted as economic entities and were visible on the national agenda only to the extent that they could be so understood.

Under Eisenhower, who presided over a domesticated and contained citizenry, those who did not fit into the national ideology were castigated (communists) or simply ignored (American Indians). Communists presented a direct threat, subversives and nonconformists a more discreet one. Throughout the cold war, issues of visible, partly visible, and invisible enemies made this a complicated and fearful time, despite Eisenhower's smiling reassurance.

For Bush, any invisibility seemed impossible. All number of groups, in all number of ways, were increasingly visible, vocal, and combative. In a political context that emphasized restricted federal resources, the president provided primarily symbolic support in the form of celebratory othering. The exclusionary aspects of this rhetoric were rendered invisible amid the very visible rhetorical commitment to so many groups.

All the presidents included here, charged with preserving the nation, did so in terms of the ideologies of their times. Those ideologies fostered the valorization of some and the vilification of others. Still others were simply erased. As civic nationalism has come to the fore in the United States, and as racialized understandings of nationalism have become less legitimate in our national politics, that erasure has proven increasingly difficult.

Diversity in the Contemporary Context

When the Fourth of July came around again in 2002, "patriotic" Americans defaced mosques; assaulted people who, regardless of their citizenship status or political beliefs, were suspected of being from the Middle East and were therefore presumed to be guilty of associating with terrorists; and urged the all-too-willing government, sometimes in the harshest and most ethnocentric of terms, to bomb large portions of the Middle East. The government inched closer to war and the new "pc," in the words of one of my colleagues, seemed to be "patriotic correctness." There were also overt exclusions that could not be traced to the events of September 11, 2001, as the issue of gay marriage caused controversy around the nation. That Fourth of July was different—and markedly less inclusive— from the one with which this book started, a fact that underlines the point that the hope and pain so eloquently expressed by Martin Luther King, Jr., remain very much a part of the American national self-understanding.

But in those days, we continued to have difficulty expressing either the hope or the pain to our satisfaction. In a single speech, therefore, George W. Bush called the perpetrators of the terrorist attacks of September 11 "murderers" and also argued that they did not represent Islamic beliefs. He vowed vengeance and asked the American people for forbearance. He pledged war and called for unity. He argued that we do not make war upon a people, but on a government, and insisted that good citizens were vigilant but also tolerant. He said, "We are in a fight for our principles, and our first responsibility is to live by them. No one should be singled out for unfair treatment or unkind words because of their ethnic background or religious faith."[3] The language of civic nationalism was clear. We had indeed come a good distance in that we tried very hard, for a variety of political reasons, to be precise about the nature of national enemies.

There were concerns about the so-called Patriot Act and its implications, worries about the requests before Congress for granting law enforcement increased surveillance powers, fears over the implications of an office of Homeland Security and its restructuring of many parts of the federal government, anxieties over the consequences of the September 11 attacks on a variety of fronts. But there was considerable cause for celebration in the restraint shown by members of the national government, and much to be proud of in the fact that despite the shock and horror generated by those attacks, the government was politically able to show at least some restraint. There was no national frenzy calling for massive retaliation; there was instead concern for the innocent civilians of Afghanistan and Iraq. Americans seemed as eager to protect the terms of civic nationalism as to protect the nation's borders. As in many other instances, that civic nationalism was in many ways reinforced by the fact of war.

At the same time, the president has refused to support civil unions for gays and lesbians, and has endorsed a restrictive view of marriage.[4] Despite the "queer eyes" directed at improving the nation's "straight guys," and the (limited) cultural acceptance of "metrosexuality," gays and lesbians are subject to harsh and exclusionary rhetoric, which the president has chosen to downplay, if not to ignore. He has, at least, not chosen to participate fully in such exclusionary rhetoric, despite its importance to his electoral and governing coalitions.

These things were, I believe, enabled by, among other things, a faith in certain national principles, principles that have been less and less available as tools of exclusion and are now, as they have always been, available as a means of arguing for inclusion. Yet then, as now, the inclusion remains incomplete; tolerance is something that presidents must still argue for, even when they choose to make such arguments, and policy continues to lag well behind rhetoric.

GEORGE H. W. BUSH AND BEYOND

In defending the status quo of the late 1980s and early 1990s, George H. W. Bush used, among other tactics, a certain sort of rhetoric that existed both before and after his tenure as president. I have labeled this rhetoric "celebratory othering" because it both complimented those who were included only in bits and pieces and at the nation's margins and reminded them of their marginality. It allowed "them" to represent "us," even while underlining the fact that "they" were therefore not "us." Unlike deferral and other presidential calls for patience, which legitimated demands while postponing their achievement, celebratory othering implies that its target groups have already been included fully, and although acknowledging a group's political visibility, has the rather perverse effect of delegitimating its demands by making it appear that a reasonable degree of inclusion has already been attained and further demands are tantamount to special rights. It is a way of ostensibly offering inclusion to everyone while also maintaining the existing political hierarchies. This style is increasingly characteristic of national political rhetoric on the subject of diversity, and it is clearly present in the rhetoric of both Bill Clinton and George W. Bush.

Bill Clinton. In Clinton's case, his famous "third way" signaled both the difficulties of national politics given divided government and the increased constraints on the federal government's budget. In many ways, Clinton may as well have been a Republican; certainly neither the North American Free Trade Agreement (NAFTA) nor welfare reform could be read as a continuation of the liberal agenda—at least not as that agenda was understood by its more optimistic proponents.[5]

Clinton was, despite his popularity among citizens of color, not terribly different in his policies from other Democratic presidents. There were many reasons for this, not least among them the fact that the political environment did not support any sweeping changes.[6] Because of budgetary constraints at home and the end of the cold war abroad, the imperatives supporting civil rights faded, and the growing ranks of the black middle class made arguments based on continued discrimination easier to resist. Clinton's attempt to put race on the national agenda with the Commission on Racial Reconciliation faltered in the wake of the intern scandal, and his vision of promoting equality remained more promise than reality.

Despite his emphasis on diversity, Bill Clinton did his fair share of celebratory othering[7] and also danced a fine line between the inclusion of immigrants as "real" Americans and promising to defend our borders against illegal immigrants, whom he tended to associate with terrorists and other threats to the national well-being.[8] In an impressionistic comparison with other recent presidents, it seems that Clinton was actually less inclined than others to speak to minority groups constituted as minority groups. By this I mean that although he did address Islamic, Jewish, and other groups—and tended to do so on holidays or other occasions special to those groups—he was more likely to speak to communities constituted by geography (the citizens of Milwaukee) than by ethnicity or religious affiliation (the Knights of Columbus).

Thus, although he showed no reluctance to engage in this rhetoric, his opportunities for celebratory othering were rather more limited than those of other presidents. He was also more likely to use celebratory othering with groups other than African Americans. With them, he was generally more overt about the contemporaneous limits of their inclusion in the national polity. When talking with, to, or about African Americans, Clinton validated both past and continuing discrimination, and tended to talk to black groups in their local vernaculars.

Even in his first term, and before his initiative on race, Clinton was willing to talk about diversity and how troubling it was to the nation. He was willing to discuss the progress the nation had made, its real achievements on the subject of inclusion, but also its limitations and the work that had yet to be done. He talked about the problems of being a diverse nation, and he talked about opening up conversations on these problems. In remarks at American University, given in his first months as president, for instance, Clinton said,

> Look now at our new immigrant Nation and think of the world which we are tending. Look at how diverse and multi-ethnic and multilingual we are, in a world in which the ability to communicate with all kinds of people from all over the world and to understand them will be critical. Look at our civic habits of tolerance and respect. They are not perfect in our own eyes. It grieved us all when there was so much trouble a year ago in Los Angeles. But Los Angeles is a country with 150 different ethnic groups of widely differing levels of education and access to capital and income. It is a miracle that we get along as well as we do. And all you have to do is look at Bosnia, where the differences were not so great, to see how well we have done in spite of our difficulties.[9]

As this quotation makes clear, Clinton was aware of the problems; he also saw in them a cause for celebration, because they were more often manageable than not; Los Angeles, for all its troubles, was not Bosnia. He sounded this theme again and again.[10]

This sort of language, which openly referred to both the positive and the negative in the national culture offers the promise of genuine inclusion, for while Clinton did not hesitate to place these issues in a positive light, there was no foreclosing debate on the negative. The pain of the excluded may not have been entirely acknowledged, but it was not entirely erased either. Moreover, Clinton did not offer an explanation of the nation's racial difficulties that placed responsibility on minorities. Rather, he acknowledged that differences are problematic; that the process of reconciling them is hard; and that both individuals and government may have roles to play in that process.

He was not entirely successful in his attempt to unite governmental with individual responsibility, as the issue of gays in the military indicated. That issue, one of the first of his presidency, threatened to derail that presidency, as it seemed to contradict much of his campaign's focus, and fed concerns that Clinton was more of an "old liberal" than a "New Democrat."[11] Many feared that he was more concerned with advancing the narrow agenda of a "special interest group" than with protecting the economic rights of the mainstream American middle class.

The evidence is that Clinton was taken by surprise by the reaction to the issue. He had campaigned on the rights of gay personnel to serve in the armed forces, and in his initial action, was simply acting on that promise. He failed to realize, however, that although he could change some aspect of the treatment of gays by executive order, congressional action would be required to change the Military Code of Conduct. He quickly realized that there was not sufficient support for any such action. Clinton thus faced a bind: he could not fulfill the letter of his campaign promise, and any action designed to accomplish part of that promise would alienate both gays and their supporters and opponents of his policy.

In facing this difficult situation, Clinton first tried to frame the issue in his preferred terms, arguing that it was not *identity*, but *behavior* that was the appropriate focus. In an exchange with reporters during his first week as president, he said, "The principle behind this for me is that Americans who are willing to conform to the requirements of conduct within the military services, in my judgment, should be able to serve in the military and that people should be disqualified from serving in the military based on something they do, not based on who they are."[12] Note that the president claimed to be operating on the basis of principle, not out of expediency. He made this argument consistently. The problem was that the principle seemed to change from one demanding inclusion to one advocating compromise.

Note also that this position directly contradicted the conception of homosexuality as a fundamental part of an individual's identity. This understanding was clear among members of the Christian communities opposed to removing the ban; it was also clear among gay rights groups, who argued that homosexuality was inherent not in what one does, but in who one is. Clinton thus offered a compromise that was no real compromise and that contravened the commonly held understanding of homosexuality.[13] His frame was untenable from the start.

When it became obvious that this issue would continue to dominate news, Clinton then tried to duck the issue. He referred the issue to a committee for study, refused to answer questions,[14] and became increasingly short-tempered as the issue seemed to control more and more of the attention the media paid to his presidency. Still, he tried to have it both ways and portrayed himself both as the protector of gays and their rights, and as a moderate member of the mainstream. When challenged by gay advocacy groups for his unwillingness to participate in a march for gay rights, he replied to a question on whether he was "snubbing" gays by saying, "I don't see how any serious person could claim that I have snubbed the gay community in this country, having taken the position I have not only on the issue of the military but of participation in Government. I have, I believe it is clear, taken a stronger position against discrimination than any of my predecessors. . . . It had nothing to do with politics and everything to do with the fact that I grew up in a segregated society and have very strong feelings about the right of everybody who is willing to work hard and play by the rules to participate in American life."[15] Note the qualification of his critics. No "serious person" would question him on this; no one should question that he acted on principle alone. Finally, note his attempt to imbue the fight over gays in the military with the legitimacy of the fight to end segregation, casting opponents of removing the ban as equal to those who supported Jim Crow.

He continued to temporize on the issue, arguing even in the same speech both that "this is not about embracing any lifestyle" and "I think the only way our country can make it is if we can find somehow strength in our own diversity, even with people with whom we profoundly disagree, as long as we can agree on how we're going to treat each other and how we're going to conduct ourselves in public forums. That is the real issue."[16] Ignoring the fact that the debate was over exactly the question of "how we're going to conduct ourselves in public forums," these positions are not inconsistent, nor were they that hard to reconcile. But Clinton's apparent attempt to placate both sides of this complicated issue, combined with his increasing reputation for "waffling,"[17] made his position unclear enough to generate challenges from both sides. Vagueness worked both for Clinton—audiences could read their preferred meanings into his words—and against him—they were liable to feel betrayed when they considered his actions less than fully accommodating of their preferred policies.

Clinton continued to insist that he did not propose any changes in the Code of Military Conduct[18] as a way of deflecting criticism that he was too liberal. In contrast to his earlier equation of the fight to include gays in the military with desegregation, he argued that the situation of gays was not analogous to that of blacks and that the situation was vastly more complicated than most realized. He tried to portray the "compromise" as reasonable, fair, and equitable.

The real thing you ought to ask is how long did it take before African Americans, in this case, were treated fully equally in the service? It didn't just happen snap with Truman's order. It didn't happen after Truman's order and it developed a long time after Truman's order. There was an explicit open involvement of the military culture with blacks in a segregated way for a very long time before this order was issued. The same thing happened with women. . . . It happened over a period of years as the military culture adapted to it. Now if I had done what you suggest, if I had just said that gays could serve and whatever they do in private is their own business—which I never committed to do in the campaign—I'll tell you exactly what would have happened. Congress would have overturned it immediately and done it on the defense bill and in ways that would have been difficult, if not impossible, for me to veto. So the situations simply aren't analogous. Congress had no intention of overturning President Truman's position, and it's something that built up over a long period of time, not something that just entered the public debate, in effect, about a year ago.[19]

So for Clinton, it was not really a matter of principle, but of what he could get through Congress; not a matter comparable to the civil rights movement or to segregation in the military, despite his earlier assertion that the situations were analogous. In effect, he was replying to gays in the military as whites long did to blacks in the segregated South—telling them that they needed to be patient, and when they had earned admission into the mainstream, they would be admitted therein. Rather than the language of celebratory othering, Clinton relied on the language of deferral.

Clinton's actions—and his rhetorical justifications of those actions—satisfied no one. He alienated many Christians, threatened many conservative supporters, and disappointed liberals.[20] He also raised considerable doubts as to his leadership style, which many saw as neatly—and disastrously—encapsulated in his bumbling management of this issue.[21] He tried to move the nation before it was ready, but also failed to enunciate a clear principle that could facilitate later inclusion. Although potentially representing some progress, it was a failure in every respect.

Not all of Clinton's rhetoric on matters of diversity could be considered in such a light, however. His rhetoric on matters of race and equality, for instance, negotiated the lines between governmental and individual action that was consistent with his campaign rhetoric and apparently more amenable to the nation's Democrats, if not to the nation's public. That rhetoric was charged with both compassion and exhortations for individual responsibility. Although Clinton tended to locate the problems of diversity in the structures of governance and the public sphere—that is, like most liberals, he considered them systemic rather than individual—he was not averse to calling on members of minority communities to improve their individual conduct. In Memphis, for instance, in one of the best speeches of his speech-laden presidency, Clinton imagined a conversation with Martin Luther King, Jr., who would, "give us a report card on the last 25 years." King, according to Clinton, would have praise for the considerable progress we have made as a nation since 1968. But he would also express sorrow:

> "But," he would say, "I did not live and die to see the American family destroyed. I did not live and die to see 13-year-old boys get automatic weapons and gun down 9-year-olds just for the kick of it. I did not live and die to see people destroy their own lives with drugs and build drug fortunes destroying the lives of others. That is not what I came here to do."
>
> "I fought for freedom," he would say, "but not for the freedom of people to kill each other with reckless abandon, not for the freedom of children to impregnate each other with babies and then abandon them, nor for the freedom of adult fathers of children to walk away from the children they created and abandon them, as if they didn't amount to anything."
>
> He would say, "This is not what I lived and died for. I

fought to stop white people from being so filled with hate that they would wreak violence on black people. I did not fight for the right of black people to murder other black people on a daily basis."[22]

For a white president to go to the city where Dr. King was assassinated and put words into Dr. King's mouth was an act breathtaking in its audacity. Yet it worked, and it worked at least in part because Clinton was adept in his use of the local vernacular—he could speak in the tones and cadences of black traditions. Equally important, in Memphis he spoke of "us" in a way that usefully constituted a white president as part of the "us" of the struggle for civil rights. He made the problems many whites relegate exclusively to "the" black community the problems of "America."

Memphis was not the only nor even the most eloquent example of this. Near the end of his first term, Clinton spoke at the University of Texas, saying, "When a child is gunned down on a street in the Bronx, no matter what our race, he is an American child. When a woman dies from a beating, no matter what our race or hers, she is our American sister. And every time drugs course through the veins of another child, it clouds the future of all our American children. Whether we like it or not, we are one nation, one family, indivisible. And for us, divorce or separation are not options."[23] Through this language, Clinton did seem to be, in Toni Morrison's famous phrase, "America's first black president," and there did seem to be a promise of the capacity for national consensus.

This is not the language of celebratory othering, which implies that the process of inclusion is complete and that the group in question can safely become politically invisible, absorbed into the mass of "Americans" without endangering their interests. In this rhetoric, Clinton clearly recognized African Americans as a uniquely and specifically threatened group, requiring both individual and governmental action to protect them. He did not envision either a present or a future in which African Americans were invisible, "like us." He recognized both the promise and the pain in their situation. In such rhetoric lies the hope of true inclusion.

Yet when it came to the details of policy, he was not as faithful to that promise, as his stance on Affirmative Action and welfare reform indicated.[24] He left the white middle class confused, ambivalent, and

resentful without cementing any real gains for minority constituencies.[25] The gains African Americans may have made under his
administration were largely symbolic and all too easily eroded.

George W. Bush. Evaluating a sitting president is always risky, and
doing justice to one impossible. As a conservative, George W. Bush
seemed to be more similar to his father in his approach to diversity
than to Clinton. He both individuated virtue (the "good hearts" of
his Cabinet) and vice ("evil doers" and their supporters). Moreover,
his presidential rhetoric was notable for its overtly Christian language, and the implications of that have been thoroughly covered
earlier in this book.

There has also been a good deal of the kind of exclusionary praise
that is associated with celebratory othering. In one case, for instance,
Bush said, "The great strength of our Nation's economy is our workforce. From teachers and entrepreneurs to factory workers and scientists, hardworking Americans serve in a wide and diverse range of
professions that are vital to protecting our health, well-being, and
quality of life. By providing important goods and services and building and generating wealth, American workers help lay the foundation for our continued progress and advancement."[26] The entire
focus here was economic; workers were valued for what they *contributed*, not for who they *were*. Absent the contribution, there was
nothing of value articulated.

In another case, he engaged in another form of marginalization
through representation. Celebrating Black Music Month, he said,

> Today we pay homage to an American tradition, a tradition
> that only America could have produced. Spirituals, jazz,
> R&B, hip-hop are performed, heard and loved in every part of
> the world—every part of the world. But they belong to our
> country in a unique way. And as the President of this coun-
> try, I'm proud to herald that uniqueness today. . . . You trace
> the roots of black American music, you arrive at the same
> place—with the people held in bondage, denied schooling
> and kept away from opportunity. Yet, out of all that suffering
> came the early spirituals, some of the sweetest praise ever
> lifted up to heaven. In those songs, humanity will always
> hear the voice of hope in the face of injustice.[27]

In placing all oppression in the past, and in claiming inclusion through appropriation of a black art form into an American one, Bush elided any continuing separation. He erased lingering discrimination and honored the absorption of African Americans into the American mainstream. By voicing only the progress and none of the pain inherent in the experiences of many contemporary African Americans, Bush erased that fact of continued exclusion. Celebratory othering exists in such pretense, for it delegitimates a group's continuing quest for inclusion even as it ostensibly legitimates the group itself.

In another example of such erasure, Bush said,

> With silver medals, we also honor the dozens more who served later, with the same courage and distinction. And with all these honors, America pays tribute to the tradition and community that produced such men, the great Navajo Nation. The paintings in this rotunda tell of America and its rise as a nation. Among them are images of the first Europeans to reach the coast, and the first explorer to come upon the Mississippi. But before all these firsts on this continent, there were the first people. They are depicted in the background, as if extras in the story. Yet, their own presence here in America predates all human record. Before others arrived, the story was theirs alone. Today we mark a moment of shared history and shared victory. [28]

Bush was assuming here that the story of European conquest had lost its significance for American Indians, that we were all Americans now, with a shared history and a shared victory. The fact that it took some sixty years for the Navajo to be recognized for their share in that victory, like the assumption that the Navajo would see themselves in the depiction of American Indians who met Europeans along the East Coast or the banks of the Mississippi, was to Bush less obvious than the unity he could claim as a result of that assumed identification and delayed recognition.

The exclusionary power of celebratory othering relies on this claim to American sameness, the expectation that the Navajo, in seeing themselves greeting the Pilgrims, would also see themselves reflected in the nation that developed from the society founded by the Pilgrims. It is less an invitation to share in the development of that nation by recognizing its multiple—and often conflicting—histories and more an invitation to join a finished nation with a singular history. The invitation is much less inclusive than it appears.

The Navajo were celebrated as different ("first people"), but that difference was then treated as trivial, and they were equated with "us," but on "our" terms. The national identity was not altered so as to encompass their identities, even as their sacrifices for the nation were ostensibly recognized. Instead, the uniqueness of their identities, and the uniqueness of their sacrifices, was erased. Genuine inclusion would celebrate the differences, acknowledge the sacrifice, and use those differences and those sacrifices to modify the national identity to accommodate them. This formulation, however, has all the accommodation moving from the Navajo to the nation and offered only erasure while ostensibly including.

As these examples indicated, the strategy of celebratory othering continues to be a viable strategy given the prevailing political context. In the post–cold war world, there are certain assumptions that all presidents, regardless of personal politics or partisan identification, seem to make: first, that the most important job of any president is to ensure that America maintains economic competitiveness in the world, and anything—or anyone—who does not contribute to that primarily economic mission is therefore not contributing to America. Second, it is the American responsibility to provide an example of democracy but not necessarily to also provide realistic levels of aid to promote it—American strategic interests trump American interests in the ideological force of its example. And finally, the United States is the sole remaining superpower; it has nothing to prove anymore and is the exemplar of democracy, the light that has illumined the world. The United States maintains its economic and strategic interests, and does not need to provide evidence of its superiority as a democratic nation—America won the cold war, and that is all the evidence required.

In the terms favored by Rogers A. Smith, the nation's ascriptive hierarchies remain, as do many of the institutional structures that support racialized rather than civic understandings of nationalism, to use Gerstle's phrases. But I think the legitimacy of those hierarchies, and of the structures that too overtly support them, is weaker now. The evidence for this can be found in the political travails of

Trent Lott (R-Miss.) as his support for Strom Thurmond led to his demise as Senate majority leader. It can also be found in the prosecution of the wars in Afghanistan and Iraq. It can even be seen in the debate over the place of gays and lesbians in the polity, indicating their political visibility and the fact that they have become politically problematic. Notions of identity based on such racialized and ascriptive hierarchies were prevalent on t-shirts and bumper stickers about the war, just as they could be found in the public discussions of gay civil unions and marriage, and in the debate over the ordination of a gay bishop in the Episcopal Church. But at least in their harshest and most obvious forms, they could not be found in the public discourse of the president. In this way, such understandings are perhaps being understood as problematic and are sometimes publicly problematized.

In addition, in the very fact of the visibility of so many groups lies considerable hope, for the process of inclusion seems to follow a path of invisibility to vilification to cultural inclusion.[29] In the present context, even vilification provides some opportunity, if only the opportunity for argument, and through argument, to some measure of acceptance. The ethic of tolerance is strong, and the accusation of intolerance is a powerful delegitimating tool. In this regard, the language of celebratory othering, while in many ways a negative, offers as did so many of its predecessors in presidential speech on national diversity, the topoi for future claims to inclusion.

Conclusion

In claiming for their polity the role of exemplar of democracy, the Puritans gave their ideological heirs a specific responsibility. In making the shining city on a hill an economically driven example, in defining "freedom" as "economic opportunity," Americans have also orchestrated an ideological oxymoron of sorts and have created no small amount of confusion as to our goals and intentions, and the degree to which those are consistent with our principles. In deciding that the key unit of analysis is the individual, Americans have individualized political processes and effects. This means that Americans often ignore the consequences of our system even while holding it up as a model to the world.

This discourse, perhaps because of its association with universal ideals, and perhaps because of the rhetorical fissures the contradictions between ideal and political practice open up, has the potential to be liberating as well as oppressive. Just as Americans were moved by hearing "The Star-Spangled Banner" being played at Buckingham Palace and by the claims emanating from around the world that "we are all Americans today" in the wake of the September 11 terrorist attacks, there is something remarkably moving about seeing people around the world adopting the form of the Declaration of Independence to present their claims, and in hearing them singing "We Shall Overcome." There is a promise in these symbols and in their international appeal that is as powerful as the attempts by those who inhabit the upper reaches of the national hierarchies to control the degree to which those promises are enacted.

Freedom is hard; obtaining equality and its promise are also hard. They will not—perhaps cannot—be given as gifts by the powerful to the powerless. But American presidential rhetoric, as flawed and exclusionary as it has often been, also provides a means by which the powerless can demand their rights of the powerful, and in that fact lies much of the promise of America, both in its idealized and its material existence.

There are implications in this sort of analysis for how Americans understand themselves as a nation. First, it affects American identity as a chosen people, the best (if not the only) real exemplar of democracy and freedom in the world. In reflecting on this issue at the time of our national bicentennial, historian Vincent Harding wrote, "Remembering errands into the wilderness which decimated the occupants of the land, remembering cities on a hill which finally sent their burning lights smashing into Hiroshima and Nagasaki, remembering Manifest Destinies which included my slavery and Vietnam's great sorrow, I avoid this idea of chosenness in most of its traditional, American, metaphysical senses of the word."[30] Instead, Harding urges Americans to look on our "history of hope, of betrayal, of vision, and of brokenness,"[31] and to make choices. He hopes that Americans will be a chosen people in the sense that they choose to learn a new sort of interdependency, based not on the entitlement of some—no mater how numerous—and the exclusion of others—no matter how few—but on the shared commitment to constitutive ideals.

I echo that hope but also understand what it would mean. It would mean really examining the idea that political and cultural power may be a zero-sum game, that the inclusion of others means the diminution of those who have such power now. To include others in the national conversation means that less discourse is reserved for the currently privileged and that the shared discourse will be different. There is a tension between maintaining one's own position and the understanding that to be part of a community of equals means to assume that the whole is always greater than the sum of its parts. And for those whose security depends on the status quo, that is asking a great deal.

It is asking them (us) to be committed to the very founding principles that they (we) claim to be defending by their (our) implicit and explicit appeals to exclusion. It is asking them (us) to do what the nation's founders and the Constitution's framers never considered doing. It is asking them (us) to recognize that common ground does not always have to be the ground upon which they (we) are most comfortable. It is asking them (us) to fully enact the vision that "all . . . are created equal." It is acknowledging that the task of forming any union, much less a more perfect one, depends on our ability to enact union, not just to pledge allegiance to it.

It is always unclear how that request will be answered, although, as this study has shown, it is usually answered slowly, incrementally, unevenly, and painfully. But if there is a singular national identity in the United States, it probably lies more in the faith that we have in asking, and asking, and asking again, than in the individual or collective tasks of enacting the answers.

Notes

Introduction: Presidential Rhetoric and National Identity

1. In fact, Fourth of July orations, by presidents and other political actors, have a long history. See Sacvan Bercovitch, *The Rites of Assent: Transformations in the Symbolic Construction of America* (New York: Routledge, 1993); John R. Gillis, ed., *Commemorations: The Politics of National Identity* (Princeton, NJ: Princeton University Press, 1996); Len Travers, *Celebrating the Fourth: Independence Day and the Rites of Nationalism in the Early Republic* (Amherst: University of Massachusetts Press, 1997).

2. See Alan Brinkley, *The Unfinished Nation: A Concise History of the American People* (New York: McGraw-Hill, 1993); Matthew Frye Jacobsen, *Whiteness of a Different Color: European Immigrants and the Alchemy of Race* (Cambridge, MA: Harvard University Press, 1998); David Roediger, *The Wages of Whiteness* (London: Verso, 1991); Alexander Saxon, *The Rise and Fall of the White Republic* (London: Verso, 1990); Michael Schudson, *The Good Citizen: A History of American Civic Life* (New York: Free Press, 1998); Ronald Takaki, *A Different Mirror: A History of Multicultural America* (Boston: Little, Brown, 1993); Howard Zinn, *A People's History of the United States* (New York: Harper & Row, 1980).

3. See among others, Edward Countryman, *Americans: A Collision of Histories* (New York: Hill and Wang, 1996), 72–3.

4. For a wonderful example of the pain and hope of the excluded, see David Halberstam, *The Children* (New York: Random House, 1998). For personal narratives see Andrew Garrod and Colleen Larimore, eds., *First Person, First Peoples: Native American College Graduates Tell Their Life Stories* (Ithaca, NY: Cornell University Press, 1997); Joseph Marshall III, *On Behalf of the Wolf and the First Peoples* (Santa Fe, NM: Red Crane, 1995); Anthony Walton, *Mississippi* (New York: Random House, 1996).

5. Kenneth Burke, of course, makes the definitive argument for the relevance of rhetorical studies to the investigation of issues of particular definitions of reality and the identities that stem from those definitions. He says, "Even if any given terminology is a *reflection* of reality, by its very nature as a terminology, it must be a *selection* of reality; and to this extent, it must function also as a *deflection* of reality." See Kenneth Burke, *Language as Symbolic Action* (Berkeley: University of California Press, 1966), 45.

6. Rogers M. Smith, *Civic Ideals: Conflicting Views of Citizenship in U.S. History* (New Haven, CT: Yale University Press, 1997).

7. American Indians form an important exception to this rule, a fact that is discussed later in the chapter.

8. Gary Gerstle, *American Crucible: Race and Nation in the Twentieth Century* (Princeton, NJ: Princeton University Press, 2001).

9. For a discussion of this point, see Wayne Fields, *Union of Words: A History of Presidential Eloquence* (New York: Free Press, 1996), 3.

10. This is part of what Thomas E. Cronin has called the "textbook presidency." See Thomas E. Cronin, *The State of the Presidency* (Boston: Little, Brown, 1975).

11. For discussion of presidential coalition building, see Lester G. Seligman and Cary R. Covington, *The Coalitional Presidency* (Chicago: Dorsey, 1989); Steven A. Shull, ed., *Presidential Policymaking: An End-of-Century Assessment* (Armonk, NY: ME Sharpe, 1999).

12. For a discussion of the conservative nature of the presidency, see Russell L. Riley, *The Presidency and the Politics of Racial Inequality: Nation-Keeping from 1831–1965* (New York: Columbia University Press, 1999), 10.

13. Riley, *Presidency*, 18.

14. This has long been a part of our politics, despite the way the issue is often treated in academic and popular circles. See, for example, Richard J. Ellis, ed., *Speaking to the People: The Rhetorical Presidency in Historical Perspective* (Amherst: University of Massachusetts Press, 1998). See also Martin J. Medhurst's distinction between "presidential rhetoric" and "the rhetorical presidency" in the introduction to his edited volume, *Beyond the Rhetorical Presidency* (College Station: Texas A&M University Press, 1996).

15. On the relationship between epideictic and ceremonial rhetoric, see Nicole Loraux, *The Invention of Athens in the Classical City* (Cambridge, MA: Harvard University Press, 1986).

16. On the functions of epideictic rhetoric, see Michael Carter, "The Ritual Functions of Epideictic Rhetoric: The Case of Socrates' Funeral Oration," *Rhetorica* 9 (1991): 209–22; J. Richard Chase, "The Classical Conception of Epideictic," *Quarterly Journal of Speech* 47 (1961): 293–300; Dale Sullivan, "The Ethos of the Epideictic Encounter," *Philosophy and Rhetoric* 26 (1993): 113–33.

17. Ernest Gellner, *Nationalism* (New York: New York University Press, 1997), 10–1; see also Benedict Anderson, *Imagined Communities: Reflections on the Origin and Spread of Nationalism* (London: Verso, 1983).

18. See also Maurice Charland, "Constitutive Rhetoric: The Case of the *Peuple Quebecois*," *Quarterly Journal of Speech* 73 (1987): 133–50; Ward Churchill, *Indians Are Us? Culture and Genocide in Native North America* (Monroe, ME: Common Courage Press, 1994), 291–357; Michael Calvin McGee, "In Search of 'The People': A Rhetorical Alternative," *Quarterly Journal of Speech* 61 (1975): 235–49.

19. For insightful discussions of this point, see M. Lane Bruner, *Strategies of Remembrance: The Rhetorical Dimensions of National Identity Construction* (Columbia: University of South Carolina University Press, 2002); Gerstle, *American Crucible*, 11; Smith, *Civic Ideals*, 9–36.

20. For a discussion of the relationship between democratic nation building

Notes to Pages 2–11 / 361

and intolerance, see Anthony W. Marx, *Faith in Nation: Exclusion Origins of Nationalism* (New York: Oxford University Press, 2003).

21. For elaboration on this point, see Murray Edelman, *Constructing the Political Spectacle* (Chicago: University of Chicago Press, 1988).

22. See, for example, Michael Calvin McGee, "The 'Ideograph,' A Link between Rhetoric and Ideology," *Quarterly Journal of Speech* 66 (1980): 1–16. See also Celeste Michelle Condit and John Louis Lucaites, *Crafting Equality: America's Anglo-African Word* (Chicago: University of Chicago Press, 1993); Eric Foner, *The Story of American Freedom* (New York: W. W. Norton, 1998); Schudson, *Good Citizen*; Kimberly K. Smith, *The Dominion of Voice: Riot, Reason, and Romance in Antebellum Politics* (Lawrence: University Press of Kansas, 1999), 139.

23. Kathleen J. Turner, "Rhetorical History as a Social Construction: The Challenge and the Promise," in *Doing Rhetorical History: Concepts and Cases*, ed. Kathleen J. Turner (Tuscaloosa: University of Alabama Press, 1998), 2.

24. On using "top down" sources to study "bottom up" history effectively, see Woody Holton, *Forced Founders: Indians, Debtors, Slaves and the Making of the American Revolution in Virginia* (Chapel Hill: University of North Carolina Press, 1999), xxi.

25. David Carroll Cochran, *The Color of Freedom: Race and Contemporary American Liberalism* (Albany, NY: SUNY Press, 1999), 2.

26. The classic examples of this tendency are Daniel Boorstin, *The Genius of American Politics* (Chicago: University of Chicago Press, 1953); Louis Hartz, *The Liberal Tradition in America: An Interpretation of American Political Thought Since the Revolution*, 2nd ed. (New York: Harvest Books, 1951–1991); Richard Hofstadter, *The American Political Tradition and the Men Who Made It* (New York: Alfred A. Knopf, 1948). This "great men" view of history still dominates elementary school, high school, and many college texts. For a typical example, see Paul S. Boyer et al., *The Enduring Vision: A History of the American People*, 4th ed. (New York: Houghton Mifflin, 2000).

27. For a good discussion of this phenomenon, see Dennis K. Davis and James Jasinski, "Beyond the Culture Wars: An Agenda for Research on Communication and Culture," *Journal of Communication* 43 (3): 141–9. For examples of it, see Allan Bloom, *The Closing of the American Mind: How Higher Education Has Failed Democracy and Impoverished the Souls of Today's Students* (New York: Simon and Schuster, 1987); Richard J. Ellis, *The Dark Side of the Left: Illiberal Egalitarianism in America* (Lawrence: University Press of Kansas, 1998); E. D. Hirsch, *Cultural Literacy: What Every American Needs to Know* (New York: Vintage, 1987); Stephen Macedo, *Diversity and Distrust: Civic Education in a Multicultural Democracy* (Cambridge, MA: Harvard University Press, 2000); Arthur Schlesinger, Jr., *The Disuniting of America: Reflections of a Multicultural Society* (New York: Norton, 1992).

28. Michael Schudson, "Good Citizens and Bad History: Today's Political Ideals in Historical Perspective," Keynote Address at Middle Tennessee State University Conference, November 11–2, 1999 (College of Mass Communication, Murfreesboro, TN, 2001), 21. See also John Patrick Diggins, *On Hallowed Ground: Abraham Lincoln and the Foundations of American History* (New Haven, CT: Yale University Press, 2000); Jim Sleeper, *Should American Journalists Make Us Americans?* (Cambridge, MA: Joan Shorenstein Center on the

Press, Politics, and Public Policy, Harvard University, Discussion Paper D-38, 1999).

29. This hold is not restricted to Americans. See Mark Hertsgaard, *The Eagle's Shadow: Why America Fascinates and Infuriates the World* (New York: Farrar, Straus, and Giroux, 2002).

30. Vine Deloria, Jr., *We Talk, You Listen: New Tribes, New Turf* (New York: Macmillan, 1970), 38–42.

31. See the detailed analysis of this by Carol Winkler, *In the Name of Terror: Presidents on Political Violence in the Post–World War II Era* (Philadelphia: Temple University Press, forthcoming), especially chapter one.

32. Foner, *Story of American Freedom*, 71.

33. See, for example, Linda K. Kerber, *No Constitutional Right to be Ladies: Women and the Obligations of Citizenship* (New York: Hill and Wang, 1995); on the complicated question of the roles of reason in politics, see Smith, *Dominion of Voice.*

34. The literature on American exceptionalism and its relationship to American national identity is immense. For canonical books or those with extensive bibliographies, see Henry Adams, *Democracy: An American Novel* (New York: Airmont, 1968); Charles A. Beard, *The American Spirit: A Study in the Idea of Civilization in the United States* (New York: Macmillan, 1942); Hector St. John Crevecoeur, *Letters from an American Farmer* (Garden City, NY: Dolphin, 1782); Seymour Martin Lipset, *American Exceptionalism: A Double-Edged Sword* (New York: Norton, 1996); Mary Nolan, "Review Essays: American Exceptionalism," *American Historical Review* 102 (1997): 748–74; Richard Rorty, *Achieving Our Country* (Cambridge, MA: Harvard University Press, 1998); Barry Alain Shane, *The Myth of American Individualism: The Protestant Origins of American Political Thought* (Princeton, NJ: Princeton University Press, 1994); Alexis de Tocqueville, *Democracy in America*, ed. J. P. Meyer, trans. George Laurence (New York: Harper, 1969).

35. For a discussion of the debate over the role ideas play in constituting political culture in the United States, see Wilfred M. McKay, "Do Ideas Matter in America?" *Wilson Quarterly* (Summer 2003): 67–84.

36. Kenneth L. Karst, *Belonging to America: Equal Citizenship and the Constitution* (New Haven, CT: Yale University Press, 1989), 32.

37. Karst, *Belonging to America*, 2.

38. Smith, *Civic Ideals*, 2–3. See also Foner, *Story of American Freedom*, xiv.

39. Smith, *Civic Ideals*, 14. See also Foner, *Story of American Freedom*, xx; Gerstle, *American Crucible*, 8.

40. Kerber, *No Constitutional Right to Be Ladies.*

41. Smith, *Civic Ideals*, 6.

42. Smith, *Civic Ideals*, 8.

43. Cochran, *Color of Freedom*, 3–12. See also Will Kymlicka, *Multicultural Citizenship* (New York: Oxford University Press, 1995); Martin E. Marty, *The One and the Many: America's Struggle for the Common Good* (Cambridge, MA: Harvard University Press, 1997).

44. Charles W. Mills, *The Racial Contract* (Ithaca, NY: Cornell University Press, 1997).

45. Desmond King, *Making Americans: Immigration, Race, and the Origins*

of the Diverse Democracy (Cambridge, MA: Harvard University Press, 2000), 2.

46. And certainly, there are those who believe that we ought to continue to contain it. See Peter Brimelow, *Alien Nation: Common Sense about America's Immigration Disaster* (New York: Random House, 1995). See also Bloom, *American Mind*; Davis and Jasinki, "Beyond the Culture Wars"; Ellis, *Dark Side of the Left*; Hirsh, *American Literacy*; Macedo, *Diversity and Distrust*; Schlesinger, *The Disuniting of America*; Schudson, "Good Citizens."

47. For an insightful discussion of such masking, see David Wilkins, *American Indian Sovereignty and the U.S. Supreme Court: The Masking of Justice* (Austin: University of Texas Press, 1997), especially 8–18.

48. Cochran, *Color of Freedom*, 55.

49. Gail Stratton first brought this idea to my attention. See Peggy McIntosh, "White Privilege: Unpacking the Invisible Knapsack," *Peace and Freedom*, July/ August 1989: 10–2; Robert Jensen, "White Privilege Shapes the U.S.," *Baltimore Sun*, July 19, 1998; Michael Wenger, "Racial Discrimination Racial Privilege," *Focus* July 1999, 3–5.

50. Gerstle, *American Crucible*, 5.

51. Marty, *The One and the Many*, 55.

52. See James Ceaser, *Reconstructing America: The Symbol of America in Modern Thought* (New Haven, CT: Yale University Press, 2000); Diggins, *Hallowed Ground*, 86–7; Gerstle, *American Crucible*, "Epilogue."

53. Large parts of this discussion reveal debts to both Richard Morris and John Sanchez, both of whom spent considerable time discussing and debating these points with me. For an interesting discussion of this in terms of welfare policy, see Peter Edelman, *Searching for America's Heart: RFK and the Renewal of Hope* (Boston: Houghton Mifflin, 2001), 179. See also Marty, *The One and the Many*, 62.

54. Karlyn Kohrs Campbell and Kathleen Hall Jamieson, *Deeds Done in Words: Presidential Rhetoric and the Genres of Governance* (Chicago: University of Chicago Press, 1990).

55. Ellis, *Dark Side*, 2–3.

56. Theodore J. Lowi, *The End of the Republican Era* (Norman: University of Oklahoma Press, 1995).

57. Walter Dean Burnham, *Critical Elections and the Mainsprings of American Politics* (New York: W. W. Norton, 1970); James L. Sundquist, *Dynamics of the American Party System: Alignment and Realignment of Political Parties in the United States* (Washington, DC: Brookings, 1983).

58. Again, the literature on this subject is extensive, even if it is restricted to issues of African-American civil rights. See, for example, Thomas Borstelman, *The Cold War and the Color Line: American Race Relations in the Global Arena* (Cambridge, MA: Harvard University Press, 2001); Mary L. Dudziak, *Cold War Civil Rights: Race and the Image of American Democracy* (Princeton, NJ: Princeton University Press, 2000); Phillip A. Klinkner with Rogers M. Smith, *The Unsteady March: The Rise and Decline of Racial Equality in America* (Chicago: University of Chicago Press, 1999); Dean J. Kotlowski, *Nixon's Civil Rights: Politics, Principle, and Policy* (Cambridge, MA: Harvard University Press, 2000); Kenneth O'Reilly, *Nixon's Piano: Presidents and Racial Politics from Washington to Clinton* (New York: Simon and Schuster, 1995); Garth

Pauley, *The Modern Presidency and Civil Rights: Rhetoric on Race from Roosevelt to Nixon* (College Station: Texas A&M University Press, 2001); Riley, *Presidency*; Steven A. Shull, *American Civil Rights Policy from Truman to Clinton: The Role of Presidential Leadership* (Armonk, NY: ME Sharpe, 1999).

59. This is even true of Ronald Reagan, who is probably the most prototypical of the cold war presidents. For relevant discussions of Reagan in this context, see Robert Dalleck, *Ronald Reagan: The Politics of Symbolism* (Cambridge, MA: Harvard University Press, 1984); Paul D. Erickson, *Reagan Speaks: The Making of an American Myth* (New York: New York University Press, 1985); Paul Michael Rogin, *Ronald Reagan, the Movie: And Other Essays in Political Demonology* (Berkeley: University of California Press, 1987); Garry Wills, *Reagan's America: Innocents at Home* (Garden City, NY: Doubleday, 1985).

60. Silence is a major theme in gay and queer scholarship. See, for example, James Creech, *Closet Writing/Gay Reading* (Chicago: University of Chicago Press, 1993); David F. Greenberg, *The Construction of Homosexuality* (Chicago: University of Chicago Press, 1993); Charles E. Morris III, "Pink Herring and the Fourth Persona: J. Edgar Hoover's Sex Crime Panic," *Quarterly Journal of Speech* 88 (2002): 228–44; Charles E. Morris III, "The Responsibilities of the Critic: F. O. Matthiessen's Homosexual Palimpsest," *Quarterly Journal of Speech* 84 (3): 261–82; Eve Kosofsky Sedgwick, *Epistemology of the Closet* (Berkeley: University of California Press, 1990). For more instrumental uses of silence as a political strategy, see Barry Brummet, "Toward a Theory of Silence as a Political Strategy," *Quarterly Journal of Speech* 67 (1980): 289–303; Keith Erickson and W. Schmidt, "Presidential Political Silence: Rhetoric and the Rose Garden Strategy," *Southern Speech Communication Journal* 47 (1982): 402–21.

Chapter 1: Land, Citizenship, and National Identity in Jackson's America

1. Smith, *Civic Ideals*, 15.

2. Smith, *Civic Ideals*, 50–67.

3. Smith, *Civic Ideals*, 123.

4. Gerstle, *American Crucible*, 8–9.

5. Michael Paul Rogin, *Fathers and Children: Andrew Jackson and the Subjugation of the American Indian*, 2nd ed. (New Brunswick, NJ: Transaction, 1995), 206.

6. "Founders" here refers to the prominent Anglo-American political leaders of the years between 1776 and 1816, beginning with the Declaration of Independence and ending with Madison's presidency. For the purposes of this argument, stress is placed on broad areas of philosophical agreement. Their ideological and pragmatic differences are largely elided.

7. Smith, *Civic Ideals*, 75.

8. E. A. Benians, *Race and Nation in the United States* (Cambridge, UK: Cambridge University Press, 1946), 26.

9. Saul Cornell, *The Other Founders: Anti-Federalism and the Dissenting Tradition in America, 1788–1828* (Chapel Hill: University of North Carolina Press, 1999), 201.

10. George Washington, "Third Annual Address," October 25, 1791, in James D. Richardson, ed., *A Compilation of the Messages and Papers of the Presidents* (Washington, DC: Bureau of National Literature and Art, 1937), 105.

11. Washington, "Proclamation," September 15, 1792, in Richardson, *Messages and Papers*, 124.

12. Washington, "Proclamation," September 15, 1792, in Richardson, *Messages and Papers*, 125.

13. The use of the term *white* to describe non–American Indians residing in the Americas is problematic at best, denoting as it does a specific race whose parameters are fluid, imprecise, and socially constructed according to different criteria at different points in time. I use it here—and throughout the book—because other terms increase, rather than diminish, analytic confusion.

14. Washington, "Fourth Annual Address," November 6, 1792, in Richardson, *Messages and Papers*, 125–6.

15. Marshall Smelser, "An Understanding of the American Revolution," in Walter Nicgorski and Ronald Weber, eds., *An Almost Chosen People: The Moral Aspirations of Americans* (Notre Dame, IN: University of Notre Dame Press), 3, 13. See also Edward Countryman, *Americans: A Collision of Histories* (New York: Hill and Wang, 1996), 51; Susan Scheckel, *The Insistence of the Indian: Race and Nationalism in Nineteenth Century America* (Princeton, NJ: Princeton University Press, 1998), 3.

16. See Kimberly K. Smith, *The Dominion of Voice: Riot, Reason, and Romance in Antebellum Politics* (Lawrence: University Press of Kansas, 1999), 16–20.

17. Publius, "Federalist No. 10," *The Federalist Papers* (New York: Modern Library, 1937), 53.

18. Publius, "Federalist No. 10," 54.

19. Publius, "Federalist No. 10," 55, 56.

20. Publius, "Federalist No. 51," 337.

21. Publius, "Federalist No. 51," 339.

22. Publius, "Federalist No. 10," 61.

23. Thomas Jefferson, "Second Inaugural," March 4, 1805, in Richardson, *Messages and Papers*, 379.

24. Jefferson, "Second Inaugural," March 4, 1805, in Richardson, *Messages and Papers*, 379.

25. Gerstle, *American Crucible*, 11; Smith, *Civic Ideals*, 9–36.

26. Anthony F. C. Wallace, *Jefferson and the Indians: The Tragic Fate of the First Americans* (Cambridge, MA: Belknap Press of Harvard University Press, 1999), 17; see also Martin Diamond, "The Idea of Equality: The View from the Founding," in Nicgorski and Weber, *Almost Chosen People*, 19–37.

27. Smith, *Civic Ideals*, 167.

28. It should also be noted that when the founders discussed "freedom of speech," it was in the context of freedom of assembly and had more to do with legislative freedoms than with those exercised by individuals. See Michael Schudson, *The Good Citizen: A History of American Civic Life* (New York: Free Press, 1998), 24.

29. Jefferson, "First Inaugural," March 4, 1801, in Richardson, *Messages and Papers*, 331.

30. Richard B. Latner, "Andrew Jackson," in Henry Graff, ed., *The Presidents: A Reference History*, 2nd ed. (New York: Simon and Schuster, 1997), 107.

31. Wallace, *Jefferson and the Indians*, 6, 11.

32. Smith, *Civic Ideals*, 198.

33. Jefferson, "First Inaugural," 332.

34. Jefferson, "First Inaugural," 333.

35. Smith, *Civic Ideals*, 182.

36. Frederick M. Binder, *The Color Problem in Early National America as Viewed by John Adams, Thomas Jefferson, and Andrew Jackson* (The Hague: Mouton, 1968), 100.

37. Quoted in Wallace, *Jefferson and the Indians*, 165.

38. Jefferson, "Fourth Annual Message," November 8, 1804, in Richardson, *Messages and Papers*, 371–2.

39. Wallace actually delineates the four elements of Jefferson's plan to use trade to garner American Indian land: create debt, bribe influential chiefs, select and invite friendly leaders to Washington, and then threaten trade embargo or war and force land cessions to alleviate the threat. This last also has four parts: white encroachment or atrocities, bloody retaliation on the part of the American Indians, military invasion to protect the settlers and punish hostile American Indians, and finally a peace treaty requiring a land cession. See *Jefferson and the Indians*, 19–20. See also Francis Paul Prucha, *The Great Father: The United States Government and the American Indians* (Lincoln: University of Nebraska Press, 1984), 139.

40. See the detailed analysis of this by Carol Winkler, *In the Name of Terror: Presidents on Political Violence in the Post–World War II Era* (Philadelphia: Temple University Press, in press), especially chapter one.

41. Jefferson, "Second Inaugural," March 4, 1805, in Richardson, *Messages and Papers*, 380.

42. S. Elizabeth Bird, ed., *Dressing in Feathers: The Construction of the American Indian in Popular Culture* (Boulder, CO: Westview, 1996); James A. Clifton, ed., *The Invented Indian: Cultural Fiction and Governmental Policies* (New Brunswick, NJ: Transaction, 1990); Brian W. Dippie, *The Vanishing American: White Attitudes and U.S. Indian Policy* (Lawrence: University Press of Kansas, 1982).

43. Jefferson, "Second Inaugural," 380.

44. See, among many others, Reginald Horsman, *Expansion and American Indian Policy 1783–1812* (Norman: University of Oklahoma Press, 1967); Bruce E. Johansen, *Debating Democracy: Native American Legacy of Freedom* (Santa Fe: Clear Light, 1998); Judith Nies, *Native American History* (New York: Ballantine Books, 1996); David E. Stannard, *American Holocaust: Columbus and the Conquest of the New World* (New York: Oxford University Press, 1992); Ian K. Steele, *Warpaths: Invasions of North America* (New York: Oxford University Press, 1994).

45. See Colin Calloway, ed., *The World Turned Upside Down: Indian Voices from Early America* (Boston: Bedford, 1994); Colin Calloway, ed., *Our Hearts Fell to the Ground: Plains Indians Views of How the West Was Lost* (Boston: Bedford, 1996); Peter Nabokov, ed., *Native American Testimony: A Chronicle of Indian-*

White Relations from Prophecy to the Present, 1492–1992 (New York: Penguin, 1993).

46. See Colin Gordon Calloway, *The American Revolution in Indian Country: Crisis and Diversity in Native American Communities* (New York: Cambridge University Press, 1995); Arthur H. DeRosier, *The Removal of the Choctaw Indians* (Knoxville: University of Tennessee Press, 1970); Clara Sue Kidwell, *Choctaws and Missionaries in Mississippi, 1818–1918* (Norman: University of Oklahoma Press, 1995); Theda Perdue and Michael D. Green, *The Cherokee Removal: A Brief History with Documents* (Boston: Bedford, 1995).

47. This is quite different from recognizing—as much contemporary scholarship does—that American Indians exercised considerable agency. Jefferson's formulation removes agency on the one hand while insisting upon it on the other, a combination that functioned to absolve the American government for responsibility by presenting false choices.

48. See, for example, Donald Cole, *The Presidency of Andrew Jackson* (Lawrence: University Press of Kansas, 1999); Richard J. Ellis and Stephen Kirk, "Jefferson, Jackson, and the Origins of the Presidential Mandate," in Richard J. Ellis, ed., *Speaking to the People: The Rhetorical Presidency in Historical Perspective* (Amherst: University of Massachusetts Press, 1998), 35–65; Latner, "Andrew Jackson."

49. Arthur M. Schlesinger, Jr., *The Age of Jackson* (Boston: Little, Brown, 1945).

50. See, for instance, Latner, "Andrew Jackson"; Robert V. Remini, *The Revolutionary Age of Andrew Jackson* (New York: Harper & Row, 1976).

51. See, for example, Rogin, *Fathers and Children;* Wendy St. John, "After Removal: Class and Ethnic Divisions in the Chickasaw Nation," *Journal of Chickasaw History* 5 (2): 7–20.

52. See, for instance, Latner, "Andrew Jackson"; Remini, *Revolutionary Age;* Robert V. Remini, *The Legacy of Andrew Jackson: Essays on Democracy, Indian Removal, and Slavery* (Baton Rouge: Louisiana State University Press, 1988); Robert V. Remini, *Andrew Jackson and His Indian Wars* (New York: Viking, 2001); Ronald N. Satz, *American Indian Policy in the Jacksonian Era* (Lincoln: University of Nebraska Press, 1975).

53. Alexis de Tocqueville, *Democracy in America,* ed. J. P. Meyer, trans. George Laurence (New York: Doubleday, 1966).

54. Rogin argues that many political developments associated with the Jacksonian era stem from the "primitive accumulation of Indian land," a similar but slightly different point from the one that I am making. My claim is rhetorical, whereas his is economically deterministic and psychological. See Rogin, *Fathers and Children,* xvii, 167.

55. Charles S. Hyneman, *The American Founding Experience: Political Community and Representative Government,* ed. Charles S. Gilbert (Urbana: University of Illinois Press, 1994), 12–3; Schudson, *The Good Citizen,* 90–1; Foner, *Story of American Freedom,* 77.

56. See Barbara Welter, "The Cult of True Womanhood," in Edward Pessen, ed., *The Many Faceted Jacksonian Era: New Interpretations* (Westport, CT: Greenwood, 1977), 47–69.

57. Schudson notes that there were forty-seven abolitionist societies in 1833; by 1837, there were more than one thousand. See Schudson, *The Good Citizen*, 105; see also Richard H. Brown, "The Missouri Crisis, Slavery, and the Politics of Jacksonianism," in Pessen, *Many Faceted Jacksonian Era*, 177–91.

58. Bird, *Dressing in Feathers*; Philip Deloria, *Playing Indian* (New Haven, CT: Yale University Press, 1988); Rogin, *Fathers and Children*; Scheckel, *Insistence of the Indian*; Raymond William Stedman, *Shadows of the Indian: Stereotypes in American Culture* (Norman: University of Oklahoma Press, 1982); Takaki, *Different Mirror*; Bruce Ziff and Pratima V. Rao, eds., *Borrowed Power: Essays in Cultural Appropriation* (New Brunswick, NJ: Rutgers University Press, 1997).

59. Scheckel, *Insistence of the Indian*, 4.

60. Deloria, *Playing Indian*.

61. Andrew Jackson, "Second Annual Message," in Richardson, *Messages and Papers*, December 6, 1830, 521.

62. For an interesting discussion of this issue, see Roger G. Kennedy, *Hidden Cities: The Discovery and Loss of Ancient North American Architecture* (New York: Penguin, 1994).

63. Jackson, "First Annual Message," December 8, 1829, in Richardson, *Messages and Papers*, 458.

64. Rogin, *Fathers and Children*.

65. Rogin, *Fathers and Children*, 159. Certainly, this position is not unusual even today. Its most famous and consistent proponent is Robert V. Remini. See especially *Indian Wars*.

66. Rogin, *Fathers and Children*, 159.

67. Jackson, "First Inaugural," March 4, 1829, in Richardson, *Messages and Papers*, 438.

68. Jackson, "Fifth Annual Message," December 3, 1833, in Richardson, *Messages and Papers*, 33.

69. Prucha, *The Great Father*, 198; Remini, *Indian Wars*.

70. Jackson, "First Annual Message," 456–7.

71. Jackson, "First Annual Message," 456–7.

72. Jackson, "Second Annual Message," December 6, 1830, in Richardson, *Messages and Papers*, 522–3.

73. Jackson, "Third Annual Message," December 6, 1831, in Richardson, *Messages and Papers*, 555.

74. Jackson, "Seventh Annual Message," December 7, 1835, in Richardson, *Messages and Papers*, 162.

75. Jackson, "Seventh Annual Message," 164–5.

76. According to Rogin, "125,000 Indians lived east of the Mississippi in 1820. 75% of these came under government removal programs in the next two decades. By 1844, less than 30,000 Indians remained in the east, mainly in the undeveloped Lake Superior region." See Rogin, *Fathers and Children*, 4.

77. Rogin, *Fathers and Children*, 79–80; Lee Francis, *Native Time: A Historical Time Line of Native America* (New York: Westview, 1996).

78. Rogin, *Fathers and Children*, 79.

79. Prucha, *The Great Father*, 195.

80. Jackson, "First Annual Message," 458–9.

81. Jackson, "Second Annual Message," 522.

82. Jackson, "Second Annual Message," 521–2.

83. Jackson, "Sixth Annual Message," December 1, 1834, in Richardson, *Messages and Papers*, 113.

84. For a discussion of the influence of the market economy on contemporaneous understandings of freedom, see Foner, *Story of American Freedom*, 57.

85. Jackson, "Second Annual Message," 521.

86. Frederick Merk, *Manifest Destiny and Mission in American History* (New York: Vintage, 1963).

87. Jackson, "Fourth Annual Message," December 4, 1832, in Richardson, *Messages and Papers*, 601.

88. Jackson, "Veto Message," July 10, 1832, in Richardson, *Messages and Papers*, 590.

89. Jackson, "Fourth Annual Message," 600.

90. Jackson, "Farewell Address," March 4, 1837, in Richardson, *Messages and Papers*, 305.

91. Jackson, "Farewell Address," 306.

Chapter 2: Temperance, Character, and Race in the Antebellum United States

1. It is also important to note that the boundaries of the groups were rigidly determined and maintained, even in the face of multiethnic identities. For an interesting case study of this point, see N. Brent Kennedy, *The Melungeons: The Resurrection of a Proud People: An Untold Story of Ethnic Cleansing in America* (Macon, GA: Mercer University Press, 1997).

2. I am obviously not counting Zachary Taylor, who served from 1849 until his death in 1850, leaving Fillmore as president. For discussions of the political travails of the presidents of the 1850s, see Phillip B. Kunhardt, Jr., Phillip B. Kunhardt III, and Peter W. Kunhardt, *The American President* (New York: Riverhead Books, 1999), 53–7, 97–100; Nathan Miller, *Star-Spangled Men: America's Ten Worst Presidents* (New York: Scribner, 1998); Richard Schenkman, *Presidential Ambition: How the Presidents Gained Power, Kept Power, and Got Things Done* (New York: HarperCollins, 1999), 108; Stephen Skowronek, *The Politics Presidents Make: Leadership from John Adams to George Bush* (Cambridge, MA: Belknap Press of Harvard University Press, 1993), 117–85.

3. Gerstle, *American Crucible*.

4. Smith, *Dominion of Voice*, 149.

5. For an insightful discussion of the national fear of intemperance, see James Darsey, *The Prophetic Tradition and Radical Rhetoric in America* (New York: New York University Press, 1997), especially 63–6.

6. Pierce, "Inaugural Address," March 3, 1853, in Richardson, *Messages and Papers*, 202.

7. Karlyn Kohrs Campbell and Kathleen Hall Jamieson, for instance, note that policy has no place in an inaugural address. See *Deeds Done in Words* (Chicago: University of Chicago Press, 1990), 14.

8. Pierce, "Inaugural Address," 202.

9. The distinction here is between federal and confederal governmental systems.

10. James Buchanan, "First Annual Message," December 8, 1857, in Richardson, *Messages and Papers*, 441.

11. Merk, *Manifest Destiny and Mission in American History*, 26.

12. Pierce, "First Annual Message," December 5, 1853, in Richardson, *Messages and Papers*, 212.

13. Brinkley, *Unfinished Nation*, 271.

14. Pierce, "First Annual Message," 213.

15. Pierce, "First Annual Message," 224.

16. Pierce, "First Annual Message," 224–5.

17. Pierce, "Veto Messages," May 3, 1854, in Richardson, *Messages and Papers*, 249. This was a view of federalism shared by the other presidents of this period as well. See Millard Fillmore, "First Annual Message," December 2, 1850, in Richardson, *Messages and Papers*, 79; Buchanan, "Inaugural Address," March 4, 1857, in Richardson, *Messages and Papers*, 435.

18. Pierce, "Third Annual Message," December 31, 1855, in Richardson, *Messages and Papers*, 341.

19. In referring to the Articles here I am arguing that these presidents generally looked back to a moment when strong state governments were the foundation of the national government rather than to the historical moments (coincident with the first and second American party systems) when the federal government seemed increasingly regnant over the states. For the classic discussion of these party systems and the ideologies that motivated them, see Walter Dean Burnham, *Critical Elections: The Mainsprings of American Politics* (New York: W. W. Norton, 1971).

20. Pierce, "Third Annual Message," 342.

21. Fillmore, "First Annual Message," 91.

22. Smith, *Civic Ideals*.

23. Pierce, "Veto Messages," 255.

24. On Daniel Webster, see "The Bunker Hill Monument Oration," in James Andrews and David Zarefsky, eds., *American Voices: Significant Speeches in American History 1640–1945* (New York: Longman, 1989), 125–38. See also his eulogy on John Adams and Thomas Jefferson, excerpted in William Safire, *Lend Me Your Ears: Great Speeches in History* (New York: W. W. Norton, 1992), 160–3. Both speeches evoked nationalist sentiment through reference to the revolutionary past. For an example of Lincoln's public speech venerating the founding, see "Address before the Springfield Young Men's Lyceum," in Richard N. Current, ed., *The Political Thought of Abraham Lincoln* (Indianapolis, IN: Bobbs Merrill, 1967), 11–21.

25. Fillmore, "First Annual Message," 92.

26. Buchanan, "Inaugural Address," 430.

27. Pierce, "First Annual Message," 222.

28. Pierce, "Third Annual Message," 342; see also Buchanan, "Message to the House and Senate," January 8, 1861, in Richardson, *Messages and Papers*, 655.

29. Buchanan, "Inaugural Address," 432.

30. Pierce, "Second Annual Message," 292.

31. Pierce, "Veto Messages," 310.

32. Pierce, "Third Annual Message," 341.

33. Fillmore, "A Proclamation," February 18, 1851, in Richardson, *Messages and Papers*, 109.

34. Pierce, "Third Annual Message," 354.

35. Fillmore, "Third Annual Message," December 6, 1852, in Richardson, *Messages and Papers*, 163; Pierce, "Fourth Annual Message," 397–8.

36. Buchanan, "Inaugural Address," 431.

37. Fillmore, "First Annual Message," December 2, 1850, in Richardson, *Messages and Papers*, 80.

38. Pierce, "Third Annual Message," 350.

39. See, for example, Fillmore, "Proclamation," February 18, 1851, in Richardson, *Messages and Papers*, 111–2; Fillmore, "Second Annual Message," December 2, 1851, in Richardson, *Messages and Papers*, 113–7; Pierce, "Proclamation," January 18, 1854, in Richardson, *Messages and Papers*, 271–2; Pierce, "Proclamation," May 31, 1854, in Richardson, *Messages and Papers*, 272–83.

40. Buchanan, "To the Senate," January 7, 1858, in Richardson, *Messages and Papers*, 469.

41. Buchanan, "To the Senate," 469.

42. Pierce, "Third Annual Message," 355.

43. Buchanan, "Third Annual Message," 553–4.

44. See Pierce, "First Annual Message," 212; Fillmore, "First Annual Message," December 2, 1850, in Richardson, *Messages and Papers*, 80; Buchanan, "First Annual Message," December 8, 1857, in Richardson, *Messages and Papers*, 436.

45. Pierce, "Third Annual Message," 328.

46. Fillmore, "Second Annual Message," 127–8.

47. Buchanan, "First Annual Message," 459.

48. James M. McPherson, *Battle Cry of Freedom: The Civil War Era* (New York: Ballantine Books, 1988), 87.

49. Buchanan, "First Annual Message," 460.

50. Buchanan, "Inaugural Address," 435.

51. Fillmore, "First Annual Message," 79.

52. Buchanan, "Second Annual Message," December 6, 1858, in Richardson, *Messages and Papers*, 498.

53. Michael Morrison, *Slavery and the American West: The Eclipse of Manifest Destiny and the Coming of the Civil War* (Chapel Hill: University of North Carolina Press, 1997), 25.

54. McPherson, *Battle Cry of Freedom*, 8.

55. Fillmore, "Third Annual Message," 165.

56. Fillmore, "Third Annual Message," 165–6.

57. Pierce, "Third Annual Message," 341.

58. Pierce, "Third Annual Message," 341.

59. Buchanan, "To the Senate," 471.

60. Mary E. Stuckey and John M. Murphy, "What's in a Name? Rhetorical Colonialism in North America," *American Indian Culture and Research Journal* 25 (2002): 73–98.

61. Fillmore, "Second Annual Message," 128.

62. Fillmore, "Third Annual Message," 174.

63. Pierce, "Second Annual Message," 286; see also Pierce, "Special Session Message," August 21, 1856, in Richardson, *Messages and Papers*, 395–6.

64. Anne Norton, *A Reading of Antebellum Political Culture* (Chicago: University of Chicago Press, 1986).

65. George Fitzhugh, "Sociology of the South," in S. T. Joshi, ed., *Documents of American Prejudice: An Anthology of Writings on Race from Thomas Jefferson to David Duke* (New York: Basic Books, 1999), 281.

66. For discussions of his rhetoric and its political significance, see Gregory P. Lampe, *Frederick Douglass: Freedom's Voice, 1818–1845* (East Lansing: Michigan State University Press, 1998); John Louis Lucaites, "The Irony of 'Equality' in Black Abolitionist Discourse: The Case of Frederick Douglass's 'What to the Slave Is the Fourth of July?'" in Thomas W. Benson, ed., *Rhetoric and Political Culture in Nineteenth Century America* (East Lansing: Michigan State University Press, 1997), 47–69; James Jasinski, "Rearticulating History in Epideictic Discourse: Frederick Douglass's 'The Meaning of the Fourth of July to the Negro'," in Benson, *Rhetoric and Political Culture*, 71–89.

67. For a discussion of the Grimke sisters, see Stephen Howard Browne, *Angelina Grimke: Rhetoric, Identity, and the Radical Imagination* (East Lansing: Michigan State University Press, 1999); Jean Yellin and John C. Van Horne, eds., *The Abolitionist Sisterhood: Women's Political Culture in Antebellum America* (Ithaca, NY: Cornell University Press, 1994).

68. For discussion of Sojourner Truth, see Suzanne Pullon Fitch and Roseann M. Mandziuk, *Sojourner Truth as Orator: Wit, Story, and Song* (Westport, CT: Greenwood, 1997).

69. For a discussion of this dynamic, see Foner, *Story of American Freedom*, 86.

70. Pierce, "Third Annual Message," 349–50.

71. Darsey, *Prophetic Tradition*, 62–63; Browne, *Angelina Grimke*, 80.

72. Pierce, "Fourth Annual Message," December 2, 1856, in Richardson, *Messages and Papers*, 399.

73. Pierce, "Third Annual Message," 340.

74. Eighteenth among the "long train of abuses and usurpations" listed in the Declaration of Independence is, "He has excited domestic Insurrections among us, and has endeavored to bring on the Inhabitants of our Frontiers, the merciless Indian Savages, whose known Rule of Warfare, is an undistinguished Destruction, of all Ages, Sexes and Conditions."

75. Richard Hofstadter, *The Paranoid Style in American Politics and Other Essays* (New York: Alfred A. Knopf, 1966).

76. Buchanan, "Veto," June 22, 1860, in Richardson, *Messages and Papers*, 611–2.

77. Tyler Anbinder, *Nativism and Slavery: The Northern Know-Nothings and the Politics of the 1850s* (New York: Oxford University Press, 1992), xiv.

78. James A. Rawley, *Race and Politics "Bleeding Kansas" and the Coming of the Civil War* (Philadelphia: Lippincott, 1969), 267; Frederick M. Binder, *The Color Problem in Early National America as Viewed by John Adams, Jefferson, and Jackson* (The Hague: Mouton, 1968), 161; Zinn, *People's History*, 170.

79. Larry Gara, *The Presidency of Franklin Pierce* (Lawrence: University Press of Kansas, 1991), 97; McPherson, *Battle Cry of Freedom*, 137.

80. McPherson, *Battle Cry of Freedom*, 156.

81. Anbinder, *Nativism and Slavery*, 19.

82. Anbinder, *Nativism and Slavery*, 45, 95.

83. Quoted in Morrison, *Slavery and the American West*, 54.

84. Pierce, "Third Annual Message," 340.

85. Buchanan, "Inaugural Address," 432.

86. Buchanan, "Inaugural Address," 432; see also Buchanan, "Third Annual Message," 557.

87. Pierce, "Third Annual Message," 344.

88. Buchanan, "Fourth Annual Message," December 3, 1860, in Richardson, *Messages and Papers*, 626–7.

89. Buchanan, "Proclamation," April 6, 1858, in Richardson, *Messages and Papers*, 494.

90. Buchanan, "First Annual Message," 455.

91. Buchanan, "First Annual Message," 455.

92. Buchanan, "First Annual Message," 456.

93. Buchanan, "First Annual Message," 456.

94. Buchanan, "Proclamation," 493.

95. Fillmore, "Third Annual Message," 181.

96. Fillmore, "Third Annual Message," 181.

97. Pierce, "Proclamation," 271–2.

98. Buchanan, "Inaugural Address," 435.

99. Fillmore, "Third Annual Message," 182.

100. Pierce, "Inaugural Address," 198–9.

101. Smith, *Civic Ideals*.

102. Peter S. Onuf, *Jefferson's Empire: The Language of American Nationhood* (Charlottesville: University Press of Virginia, 2000), 92.

Chapter 3: The Business of Government during the Democratic Interregnum of Grover Cleveland, 1885–1889

1. Skowronek, *The Politics Presidents Make*.

2. For discussions of this point, see Brinkley, *Unfinished Nation*, 465; Nell Irvin Painter, *Standing at Armageddon: The United States, 1877–1919* (New York: W. W. Norton, 1989), xxxv; Robin Kanigel, *The One, Best Way: Frederick Winslow Taylor and the Enigma of Efficiency* (New York: Viking, 1997), 5.

3. Paul W. Glad, *Progressive Century: The American Nation in Its Second Hundred Years* (Lexington, MA: D. C. Heath, 1975), 12.

4. Smith, *Civic Ideals*, 347.

5. The old hierarchies as well as the old personal networks were more stable in the white South, which had less urbanization and less industrialization than the rest of the nation. Money as a measure of an individual's place in the world was consequently less important there. This is clearly connected to both the South's increasing marginalization in the national ethos and to the importance there of its romanticized, aristocratic past. See Brinkley, *Unfinished Nation*, 431.

6. Kanigel, *One Best Way*, 8.

7. For a discussion of the roots of this aspect of national identity in the processes of nation building during the Civil War, see Melinda Lawson, *Patriot Fires: Forging a New American Nationalism in the Civil War* (Lawrence: University Press of Kansas, 2002), especially chapter 2, 40–60.

8. For a discussion of this understanding of citizenship, see Schudson, *The Good Citizen*, 182.

9. Smith, *Civic Ideals*, 402.

10. Grover Cleveland, "Inaugural Address," March 4, 1885, in Richardson, *Messages and Papers*, volume VIII (Washington, DC: Bureau of National Literature and Art, 1897), 300.

11. Cleveland, "Inaugural," 302.

12. Cleveland, "Second Annual Message," December 6, 1886, in Richardson, *Messages and Papers*, 509.

13. Painter, *Standing at Armageddon*, 37.

14. Glad, *Progressive Century*, 19; Painter, *Standing at Armageddon*, xi.

15. Both Taylorism and Darwinism were, of course, considerably more complicated than this discussion indicates. My purpose here is less to provide a nuanced social history of these ideologies and their role in American life, and more to point to ways in which they may have influenced prevailing understandings of citizenship at this particular time.

16. Cleveland, "First Annual Message," December 8, 1885, in Richardson, *Messages and Papers*, 327.

17. Cleveland, "Communication to the House and Senate," April 22, 1886, in Richardson, *Messages and Papers*, 394–5.

18. Cleveland, "Inaugural," 300.

19. Brinkley, *Unfinished Nation*, 471; Glad, *Progressive Century*, 17–8.

20. There was certainly a debate about this within the popular culture, with authors such as Louisa May Alcott actively promulgating a different, highly moralistic, standard of judging character.

21. Painter, *Standing at Armageddon*, xxxv.

22. H. W. Brands, *Theodore Roosevelt: The Last Romantic* (New York: Basic Books, 1997).

23. Gerstle, *American Crucible*, 41.

24. Cleveland, "Second Annual Message," December 6, 1886, in Richardson, *Messages and Papers*, 510–11.

25. Cleveland, "Second Annual Message," 509.

26. Cleveland, "Inaugural," 300.

27. Campbell and Jamieson, *Deeds Done in Words*, chapter 2.

28. For a discussion of these processes, see Laurie Bruce, *Artisans into Workers: Labor in Nineteenth Century America* (New York: Hill and Wang, 1989), 113.

29. Cleveland, "Second Annual Message," 526–7.

30. Brinkley, *Unfinished Nation*, 470.

31. Quoted in Bruce, *Artisans into Workers*, 116.

32. Glad, *Progressive Century*, 17–8.

33. Zinn, *People's History*, 252–4. Although the focus of this book is restricted to the executive, it is also important to note that more often than not, the presidency shares the ideological predilections of the other branches. For an astute rendering of the role of the judiciary in weakening the American labor

movement, see Victoria C. Hattam, *Labor Visions and State Power: The Origins of Business Unionism in the United States* (Princeton, NJ: Princeton University Press, 1993).

34. Bruce, *Artisans into Workers*, 139; trans. Kai Schoenhals, *Friedrich A. Sorge's Labor Movement in the United States: A History of the American Working Class from 1890 to 1896* (New York: Greenwood, 1987), 2.

35. Cleveland, "Fourth Annual Message," December 3, 1888, in Richardson, *Messages and Papers*, 774.

36. Cleveland, "First Annual Message," 359.

37. Cleveland, "Fourth Annual Message," 775.

38. Cleveland, "Fourth Annual Message," 776.

39. Cleveland, "Fourth Annual Message," 774.

40. Cleveland, "Communication to the House and Senate," 395.

41. Cleveland, "Communication to the House and Senate," 395.

42. Cleveland, "Communication to the House and Senate," 395–6.

43. For a discussion of the mechanisms of exclusion, see Smith, *Civic Ideals*, 357.

44. Takaki, *Different Mirror*, 150.

45. Cleveland, "Inaugural," 302.

46. Zinn, *People's History*, 239.

47. Zinn, *People's History*, 263.

48. Brinkley, *Unfinished Nation*, 482.

49. Cleveland, "First Annual Message," 329.

50. Cleveland, "First Annual Message," 329.

51. Cleveland, "First Annual Message," 336.

52. Cleveland, "First Annual Message," 336.

53. Cleveland, "First Annual Message," 348.

54. Painter, *Standing at Armageddon*, xxv.

55. Augustus Sartorious von Walterschausen, *The Workers' Movement in the United States, 1879–1885*, ed. David Montgomery, trans. Marcel van der Linden (Cambridge, UK: Cambridge University Press, 1998), 171–2.

56. von Walterschausen, *Workers' Movement*, 172; see also Painter, *Standing at Armageddon*, xxxvi.

57. Cleveland, "First Annual Message," 345.

58. Cleveland, "Proclamation," November 1, 1886, in Richardson, *Messages and Papers*, 491.

59. Cleveland, "Veto Message," February 16, 1887, in Richardson, *Messages and Papers*, 557.

60. Cleveland, "Veto Message," February 4, 1887, in Richardson, *Messages and Papers*, 554.

61. Cleveland, "Fourth Annual Message," 797.

62. Cleveland, "Veto Message," April 18, 1888, in Richardson, *Messages and Papers*, 645.

63. Cleveland, "Veto Message," August 10, 1888, in Richardson, *Messages and Papers*, 702. See also "Veto Message," May 10, 1888, in Richardson, *Messages and Papers*, 668.

64. Painter, *Standing at Armageddon*, xxxviii.

65. Painter, *Standing at Armageddon*, xxxiv.

66. Brinkley, *Unfinished Nation*, 485; Bruce, *Artisans into Workers*, 4; Zinn, *People's History*, 259.

67. Foner, *Story of American Freedom*, 134.

68. Klinkner with Smith, *Unsteady March*, 90.

69. Bruce, *Artisans into Workers*, 27.

70. Cleveland, "Inaugural," 302.

71. Quoted in Takaki, *Different Mirror*, 37.

72. Brinkley, *Unfinished Nation*, 458.

73. Darsey, *Prophetic Tradition*, 87.

74. Foner, *Story of American Freedom*, 147.

75. Montgomery, "Introduction," in *Workers' Movement*, 19; emphasis in original. For an insightful discussion of manliness and the labor movement, see Darsey, *Prophetic Tradition*, 88.

76. Bruce, *Artisans into Workers*, 185.

77. Henry George, "The Chinese in California," in Joshi, *Documents of American Prejudice*, 431–2.

78. Cleveland, "First Annual Message," 329.

79. Cleveland, "First Annual Message," 329.

80. Cleveland, "First Annual Message," 361.

81. Cleveland, "First Annual Message," 361.

82. For a discussion of this point, see Smith, *Civic Ideals*, 385–6.

83. Cleveland, "Veto Message," September 7, 1888, in Richardson, *Messages and Papers*, 721.

84. For a discussion of these processes, see Kerber, *No Constitutional Right to Be Ladies*, 112.

85. Cleveland, "Inaugural," 302.

86. Cleveland said for instance, "Among the Indians upon these several reservations there exist the most marked differences in natural traits and disposition and in their progress toward civilization. While some are lazy, vicious, and stupid, others are industrious, peaceful, and intelligent." "First Annual Message," 356.

87. Cleveland, "Second Annual Message," 519.

88. Cleveland, "Fourth Annual Message," 796.

89. Traditional American Indian nations did not understand land to be "owned" in the Anglo, legal sense of the word. See Vine Deloria, Jr., *God Is Red: A Native View of Religion* (Golden, CO: Fulcrum, 1994), especially chapter 4; see also Ward Churchill, *Struggle for the Land: Indigenous Resistance to Genocide, Ecocide, and Expropriation in Contemporary North America* (Monroe, ME: Common Courage Press, 1993); Wilcomb E. Washburn, *Red Man's Land, White Man's Law: The Past and Present Status of the American Indian*, 2nd ed. (Norman: University of Oklahoma Press, 1994).

90. Smith, *Civic Ideals*, 390–1.

91. For details on this process, see David Wallace Adams, *Education for Extinction: American Indians and the Boarding School Experience* (Lawrence: University Press of Kansas, 1995).

92. The individual stories of those who experienced this form of education are deeply moving. For some examples, see Adams, *Education for Extinction*; Nabokov, *Native American Testimony*, especially 213–32, 388–90; *The Journal of Chickasaw History* 6 (2), 2000.

93. See Cleveland, "Second Annual Message," 514.

94. Cleveland, "Fourth Annual Message," 790.

95. The Apache were the first Americans to be incarcerated as prisoners of war on American soil. Their anonymous graves, marked only "Apache Prisoner of War," can still be seen at Fort Sill, Oklahoma. For details on Apache history, see Donald E. Worcester, *The Apaches: Eagles of the Southwest* (Norman: University of Oklahoma Press, 1979); H. Henrietta Stockel, *Women of the Apache Nation: Voices of Truth* (Reno: University of Nevada Press, 1991).

96. For example, Cleveland signed into law the 1888 White Men and Indian Women Marriage Act, regulating marital relations between races and preventing "illegal benefits" of interracial marriage. For details on this legislation, see Duane Champagne, ed., *Native North American Almanac* (Detroit, MI: Gale Research, 1994), 494. See also Francis Paul Prucha, ed., *Documents of American Indian Policy*, 2nd ed. (Lincoln: University of Nebraska Press, 1990), 176–7. ·

97. Cleveland, "Inaugural," 301.

98. Cleveland, "First Annual Message," 325.

99. Cleveland, "Inaugural," 299.

100. Cleveland, "Fourth Annual Message," 800. See also Cleveland, "First Annual Message," 363–4; Cleveland, "Second Annual Message," 527.

101. Cleveland, "To the Heads of Departments in the Service of Good General Government," July 14, 1886, in Richardson, *Messages and Papers,* 494.

102. Cleveland, "To the Congress of the United States," July 23, 1888, in Richardson, *Messages and Papers,* 618.

103. For a brief discussion of this point, see Takaki, *Different Mirror,* 204–6.

Chapter 4: Establishing a Transcendent International Order under Woodrow Wilson, 1913–1921

1. For a discussion of the tensions between civic and racial nationalism, see Gerstle, *American Crucible.*

2. For a discussion of Wilson's role in developing institutional power, see Jeffrey Tulis, *The Rhetorical Presidency* (Princeton, NJ: Princeton University Press, 1987). For a discussion of the ideological power of definition, see David Zarefsky, C. Miller-Tutzauer, and F. Tutzauer, "Reagan's Safety Net for the Truly Needy: The Rhetorical Uses of Definition," *Central States Communication Journal* 35 (1984): 113–9.

3. Kenneth Burke, *A Rhetoric of Motives* (Berkeley: University of California Press, 1950), 10–3.

4. Burke, *Rhetoric of Motives,* 21.

5. John Milton Cooper, Jr., *The Warrior and the Priest: Woodrow Wilson and Theodore Roosevelt* (Cambridge, MA: Belknap Press of Harvard University Press, 1983), 229; Arthur Link, *Woodrow Wilson: Revolution, War, and Peace* (Arlington Heights, IL: AHM Publishing, 1979), 2.

6. Herbert Croly, *The Promise of American Life* (New York: Macmillan, 1912), 443.

7. Louis Auchincloss, *Woodrow Wilson* (New York: Lipper/Viking, 2000), 44; Sigmund Freud and William C. Bullitt, *Thomas Woodrow Wilson, Twenty-*

Eighth President of the United States: A Psychological Study (Boston: Houghton Mifflin, 1967), 117.

8. David H. Burton, *The Learned Presidency: Theodore Roosevelt, William Howard Taft, Woodrow Wilson* (Rutherford, NJ: Fairleigh Dickinson University Press, 1988), 178.

9. Wilson, "An Inaugural Address," March 14, 1913, in Arthur S. Link, ed., *The Papers of Woodrow Wilson* (Princeton, NJ: Princeton University Press), volumes 27–67, 1978–1992, 148.

10. Wilson, "An Inaugural Address," 149.

11. Edwin A. Weinstein, *Woodrow Wilson: A Medical and Psychological Biography* (Princeton, NJ: Princeton University Press, 1981), 245.

12. Smith, *Civic Ideals,* 74.

13. Link, *Woodrow Wilson,* 1.

14. Arthur Walworth, *Woodrow Wilson,* 3rd ed. (New York: W. W. Norton, 1978 [1965, 1958]), 342.

15. Wilson, "An Inaugural Address," 149–50.

16. Wilson, "An Inaugural Address," 151.

17. Wilson, "An Address in St. Paul to a Joint Session of the Legislature of Minnesota," September 9, 1919, in Link, *Papers of Woodrow Wilson,* 131.

18. Burton, *Learned Presidency,* 138–9.

19. Wilson, "Remarks to Reporters at the First Press Conference," March 22, 1913, in Link, *Papers of Woodrow Wilson,* 211.

20. He took this position so far, in fact, as to make public appeals for a Democratic Congress during the war—despite Republican support for the war effort. He failed to see the resulting Republican Congress as a repudiation of either his leadership or his party, however. See Wilson, "An Appeal for a Democratic Congress," in Link, *Papers of Woodrow Wilson,* October 19, 1918, 381–2; Wilson, "Remarks to the Democratic National Committee," February 28, 1919, in Link, *Papers of Woodrow Wilson,* 309–11.

21. Wilson, "An Address on Jury Reform at Jersey City, NJ," May 2, 1913, in Link, *Papers of Woodrow Wilson,* 392–3.

22. Wilson, "Remarks to the Associated Press in New York," April 20, 1915, in Link, *Papers of Woodrow Wilson,* 41.

23. Wilson, "A Luncheon Address in Detroit," July 10, 1916, Link, *Papers of Woodrow Wilson,* 389.

24. Michael Kazin, *The Populist Persuasion: An American History* (New York: Basic Books, 1995), 52.

25. Wilson, "An Interview," April 27, 1914, in Link, *Papers of Woodrow Wilson,* 522.

26. Cooper, *Warrior and the Priest,* 236–7.

27. For commentary on this aspect of his presidency, see Leon H. Canfield, *The Presidency of Woodrow Wilson: Prelude to a World in Crisis* (Rutherford, NJ: Fairleigh Dickinson University Press, 1966), 41; Walworth, *Woodrow Wilson,* 354. For examples of it in his own words see, "Remarks to the Gridiron Club of Washington," April 12, 1913, in Link, *Papers of Woodrow Wilson,* 304–5; "Remarks at a Press Conference," January 29, 1914, in Link, *Papers of Woodrow Wilson,* 199.

28. See his language to that effect, quoted in Walworth, *Woodrow Wilson*, 326–7.

29. Wilson, "Remarks to a Delegation from the National Women's Suffrage Convention," December 8, 1913, in Link, *Papers of Woodrow Wilson*, 22. See also Wilson, "Remarks to a Committee of Working Women," February 2, 1914, in Link, *Papers of Woodrow Wilson*, 215; Wilson, "Remarks to a Delegation of Democratic Women," January 6, 1915, in Link, *Papers of Woodrow Wilson*, 22.

30. Wilson, "Remarks to a Women's Suffrage Delegation," June 30, 1914, in Link, *Papers of Woodrow Wilson*, 226. See also "Remarks in New York to a Suffrage Delegation," January 27, 1916, in Link, *Papers of Woodrow Wilson*, 3.

31. Wilson, "Remarks to a Women's Suffrage Delegation," June 30, 1914, in Link, *Papers of Woodrow Wilson*, 229.

32. Wilson, "Remarks upon Signing the Federal Reserve Bill," December 23, 1913, in Link, *Papers of Woodrow Wilson*, 65.

33. Wilson, "A Fourth of July Address," July 4, 1914, in Link, *Papers of Woodrow Wilson*, 251.

34. Walworth, *Woodrow Wilson*, 287.

35. Wilson, "An Address on Jury Reform in Jersey City, NJ," 393.

36. For a discussion of the exclusionary potential of progressivism inclusions, see Gerstle, *American Crucible*, 79–84.

37. Wilson, "An Address to the United States Chamber of Commerce," February 3, 1915, in Link, *Papers of Woodrow Wilson*, 179.

38. Wilson, "A Luncheon Address to the Chamber of Commerce of Columbus, Ohio," December 10, 1915, in Link, *Papers of Woodrow Wilson*, 327.

39. Wilson, "An Annual Message on the State of the Union," December 2, 1919, in Link, *Papers of Woodrow Wilson*, 110–1.

40. Elson J. Eisenach, *The Lost Promise of Progressivism* (Lawrence: University Press of Kansas, 1994), 224.

41. Burton, *Learned Presidency*, 139.

42. Eisenach, *Lost Promise*, 242.

43. Kendrick A. Clements, *The Presidency of Woodrow Wilson* (Lawrence: University Press of Kansas, 1992), 1.

44. Wilson, "An Address to the Federal Council of Churches in Columbus," December 10, 1915, in Link, *Papers of Woodrow Wilson*, 329. For secondary sources who discuss Wilson's commitment to Christian principles and their relationship to his government, see Burton, *Learned Presidency*, 140–1; Link, *Woodrow Wilson*, 45; and Walworth, *Woodrow Wilson*, 407.

45. Wilson, "An Address to the Pittsburgh Young Man's Christian Association," October 24, 1914, in Link, *Papers of Woodrow Wilson*, 221.

46. Wilson, "A Statement," July 23, 1917, in Link, *Papers of Woodrow Wilson*, 244.

47. Wilson, "A Statement," January 20, 1918, in Link, *Papers of Woodrow Wilson*, 42.

48. Wilson, "Remarks to the Gridiron Club," December 11, 1915, in Link, *Papers of Woodrow Wilson*, 343.

49. Wilson, "A Welcome to the Daughters of the American Revolution," April 14, 1913, in Link, *Papers of Woodrow Wilson*, 306.

50. Wilson, "Remarks upon Signing the Federal Reserve Bill," 65.

51. Wilson, "An Annual Address to Congress," December 2, 1913, in Link, *Papers of Woodrow Wilson*, 5–6.

52. Wilson, "A Memorial Address," May 11, 1914, in Link, *Papers of Woodrow Wilson*, 14–5.

53. Wilson, "An Address to the Daughters of the American Revolution," 50–1.

54. Wilson, "An Address in Buffalo to the American Federation of Labor," November 12, 1917, in Link, *Papers of Woodrow Wilson*, 16.

55. See Wilson, "Remarks to the Clerical Conference of the New York Federation of Churches," January 27, 1916, in Link, *Papers of Woodrow Wilson*, 6.

56. Wilson, "A Statement to the American People," June 26, 1918, in Link, *Papers of Woodrow Wilson*, 98.

57. Burke says, "To say that hierarchy is inevitable is not to say that any particular hierarchy is inevitable." See *Rhetoric of Motives*, 141.

58. Wilson, "An Address to Newly Naturalized Citizens," May 10, 1915, in Link, *Papers of Woodrow Wilson*, 148.

59. Wilson, "Remarks to the National Press Club," May 15, 1916, in Link, *Papers of Woodrow Wilson*, 47.

60. Wilson, "Remarks at the National Service School for Women," May 1, 1916, in Link, *Papers of Woodrow Wilson*, 574.

61. Wilson, "An Address on Commodore John Barry," May 16, 1914, in Link, *Papers of Woodrow Wilson*, 36.

62. For a discussion of how immigrants used "homemaking myths," see Orm Overland, *Immigrant Minds, American Identities: Making the United States Home, 1870–1930* (Urbana: University of Illinois Press, 2000), 15.

63. Overland, *Immigrant Minds*, 102–11.

64. Wilson, "Remarks to a Group of Hungarian Americans," February 23, 1916, in Link, *Papers of Woodrow Wilson*, 205; "A Memorial to the President," April 20, 1917, in Link, *Papers of Woodrow Wilson*, 113–6; "From Samuel Gompers," April 20, 1917, in Link, *Papers of Woodrow Wilson*, 135.

65. American Indian veterans were granted citizenship on November 6, 1919. The Indian Citizenship Act, which gave all American Indians citizenship, was passed on June 2, 1924. See Francis Paul Prucha, ed., *Documents of United States Indian Policy*, 2nd ed., expanded (Lincoln: University of Nebraska Press, 1990), 215, 218.

66. Wilson, "An Address to the Senate," September 30, 1918, in Link, *Papers of Woodrow Wilson*, 159–60.

67. Leonard Dinnerstein and David M. Reimers, *Ethnic Americans: A History of Immigration*, 4th ed. (New York: Columbia University Press), 56; Takaki, *Different Mirror*, 308.

68. For a fuller discussion of these points, see Robert A. Rockaway, *Words of the Uprooted: Immigrants in Early Twentieth Century America* (Ithaca, NY: Cornell University Press, 1998); Gerald Sorin, *A Time for Building: The Third Migration 1880–1920* (Baltimore: Johns Hopkins University Press, 1992).

69. Wilson, "To Various Ethnic Societies," May 23, 1918, in Link, *Papers of Woodrow Wilson*, 117.

70. Wilson, "A Memorial Day Address," May 30, 1916, in Link, *Papers of Woodrow Wilson*, 125.

71. See the excerpts that appear in S. T. Joshi, ed., *Documents of American Prejudice: An Anthology of Writings on Race from Thomas Jefferson to David Duke* (New York: Basic Books, 1999), 304–30. See also Dinnerstein and Reimers, *Ethnic Americans*, 80; Desmond King, *Making Americans: Immigration, Race, and the Origins of a Diverse Democracy* (Cambridge, MA: Harvard University Press, 2000), 12; Painter, *Standing at Armageddon*, 228.

72. Wilson, "A Message to American Indians," May 19, 1913, in Link, *Papers of Woodrow Wilson*, 469.

73. For a discussion of this history, see Dippie, *Vanishing American*, 211; Peter Iverson, *"We are Still Here": American Indians in the Twentieth Century* (Wheeling, IL: Harlan Davidson, 1998), 18–9; Judith Nies, *Native American History: A Chronology of a Culture's Vast Achievements and Their Links to World Events* (New York: Ballantine Books, 1996), 318–24.

74. Wilson did believe in the frontier myth, even if it played but a small role in his public speech. See Walworth, *Woodrow Wilson*, 343.

75. Wilson, "An Address on Behalf of the American Red Cross," May 18, 1918, in Link, *Papers of Woodrow Wilson*, 56–7. The paragraph containing this story was omitted from the official text of the address.

76. For a good historical discussion of depictions of American Indians and their speech, see Raymond William Stedman, *Shadows of the Indian: Stereotypes in American Culture* (Norman: University of Oklahoma Press, 1982), 58–73.

77. Walworth, *Woodrow Wilson*, 325.

78. On Wilson's comparative liberality on race, see Cooper, *Warrior and the Priest*, 210; Weinstein, *Woodrow Wilson*, 248–9; On Brownsville in particular, see Mary E. Stuckey, "Maintaining Democratic Power through Silencing: Theodore Roosevelt and the Brownsville Raid," presented at the annual meeting of the National Communication Association, New Orleans, LA, 2002.

79. Wilson, "Remarks at a Press Conference," March 30, 1914, in Link, *Papers of Woodrow Wilson*, 386.

80. Wilson, "Remarks at a Press Conference," May 19, 1913, in Link, *Papers of Woodrow Wilson*, 452.

81. Wilson, "Remarks upon the Clause for Racial Equality," April 11, 1919, in Link, *Papers of Woodrow Wilson*, 268.

82. Wilson, "Remarks to a Group of American Blacks," October 1, 1918, in Link, *Papers of Woodrow Wilson*, 168.

83. Burton, *Learned Presidency*, 181; Walworth, *Woodrow Wilson*, 338–9.

84. John Whiteclay Chambers II, *The Tyranny of Change: America in the Progressive Era, 1890–1920*, 2nd ed. (New Brunswick, NJ: Rutgers University Press, 2000), 88.

85. Clements, *Presidency of Woodrow Wilson*, 74.

86. Wilson, "An Address at the Dedication of the American Federation of Labor Building," April 4, 1916, in Link, *Papers of Woodrow Wilson*, 355.

87. Wilson, "An Address on Tariff Reform to a Joint Session of Congress," April 18, 1913, in Link, *Papers of Woodrow Wilson*, 271.

88. Wilson, "An Address on Tariff Reform to a Joint Session of Congress," 271.

89. Wilson, "To the American Alliance for Labor and Democracy," June 10, 1918, in Link, *Papers of Woodrow Wilson*, 275.

90. Chambers, *Tyranny of Change*, 81.

91. Chambers, *Tyranny of Change*, 82.

92. Wilson, "Remarks to the Associated Press in New York," 38.

93. Wilson, "An Annual Message on the State of the Union," December 7, 1915, in Link, *Papers of Woodrow Wilson*, 307.

94. For a discussion of the Klan and the implications of its growth during these years, see Dinnerstein and Reimers, *Ethnic Americans*, 84–6. For discussion of the Leo Frank case, see Sorin, *Time for Building*, 167.

95. Chambers, *Tyranny of Change*, 196; Clements, *Presidency of Woodrow Wilson*, xi.

96. Klinkner with Smith, *Unsteady March*, 110.

97. Wilson, "Remarks by Wilson and a Dialogue," November 12, 1914, in Link, *Papers of Woodrow Wilson*, 302.

98. Burke, *Rhetoric of Motives*, 141.

99. John Morton Blum, *Woodrow Wilson and the Politics of Morality*, Oscar Handlin, ed. (Boston: Little, Brown, 1956), 119.

100. Wilson, "An Address on Latin American Policy in Mobile, Alabama," October 27, 1913, in Link, *Papers of Woodrow Wilson*, 451.

101. Wilson, "A Welcome to the Daughters of the American Revolution," 306.

102. Link, *Woodrow Wilson*, 5.

103. Wilson, "An Address on Latin American Policy in Mobile, Alabama," 448. See also Wilson, "An Address to a Joint Session of Congress," February 11, 1918, in Link, *Papers of Woodrow Wilson*, 321–3; Wilson, "Remarks to Mexican Editors," June 7, 1918, in Link, *Papers of Woodrow Wilson*, 256.

104. For a discussion of Wilson's efforts to get self-determination for the Filipino people, for instance, see Link, *Woodrow Wilson*, 10.

105. Wilson, "An Annual Message to Congress on the State of the Union," December 2, 1913, in Link, *Papers of Woodrow Wilson*, 8.

106. For an insightful discussion of this point, see Richard Drinnon, *Facing West: The Metaphysics of Indian-Hating and Empire Building* (Norman: University of Oklahoma Press, 1980).

107. Wilson, "A Statement on the Chinese Loan," March 18, 1913, in Link, *Papers of Woodrow Wilson*, 193.

108. Wilson, "Remarks at a Luncheon," May 17, 1915, in Link, *Papers of Woodrow Wilson*, 210.

109. Wilson, "An Address on Preparedness to the Manhattan Club," November 4, 1915, in Link, *Papers of Woodrow Wilson*, 169.

110. Chambers, *Tyranny of Change*, 213. See also Blum, *Woodrow Wilson*, 85; Alexander L. George and Juliette L. George, *Woodrow Wilson and Colonel House: A Personality Study* (New York: Dover, 1964), 159.

111. Wilson, "An Address to the Daughters of the American Revolution," 49.

112. Wilson, "An Address on Latin American Policy in Mobile, Alabama," 451.

113. Wilson, "A Luncheon Address in Detroit," July 10, 1916, in Link, *Papers of Woodrow Wilson*, 394–5.

114. Wilson, "A Luncheon Address in Portland," September 15, 1919, in Link, *Papers of Woodrow Wilson*, 280.

115. Burke, *Rhetoric of Motives*, 187; emphasis in original.

116. Tulis, *Rhetorical Presidency.*

117. For a discussion of Wilson's legacy, especially in terms of its impact on FDR, see Cooper, *Warrior and the Priest,* 348–9.

Chapter 5: Balancing the Nation: Brokering FDR's Economic Union, 1932–1940

1. Gerstle, *American Crucible,* 133.

2. George McJimsey, *The Presidency of Franklin Delano Roosevelt* (Lawrence: University Press of Kansas, 2000), xii.

3. Roosevelt, "Radio Address on Brotherhood Day," February 23, 1936, in Samuel I. Rosenman, ed., *The Public Papers and Addresses of Franklin D. Roosevelt* (New York: Macmillan, 1938), 86.

4. McJimsey, *Presidency of Franklin Delano Roosevelt,* 7.

5. Roosevelt, "Inaugural Address," March 4, 1933, in Rosenman, *Public Papers,* 14.

6. For a discussion of pluralism and pluralists, see A. J. Beitzinger, *A History of American Political Thought* (New York: Harper & Row, 1972), 500–5; 545–51.

7. Gareth Davis, "The Unsuspected Radicalism of the Social Security Act," in Robert A. Garson and Stuart S. Kidd, eds., *The Roosevelt Years: New Perspectives on American History* (Edinburgh: Edinburgh University Press, 1999), 56. See also James McGregor Burns, *The Lion and the Fox, 1882–1940* (New York: Harcourt Brace, 1940), 403; Mary E. Stuckey, *Strategic Failures in the Modern Presidency* (Cresskill, NJ: Hampton Press, 1997), 94.

8. Roosevelt, "A Call to War Veterans to Rally to the Colors in a Peacetime Sacrifice. Address before the American Legion Convention," Chicago, Illinois, October 2, 1933, in Rosenman, *Public Papers,* 374.

9. Roosevelt, "Address at the Jackson Day Dinner, Washington, D.C., Broadcast to 3,000 Similar Dinners throughout the Nation," January 8, 1936, in Rosenman, *Public Papers,* 39. See also Roosevelt, "Radio Address on Current Events," October 5, 1937, in Rosenman, *Public Papers,* 412.

10. Roosevelt, "A Greeting to the National Conference of Social Work," May 23, 1936, in Rosenman, *Public Papers,* 189.

11. Sean Dennis Cashman, *America Ascendant: From Theodore Roosevelt to FDR in the Century of American Power, 1901–1945* (New York: New York University Press, 1998), 299–300. See also Gary Dean Best, *Pride, Prejudice, and Politics: Roosevelt versus Recovery, 1933–1938* (New York: Praeger, 1991), 25, 52; Irwin F. Gellman, *Secret Affairs: Franklin Roosevelt, Cordell Hull, and Sumner Welles* (Baltimore: Johns Hopkins University Press, 1995), 11; Stuckey, *Strategic Failures,* 131. For details on his critics, see Albert Fried, *FDR and His Enemies* (New York: St. Martin's Press, 1999), 6; and George Wolfskill and John A. Hudson, *All But the People: Franklin D. Roosevelt and His Critics, 1933–1939* (New York: Macmillan, 1969), x.

12. Foner, *Story of American Freedom,* 205.

13. Fried, *FDR and His Enemies,* 6.

14. Roosevelt, "'All of Us—You and I Especially, Are Descended from Immigrants and Revolutionists.' Extemporaneous Remarks before the Daughters of the

American Revolution, Washington, D.C.," April 21, 1938, in Rosenman, *Public Papers*, 259.

15. David M. Kennedy, *Freedom from Fear: The American People in Depression and War, 1929–1945* (New York: Oxford University Press, 1999), 174–5; Wolfskill and Hudson, *All But the People*, 61–2.

16. Harry Hopkins, "Federal Relief," September 9, 1936, in Richard Polenberg, *The Era of Franklin D. Roosevelt, 1933–1945* (New York: Bedford/St. Martin's, 2000), 86.

17. For a discussion of FDR's responsiveness to group demands, see McJimsey, *Presidency of Franklin Delano Roosevelt*, 151.

18. McJimsey, *Presidency of Franklin Delano Roosevelt*, 80.

19. Gerstle, *American Crucible*, 130.

20. Roosevelt, "The Goal of the National Industrial Recovery Act—A Statement by the President on Signing it," June 16, 1933, in Rosenman, *Public Papers*, 246.

21. Roosevelt, "Presidential Statement on the National Industrial Recovery Act—'To Put People Back to Work'," June 16, 1933, in Rosenman, *Public Papers*, 251–2.

22. Roosevelt, "The Third 'Fireside Chat'—'The Simple Purposes and the Solid Foundations of Our Recovery Program'," July 24, 1933, in Rosenman, *Public Papers*, 302.

23. Roosevelt, "Annual Message to Congress," January 4, 1935, in Rosenman, *Public Papers*, 17.

24. For a discussion of the Wagner Act, see Kennedy, *Freedom from Fear*, 290.

25. For a discussion of labor issues and FDR's relationship with labor, see Kennedy, *Freedom from Fear*, 290–6.

26. For a discussion of the Flint strike, see Cashman, *America Ascendant*, 327–8; Kennedy, *Freedom from Fear*, 312.

27. Best, *Pride, Prejudice, and Politics*, 154–5.

28. Burns, *Lion and the Fox*, 216.

29. Cashman, *America Ascendant*, 327–30, 305.

30. Roosevelt, "Address at the Dedication of the Samuel Gompers Memorial Monument, Washington, D.C.," October 7, 1933, in Rosenman, *Public Papers*, 387.

31. Roosevelt, "The President Urges Cooperation between the Management and Employees of the Railroads," March 6, 1936, in Rosenman, *Public Papers*, 109.

32. Roosevelt, "The First 'Fireside Chat' of 1936, following the Drought Inspection Trip—'We Are Going to Conserve Soil, Conserve Water, Conserve Life'," September 6, 1936, in Rosenman, *Public Papers*, 338–9.

33. See, for example, Roosevelt, "Radio Address in Honor of General Kryanowski of Poland," October 11, 1937, in Rosenman, *Public Papers*, 427.

34. This may well be among the earliest examples of what later comes to characterize presidential speech on diversity, the rhetoric of celebratory othering.

35. Kennedy, *Freedom from Fear*, 86.

36. Roosevelt, "A Christmas Greeting to the Nation," December 24, 1935, in Rosenman, *Public Papers*, 506.

37. For a discussion of how this sort of language may have operated among

members of European immigrant communities, see Gerstle, *American Crucible,* 168.

38. Wolfskill and Hudson, *All But the People,* 316.

39. Roosevelt, "Radio Address on Maryland Tercentenary Celebration," November 22, 1933, in Rosenman, *Public Papers,* 497.

40. Roosevelt, "'A Wider Opportunity for the Average Man'—Address Delivered at Green Bay, Wisconsin," August 9, 1934, in Rosenman, *Public Papers,* 370. See also Roosevelt, "On the Importance of Teaching the English Language in Puerto Rico," April 17, 1937, in Rosenman, *Public Papers,* 161; Roosevelt, "Address on Hemisphere Day," October 12, 1940, in Rosenman, *Public Papers,* 461–2.

41. Roosevelt, "'The Fight for Social Justice and Economic Democracy . . . Is a Long, Weary, Uphill Struggle.' Radio Address on Electing Liberals to Public Office," November 11, 1938, in Rosenman, *Public Papers,* 593.

42. Roosevelt, "Address on the Occasion of the Fiftieth Anniversary of the Statue of Liberty, 'Carry Forward American Freedom and American Peace by Making Them Living Facts in a Living Present'," October 28, 1936, in Rosenman, *Public Papers,* 541.

43. See Skowronek, *The Politics Presidents Make,* chapters 2–3 on reconstructive presidents, and chapter 7 on FDR specifically.

44. Roosevelt, "Address on the Occasion of the Fiftieth Anniversary of the Statue of Liberty," 543.

45. S. Jay Kleinberg, "Widows' Welfare in the Great Depression," in Garson and Kidd, *Roosevelt Years,* 72–3.

46. Kleinberg, "Widows' Welfare," 85; See also Brinkley, *Unfinished Nation,* 661–4, 703.

47. Molly Dewson, "Women and the New Deal," April 8, 1936, in Polenberg, *Era of Franklin D. Roosevelt,* 101.

48. Wolfskill and Hudson, *All But the People,* 145.

49. Halford R. Ryan notes FDR's propensity to scapegoat in "Roosevelt's First Inaugural: A Study of Technique," in Halford R. Ryan, ed., *American Rhetoric from Roosevelt to Reagan: A Collection of Speeches and Critical Essays* (Prospect Heights, IL: Waveland, 1983), 11–3.

50. Burns, *Lion and the Fox,* 195.

51. Roosevelt, "The Fourth 'Fireside Chat'—'We Are on Our Way, and We Are Headed in the Right Direction'," October 22, 1933, in Rosenman, *Public Papers,* 424.

52. Roosevelt, "Address Delivered at Savannah, Georgia, 'The American March of Progress'," November 18, 1933, in Rosenman, *Public Papers,* 499.

53. Roosevelt, "The First 'Fireside Chat' of 1934—'Are You Better Off Than You Were Last Year?'" June 28, 1934, in Rosenman, *Public Papers,* 315.

54. Roosevelt, "'We Are Fighting to Save a Great and Precious Form of Government for Ourselves and for the World'—Acceptance of the Renomination for the Presidency, Philadelphia, Pennsylvania," June 27, 1936, in Rosenman, *Public Papers,* 232.

55. Roosevelt, "'New Approaches to Old Problems'—Address at Rollins College, Florida, on Receiving Honorary Degree," March 23, 1936, in Rosenman, *Public Papers,* 147.

56. Frank Freidel, *F.D.R. and the South* (Baton Rouge: Louisiana State University Press, 1965), 2. See also Brinkley, *Unfinished Nation*, 701; Foner, *Story of American Freedom*, 196.

57. Kennedy, *Freedom from Fear*, 128.

58. Ronald L. Feinman, *Twilight of Progressivism: The Western Republican Senators and the New Deal* (Baltimore: Johns Hopkins University Press, 1981), 64; see also McJimsey, *Presidency of Franklin Delano Roosevelt*, 135.

59. For an evocative description of a life lived with these tensions, see Jimmy Carter, *An Hour before Daylight: Memories of a Rural Boyhood* (New York: Simon and Schuster, 2001). For discussion of the politics of Jim Crow, see Ralph J. Bunche, *The Political Status of the Negro in the Age of FDR*, Dewey W. Grantham, ed. (Chicago: University of Chicago Press, 1973); Nancy J. Weiss, *Farewell to the Party of Lincoln: Black Politics in the Age of FDR* (Princeton, NJ: Princeton University Press, 1983).

60. Freidel, *F.D.R. and the South*, 73; Klinkner with Smith, *Unsteady March*, chapters 4–5; Pauley, *Modern Presidency*, 18–30; Shull, *American Civil Rights Policy*.

61. See Weiss, *Farewell to the Party of Lincoln*, 35. For a more personalized discussion of the economic aspects of lynching and Jim Crow, see Carter, *An Hour before Daylight*, 149.

62. Bunche, *Political Status of the Negro*, 109.

63. Foner, *Story of American Freedom*, 207.

64. Gerstle, *American Crucible*, 130–1.

65. Gunnar Myrdal, *An American Dilemma: The Negro Problem and American Democracy* (New York: McGraw-Hill, 1964 [1924]).

66. Graham J. White, *FDR and the Press* (Chicago: University of Chicago Press, 1979), 18.

67. Roosevelt, "Congratulations to Negroes of the United States upon the Seventieth Anniversary of the Proclamation of Emancipation," September 22, 1933, in Rosenman, *Public Papers*, 364.

68. Roosevelt, "A Letter on the Progress Made by the Negro Race Since the Proclamation of Emancipation," December 26, 1935, in Rosenman, *Public Papers*, 507.

69. Roosevelt, "A Greeting to the NAACP," June 13, 1939, in Rosenman, *Public Papers*, 370.

70. Roosevelt, "A Special Press Conference with the Members of the American Society of Newspaper Editors, Washington, D.C.," April 21, 1938, in Rosenman, *Public Papers*, 263.

71. Roosevelt, "Informal, Extemporaneous Remarks at Tuskegee Institute, Tuskegee, Alabama," March 30, 1939, in Rosenman, *Public Papers*, 178.

72. For a discussion of New Deal policies affecting African Americans, see Wolfskill and Hudson, *All But the People*, 86–9.

73. For a discussion of the Black Cabinet, see Weiss, *Farewell to the Party of Lincoln*, 136–9.

74. Roosevelt, "The Fourth 'Fireside Chat'," 420.

75. Roosevelt, "The Annual Message to Congress," in Rosenman, *Public Papers*, 636.

76. Roosevelt, "Extemporaneous Remarks to the State Directors of the National Emergency Council," February 2, 1934, in Rosenman, *Public Papers,* 83.

77. Roosevelt, "The Golden Rule in Government—An Extemporaneous Address at Vassar College, Poughkeepsie, New York," August 26, 1933, in Rosenman, *Public Papers,* 342; see also Roosevelt, "Annual Message to Congress," January 3, 1938, in Rosenman, *Public Papers,* 4.

78. See, for example, Roosevelt, "Annual Message to Congress," January 4, 1935, in Rosenman, *Public Papers,* 16.

79. White, *FDR and the Press,* viii–ix.

80. Best, *Pride, Prejudice, and Politics,* 25, 52.

81. Roosevelt, "'Self-Government We Must and Shall Maintain', Address at Little Rock, Arkansas," June 10, 1936, in Rosenman, *Public Papers,* 198.

82. Roosevelt, "The Need for Patriotic and Religious Faith—An Address before the National Conference of Catholic Charities," October 4, 1933, in Rosenman, *Public Papers,* 380.

83. Roosevelt, "The President Vetoes the Bonus Bill," May 22, 1935, in Rosenman, *Public Papers,* 191.

84. Kennedy, *Freedom from Fear,* 183.

85. Roosevelt, "A Radio Invitation to All Veterans for Cooperation," March 5, 1933, in Rosenman, *Public Papers,* 17–8.

86. Roosevelt, "Inaugural Address," March 4, 1933, in Rosenman, *Public Papers,* 14.

87. Roosevelt, "Address at the Dedication of the Samuel Gompers Memorial Monument, Washington, D.C.," October 7, 1933, in Rosenman, *Public Papers,* 387.

88. McJimsey, *Presidency of Franklin Delano Roosevelt,* 164.

89. Quoted in Wolfskill and Hudson, *All But the People,* 17. On the issue of Eleanor's importance to the administration, see also Burns, *Lion and the Fox,* 173.

90. For a discussion of the Indian Reorganization Act and Collier's role in it, see Kenneth R. Philp, "Introduction: The Indian Reorganization Act Fifty Years Later," in Kenneth R. Philp, ed., *Indian Self-Rule: First-Hand Accounts of Indian White Relations from Roosevelt to Reagan* (Logan: Utah State University Press, 1995), 16.

91. John Collier, "A New Deal for American Indians," in Polenberg, *Era of Franklin D. Roosevelt,* 152.

92. Wilcomb E. Washburn, *Red Man's Land, White Man's Law,* 2nd ed. (Norman: University of Oklahoma Press, 1994), 76.

93. Dippie, *Vanishing American,* 307–8.

94. E. Richard Hart, "Introduction," in Philp, *Indian Self-Rule,* 9.

95. For a discussion of these issues, see Rupert Costo, in Rupert Costo, Benjamin Reifel, Kenneth R. Philp, Dave Warren, Afonso Ortiz, "Federal Indian Policy, 1933–1945," in Philp, *Indian Self-Rule,* 48; for an opposing view, see the remarks by Philp, 59; Dippie, *Vanishing American,* 325.

96. For an overview of some of the issues involved in these complicated questions, see Bird, *Dressing in Feathers;* Ward Churchill, *Indians Are Us? Culture and Genocide in Native North America* (Monroe, ME: Common Courage Press, 1994); Philip J. Deloria, *Playing Indian* (New Haven, CT: Yale University Press,

1998); Bruce Ziff and Pratima V. Rao, eds., *Borrowed Power: Essays on Cultural Appropriation* (New Brunswick, NJ: Rutgers University Press, 1997).

97. Floyd A. O'Neil, "The Indian New Deal: An Overview," in Philp, *Indian Self-Rule*, 42; William N. Thompson, *Native American Issues* (Santa Barbara, CA: ABC-CLIO, 1996), 11.

98. Those tensions became extreme in the 1960s and 1970s, during the era of Red Power, and were especially virulent on the Pine Ridge Reservation in South Dakota. There is a voluminous literature on Red Power, and its causes and consequences. See, for example, Vine Deloria, Jr., *Behind the Trail of Broken Treaties: An Indian Declaration of Independence* (Austin: University of Texas Press, 1985); Troy Johnson, Joane Nagel, and Duane Champagne, eds., *American Indian Activism: From Alcatraz to the Longest Walk* (Urbana: University of Illinois Press, 1997); Joane Nagel, *American Indian Ethnic Renewal: Red Power and the Resurgence of Identity and Culture* (New York: Oxford University Press, 1996). It is important to note that many nations are now working to rewrite their constitutions to bring tribal governance more in line with traditions. For the most recent general work on tribal constitutions, see Sharon O'Brien, *American Indian Tribal Governments* (Norman: University of Oklahoma Press, 1989).

99. Roosevelt, "Presidential Statement Endorsing the Wheeler-Howard Bill to Aid the Indians," April 28, 1934, in Rosenman, *Public Papers*, 202.

100. Quoted in Kennedy, *Freedom from Fear*, 131.

101. Roosevelt, "The President Hails the Four Hundredth Anniversary of the Printing of the First English Bible," October 6, 1935, in Rosenman, *Public Papers*, 420. See also Roosevelt, "'The Need for Patriotic and Religious Faith'—An Address before the National Conference of Catholic Charities," October 4, 1933, in Rosenman, *Public Papers*, 379; Roosevelt, "Address on the White House Conference on Children in a Democracy," April 23, 1939, in Rosenman, *Public Papers*, 244.

102. Roosevelt, "Extemporaneous Speech at the Hyde Park Methodist Episcopal Church, 'Cooperation from Churches'," September 29, 1933, in Rosenman, *Public Papers*, 368.

103. Roosevelt, "An Acknowledgment of the Award of the American Hebrew Medal," March 6, 1939, in Rosenman, *Public Papers*, 154.

104. Roosevelt, "Informal Extemporaneous Remarks to a Number of Visiting Protestant Ministers, Washington, D.C.," January 1, 1938, in Rosenman, *Public Papers*, 75. See also Roosevelt, "An Annual Message to Congress," January 4, 1939, 1.

105. Roosevelt, "Radio Address on Behalf of the Annual Mobilization for Human Needs, Poughkeepsie, New York," October 18, 1937, in Rosenman, *Public Papers*, 441–2.

106. See, for example, Roosevelt, "Inaugural Address," 11, where he says, "Our distress comes from no failure of substance."

107. Roosevelt, "Extemporaneous Speech to the Civilian Works Administration Conference in Washington," November 15, 1933, in Rosenman, *Public Papers*, 469.

108. Stuckey, *The President as Interpreter-in-Chief* (Chatham, NJ: Chatham

House, 1991), 34. It is significant that Roosevelt claimed his favorite song was "Home on the Range," a paean to the frontier experience. For a discussion of the ideological role this song played during the Depression and its congruence with the argument being made here, see Gary Giddens, *Bing Crosby: A Pocketful of Dreams, The Early Years 1903–1940* (Boston: Little, Brown, 2001), especially 339–40.

109. Roosevelt, "'A Wider Opportunity for the Average Man'—Address Delivered at Green Bay, Wisconsin," August 9, 1934, in Rosenman, *Public Papers*, 371. See also Roosevelt, "'The Period of Social Pioneering Is Only at Its Beginning'— Address at the Young Democratic Club, Baltimore, Maryland," April 13, 1936, in Rosenman, *Public Papers*, 165.

110. For a discussion of how language works in these instances, see Mary E. Stuckey and John M. Murphy, "By Any Other Name: Rhetorical Colonialism in North America," *American Indian Culture and Research Journal* 25 (2002): 73–98.

111. Roosevelt, "The Uses of an Education—Extemporaneous Speech at Washington College, Chestertown, Maryland, on Receipt of Honorary Degree," October 21, 1933, in Rosenman, *Public Papers*, 418.

112. See also Roosevelt, "Address at George Rogers Clark Celebration, Harrodsburg, Kentucky—'Survival Calls for a New Pioneering on Our Part'," November 6, 1934, in Rosenman, *Public Papers*, 457; Roosevelt, "A Suggestion for Legislation to Create the Tennessee Valley Authority," April 10, 1933, in Rosenman, *Public Papers*, 122–3; Roosevelt, "Address upon Receiving Honorary Degree at the College of William and Mary, Williamsburg, VA," October 20, 1934, in Rosenman, *Public Papers*, 434; Roosevelt, "A Labor Day Statement by the President," September 5, 1937, in Rosenman, *Public Papers*, 349.

113. Roosevelt, "An Address on the Accomplishments and Future Aims for Agriculture, Fremont, Nebraska," September 28, 1935, in Rosenman, *Public Papers*, 380.

114. Roosevelt, "'We Believe That the Only Whole Man Is a Free Man'— Address at a Dedication of Great Smoky Mountains National Park," September 2, 1940, in Rosenman, *Public Papers*, 371.

115. See Deloria, *Playing Indian*.

116. For a discussion of the consequences of this understanding, see Richard Drinnon, *Facing West: The Metaphysics of Indian-Hating and Empire Building* (Norman: University of Oklahoma Press, 1980).

117. Kennedy, *Freedom from Fear*, 296.

118. Gerstle, *American Crucible*, 163.

Chapter 6: Citizenship Contained: Domesticating God, Family, and Country during the Eisenhower Years

1. For a discussion of the rhetorical implications of containment during Eisenhower's presidency, see Robert L. Ivie, "Eisenhower as Cold Warrior," in Martin J. Medhurst, ed., *Eisenhower's War of Words: Rhetoric and Leadership* (East Lansing: Michigan State University Press, 1994), 10.

2. For a different, but related, discussion of this point, see Ira Chernus, *General Eisenhower: Ideology and Discourse* (East Lansing: Michigan State University Press, 2002).

3. Eisenhower, "Annual Message to the Congress on the State of the Union," January 6, 1955, *Public Papers of the Presidents of the United States* (Washington, DC: United States Government Printing Office), 7–8.

4. See Ira Chernus, *Eisenhower's Atoms for Peace* (College Station: Texas A&M University Press, 2002), 9–56.

5. Eisenhower, "Inaugural Address," January 20, 1953, *Public Papers*, 2.

6. Eisenhower, "Inaugural Address," 4.

7. Eisenhower, "Annual Message to the Congress on the State of the Union," January 10, 1957, *Public Papers*, 18.

8. Eisenhower, "Address at the Anniversary Dinner of the Brotherhood of Carpenters and Joiners," October 23, 1956, *Public Papers*, 996.

9. Eisenhower, "Remarks at the Annual Meeting of the United States Chamber of Commerce," May 2, 1955, *Public Papers*, 449.

10. Eisenhower, "Address at the Cow Palace Accepting the Nomination of the Republican National Convention," August 23, 1956, *Public Papers*, 712.

11. Eisenhower, "The President's News Conference of May 28, 1953," *Public Papers*, 88. See also Eisenhower, "Statement by the President on the 4th Anniversary of the Signing of the North Atlantic Treaty," April 4, 1953, *Public Papers*, 161; Eisenhower, "Remarks to a Delegation from the National Council of Churches," September 9, 1959, *Public Papers*, 655.

12. Foner, *Story of American Freedom*, 254.

13. H. W. Brands, *Cold Warriors: Eisenhower's Generation and American Foreign Policy* (New York: Columbia University Press, 1988), xi.

14. For a discussion of this point, see David L. Snead, *The Gaither Committee, Eisenhower, and the Cold War* (Columbus: Ohio State University Press, 1999), 17.

15. Robert H. Ferrell, ed., *The Eisenhower Diaries* (New York: W. W. Norton, 1981), 223.

16. Eisenhower, "Address before the Council of the Organization of American States," April 12, 1953, *Public Papers*, 173.

17. Eisenhower, "Remarks at the Twelfth Annual Washington Conference for the Advertising Council," April 3, 1956, *Public Papers*, 359.

18. Eisenhower, "Address at the New York Republican State Committee Dinner, Astor Hotel, New York City," May 7, 1953, *Public Papers*, 263.

19. For work that details Eisenhower's civil rights policies and attitudes, see among others, Robert Frederick Burk, *The Eisenhower Administration and Civil Rights* (Knoxville: University of Tennessee Press, 1984); Dudziak, *Cold War Civil Rights*; Klinkner with Smith, *Unsteady March*; Pauley, *Modern Presidency*, 18–30; Shull, *American Civil Rights Policy*.

20. Eisenhower, "Annual Message to the Congress on the State of the Union," January 5, 1956, *Public Papers*, 25.

21. Eisenhower, "Inaugural Address," 2. On the importance of science to this ideology, see David J. Tietge, *Flash Effect: Science and the Rhetorical Origins of the Cold War* (Athens: Ohio University Press, 2002).

22. Gerstle, *American Crucible*, 240–1.

23. Gerstle, *American Crucible*, 246.

24. Eisenhower, "Annual Message to the Congress on the State of the Union," January 7, 1954, *Public Papers*, 22. See also Eisenhower, "Address 'Science: Handmaiden of Freedom,' New York City," May 14, 1959, *Public Papers*, 400.

25. Eisenhower, "Special Message to the Congress on Labor-Management Relations," January 11, 1954, *Public Papers*, 40.

26. Eisenhower, "Address at Transylvania College, Lexington, Kentucky," April 23, 1954, *Public Papers*, 417.

27. Eisenhower, "Annual Message," January 6, 1955, *Public Papers*, 22.

28. Eisenhower, "Letter to Representative Auchincloss on the Second Anniversary of the President's Inauguration," January 20, 1955, *Public Papers*, 206. See also Eisenhower, "Annual Message," January 5, 1956, *Public Papers*, 20.

29. Eisenhower, "Remarks at the Governors' Conference, Seattle, Washington," August 4, 1953, *Public Papers*, 536.

30. Eisenhower, "Statement by the President on Compliance with Final Orders of the Courts," August 20, 1958, *Public Papers*, 631.

31. Eisenhower, "Remarks at Rice Park, St. Paul, Minnesota," October 16, 1956, *Public Papers*, 932.

32. Eisenhower, "Annual Message," January 10, 1957, *Public Papers*, 21.

33. Eisenhower, "Address at the Inauguration of the 22nd President of the College of William and Mary at Williamsburg," May 15, 1953, *Public Papers*, 300–1.

34. Martin J. Medhurst, *Dwight D. Eisenhower: Strategic Communicator* (Westport, CT: Greenwood, 1993), 119.

35. Eisenhower, "Address at the Cow Palace," 705.

36. Eisenhower, "Inaugural Address," 3.

37. Eisenhower, "Address, 'The Chance for Peace,' Delivered before the American Society of Newspaper Editors," April 16, 1953, *Public Papers*, 182; emphasis in original.

38. Eisenhower, "Remarks at a Meeting of Negro Leaders Sponsored by the National Newspaper Publishers Association," May 12, 1958, *Public Papers*, 392.

39. Eisenhower, "The President's News Conference of March 14, 1956," *Public Papers*, 304.

40. Klinkner with Smith, *Unsteady March*, 253.

41. Quoted in James C. Duram, *A Moderate among Extremists: Dwight D. Eisenhower and the School Desegregation Crisis* (Chicago: Nelson-Hall, 1981), 108–9.

42. Eisenhower, "Remarks to Members of the Orthopaedic Association of the English-Speaking World," May 14, 1958, *Public Papers*, 406.

43. It is worth pointing out that this group is not confined to African Americans. People could be easily and facilely excluded from the American consensus based on sexual orientation, political preferences, and an infinite number of other reasons.

44. David Halberstam, *The Fifties* (New York: Fawcett Columbine, 1993), 686.

45. Shull, *American Civil Rights Policy*, 36. See also Pauley, *Modern Presidency*, 59.

46. Burk, *Eisenhower Administration*, 69.

47. Burk, *Eisenhower Administration*, 80–6; E. Frederic Morrow, *Black Man in the White House* (New York: McFadden, 1969 [1969]).

48. Morrow, *Black Man*, 32.

49. Morrow, *Black Man*, 162–3. For a discussion of the events surrounding King and integration at the University of Mississippi, see Nadine Cohodas, *The Band Played Dixie: Race and the Liberal Conscience at Ole Miss* (New York: Free Press, 1997).

50. Chester J. Pach and Elmo Richardson, *The Presidency of Dwight D. Eisenhower*, rev. ed. (Lawrence: University Press of Kansas, 1991), 146.

51. For an example of the latter argument, see Theodore G. Bilbo, "Take Your Choice: Separation or Mongrelization," in S. T. Joshi, ed., *Documents of American Prejudice: An Anthology of Writings on Race from Thomas Jefferson to David Duke* (New York: Basic Books, 1999), 334–7.

52. For a discussion of the Klan's growth during these years, see Pach and Richardson, *Presidency of Dwight D. Eisenhower*, 145.

53. For a discussion of these issues, see Klinkner with Smith, *Unsteady March*, 231.

54. Eisenhower, "The President's News Conference of March 16, 1960," *Public Papers*, 294.

55. See, for example, the activities of COINTELPRO, discussed in Blanche Wiesen Cook, *The Declassified Eisenhower: A Divided Legacy* (New York: Doubleday, 1981), 163; William Bragg Ewald, Jr., *Eisenhower the President: Crucial Days* (Englewood Cliffs, NJ: Prentice Hall, 1981), 256.

56. Burk, *Eisenhower Administration*, 204; Pauley, *Modern Presidency*, 73.

57. Eisenhower, "The President's News Conference of September 11, 1956," *Public Papers*, 758–9.

58. Stanley I. Cutler, "Eisenhower, the Judiciary, and Desegregation: Some Reflections," in Gunter Bischof and Stephen E. Ambrose, eds., *Eisenhower: A Centenary Assessment* (Baton Rouge: Louisiana State University Press, 1995), 88–9. See also Ewald, *Crucial Days*, 85.

59. For discussions of this point, see Duram, *Moderate among Extremists*, 156–71; Dudziak, *Cold War Civil Rights*, chapter 4.

60. Eisenhower, "Radio and Television Address to the American People on the Situation in Little Rock," September 24, 1957, *Public Papers*, 692.

61. Eisenhower, "Address at the New England 'Forward to '54' Dinner, Boston, Massachusetts," September 21, 1953, *Public Papers*, 598. See also Eisenhower, "Address at the New York Republican State Committee Dinner, Astor Hotel, New York City," May 7, 1953, *Public Papers*, 262.

62. Eisenhower, "Address at the Jewish Tercentenary Dinner, New York City," October 20, 1954, *Public Papers*, 920; Eisenhower, "Remarks at the Dedication of the Washington Hebrew Congregation Temple," May 6, 1955, *Public Papers*, 477; Eisenhower, "Statement by the President on the Occasion of Rosh Hashanah," September 5, 1956, *Public Papers*, 746.

63. Eisenhower, "Annual Message to the Congress on the State of the Union," January 5, 1956, *Public Papers*, 26.

64. For discussions of federal policy toward American Indians during these years, see Vine Deloria, Jr., and Clifford M. Lytle, *American Indians, American Justice* (Austin: University of Texas Press, 1983), 16–9; Dippie, *Vanishing American*, 336.

65. Dippie, *Vanishing American*, 337.

66. For a discussion of the effects of termination on Menominee and Klamath nations and the fights for the restoration of their tribal status, see Stephen Cornell, *The Return of the Native: American Indian Political Resurgence* (New York: Oxford University Press, 1988), 121–3, 160–1; Joane Nagel, *American Indian Ethnic Renewal: Red Power and the Resurgence of Identity and Culture* (New York: Oxford University Press, 1996), 118–21; James Wilson, *The Earth Shall Weep: A History of Native America* (New York: Atlantic Monthly Press, 1998), 361–9.

67. Cornell, *Return of the Native*, 128–32; Nagel, *American Indian Ethnic Renewal*, 119–21.

68. For a discussion of these issues, see among many others, Troy Johnson, *The Occupation of Alcatraz Island: Indian Self-Determination and the Rise of Indian Activism* (Urbana: University of Illinois Press, 1996); Adam (Nordwall) Fortunate Eagle, *Alcatraz! Alcatraz! The Indian Occupation of 1969–1971* (Berkeley, CA: Heyday Books, 1992); Russell Means, *Where White Men Fear to Tread: The Autobiography of Russell Means* (New York: St. Martin's, 1995); Nagel, *American Indian Ethnic Renewal*, 131–7.

69. Eisenhower, "Remarks at the Dedication of the Boulder, Colorado, Laboratories of the National Bureau of Standards," September 14, 1954, *Public Papers*, 849.

70. Eisenhower, "Remarks at the Dedication of the Hiawatha Bridge, Red Wing, Minnesota," October 18, 1960, *Public Papers*, 781. For another example of such casual racism, see Eisenhower, "Remarks to the National 4-H Conference," June 19, 1958, *Public Papers*, 488.

71. For information about the "real" Hiawatha and his legacy, see, among many others, Laurence M. Hauptman, *The Iroquois Struggle for Survival: World War II to Red Power* (Syracuse, NY: Syracuse University Press, 1986); Dean R. Snow, *The Iroquois* (Cambridge, MA: Blackwell, 1994).

72. For a complete discussion of this point, see Deloria, *Playing Indian*.

73. Raymond J. Saulnier, "The Philosophy Underlying Eisenhower's Economic Policies," in Joan P. Krieg, ed., *Dwight D. Eisenhower: Soldier, President, Statesman* (Westport, CT: Greenwood, 1987), 99.

74. Medhurst, *Strategic Communicator*, 12.

75. Rachel Holloway, "Keeping the Faith": Eisenhower Introduces the Hydrogen Age," in Medhurst, *War of Words*, 47–71.

76. Dwight D. Eisenhower, *Mandate for Change, 1953–1956* (New York: Doubleday, 1963), 100.

77. Takaki, *Different Mirror*, 374.

78. On the Nazis, see Takaki, *Different Mirror*, 375.

79. On the Hungarian uprising, see Takaki, *Different Mirror*, 375. See also Kenneth Kitts and Betty Glad, "Presidential Personality and Improvisational Decision-Making: Eisenhower and the Hungarian Crisis," in Shirley Anne Warshaw, ed., *Reexamining the Eisenhower Presidency* (Westport, CT: Greenwood, 1993), 183–208; Pach and Richardson, *Presidency of Dwight D. Eisenhower*, 132.

80. Eisenhower, "Inaugural Address," 1, 7.

81. Eisenhower, "Remarks at Twelfth Annual Washington Conference for the Advertising Council," April 3, 1956, *Public Papers*, 362.

82. Eisenhower, "Annual Message," January 10, 1957, *Public Papers*, 19.

83. Eisenhower, "Second Inaugural Address," January 21, 1957, *Public Papers*, 62.

84. Eisenhower, "Inaugural Address," 4.

85. Robert F. Burk, *Dwight D. Eisenhower: Hero and Politician* (Boston: Twayne, 1986), 127.

86. Eisenhower, "Annual Message," February 2, 1953, *Public Papers*, 13.

87. On the establishment of a secret government, see Halberstam, *The Fifties*, 372; Piers Brendon, *Ike: His Life and Times* (New York: Harper & Row, 1986), 257; Cook, *Declassified Eisenhower*, 182–3.

88. Eisenhower, "The President's News Conference of November 11, 1953," *Public Papers*, 760.

89. Eisenhower, "Letter on Intellectual Freedom to the President of the American Literary Association," June 26, 1953, *Public Papers*, 456.

90. Pach and Richardson, *Presidency of Dwight D. Eisenhower*, 62.

91. Ferrell, *Eisenhower Diaries*, 234.

92. Eisenhower, "Remarks by the President upon Signing the Communist Control Act of 1954," August 24, 1954, *Public Papers*, 756.

93. Eisenhower, "Address at the Annual Luncheon of the Associated Press, New York City," April 25, 1955, *Public Papers*, 419.

94. Eisenhower, "Annual Message," January 7, 1954, *Public Papers*, 22–3.

95. Eisenhower, "Radio and Television Address to the American People on the State of the Union," April 5, 1954, *Public Papers*, 373.

96. Brinkley, *Unfinished Nation*, 778.

97. Stephanie Coontz, *The Way We Never Were: American Families and the Nostalgia Trap* (New York: Basic Books, 1992), 29.

98. For a discussion of the nation's economy during the Eisenhower administration, see Brinkley, *Unfinished Nation*, 787–8. See also Louis Galambos, "Foreword," in Warshaw, *Eisenhower Presidency*, vii.

99. Stephen E. Ambrose, *Eisenhower: Soldier and President* (New York: Simon and Schuster, 1990), 292.

100. Burk, *Hero and Politician*, 150.

101. Brinkley, *Unfinished Nation*, 781.

102. For a discussion of the middle class of the 1950s, see Brinkley, *Unfinished Nation*, 782.

103. Eisenhower, "Remarks at the Republican Women's National Conference," May 10, 1955, *Public Papers*, 484.

104. Eisenhower, "Radio and Television Address to the American People on the Administration's Purposes," January 4, 1954, *Public Papers*, 2.

105. Eisenhower, "Special Message to Congress on Housing," January 25, 1954, *Public Papers*, 193.

106. Eisenhower, "Address to the National Council of Catholic Women, Boston, Massachusetts," November 8, 1954, *Public Papers*, 1024.

107. Elaine Tyler May, *Homeward Bound: American Families in the Cold War Era* (New York: Basic Books, 1988), 3.

108. May, *Homeward Bound*, 208–9.

109. Eisenhower, "Address at a Dinner of the American Newspaper Publishers Association," April 22, 1954, *Public Papers*, 408.

110. Eisenhower, "Remarks at a Meeting of Negro Leaders," 393.

111. Joanne Meyorwitz, "Introduction," in Joanne Meyerowitz, ed., *Not June Cleaver: Women and Gender in Postwar America* (Philadelphia: Temple University Press, 1994), 1–18.

112. Meyerowitz, "Introduction," 4.

113. For a discussion of gender roles in the 1950s, see Halberstam, *The Fifties*, 590.

114. Ambrose, *Eisenhower*, 293.

115. Gerstle, *American Crucible*, 255.

116. Halberstam, *The Fifties*, 269–96.

117. Gerstle, *American Crucible*, 254; Charles E. Morris III, "Pink Herring and the Fourth Persona: J. Edgar Hoover's Sex Crime Panic," *Quarterly Journal of Speech* 88 (2002): 228–44.

118. Halberstam, *The Fifties*, 129.

119. R. Alton Lee, *Eisenhower and Landrum-Griffin: A Study in Labor–Management Politics* (Lexington: University Press of Kentucky, 1990), 18–9.

120. One of the ways in which labor was prevented from developing was by connecting fears of racial progress and anticommunism to the labor movement. For a discussion of these tactics, see Klinkner with Smith, *Unsteady March*, 231.

121. Brinkley, *Unfinished Nation*, 780.

122. Brinkley, *Unfinished Nation*, 781; Lee, *Landrum-Griffin*, 45.

123. Lee, *Landrum-Griffin*, 9.

124. Eisenhower, "Carpenters and Joiners," 993. See also Eisenhower, "Telephone Broadcast to the AFL-CIO Merger Meeting in New York City," December 5, 1955, *Public Papers*, 851.

125. Eisenhower, "Remarks at Dedication of AFL-CIO Building," June 4, 1956, *Public Papers*, 550.

126. Cook, *Declassified Eisenhower*, 157. See also Eisenhower, "The President's News Conference of June 3, 1959," *Public Papers*, 428.

127. Lee, *Landrum-Griffin*, 19.

128. Ferrell, *Eisenhower Diaries*, 229.

129. Eisenhower, "Annual Message to the Congress on the State of the Union," January 9, 1959, *Public Papers*, 5.

130. Karlyn Kohrs Campbell and Kathleen Hall Jamieson, *Deeds Done in Words: Presidential Rhetoric and the Genres of Governance* (Chicago: University of Chicago Press, 1990).

131. Eisenhower, "Remarks at the National Conference on Civil Rights," June 9, 1959, *Public Papers*, 448.

132. Eisenhower, "Address to the Republican National Conference," June 7, 1957, *Public Papers*, 450.

133. Eisenhower, "Address to the 1959 Governor's Conference, Williamsburg, Virginia," June 24, 1957, *Public Papers*, 486.

134. In Chernus' terms, this amounted to "a yearning for permanent stasis." See Chernus, *Atoms for Peace*, 128.

135. Ivie, "Eisenhower as Cold Warrior," 21.

136. Eisenhower, "Remarks for the White House Conference on Education," November 28, 1955, *Public Papers*, 848.

Chapter 7: Managing Diversity in a Fragmented Polity:
The Post–Cold War World of George H. W. Bush

1. For a discussion of lobbying, see Robert M. Stein and Kenneth N. Bickers, *Perpetuating the Pork Barrel: Policy Subsystems and American Democracy* (New York: Cambridge University Press, 1995).

2. For a discussion of social movements and their historical trajectories, see among numerous others, Jo Freeman and Victoria Johnson, eds., *Waves of Protest* (New York: Rowman and Littlefield, 1999); David S. Meyer and Sidney Tarrow, eds., *The Social Movement Society* (New York: Rowman and Littlefield, 1997); Herbert Simons, "Requirements, Problems, Strategies: A Theory of Persuasion for Social Movements," *Quarterly Journal of Speech* 56 (1970): 1–11.

3. Gerstle, *American Crucible*, 312.

4. Erwin C. Hargrove, *The President as Leader: Appealing to the Better Angels of Our Nature* (Lawrence: University Press of Kansas, 1998), 62; Paul Johnson, *A History of the American People* (New York: HarperCollins, 1997), 931.

5. Bush did try to appease conservatives, who remained suspicious of him. See, for example, Matthew C. Moen and Kenneth T. Palmer, "'Poppy' and His Conservative Passengers," in Ryan J. Barilleaux and Mary E. Stuckey, eds., *Leadership and the Bush Presidency: Prudence or Drift in an Era of Change?* (New York: Praeger, 1992), 133–46.

6. Richard Rose, *The Post-Modern Presidency: George Bush Meets the World* (Chatham, NJ: Chatham House, 1991). See also David Mervin, *George Bush and the Guardianship Presidency* (New York: St. Martin's, 1996).

7. I am indebted to Greg M. Smith for this phrase.

8. For a discussion of Bush's differences with Reagan, see William W. Lammers and Michael A. Genovese, *The Presidency and Domestic Policy: Comparing Leadership Styles, FDR to Clinton* (Washington, DC: CQ Press, 2000), 279. Stephen Skowronek, on the other hand, refers to Bush as Reagan's "faithful son." See Skowronek, *The Politics Presidents Make*, 429.

9. On Bush's style, see, among many others, Lance Blakesley, *Presidential Leadership from Eisenhower to Clinton* (Chicago: Nelson-Hall, 1995); George C. Edwards III, "George Bush and the Public Presidency: The Politics of Inclusion," in Colin Campbell and Bert Rockman, eds., *The Bush Presidency: First Appraisals* (Chatham, NJ: Chatham House, 1991), 191–7; Carol Gelderman, *All the Presidents' Words: The Bully Pulpit and the Creation of the Virtual Presidency* (New York: Walker & Co., 1997), 143; Johnson, *History of the American People*, 931. Kerry Mullins and Aaron Wildavsky, "The Procedural Presidency of George Bush," *Political Science Quarterly* 107 (1992): 39–40; Bert Rockman, "The Leadership Style of George Bush," in Campbell and Rockman, *Bush Presidency*; Mary E. Stuckey and Frederick J. Antczak, "Governance as Political Theater: George Bush and the MTV Presidency," in Barilleaux and Stuckey, *Leadership and the Bush Presidency*, 24–34.

10. For a (biased) account of that campaign, see Sidney Blumenthal, *Pledging Allegiance: The Last Campaign of the Cold War* (New York: HarperCollins, 1990). See also Hargrove, *President as Leader*, 171; Bob Woodward, *The Commanders* (New York: Simon and Schuster, 1991), 47.

11. Michael Duffy and Dan Goodgame, *Marching in Place: The Status Quo Presidency of George Bush* (New York: Simon and Schuster, 1992), 65–6.

12. George Bush, "Remarks at the Texas A&M University Commencement Ceremony in College Station, TX," May 12, 1989, *Public Papers of the Presidents of the United States* (Washington, DC: United States Government Printing Office, 1990), 541.

13. Bush, "Inaugural Address," January 20, 1989, *Public Papers*, 3.

14. Bush, "Remarks to the Chamber of Commerce in Cincinnati, Ohio," January 12, 1990, *Public Papers*, 43.

15. Quoted in Duffy and Goodgame, *Marching in Place*, 70.

16. Bush, "Address on Administration Goals before a Joint Session of Congress," February 8, 1989, *Public Papers*, 79.

17. Bush, "Address before a Joint Session of Congress on the State of the Union," January 29, 1991, *Public Papers*, 74.

18. Bush, "Address before a Joint Session of Congress on the State of the Union," January 28, 1992, *Public Papers*, 157.

19. Blumenthal, *Pledging Allegiance*, 5.

20. Stuckey, *Interpreter-in-Chief*, 131. See also Gelderman, *Presidents' Words*, 147.

21. Bush, "Remarks at a Meeting of the American Society of Association Executives," February 27, 1991, *Public Papers*, 185.

22. Nelson Polsby, quoted in Charles O. Jones, *Separate but Equal Branches: Congress and the Presidency* (Chatham, NJ: Chatham House, 1995), 220.

23. Bush, "Remarks to the Kentucky Fried Chicken Convention in Nashville, Tennessee," October 30, 1992, *Public Papers*, 2093.

24. Bush, "Remarks to the American Society of Association Executives," March 6, 1990, *Public Papers*, 325.

25. It is interesting that he dates "America's" age from the Pilgrims. As with earlier versions of the frontier myth, this serves to erase the American Indian presence and the genocidal actions of the "American" government regarding them. For a discussion of this point, see Wilson, *And the Earth Shall Weep*.

26. Bush, "Remarks to the Annual Convention of the National Fraternal Congress of America," October 3, 1991, *Public Papers*, 1255.

27. Bush, "Remarks at the *American Spectator* Annual Dinner," January 22, 1990, *Public Papers*, 72.

28. Bush, "Remarks on Signing the Martin Luther King, Jr., Federal Holiday Proclamation in Atlanta, Georgia," January 17, 1992, *Public Papers*, 118.

29. Bush, "Remarks at the University of Michigan Commencement Ceremony in Ann Arbor, Michigan," May 4, 1991, *Public Papers*, 472.

30. Bush, "Remarks to Students at Washington University in St. Louis, Missouri," February 17, 1989, *Public Papers*, 108.

31. Bush, "Remarks at the United Negro College Fund Dinner in New York, New York," March 9, 1989, *Public Papers*, 202.

32. Bush, "State of the Union," 1991, *Public Papers*, 75.

33. Bush, "Remarks to Representatives of the Future Farmers of America," July 27, 1989, *Public Papers*, 1021–2.

34. John Robert Greene, *The Presidency of George Bush* (Lawrence: University Press of Kansas, 2000), 144.

35. Bush, "Remarks at the *American Spectator* Annual Dinner," 72.

36. Bush, "Remarks to the United Nations Security Council in New York City," January 31, 1992, *Public Papers*, 176.

37. Bush, "Remarks to Members of the Small Business Legislative Council," March 1, 1989, *Public Papers*, 159.

38. Shull, *American Civil Rights Policy*, xiii.

39. For example, as a member of Congress, Bush denounced the Civil Rights Act of 1964, but did create something of a stir in conservative circles with his support for the Fair Housing Act of 1968. See Klinkner with Smith, *Unsteady March*, 284–5.

40. Shull, *American Civil Rights Policy*, 96–100.

41. Bush, "Exchange with Reporters in San Francisco, California," October 29, 1990, *Public Papers*, 1487.

42. Bush, "State of the Union," 1991, 77.

43. Bush, "Remarks at the Council of the Americas," May 2, 1989, *Public Papers*, 505.

44. Bush, "The President's News Conference," June 5, 1989, *Public Papers*, 669.

45. Bush, "News Conference," 669–70.

46. For a discussion of human rights and China, see Duffy and Goodgame, *Marching in Place*, 183.

47. Bush, "Exchange with Reporters at the Holly Hills Country Club in Ijamsville, NY," October 13, 1991, *Public Papers*, 1285.

48. Bush, "Remarks at the Cheltenham High School Commencement Ceremony at Wyncote, PA," June 19, 1989, *Public Papers*, 757.

49. Bush, "*American Spectator* Annual Dinner," 70–1.

50. Duffy and Goodgame, *Marching in Place*, 63.

51. For discussions of Willie Horton, see among others, Greene, *Presidency of George Bush*, 39; Klinker with Smith, *Unsteady March*, 305.

52. Bush, "The President's News Conference," July 10, 1991, *Public Papers*, 857.

53. Klinkner with Smith, *Unsteady March*, 305. See also Augustus J. Jones, Jr., "Kinder, Gentler? George Bush and Civil Rights," in Barilleaux and Stuckey, *Leadership and the Bush Presidency*, 180–5.

54. Bush, "Remarks to the Law Enforcement Community in Wilmington, DE," March 22, 1989, *Public Papers*, 297.

55. Bush, "Address to the Nation on the National Drug Control Strategy," September 5, 1989, *Public Papers*, 1138.

56. Greene, *Presidency of George Bush*, 9.

57. Greene, *Presidency of George Bush*, 72; Woodward, *Commanders*, 116.

58. Bush, "Remarks at the International Drug Enforcement Conference in Miami, Florida," April 27, 1989, *Public Papers*, 486.

59. Bush, "Remarks at the Urban League National Conference," August 8, 1989, *Public Papers*, 1069.

60. I am not arguing here that the problems of the inner cities are the responsibility of the federal government; only that in Bush's rhetoric that possibility is precluded.

61. Bush, "Radio Address to the Nation on Welfare Reform," April 11, 1992, *Public Papers*, 592.

62. Bush, "Remarks to the Knights of Columbus Supreme Council Convention in New York City," August 5, 1992, *Public Papers*, 1305.

63. Bush, "Remarks to the Illinois Farm Bureau in Chicago, Illinois," December 10, 1991, *Public Papers*, 1585. See also Bush, "Remarks to Representatives of the Future Farmers of America," July 27, 1989, *Public Papers*, 1021.

64. Bush, "Remarks on Signing the National Agriculture Day Proclamation," March 20, 1990, *Public Papers*, 392.

65. For a discussion of how these messages work in the media, see Robert M. Entman and Andrew Rojecki, *The Black Image in the White Mind: Media and Race in America* (Chicago: University of Chicago Press, 2001).

66. For a discussion of the violence in Los Angeles, see Brinkley, *Unfinished Nation*, 904.

67. Sergeant Stacy C. Koon, "Presumed Guilty," in S. T. Joshi, ed., *Documents of American Prejudice: An Anthology of Writings on Race from Thomas Jefferson to David Duke* (New York: Basic Books, 1999), 347.

68. Bush, "Statement on the Verdict of the Los Angeles Police Trial," April 30, 1992, *Public Papers*, 668–9.

69. Bush, "Remarks on Civil Disturbances in Los Angeles, California," April 30, 1992, *Public Papers*, 669.

70. Bush, "Address to the Nation on the Civil Disturbance in Los Angeles, California," May 1, 1992, *Public Papers*, 685.

71. Not least among the elements of this contention is the terminology used to describe the violence: was it a "riot," implying angry and unorganized disorder, or was it a "rebellion," a term that politicizes the anger as well as the violence?

72. Dudziak, *Cold War Civil Rights*, 253; Klinkner with Smith, *Unsteady March*, 288; Shull, *American Civil Rights Policy*, 193.

73. Quoted in Klinkner with Smith, *Unsteady March*, 307.

74. Klinkner with Smith, *Unsteady March*, 288.

75. For a discussion of this issue, see Gerstle, *American Crucible*, 359.

76. Bush, "Address to the Nation on the Federal Budget Agreement," October 2, 1990, *Public Papers*, 1349.

77. Bush, "University of Michigan Commencement Ceremony," 470–1.

78. American Indians have little reason to admire his liberalism. See John R. Wunder, *"Retained by the People": A History of American Indians and the Bill of Rights* (New York: Oxford University Press, 1994), 180.

79. Greene, *Presidency of George Bush*, 159.

80. Greene, *Presidency of George Bush*, 159–60; Klinkner with Smith, *Unsteady March*, 306.

81. Bush, "The President's News Conference at Kennebunkport, Maine," July 1, 1991, *Public Papers*, 801.

82. Bush, "The President's News Conference at Kennebunkport, Maine," 802.

83. Bush, "Remarks and an Exchange with Reporters on the Nominations of Robert M. Gates and Clarence Thomas," July 24, 1991, *Public Papers*, 951.

84. Duffy and Goodgame, *Marching in Place*, 97.

85. Bush, "Annual Meeting of the United States Chamber of Commerce," April 30, 1990, *Public Papers*, 585.

86. Duffy and Goodgame, *Marching in Place*, 21; emphasis in original. See also Lammers and Genovese, *Presidency and Domestic Policy*, 282.

87. Bush, "Remarks at the Frontier Days and State Centennial Parade in Cheyenne, Wyoming," July 20, 1990, *Public Papers*, 1039.

88. Bush, "State of the Union," 1991, 75.

89. Bush, "Remarks Accepting the Presidential Nomination at the Republican National Convention in Houston, Texas," August 20, 1992, *Public Papers*, 1382.

90. Bush, "Address on Administration," 75.

91. For discussions of these cultural shifts and their implications, see Brinkley, *Unfinished Nation*, 904–12; Johnson, *History of the American People*, 963–72.

92. Bush, "Remarks at an Independence Day Celebration in Faith, North Carolina," July 4, 1992, *Public Papers*, 1081.

93. Bush, "Remarks at the National Prayer Breakfast," January 30, 1992, *Public Papers*, 169.

94. Bush, "Remarks to the National Baptist Convention in New Orleans, Louisiana," September 8, 1989, *Public Papers*, 1169.

95. Duffy and Goodgame, *Marching in Place*, 211.

96. Bush, "Remarks at an Independence Day Celebration," 1081.

97. Bush, "Remarks to the National Governor's Association in Chicago, Illinois," July 31, 1989, *Public Papers*, 1037.

98. Duffy and Goodgame, *Marching in Place*, 211.

99. Stuckey, *Interpreter-in-Chief*, 125.

100. Bush, "Remarks at the Associated Press Business Luncheon in Chicago, Illinois," April 24, 1989, *Public Papers*, 467.

101. Bush, "University of Michigan Commencement Ceremony," 470.

102. Bush, "Remarks at the Electronics Industries Association's Government-Industry Dinner," March 15, 1989, *Public Papers*, 243.

103. Bush, "Remarks at the American Association of University Women," June 26, 1989, *Public Papers*, 797.

104. Bush, "National Governor's Association," 1038.

105. Bush, "Remarks at the Biannual Convention of the American Federation of Labor and the Congress of Industrial Organizations," November 15, 1989, *Public Papers*, 1526.

106. Bush, "Message on the Observance of Labor Day," September 1, 1989, *Public Papers*, 1131.

107. Bush, "Message on the Observance of Labor Day," 1132.

108. Bush, "Message on the Observance of Labor Day," September 1, 1990, *Public Papers*, 1187.

109. Brinkley, *Unfinished Nation*, 902.

110. Johnson, *History of the American People*, 947.

111. Brinkley, *Unfinished Nation*, 902; Greene, *Presidency of George Bush*, 5.

112. Greene, *Presidency of George Bush*, 83.

113. Brinkley, *Unfinished Nation*, 895–7; Hargrove, *President as Leader*, 71–2.

114. Shull, *American Civil Rights Policy*, 42.

115. Bush, "Remarks Commemorating the First Anniversary of the Signing of the Americans with Disabilities Act of 1990," July 26, 1991, *Public Papers*, 963–4.

116. Bush, "Message on the Observance of National Afro-American (Black) History Month," February 25, 1991, *Public Papers*, 129.

117. Bush, "Message on the Observance of National Afro-American (Black) History Month," February 1, 1989, *Public Papers*, 39.

118. Bush, "Message on the Observance of Passover," March 29, 1991, *Public Papers*, 319.

119. Bush, "Message on the Observance of St. Patrick's Day," March 7, 1991, *Public Papers*, 224.

120. Bush, "Remarks at the Annual Convention of the United States Hispanic Chamber of Commerce in Chicago, Illinois," September 20, 1991, *Public Papers*, 1195–6. See also Bush, "Remarks at a Cinco de Mayo Celebration," May 5, 1989, *Public Papers*, 520; Bush, "Remarks to the United States Hispanic Chamber of Commerce," September 8, 1989, *Public Papers*, 1165.

121. Bush, "Remarks to the Hispanic-American Community in Los Angeles, California," April 25, 1989, *Public Papers*, 477.

122. Bush, "Remarks at the Asian Pacific American Heritage Dinner in Los Angeles," May 29, 1992, *Public Papers*, 857. See also Bush, "Statement on Signing Legislation Establishing Asian/Pacific American Heritage Month," October 23, 1992, *Public Papers*, 1938.

123. For a discussion of these stereotypes and how they function, see Bird, *Dressing in Feathers*; Deloria, *Playing Indian*; Scheckel, *Insistence of the Indian*; Stedman, *Shadows of the Indian*.

124. Bush, "Remarks at the Washington Centennial Celebration in Spokane, Washington," September 19, 1989, *Public Papers*, 1228.

125. See Christian F. Feest, "Europe's Indians," in James A. Clifton, ed., *The Invented Indian: Cultural Fictions and Government Policies* (New Brunswick, NJ: Transaction, 1994), 317–8.

126. Churchill, *Struggle for the Land*; Peter Eichstaedt, *If You Poison Us: Uranium and Native Americans* (Santa Fe, NM: Red Crane, 1994); Donald A. Grinde and Bruce E. Johansen, *Ecocide of Native America: Environmental Destruction of Indian Lands and Peoples* (Santa Fe, NM: Clear Light, 1995).

127. Bush, "Remarks at the Texas A&I Commencement Ceremony in Kingsville, Texas," May 11, 1990, *Public Papers*, 643.

128. Bush, "Remarks at a White House Briefing for the Leadership of Small Business United at the National Association of Women Business Owners," May 1, 1990, *Public Papers*, 597.

129. Bush, "Remarks at a Meeting of the American Society of Association Executives," February 27, 1991, *Public Papers*, 184.

130. Bush, "Remarks to Arab-American Leaders," January 25, 1991, *Public Papers*, 62.

131. Bush, "Remarks on Signing the Civil Rights Act of 1991," November 21, 1991, *Public Papers*, 1502.

132. Greene, *Presidency of George Bush*, 48.

133. Bush, "Afro-American (Black) History Month," 1991, 172.

134. Bush, "Remarks on Signing the Asian/Pacific American Heritage Month Proclamation," May 7, 1990, *Public Papers*, 632.

135. Duffy and Goodgame, *Marching in Place*, 103.

Conclusion: Choosing Our National Identity

1. For one of the best such analyses, see Skowronek, *The Politics Presidents Make.*

2. Gerstle, *American Crucible.* See also Smith, *Civic Ideals,* 9–36.

3. George W. Bush, "Address to a Joint Session of Congress," *Atlanta Journal and Constitution,* September 21, 2001, A17.

4. In a press conference on July 31, 2003, Scott McClellan summed up the president's position: "Well, the President believes strongly in the sanctity of marriage, and he believes strongly that marriage is a sacred institution between a man and a woman. And the President is strongly committed to protecting and defending the sanctity of marriage. And there has been a lot of discussion raised recently because of some court cases about this issue. The President strongly supports the Defense of Marriage Act, and the President remains committed to making sure we protect the sanctity of marriage. So we are looking at what may be needed in the context of the court cases that are pending now." See the transcript of that press conference at www.whitehouse.gov/news/releases/2003/07/20030731-9.html#7 (accessed March 23, 2004).

5. For an extended discussion of this point, see Edelman, *Searching for America's Heart.*

6. Shull, *American Civil Rights Policy,* 202.

7. See, for example, William Jefferson Clinton, "Remarks at the Ireland Fund Dinner," March 16, 1993, *Public Papers of the Presidents of the United States* (Washington, DC: United States Government Printing Office, 1994), 312; Clinton, "Remarks on Signing the Greek Independence Day Proclamation," March, 25, 1993, *Public Papers,* 357–8; Clinton, "Remarks on Signing the Asian/Pacific American Heritage Month Proclamation," May 3, 1993, *Public Papers,* 554.

8. See, for example, Clinton, "Remarks and an Exchange with Reporters on Immigration Policy," July 27, 1993, *Public Papers,* 1194; Clinton, "Interview with the California Media," July 30, 1993, *Public Papers,* 1245; Clinton, "Interview with the Nevada Media," August 3, 1993, *Public Papers,* 1319.

9. Clinton, "Remarks at the American University Centennial Celebration," February 26, 1993, *Public Papers,* 214.

10. Clinton, "Remarks and a Question and Answer Session at the Adult Learning Center in New Brunswick, NJ," March 1, 1993, *Public Papers,* 220; Clinton, "Remarks to the Community in Milwaukee, WI," June 1, 1993, *Public Papers,* 788; Clinton, "Remarks at a Children's Town Meeting," March 19, 1994, *Public Papers,* 490.

11. James MacGregor Burns and Georgia J. Sorenson, with Robin Gerber and Scott W. Webster, *Dead Center: Clinton-Gore Leadership and the Perils of Moderation* (New York: Scribner, 1999), 99; Charles O. Jones, *Clinton and Congress, 1993–1996: Risk, Restoration, and Reelection* (Norman: University of Oklahoma Press, 1999), 76; John Kenneth White, *Still Seeing Red: How the Cold War Shapes the New American Politics* (Boulder, CO: Westview, 1997), 221.

12. Clinton, "Remarks Honoring the School Principal of the Year and an Exchange with Reporters," January 28, 1993, *Public Papers,* 18.

13. Denise M. Bostdorff, "Clinton's Characteristic Issue Management Style:

Caution, Conciliation, and Conflict Avoidance in the Case of Gays in the Military," in Robert E. Denton, Jr., and Rachel L. Holloway, eds., *The Clinton Presidency: Images, Issues, and Communication Strategies* (New York: Praeger, 1996), 199.

14. Clinton, "The President's News Conference," March 23, 1993, *Public Papers*, 337, 338; Clinton, "Interview with Dan Rather of CBS News," March 24, 1993, *Public Papers*, 352–3; Clinton, "Remarks on the Appointment of Kristine M. Gebbie as AIDS Policy Coordinator and Exchange with Reporters," June 25, 1993, *Public Papers*, 933.

15. Clinton, "Remarks to Law Enforcement Organizations and an Exchange with Reporters," April 15, 1993, *Public Papers*, 443–4.

16. Clinton, "Remarks to the Newspaper Association of America in Boston, Massachusetts," April 25, 1993, *Public Papers*, 504.

17. Colin Campbell, "Management in a Sandbox: Why the Clinton White House Failed to Cope with Gridlock," Colin Campbell and Bert A. Rockman, eds., *The Clinton Presidency* (New York: Chatham House, Seven Bridges Press, 2000), 64; George C. Edwards III, "Frustration and Folly: Bill Clinton and the Public Presidency," in Campbell and Rockman, *First Appraisals*, 241; Stanley Renshon, *High Hopes: The Clinton Presidency and the Politics of Ambition* (New York: New York University Press, 1996), 75.

18. Clinton, "Question and Answer Session with the Cleveland City Club," May 10, 1993, *Public Papers*, 610.

19. Clinton, "Interview with Larry King," July 20, 1993, *Public Papers*, 1146.

20. Rita K. Whillock, "The Compromising Clinton: Images of Failure, a Record of Success," 124–38, in Denton and Holloway, *Clinton Presidency*, 134; Graham K. Wilson, "The Clinton Administration and Interest Groups," in Campbell and Rockman, *First Appraisals*, 223.

21. Bostdorff, "Issue Management Style," 203; Jones, *Clinton and Congress*, 76; Whillock, "Compromising Clinton," 131.

22. Clinton, "Remarks to the Convocation of the Church of God in Memphis," November 13, 1993, *Public Papers*, 1983.

23. Clinton, "Remarks to the Convocation of the Church of God," 1983–4.

24. Burns and Sorenson, *Dead Center*, 228–9; Edelman, *Searching for America's Heart*, 142; Virginia Shapiro and David T. Canon, "Race, Gender, and the Clinton Presidency," in Campbell and Rockman, *The Clinton Presidency*, 192–3; Michael Waldman, *POTUS Speaks: Finding the Words That Defined the Clinton Presidency* (New York: Simon and Schuster, 2000), 128.

25. Stanley Greenberg, *Middle Class Dreams: The Politics and Power of the New American Majority*, revised and updated edition (New Haven, CT: Yale University Press, [1995] 1996), 21; Harold W. Stanley, "The Parties, the President, and the 1994 Midterm Elections," in Campbell and Rockman, *First Appraisals*, 194.

26. George W. Bush, "President's Message for Labor Day," August 31, 2001. Available at: www.whitehouse.gov/news/releases/2001/08/20010831-2.html.

27. George W. Bush, "Remarks by the President in Honor of Black Music Month," July 29, 2001. Available at: www.whitehouse.gov/news/releases/2001/06/20010629-8.html.

28. George W. Bush, "President Bush Honors Navajo Code Talkers," July 26,

2001. Available at: www.whitehouse.gov/news/releases/2001/07/20010726-5. html.

29. The experiences of American Indians do not conform to this pattern.

30. Vincent Harding, "Is America in Any Sense Chosen?" in Nicgorski and Weber, *Almost Chosen People*, 122.

31. Harding, "Any Sense Chosen," 126.

Index

Abolitionists, 64, 77, 81, 91–2, 94,
98, 100, 101, 104
Adams, John, 31, 34
African Americans. *See also*
Slavery
Affirmative Action and, 289,
324–5, 351
George H. W. Bush on, 298,
308–10, 312–3, 315–7, 328,
331–2
George W. Bush on, 352–3
Cleveland on, 135–7
Clinton on, 345–6, 349, 350–2
Eisenhower on, 256, 259–64,
271, 279
as examples of citizenship, 139,
141
as excluded group, 24, 61, 93,
102, 104, 126, 217, 339
issues of visibility in presidential rhetoric on, 135–6, 213,
224, 260–3, 264, 304, 312,
315
paternalism toward, 89
Pierce on, 90
Franklin Roosevelt on, 214,
220–5
Wilson on, 152, 153, 161, 163,
165, 169, 177, 180–2, 188–9,
193, 197
Alien and Sedition Acts, 30–1
American Indians
Apache, 144–6
assimilation of, 37, 45, 49,
142–4, 233–4, 269

George H. W. Bush on, 329
George W. Bush on, 353–4
citizenship and, 37, 55–6, 64, 83,
87–9, 139, 141, 144–5
Cleveland on, 130, 142–6
economic issues and, 36–7,
233–4, 269
Eisenhower on, 268–71
as excluded group, 2, 24, 53, 54,
102, 104, 217, 234, 339–40
Fillmore on, 87
issues of visibility in presidential rhetoric and, 19, 35, 42,
49–51, 53–4, 59–60, 88,
142–6, 234, 269
Jackson on, 21, 42–52, 99
Jefferson on, 34–9, 366n39
land issues and, 34, 35, 43, 50, 53
as military problem, 25, 34, 88,
92, 130
comparisons to Mormons of,
97–9
Navajo, 353–4
paternalism toward, 36, 37, 52,
143–4
Pierce on, 88
removal of, 32, 40, 41, 46, 54–5,
161, 269
Franklin Roosevelt on, 214,
232–5, 239–40
termination of reservations of,
268–71
"Vanishing" of, 34–6, 43, 270
Wilson on, 34, 152, 153, 163,
166, 175, 177–80, 193

Americanization. *See* Assimilation
Americans with Disabilities Act,
   303, 327
Articles of Confederation, 63,
   65–71, 370n19
Asian Americans, 104, 217, 268
   George H. W. Bush on, 328–9,
   332
Assimilation, 16, 119–20, 138–9,
   174–6, 213, 268
   of American Indians, 45, 49,
   142–4, 233–4, 269
Balance, national, in presidential
   rhetoric, 4, 20, 28, 38, 62,
   106. *See also* Stability
   antebellum president on, 78,
   100
   Cleveland and, 111, 118, 121,
   124
   Eisenhower and, 257–8
   Jackson and, 22, 47, 51, 57–8,
   339
   Franklin Roosevelt and,
   199–200, 202, 220, 226
   Wilson and, 156, 163

Black Cabinet, 224
Brown, John, 97
Buchanan, James, 18, 337, 339, 341
   on founding principles, 65, 71,
   74, 76, 77–8, 86, 95, 100, 103
   and frontier myth, 80, 88, 100
   issues of visibility and, 78, 103
   Jackson and, 63–4, 65, 72, 76,
   79, 83, 88, 103
   Jefferson and, 63–4, 65, 77, 79,
   88
   on Mormons, 97–9
   national balance and, 78
   national identity and, 74
   philosophy of government of,
   71, 74, 76, 83
   on political coalition, 71, 90,
   103
   on states' rights, 66–9, 73, 96–7
   use of history by, 73–4

Bush, George H. W., 18, 20
   on African Americans, 298, 304,
   308–10, 312–3, 315–7, 328,
   331–2
   on American Indians, 329
   on Asian Americans, 328–9, 332
   as conservative, 291, 293–4, 295,
   297, 324
   celebratory othering and, 322–33
   on China, 305–6
   on Christianity, 319–21
   on citizenship, 289, 298, 301,
   302, 311–2, 318–22, 333–4
   on civil rights, 303–5
   on class and economic issues,
   326–7
   Cleveland and, 307, 311
   deferral tactics of, 301
   differentiation tactics of, 310–1,
   312, 317
   drug issues and, 308–10, 322
   Eisenhower and, 292, 293, 295,
   297, 300, 304, 305, 317, 319,
   320
   frontier myth and, 296, 320, 330
   on Hispanics/Latino/as, 328,
   331
   on immigrants, 329–30
   on labor, 325–6
   on minorities, 298, 302, 315,
   321, 328, 331–2
   on Muslims, 331–2
   national identity and, 289–90,
   291–2, 298, 299, 306–7, 309,
   312, 320–1
   on political coalition, 297,
   324–5
   political philosophy of, 293,
   338, 340
   Franklin Roosevelt and, 268,
   297, 301, 302, 304, 307, 330
   use of history by, 295–9, 331
   visibility of minorities and, 289,
   310–1, 342
   on voluntarism, 300–1, 318–9,
   321

Wilson and, 301, 303, 304, 307, 312, 314, 320
Bush, George W., 20, 343, 344, 352–6

Catholics, 93, 213, 311
Celebratory othering
George H. W. Bush's use of, 322–33
George W. Bush's use of, 353–4
Clinton's use of, 345, 351
as rhetorical tactic, 6, 290, 322–3, 333
Central America, 77, 84–5
China, 193, 305–6
Chinese immigrants, 128, 130, 138–40
Christianity
George H.W. Bush and, 319–21
George W. Bush and, 352
Eisenhower and, 245, 246, 251, 253–4, 271, 272–7
Franklin Roosevelt and, 212–3, 235–7
Wilson and, 167–70, 176
Citizenship
antebellum presidents on, 23, 63–4, 85–6, 102
George H. W. Bush on, 289, 298, 301, 302, 311–2, 318–22, 333–4
Cleveland on, 109, 119, 124, 127–9, 130, 137–8, 147–9
Eisenhower on, 245–51, 252, 256–7, 260, 274, 275–6, 278, 279–83, 341–2
Fillmore on, 20, 23
Founders on, 23–32, 63
Jackson on, 21, 22, 41–2, 52–57, 92
Jefferson on, 29, 30–9
national disciplinary project and, 4, 16, 19, 29–30, 48–9, 64, 92, 107, 124, 127
in presidential rhetoric, 4–5
Franklin Roosevelt on, 199–200,

201, 205, 206, 210, 215, 225–6, 227, 229, 237
Wilson on, 152, 157, 159, 160, 162, 163, 166, 169–70, 171–2, 174–5, 196
Civil Rights
Bush and, 303–5
Eisenhower and, 250, 255, 258, 259–60, 261–2, 265–6, 284–5
Franklin Roosevelt and, 221–3
Civil Rights Act, 303–4
Class, 14, 24, 27–8, 58, 81, 123–4
Clay, Henry, 84
Cleveland, Grover, 18, 20
on African Americans, 135–7
on American Indians, 130, 142–6
antebellum presidents and, 108, 110, 112, 118, 120, 125
on business, 107, 108, 110, 114–7, 149, 337
on citizenship, 109, 119, 124, 127–9, 130, 137–8, 147–9
on civil service, 146–9
on class, 127
on founding principles, 108
on immigrants, 119, 126, 127–9, 134–5, 138–40
on individualism, 121, 123
on issues of visibility, 106, 124, 129–30, 133, 135–6, 138, 149–50
Jackson and, 107, 108, 113, 118, 120, 138
Jefferson and, 107, 118, 120, 138
on labor, 116–7, 119, 120, 123–4, 124–5, 126, 128, 134–5, 137–8
on manliness, 128, 133, 137–8
on Mormons, 140–1, 142,
national balance and, 111, 118, 121, 124, 339
national identity and, 107, 109, 111, 115, 118, 120, 126–7, 128, 135, 137, 139, 141
on organic union, 107, 110, 112, 118–9, 123, 136, 14

Cleveland, Grover (continued)
  as party leader, 117–8
  philosophy of government of,
    110
  on political coalition, 107, 109,
    124
  on the poor, 131–3
  on race,127, 149, 339
  on standardization, 111, 112,
    114–5, 117–20, 134, 146–7
  use of history by, 113, 143
  on women's issues, 141–2
Clinton, Bill, 20, 345–6, 349, 350–2
Cold War, 19, 243, 245–51, 258–9,
  265–6, 271, 272, 274, 275,
  286, 292, 294
Collier, John, 232–4
Communism (see Cold War)
Constitution, U. S., 24, 63, 65–71,
  76, 82–3, 95–6, 101, 104,
  109–10, 126, 252

Declaration of Independence, U.S.,
  65, 69, 104, 173, 356
Deferral as presidential tactic, 6,
  183–90, 206, 301
Democratic Party, 18, 84, 103, 117,
  160, 222, 314
Differentiation as presidential tac-
    tic, 6
  in George H. W. Bush's rhetoric,
    310–1, 312, 317
  in Cleveland's rhetoric, 124,
    125, 126–7, 133–5, 138–40,
    145
  in Franklin Roosevelt's rhetoric,
    208
  in Wilson's rhetoric, 153, 178
Disabled Americans, 19, 303, 327
Douglass, Frederick, 89, 330

Eisenhower, Dwight, 18, 20
  on African Americans, 256,
    259–61, 262–5, 271, 279
  on American Indians, 268–71
  antebellum presidents and, 243,

    254, 255, 256, 263
  on Christianity, 245, 246, 251,
    253–4, 271, 272–7
  on citizenship, 245–51, 252,
    256–7, 260, 274, 275–6, 278,
    279–83, 341–2
  Civil Rights and, 250, 255, 258,
    259–60, 261–2, 265–6, 284–5
  Cleveland and, 254, 255–6
  economy and, 276–7
  frontier myth and, 268, 269–70
  Jackson and, 243, 249, 252, 254,
    279
  Jefferson and, 243, 249, 254, 271
  on Jews, 267–8
  on labor, 252–3, 281–3
  Lincoln and, 244, 284
  McCarthyism and, 275, 281
  on minorities, 250, 259–60,
    262–71, 279, 286, 287
  national balance and, 257–8
  national identity and, 257, 267,
    280–1, 84–6, 286, 287
  on political coalition, 264,
    266–74, 282
  political philosophy of, 246,
    249, 251–5, 257–61, 266–7,
    338
  Franklin Roosevelt and, 252,
    254, 256, 268, 272, 278, 283,
    284
  on states' rights, 254–5
  use of history by, 243, 245, 254,
    269–71, 283–6
  visibility of minorities and, 254,
    261, 268, 282, 287
  Wilson and, 247, 248, 249, 252,
    253, 267, 271, 273, 279, 283
  on women's issues, 277–8,
    280–1
Ethnicity, 14. See also Race
Expansion, geographical
  Jefferson on, 28, 29, 35–6
  as political problem, 28, 32,
    61–2, 66, 71, 74, 77–8, 81, 93,
    106

Fillmore, Millard
  on American Indians, 87
  on citizenship, 20, 23
  on founding principles, 65, 71–9,
    86, 95, 100, 103
  frontier myth, 80, 88, 100
  on issues of visibility, 78, 103
  Jackson and, 63–4, 65, 72, 76,
    79, 83, 88, 103
  Jefferson and, 63–4, 65, 77, 79, 88
  national balance and, 100
  national identity and, 74
  philosophy of government of,
    71, 74, 76, 83
  on political coalition, 71, 90, 103
  on states' rights, 66–9, 73, 96–7
  use of history by, 73–4

Founders, 46–7, 90, 354n6. *See also*
    Adams; Jefferson; Madison;
    Washington
  on citizenship, 23–32, 63
  as myth, 71–9, 215–6
  national identity and, 23–4,
    26–7, 29–30, 32, 33–4
  philosophy of citizenship by,
    23–32, 63
Frank, Leo, 188
Free Soil Party, 94
Frontier myth
  Buchanan and, 80, 88, 100
  George H. W. Bush and, 296,
    320, 330
  Eisenhower and, 268, 269–70
  Fillmore and, 80, 88, 100
  Jackson and, 23, 39, 40, 41, 44,
    52, 56, 57, 88, 116, 128, 341
  Jefferson and, 23, 39
  Pierce and, 80, 88, 100
  Franklin Roosevelt and, 215,
    235, 237–40
  Wilson and, 179, 194–5
Fugitive Slave Law, 75, 104

Gays, 335
  as excluded group, 2, 343

issues of visibility in presiden-
    tial rhetoric on, 19, 281
  in military, 346–9
Gender (*see also* Women), 24, 56,
    81

Hill, Anita, 317
Hispanics
  George H. W. Bush and, 328,
    331
  as excluded group, 214, 217
  issues of visibility in presiden-
    tial rhetoric on, 19
  Wilson and, 173
History, U.S., 23, 62
  national identity and, 14–7, 73,
    82–3
  in presidential rhetoric, 48–9,
    50, 54, 69–70, 101, 110, 112
Horton, Willie, 308
Homestead Act, 92
Hopkins, Harry, 205

Immigrants
  George H. W. Bush on, 329–30
  Chinese, 128, 130, 138–40
  Cleveland on, 119, 126, 127–9,
    134–5, 138–40
  as excluded group, 2, 24, 64, 98,
    102, 126
  Irish, 61, 104
  issues of visibility in presiden-
    tial rhetoric and, 5, 175–6
  Jewish, 61, 167, 175–6, 188, 213,
    235, 267–8
  as political problem, 30–1, 92
  Franklin Roosevelt on, 201,
    211–7, 239
  Wilson on, 129, 153, 163, 165–6,
    172–3, 185–6, 187–8
Inaugurals, 9, 117, 157, 292
Irish immigrants, 61, 104

Jackson, Andrew
  on American Indians, 21, 42–52,
    99, 339, 341

Jackson, Andrew (continued)
  on Bank of the United States,
    40, 59
  on citizenship, 21, 22, 41–2,
    52–7, 92 21, 22, 41–2, 52–7,
    92
  on founding principles, 20, 22,
    32, 58
  frontier myth and, 23, 39, 40,
    41, 44, 52, 56, 57, 88, 116,
    128, 341
  Jefferson and, 21, 22, 32, 41, 44,
    52, 61–2, 337
  on land ownership, 21, 22, 41–2,
    52–7, 92, 337
  national balance and, 22, 47, 51,
    57–8 22, 47, 51, 57–8, 337,
    339
  national identity and, 17–8, 21,
    22, 32, 41–2, 46–7, 48, 53, 56,
    57–8, 339, 340–1
  on political coalition, 19, 21
  on states' rights, 40
Jefferson, Thomas
  on Alien and Sedition acts, 31
  on American Indians, 34–9,
    366n39
  on citizenship and national
    identity, 29, 30–9
  frontier myth and, 23, 39
  influence of, on Jackson, 21, 22,
    32, 41, 44, 52, 61–2, 337
  on national expansion and cul-
    ture, 28, 29, 35–6
Jewish immigrants, 61, 167, 175–6,
    188, 213, 235, 267–8

Khruschchev, Nikita, 280
King, Martin Luther, Jr., 1–2, 298,
    342, 350–1
King, Rodney, 312–3
Know-Nothing Party, 93–4

Labor
  George H. W. Bush on, 325–6
  Cleveland on, 116–7, 119, 120,

    123–4, 124–5, 126, 128,
    134–5, 137–8
  Eisenhower on, 252–3, 281–3
  Franklin Roosevelt on, 206–11
  Wilson on, 152, 186–7
Lesbians
  as excluded group, 2, 10, 343
  gays in military and, 346–9
  issues of visibility in presiden-
    tial rhetoric, 19, 281
Lincoln, Abraham, 71, 244, 284

Madison, James, 26–7, 28, 29–30,
    75
Manifest Destiny, 102
Minorities, 10, 11–2, 16, 17, 20,
    184, 288. See also African
    Americans; American
    Indians; Gays; Lesbians;
    Hispanics; Immigrants;
    Women
  George H. W. Bush on, 298, 302,
    315, 321, 328, 331–2
  Eisenhower on, 250, 259–60,
    262–71, 279, 286, 287
  Franklin Roosevelt on, 198, 199,
    205, 214, 217, 219, 231, 241
  Wilson on, 183, 188, 192
Mob violence, 25, 26, 75–6, 94–5,
    170, 171, 264
Monroe, James, 75
Morrow, E. Frederick, 263–4
Muslims, 61, 343, 331–2, 355
Mormons, 61, 64, 97–9, 102, 104,
    119, 140–1, 142, 166

National identity, American, 11–2,
    13–7, 355–6, 362n34
  antebellum presidents and,
    63–4, 69, 72–3, 81–2, 85, 90,
    97–9, 102
  ascriptive hierarchies and, 5, 6,
    14, 76, 339, 354–5
  George H. W. Bush and, 289–90,
    291–2, 298, 299, 306–7, 309,
    312, 320–1

George W. Bush and, 354
Cleveland and, 107, 109, 111,
    115, 118, 120, 126–7, 128,
    135, 137, 139, 141
Eisenhower and, 257, 267,
    280–1, 84–6, 286, 287
Founders and, 23–4, 26–7,
    29–30, 32, 33–4
inclusive and exclusive, 9, 29,
    72, 267
mission, 16, 272–6
Jackson and, 17–8, 21, 22, 32,
    41–2, 46–7, 48, 53, 56, 57–8,
    339, 340–1
in presidential rhetoric, 2–3
religion and, 24
Franklin Roosevelt and, 198–9,
    200, 201, 203, 206–7, 211–2,
    213–4, 216, 217, 221–2, 227,
    230, 232, 239–40
Wilson and, 152–4, 159, 161,
    162–3, 164–6, 168, 174–5,
    181–2, 183, 189, 196
Nationalism, civic, 7, 15–6, 336,
    339, 354
in antebellum presidents' rheto-
    ric, 72, 85, 90
in George H.W. Bush's rhetoric,
    296–7, 304
in George W. Bush's rhetoric, 343
in Cleveland's rhetoric, 129,
    136, 139
in Eisenhower's rhetoric, 257,
    285
in Jackson's rhetoric, 31, 48
in Franklin Roosevelt's rhetoric,
    235, 240, 242
in Wilson's rhetoric, 151–2, 153,
    155, 158, 163, 165, 169, 176
Nationalism, racial, 7, 16, 336,
    339, 354
in antebellum presidents' rheto-
    ric, 72, 81, 85, 88,
in Cleveland's rhetoric, 126, 139
in Jackson's rhetoric, 31, 48
in Wilson's rhetoric, 151–2, 153

Native Americans. *See* American
    Indians
Naturalization Act, 30–1
New Deal, 198, 207, 217, 221, 224
Nixon, Richard, 280

Pierce, Franklin, 18, 20
on African Americans, 90
on American Indians, 88
on founding principles, 65, 71–9,
    86, 95, 100, 103
frontier myth and, 80, 88, 100
on issues of visibility, 78, 103
Jackson and, 63–4, 65, 72, 76,
    79, 83, 88, 103
Jefferson and, 63–4, 65, 77, 79,
    88
national balance and, 78, 100
national identity and, 74
philosophy of government, 71,
    74, 76, 83
political coalition, 71, 90, 103
states' rights, 66–9, 73, 96–7
use of history by, 73–4
Presidency, U.S. *See also*
    Presidents, U.S.; *listings of*
    individual presidents
as conservative institution, 3,
    7–8, 65, 104, 183, 267, 332,
    337
as repository of cultural power,
    16, 336
as representative institution, 7,
    8–9, 10, 46–7
as rhetorical institution, 4, 5–6,
    10, 11–2, 196–7, 332–3
Presidents, U.S. *See*
    also Presidency, U.S.; *listings*
    of individual presidents
as articulators of national iden-
    tity, 2, 3, 7–10, 17, 160
leadership of, 3
Progressive Party, 154, 158, 166

Race, 56, 58, 65, 81, 85, 183–4,
    365n13. *See also* African Amer-

icans; American Indians; Asian
Americans; Chinese immi-
grants; Nationalism, racial
Cleveland and, 127, 149, 339
Franklin Roosevelt and, 199
Wilson and, 195–6
Reagan, Ronald, 289, 290–1, 314,
317, 338
Religion 33, 34, 81, 194. *See also*
Catholics; Christianity;
Jewish Immigrants;
Mormons; Muslims
George H. W. Bush on, 319–21
George W. Bush on, 352
Eisenhower, and, 245, 246, 251,
253–4, 271, 272–7
inclusive and exclusive, 72–3, 23
Franklin Roosevelt and, 212–3,
235–7
Wilson and, 167–8, 170
Republican Party, 18, 61, 156, 157
Roosevelt, Alice Longworth, 232
Roosevelt, Eleanor, 221, 232
Roosevelt, Franklin, 18, 20, 66,
338, 339, 341
on African Americans, 214, 217,
220–5
on American Indians, 214, 217,
232–5, 239–40
antebellum presidents and, 199
on business, 208–9, 218
on Christianity, 212–3, 235–7
on citizenship, 199–200, 201,
205, 206, 210, 215, 225–6,
227, 229, 237
on Civil Rights, 221–3
on class, 204, 205, 227–8
Cleveland and, 109, 200, 201,
211, 225, 230, 237, 240
co-option and, 206–17, 220
deferral tactics of, 206, 219,
220–31
deflection tactics of, 232–5
exclusion and, 206, 217–9
frontier myth and, 215, 235,
237–40

on immigrants, 201, 211–7, 239
Jackson and, 201, 215, 219, 227,
228, 230, 237, 238, 239
Jefferson and, 228, 237, 238, 239
on labor, 206–11
on minorities, 198, 199, 205,
214, 217, 219, 231, 241
national balance and, 199–200,
202, 220, 226
on national unity, 203, 215,
229–30
on political coalition, 198–9,
206, 212, 220, 222
political philosophy of, 200–6
on race, 199
on stability, 200
visibility of minorities and, 203,
206, 231, 232
Wilson and, 158, 198, 199, 200,
201, 203, 204, 205, 214, 216,
219, 227, 230, 231, 238, 240
on women's issues, 216–7
Roosevelt, Theodore, 115, 129,
179, 181, 194
"Rooseveltian Nation," 22–3, 31,
129, 289, 298, 302

Sherman Act, 121
Slavery, 22, 33–4, 42, 53, 62, 66–7,
70, 73, 75, 101, 104, 105, 126,
163
Social Darwinism, 111–3
Sovereignty, popular, 95
Soviet Union. *See Cold War*
Stability, national need for, 26–7,
44, 64, 79–86, 96, 106, 200,
258. *See also* Balance,
national

Thomas, Clarence, 315–7
Tower, John, 303
Truth, Sojourner, 89–90

Visibility, political, 4, 20
in antebellum presidents' rhetoric, 78, 81–2, 103

in Cleveland's rhetoric, 106,
124, 129, 135–6, 149–50
in Wilson's rhetoric, 163, 188–9

Wagner Act, 209
Washington, Booker T., 136, 181
Washington, George, 19, 23, 34
Webster, Daniel, 71
Wheeler–Howard Act, 233
Whiskey Rebellion, 24–5, 166
Wilson, Woodrow, 18, 20, 66, 338,
339–40, 341
on African Americans, 152, 153,
161, 163, 165, 169, 177,
180–2, 188–9, 193, 197
on American Indians, 34, 152,
153, 163, 166, 175, 177–80, 193
antebellum presidents, 154, 162,
166, 171
on Christianity, 167–70, 176
on citizenship, 152, 157, 159,
160, 162, 163, 166, 169–70,
171–2, 174–5, 196
Cleveland and, 154, 156, 159,
162, 163, 166, 179, 193
deferral tactics of, 183–90
on economic class, 162, 163
on founding principles, 156, 164
frontier myth and, 179, 194–5
on immigrants, 129, 153, 163,
165–6, 172–3, 185–6, 187–8
Jackson and, 154, 157–58, 159,
161–2, 171, 190, 193

Jefferson and, 154, 159, 162,
178, 190, 193
on labor, 152, 186–7
on minorities, 183, 188, 192
national balance and, 156, 163
on national diversity, 173–4
on nationalism, 157
on national unity, 151, 162–71,
190
as party leader, 153–60
on political coalition, 151, 185
political philosophy of, 152,
158, 161, 171, 172
on race, 195–6
on states' rights, 160
use of history by, 190–2
visibility of minorities and, 166,
171, 177
Washington and, 166
on women's issues, 160–61, 162,
163, 165, 173–4, 175, 182
Women, 106, 316
Cleveland on, 141–2
Eisenhower on, 277–8, 280–1
as excluded group, 11–2, 22, 42,
53, 64, 104, 119
issues of visibility in presidential rhetoric, 5, 12, 141–2
Franklin Roosevelt on, 216–7
Wilson on, 160–61, 162, 163,
165, 173–4, 175, 182
World War I, 155, 167, 248
World War II, 248, 272, 286